WEBSTER
SCIENCE YEARBOOK

WEBSTER
SCIENCE YEARBOOK

This book is also published as
THE FACTS ON FILE SCIENTIFIC YEARBOOK–1988

Meredith Corporation
New York

The Facts On File Scientific Yearbook 1988

The Facts on File scientific yearbook. — 1985- — New York, N.Y. : Facts on File Publications, c1985-

v. : ill. ; 29 cm.

Annual.
Spine title: Scientific yearbook
Continues: Young students science yearbook.
ISSN 0883-0800 = The Facts on File scientific yearbook.

1. Science—Yearbooks. I. Facts on File, Inc. II. Title: Scientific yearbook.

Q9.F32 505 85-642413
AACR 2 MARC-S

Library of Congress [8706]

ISBN 0-8160-1889-8

British CIP data available on request

Printed in the United States of America

10 9 8 7 6 5 4 3 2 1

Contents

WEBSTER
SCIENCE YEARBOOK

Part One

Life Science

The black-footed ferret found in the western United States.

EVENTS AND TRENDS IN LIFE SCIENCE

The year 1987 was filled with promising developments in biology and medicine—but the fate of many animal species and the environment continued to be troubled.

Animals and Plants

Fifteen years ago, Jared Diamond, an ecologist at the University of California at Los Angeles, along with other ecologists, proposed the analogy that national parks were like "land-bridge islands" cut off from continents by rising seas or changing topography. On real land-bridge islands, the full ecological diversity of the mainland cannot be sustained, resulting in "faunal collapse." In bad times, isolated populations become less robust and their numbers dwindle, and then they are apt to be killed off by a storm or an epidemic.

Bearing out Diamond's hypothesis, North America's national parks, even those covering hundreds of thousands of acres, have become isolated islands too small to support many of the animals that live in them. Research by William Newmark, an ecologist now at the College of African Wildlife Management in Moshi, Tanzania, found an alarming loss of species in the great western parks on a scale that had gone unrecognized by wildlife officials.

In regions that seemed spacious three-quarters of a century ago, when the parks were founded, roads, housing developments, and deforestation now isolate animal populations. By the time the parks were established, some species had been killed off or already driven out of the park area. Dr. Newmark's study, the first complete survey of major mammal populations throughout the great western parks, found that the loss of entire species continues.

Although individual park managers and scientists were aware of some local extinctions, few recognized that the trend had gone on for most of the century. No one had sensed the universal pattern in species loss across the continent.

Animals that have vanished from some parks are still flourishing in others. However, some ecologists view Newmark's study as an omen for the future. They fear that certain species may be prone to extinction. If they become extinct in one park, their demise may signal an impending loss in other parks.

In conducting the survey as part of his doctoral dissertation, Newmark visited all the parks. He developed and used checklists, and reviewed sighting records that go back decades. A species was listed as locally extinct only when it had not been sighted for at least 10 years.

Larger animals proved to be most in jeopardy, and older parks had sustained the greatest losses. The only park that seemed immune to loss was the largest grouping, the combination of Kootenay, Banff, Jasper, and Yoho parks in Canada.

Newmark's study was confined to mammals, which are the species most reliably observed by park scientists and visitors. Faunal collapse on land-bridge islands also affects small animals, birds, and plants. Their fate in the national parks remains unknown.

Newmark's findings have intensified the already heated debate about the operation of parks and their surrounding lands. Some ecologists, including some who had staunchly preached nonintervention, have begun to argue in favor of creative management.

Other ecologists are advocating that attention be given to the management of land adjacent to the parks. Despite the fact that much of the surrounding land is federally owned, theirs is a controversial position.

Compensatory park management techniques have been tried or are being debated. These include the introduction of new animals, genetic manipulation to combat inbreeding due to dwindling populations, control of vegetation for the benefit of imperiled species, the creation of nest sites, and the removal of unwanted animals. However, active intervention tends to make ecologists uneasy, since human judgments about "pieces" of nature have often been unreliable in the past.

Health and Medicine

Sudden death syndrome, or sudden cardiac arrest, claims 400,000 lives annually, more than any other natural disease. Among the 1,100 people who die each day, some are dead within minutes of the symptoms' first appearance. The heart's rhythm increases uncontrollably and deteriorates into a state in which it trembles and jerks instead of pumping blood.

Twice as many men as women are victims of sudden death syndrome. Researchers suspect that their female hormones protect women from sudden death syndrome until menopause.

Harvard Medical School cardiologist Bernard Lown believes the wildly erratic heart arrhythmias characteristic of the syndrome are set off by stress-activated, improper electrical impulses from the brain. When Lown interviewed survivors of life-threatening arrhythmias, he discovered that 21 percent had experienced acute emotional upset during the 24 hours before the onset of the irregular heartbeats. For two-thirds of the 21 percent, the stressful incident occurred less than an hour before the attack.

The director of the National Center of Preventive and Stress Medicine in Phoenix, Arizona, Robert Eliot, has been tracking the stress death linkage since 1968, when he was called in as a cardiovascular consultant at Cape Kennedy. NASA engineers between the ages of 28 and 35 were dropping dead at 2 and a half times the sudden death rate for the rest of the state of Florida. The CIA even wondered if the young men were being poisoned.

The victims' original autopsies did not reveal coronary disease. But Eliot repeated the autopsies, and found that 90 percent of the engineers had ruptured heart-muscle fibers. At the time, NASA was undergoing sporadic employee layoffs, and rates were high for alcoholism, drug abuse, divorce, and suicide.

Ten years of animal experimentation followed Eliot's Cape Kennedy findings. He was able to establish that injections of excessive amounts of adrenaline in lab animals caused chaotic electrical storms, after which the heart stopped pumping blood.

Fear and other types of stress can trigger extra secretions of adrenaline. Eliot's studies did not answer the question of whether adrenaline injections precipitated the same response as stress-induced adrenaline. Nor did they answer whether healthy persons were as affected as cardiac patients.

A professor of neurosciences at the New Jersey Medical School in Newark, Benjamin Natelson, conducted studies to address the unanswered questions. During a week of training, Natelson's research team administered mild electric shocks, preceded by light signals, to one group of guinea pigs to establish that light preceded shock. A second group received only the light signal. All the animals were given digitalis, a powerful cardiac stimulant that in high doses can cause arrhythmias.

After the injection, all the animals were given the light signal. The group conditioned to receiving a shock responded as if to stress, although there was no shock. They developed arrhythmias much more quickly than the group that was not conditioned. Guinea pigs who received shock and not digitalis did not develop arrhythmias.

A colleague of Lown's at Harvard, Thomas Graboys, points to the flood of chemicals called catecholamines, of which adrenaline is only one, that are released during periods of extreme stress. These he thinks may rupture tiny cardiac muscle fibers, which in turn may set off the electrical storm thought to result in arrhythmia.

Eliot hopes to expand the National Center of Stress and Preventive Medicine into 20 regional centers where physicians could identify those at risk for sudden death. He and his colleagues have developed precise testing systems to measure physiological overreactions to stress among the one in every five "hot reactors" who respond to stress as if challenged by a saber-toothed tiger.

Biology

While staring at an African clawed frog recovering from a surgical incision in tank water murky with bacteria, pediatrician and microbiologist Michael Zasloff wondered why the frog healed so easily. Dr. Zasloff examined another healing wound to look for the white cells that fight off infection. He found none, which meant the frog's immune system was not involved in the healing process. He speculated that some potent chemical in the frog's skin might be protecting the wound from bacterial invasion.

When Zasloff ground up the frog's skin and screened it for chemicals, he found two peptides of 23 amino acids each, which he described as functionally distinct from any substance so far detected in animals. He named the substances *magainins* after the Hebrew word for shields.

In low concentration, the frog magainins kill various, though not all, invading bacteria, fungi, and protozoa, but they leave human red cells intact. Zasloff does not know how magainins distinguish between invaders and normal cells, but he does have clues as to how they attack infecting microbes. The peptides are amphiphilic: That is, half the molecule is oily and half is water-loving. A paramecium exposed to magainins swelled and burst within seconds. Apparently, the magainin dramatically affected the paramecium's discharge of water.

Zasloff suspects that magainins may be the vertebrate counterpart of cecropins, antibacterial peptides made up of 37 amino acids found circulating in some insects that lack antibodies and lymphocytes. Substances such as these were not thought to be found in vertebrates: Nevertheless, they are a major component of the frog's skin and probably circulate throughout the frog's body. They likely represent a first-line defense system developed early in evolution.

The frog magainins are made by the granular gland, which also produces neurotransmitters and hormones. Many proteins isolated from this gland have been found to have analogues in the gut and nervous system of mammals.

Zasloff has cloned the genetic message of the frog magainins and is using the clone probes to look for similar peptides in humans. If such peptides are discovered, they could help to explain how corneas are able to heal without the inflammation normally associated with the presence of white cells invoked by the immune system. Study of the properties of magainin also may help explain the folk practice in Argentina of strapping a frog onto a wound to induce healing.

In addition, synthesized magainins may be useful in the treatment of burns. But for Zasloff, the most exciting implication of his discovery is a long-sought explanation for cystic fibrosis.

From the time of birth, the lungs of a child with cystic fibrosis become colonized by bacteria that do not infect the rest of the body. The mucus-secreting cells in the child's airways, and secreting cells elsewhere, have difficulty transporting water and ions across their membranes. If magainins are found in humans, Zasloff suspects that a defect in the magainin system could underlie some of the symptoms of cystic fibrosis, and therefore the discovery offers an entry into the cure of the disease.

If magainins can help fight disease, and if they can safely be tested on people, and if humans produce the substance naturally, then a successor to antibiotics may have been found.

The Changing Environment

Residents of arid farm areas in the Southwest grow apprehensive as burgeoning cities buy farmland. Phoenix recently bought 14,000 acres of farmland 100 miles west of the city, not to grow crops but to secure the water beneath the land. Other fast growing cities such as Tucson, Mesa, and Scottsdale have also been buying land far from their city limits. Arizonans call the practice ''water ranching.''

These rural citizens see their lifeblood being drained away, and they fear that removal of water from rural areas may upset the ecological balance. Since the population of the Phoenix metropolitan area rose 26 percent between 1980 and 1986, the nation's highest growth rate, and the demand for water in Phoenix is expected to double over the next 40 years, city officials view their land purchases as prudent preparation for future growth.

Rural officials on the other hand, are pressing the state legislature to restrict efforts to buy agricultural water. Under western water law, when land is sold, whatever rights the owner has had to draw water from a river or from the ground are generally sold with the property. This legal tradition, along with a 1980 Arizona state law regulating the use of subterranean water, make water ranching possible. In La Paz County, Arizona, 22,000 of 140,000 privately owned acres have been sold or leased solely for their water rights.

But rural officials point to the real-life precedent dramatized in the movie *Chinatown* in which Los Angeles water officials purchased huge tracts of land in the scenic Owens Valley and then built an aqueduct to bring the water to the city. Owens Valley residents have claimed ever since that the ''pirating'' of their water left them too parched to ever achieve prosperity.

Some environmentalists support the actions of city officials, contending that farmers often use available water inefficiently. Moreover, they claim that shifting some of the water marked for agriculture would reduce urban demands for environmentally damaging new dams and canal systems. Others contend that removal of rural areas' water resources increase the pressure on people to congregate in crowded cities, thereby intensifying the strain on resources, both natural and social, including water. One hopeful solution can be found in the precedent set in 1987 by the city of Albuquerque, New Mexico, where citizens have voted to plan for growth in such a way that best conserves the natural resources and beauty of its setting.

1

Animals and Plants

VETERINARY HIGH TECHNOLOGY

Treatment of a Diverse Population Comes of Age

The owner of Ernie, a 4-month old tabby kitten brought home from an animal shelter, spent money she had saved for her honeymoon for Ernie's intensive care at Tufts University School of Veterinary Medicine (TUSVM) Foster Hospital for Small Animals. The kitten had been burned over 40 percent of his 2-pound body. Ernie was cared for by Dr. Michael Pavlectic, a surgeon whose rare speciality is veterinary reconstructive surgery. Burn victims, whether human or animal, face life-threatening problems, including infection and deterioration of muscle mass. Tissue must be restored, and the victim must be kept in a germ-free environment. For 2 weeks prior to surgery, Ernie was placed on a high-protein liquid diet created especially for him. During two procedures, which took a total of 6 hours, "islands" of skin transplanted from healthy tissue on the kitten's body were used to cover the area left without skin. Dr. Lisa Alexander, a surgical resident who participated in Ernie's care, described the kitten's will to live as extraordinary.

The Patient Population and a Profile of Two Sources of Care

More than 60 percent of U.S. households have "companion animals": over 110 million dogs and cats; 10 million horses owned by 3 million owners who spend $9 billion annually for feed, tack, veterinary medicine, and related services; 62 million Americans spend $600 million annually on seed, feeders, and bird houses for a portion of the nation's 6 billion wild birds.

In veterinary terms, "large animals" are those having to do with food, farm, or fiber; that is, horses, cattle, sheep, swine, goats, and so on. "Small animals" are those viewed as pets; that is, dogs, cats, hamsters, mice, birds, reptiles, etc.

The United States and Canada have a combined total of 32 veterinary schools: The newest school is on Prince Edward Island in Canada. Tufts University School of Veterinary Medicine (TUSVM), the third newest school, graduated its first class of 35 in 1983. The TUSVM facility, which is spread over 634 acres in Grafton, Massachusetts, includes the Henry and Lois Foster Hospital for Small Animals, the Hospital for Large Animals, a Wildlife Clinic, poultry and sheep operations, a piggery, and several fields of corn and hay.

The University of Pennsylvania School of Veterinary Medicine (Penn) is the nation's second oldest veterinary school. Begun in 1884, it opened in the midst of devastating plagues that took an awful toll of the nation's livestock populations. Like TUSVM, Penn has two hospitals, but unlike TUSVM, they are separated into an urban and a rural setting. Large animals are cared for at New Bolton Center, about 35 miles west of Philadelphia. Small animals are treated at a three-building complex called the Veterinary Hospital of the University of Pennsylvania (VHUP) on Spruce Street in downtown Philadelphia.

Treatment and Care

The modern veterinary school over the last decade has increasingly become the site of high-technology medicine. In addition to traditional concerns, students must be introduced to new and emerging fields: environmental science; toxicology; wildlife medicine; genetic engineering; comparative medicine; bioengineering; cell biology; human and animal nutrition; animal welfare and ethology (applied ethics); and international veterinary medicine.

The impact of high technology has been particularly visible in radiology. In the late summer of 1987, TUSVM received an anonymous gift of a CT (computerized tomography) scan. CT scans serve the same diagnostic purpose for animals as they do for humans. Finely focused X-rays divide the patient's body into visual slices, or sections, for

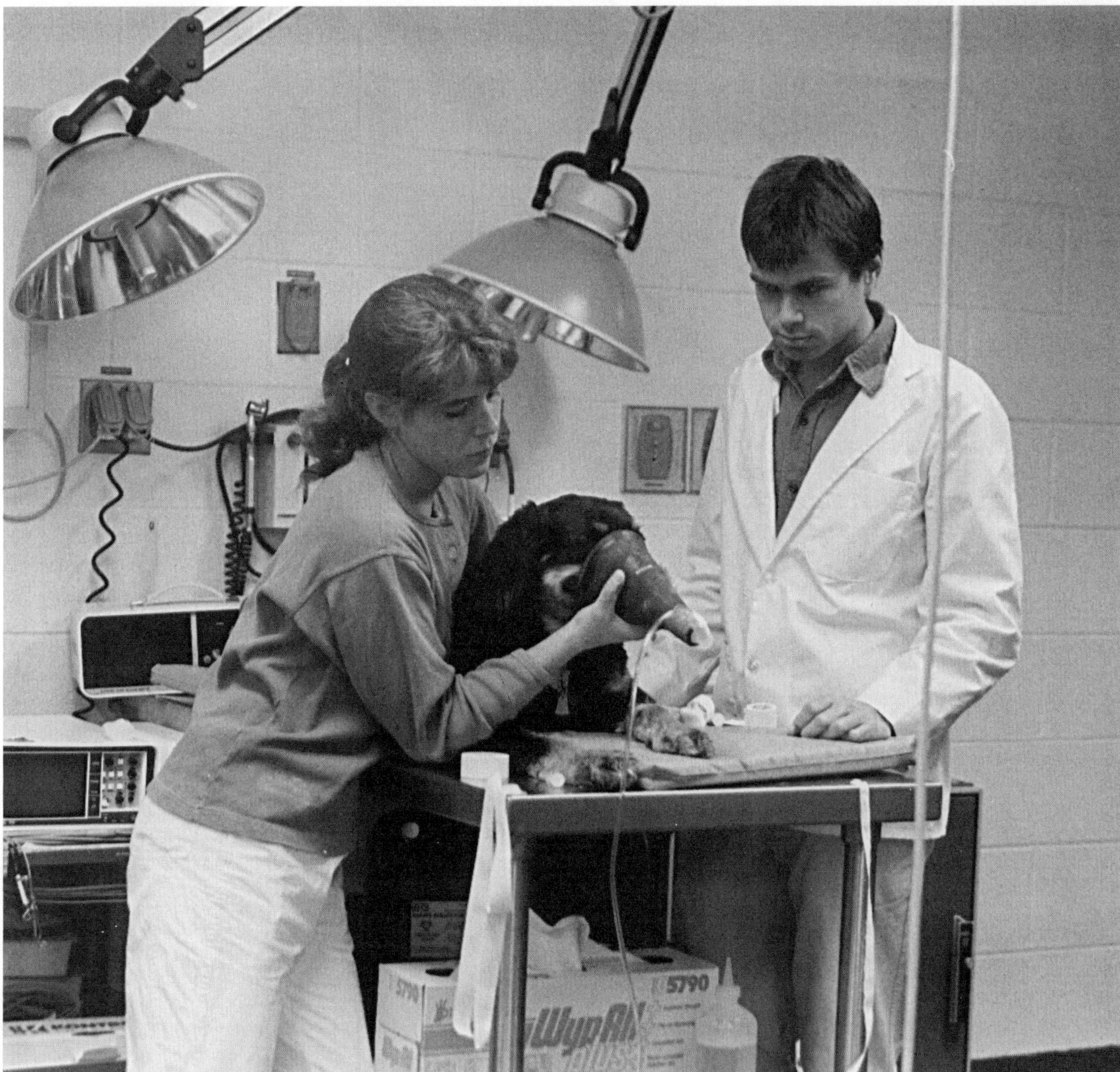

A patient receives oxygen in the Intensive Care Unit of TUSVM's Foster Hospital for Small Animals.

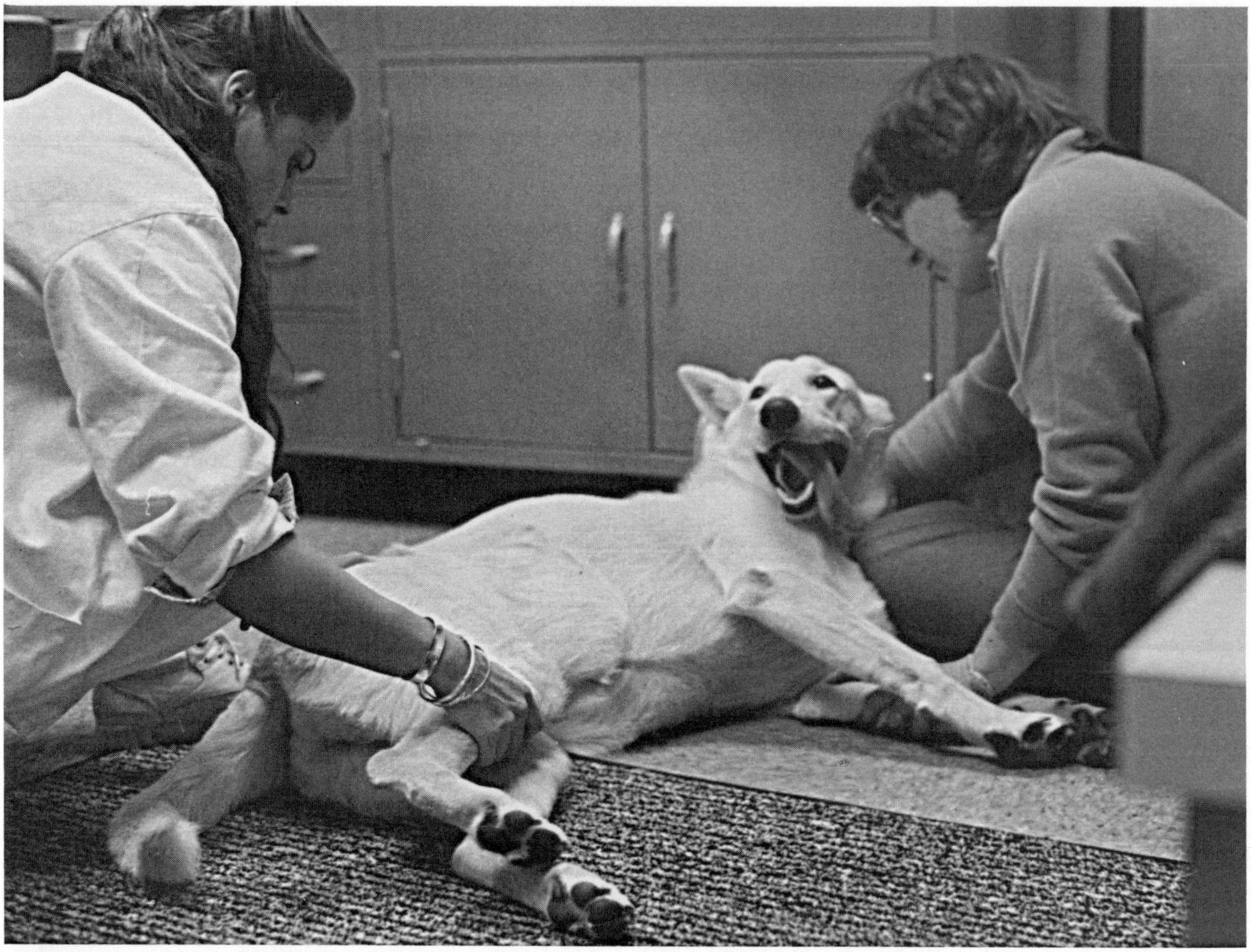

Large dogs frequently suffer from hip dysplasia, a condition in which the ball and socket of the hip joint do not fit together properly. Here, while her owner is soothing her, a TUSVM veterinarian rotates the hind leg of Stella, an eight-month-old German shepherd.

examination. The slices are processed by computer rather than developed as they would be with ordinary X-ray film, and they can be analyzed on the computer screen to reveal abnormalities such as tumors. TUSVM's CT scan is in the Hospital for Large Animals but is used more often for smaller animals. It is not large enough to accommodate the entire body of a horse, but it can be used for a horse's head or legs.

Tumors are one of the most common problems seen by the TUSVM staff. In the near future, the radiology department hopes to create a wing that will house a cobalt unit to provide radiation therapy for animals that have cancer. Animals already receive other traditional cancer treatments such as chemotherapy and cryosurgery (the use of subfreezing temperature to destroy tissue).

Orthopedic problems are common in veterinary practice. Using a technique developed at the Ohio State Veterinary Teaching Hospital, TUSVM small-animal orthopedic surgeon Randy Boudrieau provides dogs with artificial hip joints made of steel instead of bone. The hip joint is essentially a ball and socket. During surgery, the animal's socket is replaced with a plastic cup, and the ball of the thigh bone is replaced with a stainless steel ball. Special acrylic cement attaches the implants to the bone.

Hip joint diseases are a frequent occurrence in large dogs such as German shepherds, Irish setters, Old English sheepdogs, Rottweilers, and Labrador retrievers. The diseases keep their canine victims in constant, debilitating pain. An 8-month-old white German shepherd named Stella was referred to the Foster Hospital for a possible hip replacement. Stella had learned to compensate for her painful hips by "bunnyhopping" up the stairs. Stella's owner built a ramp to her home's "dog door" to make it easier for Stella to come in and out. Because of Stella's young age, measures short of a hip replacement would be tried first; a replacement would be only a last resort.

9

ANIMALS AND PLANTS

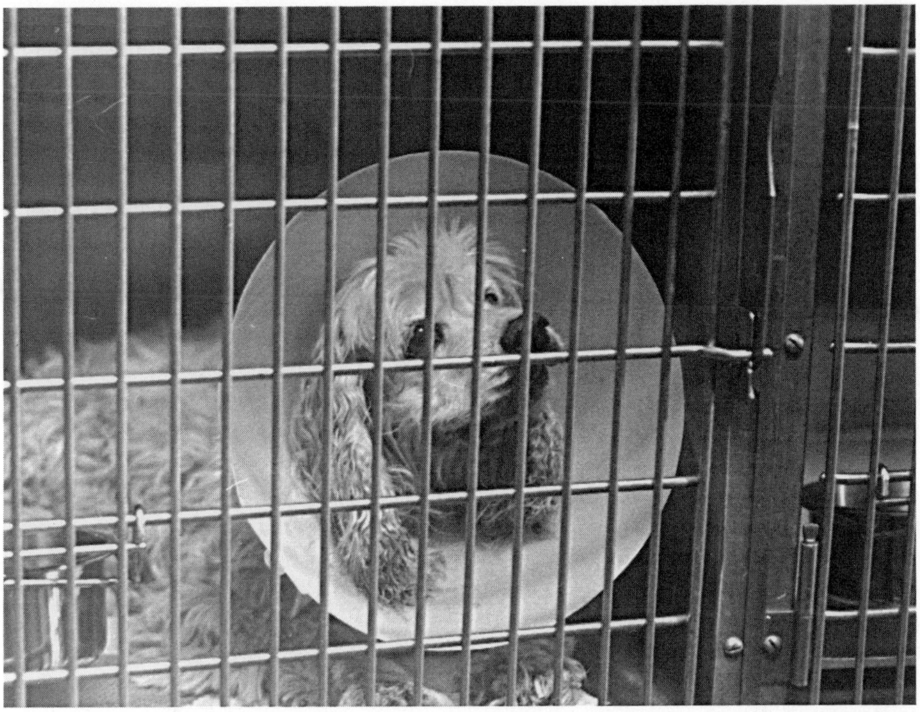

A megaphone collar keeps an animal from gnawing at sutures or licking a rash.

A golden retriever named Brandy was given a hip replacement in an operation that cost about $1,500, approximately one-tenth the cost of the procedure in a human. Brandy was out of the hospital in 4 days. Although both hips are frequently involved, usually one hip is replaced. The dogs learn to depend upon the sound, pain-free leg.

The Foster Hospital has a 24-hour emergency service with a busy intensive care unit. Harry is an example of a veterinary emergency. He is a curious kitten who bit an electrical cord, received a severe shock, and stopped breathing. Harry's owner had recently taken a course in CPR (cardiopulmonary resuscitation). She felt it might work on Harry. After about five tries, the kitten resumed

Animal blood is handled in much the same way human blood is. It can be frozen, and its parts can be separated. In an emergency, a donation of blood at the proper temperature can be secured from one of TUSVM'S in-house donors rather than wait for frozen blood to be warmed.

breathing. A call to the emergency number at Foster Hospital prompted the recommendation that Harry be brought in immediately. After fluids, oxygen, several days in intensive care, and treatment for burns to his gums, Harry regained his curiosity.

At any one time the Foster Hospital intensive care unit might include pets recovering from serious surgery, critical injury, or treatment for cancer. Post-surgery recovery patients are likely to be wearing megaphone-shaped collars to prevent them from tampering with their incisions. Animals are aroused from anesthesia on heated waterbeds or hot water bottles, or are warmed by heating lamps to offset the coolness of air-conditioning that exchanges the air 12 to 18 times an hour.

Blood Banking

For animals that are anemic, that sustain severe trauma, or that have extensive surgery, blood replacement is a critical concern. The TUSVM section head of small-animal medicine, Dr. Susan Cotter, was awarded a 5-year grant from the National Institute of Health to develop a model blood bank.

Foster Hospital has dogs and cats that act as blood donors. Three dogs and two cats are permanent residents of the hospital, and each in-house donor may donate 1 unit of blood, 450 ccs, no more than once each month. In addition to the in-house donors, the hospital has a list of employees' dogs and cats who also donate.

The dog donors must weigh at least 50 pounds, be in good health, and have a placid temperament. The cats must weigh 8 to 10 pounds, but a placid temperament is not enough to make a cat a willing donor: A cat usually needs to be mildly tranquilized. In exchange for donating blood the animal receives a free exam before donation. The dogs' blood types are either A negative, a universal donor, or A positive. Cats' blood types are either A or B. (B is extremely rare.) Most of the blood is needed for small animals. In the future, increasing use of "autotransfusion," which uses the patient's own blood for a transfusion, is expected in veterinary medicine. For example, from a patient with blood that has pooled as a result of a wound in the abdomen, the blood can be collected, filtered, and returned to the patient.

Animal Sports Medicine

Until recently, handed-down remedies and ancient theories about injuries to horses contributed little to increased understanding or prevention. As a remedy, the TUSVM developed a sports-medicine program for equine athletes. The program, called Equisport, is directed by Dr. Howard Seeherman, a veterinary surgeon who has a master's degree in physiology and who uses computerized equipment in his study of the horse in athletic competition.

In the small geographic area of New England, New York, and New Jersey, there are over a half million horses. Approximately 20,000 participate in racing, dressage, jumping, polo, or other competitions. The value of more than 18,000 of those horses is in excess of $50,000 apiece. Given the earning potential of horses who compete, those responsible for their care have sought ways to discover and modify the causes of lameness before they interfere with performance. The TUSVM's Hospital for Large Animals offers diagnosis, tailored therapy, convalescent care, and sport-specific research. The program takes techniques found to be effective in improving human performance and applies them to horses.

For example, a new piece of equipment is an in-ground, high-speed Sato treadmill. On a platform, a horse is put through every gait, including a gallop. Monitors analyze locomotion, respiration, and heart rate. Researchers can stand within a few feet of a horse who is running a two-minute mile. Gait and locomotion (movement) studies bring together engineers, orthopedists, and physiologists. Given the horse's specific anatomy—a large muscular body supported by slender limbs—musculoskeletal problems are frequent. Diagnostic methods to detect these problems include tracked motion data, force-plate gait analysis, and treadmill data.

Tracked motion data ("stick figure" data) allow the diagnosticians and researchers to picture accurately the angles of joints. Force-plate data depict the degree of force applied simultaneously in three directions to the ground by the limb. Treadmill data permit the repetition of a gait cycle, at the same velocity again and again, until an irregularity can be detected.

The treadmill, in addition to routine locomotion, heart, and respiration examination, is used for stress testing to find muscle abnormalities that may appear only at higher speed. The output of the heart is tested using radioactive isotope scintigraphy (nuclear medicine scan). An endoscope (an instrument to examine a hollow organ) can be introduced to observe obstructions of the upper airway.

The arthroscope, an instrument used in 200 procedures each year at Penn's New Bolton Center, has gained widespread use in horses in the 1980s. A slender optical instrument, the arthroscope permits an orthopedic surgeon to look inside a joint by using fiber optics to illuminate the joint and a lens to permit wide visualization. Infected joints can be examined and flushed out, and bone chips or damaged cartilage can be removed.

A rule of thumb about racehorses in the past was "no hoof, no horse." A new rule of thumb is becoming "no lung, no horse," as the ability to measure how well oxygen is being used improves. An old problem, exercise-induced

11

ANIMALS AND PLANTS

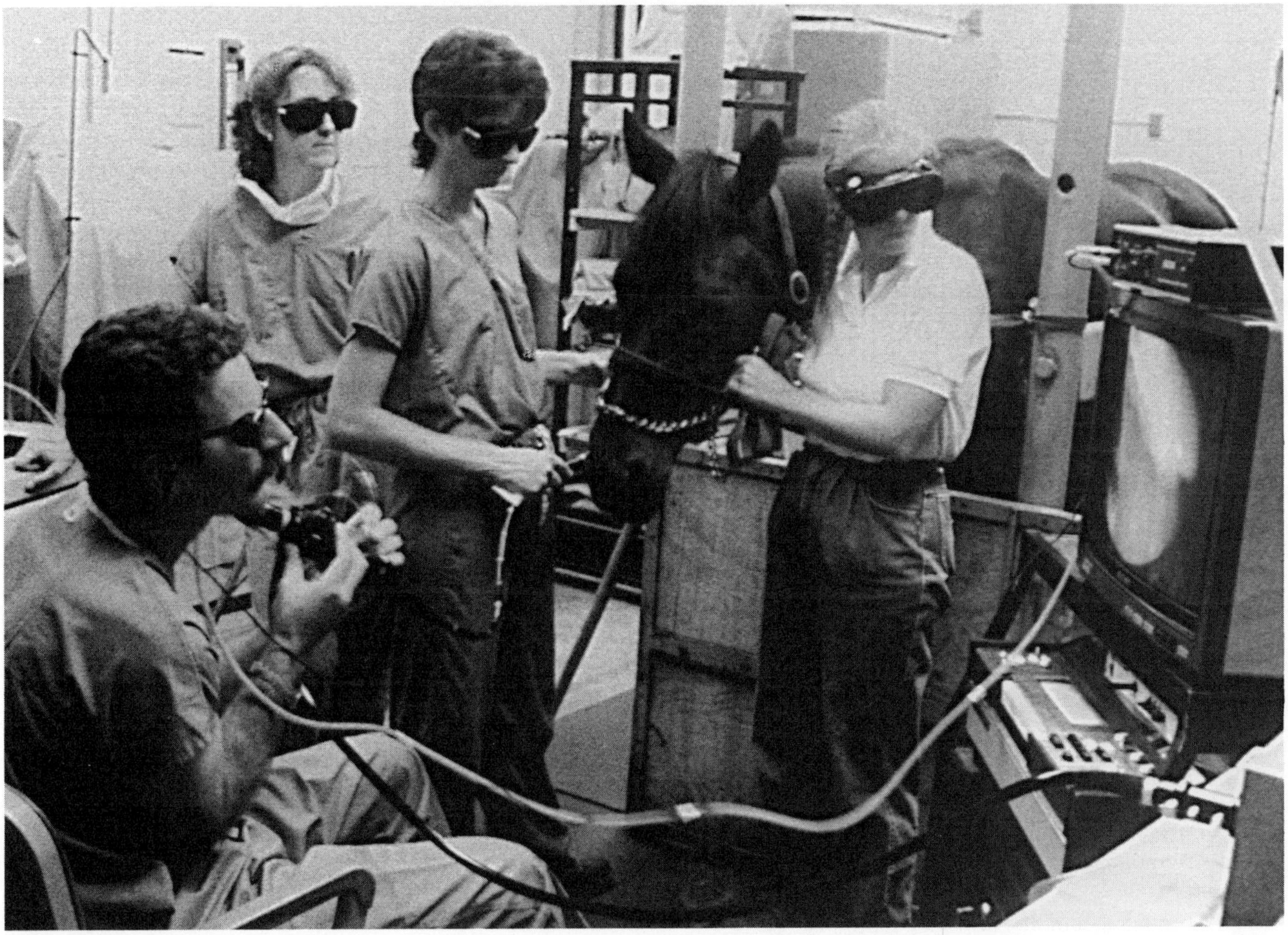

Laser surgery is being performed on a horse at the University of Pennsylvania School of Veterinary Medicine.

pulmonary hemorrhage (EIPH), is receiving increased attention. Two researchers at the New Bolton Center, Drs. Corinne Sweeney and Lawrence Soma, investigated EIPH at a large number of racetracks in Pennsylvania and New Jersey, and Dr. Soma reported that EIPH occurs in racehorses when high speed is demanded in a short period of time but does not appear in horses running long-distance endurance races.

One theory is that in EIPH, the small airways that terminate into minute air sacs may be partially obstructed. When the horse is breathing hard, the small terminal airways may collapse during exhalation and not reopen with inhalation. Unequal expansion of the lungs may cause capillaries (the smallest blood vessels) to break.

As a part of its own sports equine research program, TUSVM raised and trained its own yearling and scheduled it to race during the fall of 1987. As a part of the ongoing research into performance, owners who felt their horses were not doing as well as expected have brought the horses in for diagnosis and training. The performance of those animals will be followed in their subsequent careers.

Neonatal and Intensive Care

Given the costly investment that owners of large animals have made in their animals and in their animals' offspring, neonatal care for large animals, mostly foals (newborn horses) and calves (newborn cows), has started at TUSVM. Newborns with a problem, or newborns who are orphans, are cared for in a padded stall whose floor is a heated water bed. The stall is equipped with a Bennet respirator, oxygen, and temperature and humidity controls. A resident goat named Patty Cakes supplies the newborns with goat's milk, which is palatable to foals as well.

The practice of large animal neonatology was pioneered at the University of Florida, where the Thoroughbred Breeder's Association supported its development. Only in the past 5 or 6 years have the techniques been used in large veterinary clinics and in veterinary medical schools.

In October of 1987, the New Bolton Center opened the "state of the art" Connelly Intensive Care Unit and the Graham French Neonatal Section for the care of horses. The 11,200-square-foot building features an electric monorail designed to move horses weighing more than 1,000 pounds, and a central nurses' station that permits continuous observation of patients in both units.

In many ways, caring for a horse in intensive care is comparable to caring for a human. Heart rate, pulse, and blood pressure are electronically monitored, and the animal is closely observed. On the other hand, a 1,000-pound horse is apt to thrash about and require 70 to 100 liters of fluid every 24 hours.

Problems Unique to Veterinary Medicine

Despite the technological advances that create parallels with human medicine, veterinarians are often faced with problems uncommon in human medicine. One problem relates to the size of the patients. A horse about to have surgery may have to be lifted onto a table by a hoist. Equally likely is that the horse will be placed in a padded room, crowded against a padded wall, given a sedative, and then as the sedative takes effect be eased into a lying down position by human muscle power, onto a hydraulic table.

At the other extreme of size is a sparrow with a broken leg. In this case, veterinarians at the TUSVM Wildlife Clinic have to delicately insert a slender, steel hypodermic needle inside the shaft of the bird's leg to hold the broken pieces together.

Restraints are another routine veterinary problem. When in pain, even the gentlest animal may bite. The radiology department at the TUSVM remembers a mule that dragged the staff through a door and down the hall. Dogs being examined may have to wear crossed strips of gauze around their muzzle. A horse whose broken leg is rebuilt with metal implants is apt to wake up kicking. At Penn's New Bolton Center, horses with leg implants are hoisted from the operating table into a rubber raft with holes for the legs and floated in a warm pool until they revive and calm down.

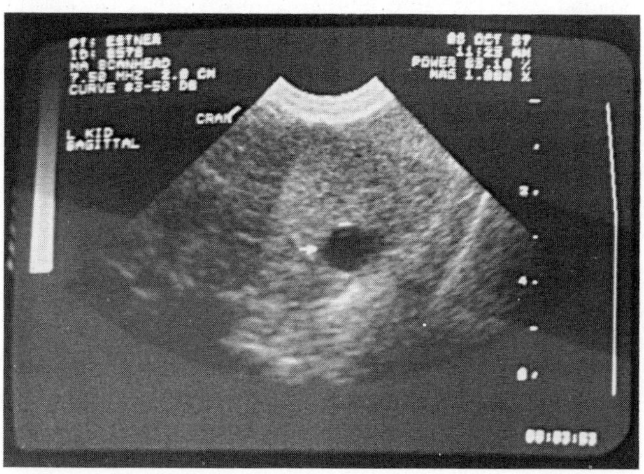

An ultrasound scan of Skippy, a 15-year-old minature dog, at Foster Hospital reveals a cyst on his liver.

Technological Reproduction

The cost of purchasing and/or raising a farm or a performance animal is so great that owners have a strong interest in the outcomes of reproduction. Long before their recent consideration in humans, artificial insemination and embryo transfer techniques were used in animals, particularly in the dairy industry. Improvements in breeding animals are a continuing interest to owners and to the researchers at the TUSVM. During breeding season, whole herds are brought into the Large Animal Hospital to be examined.

Because pregnancy interferes with a mare's training and performance schedule, the technique of embryo transfer is used increasingly to produce high-quality performance horses. Dr. Patricia Sertich, a specialist in reproduction at the George and Philip Hoffman Center for Reproduction at New Bolton Center, works mostly with show jumpers and dressage horses. The reproductive cycles of the mare who is to be bred (the donor) and the mare who will carry the foal (the recipient) are synchronized using hormones. Seven days after artificial insemination and ovulation, the donor mare's uterus is flushed and the embryo, no larger than a pinhead, is transferred nonsurgically into the recipient mare. The donor is then free to continue with her schedule, while the recipient mare bears the foal. Another advantage of embryo transfer is that it allows the high quality donor mare to produce more offspring than the horse's 11-month gestation period would normally allow.

Specialized Treatment

A 1987 treatment breakthrough at UC Davis was the first successful kidney transplant in cats. The surgery was performed in April. The recipient cat, Queenie, and the donor cat, Lily, were still doing well in October.

Another treatment first at UC Davis in 1987 was a corneal transplant in an eagle. The eagle had run into a cactus, damaging one eye. The corneal transplant surgery went perfectly but the bird had sustained too much other damage to the eye to be able to see well, even after the operation. The bird, who was at first thought to be a male, turned out to be a female, and the staff hoped to use her for breeding.

Neurologic examinations are particularly important to animal breeders, whose livelihood depends upon the soundness of the animals they breed. A new litter can be brought in for examination to determine which animals should not be sold.

Dental care is rapidly being recognized as important to an animal's well-being. For example, an animal who cannot chew or eat properly may develop colic. Dental bridges and crowns for both large and small animals are becoming commonplace. Police dogs are particularly apt to break a tooth in the line of duty and need a replacement. Cats can be fitted with braces to realign crooked fangs. The TUSVM has a veterinarian who is doing a residency in animal denistry.

Periodontal disease caused by the bacteria that form plaque is common among animals. The disease attacks the gum and bone tissues and, in advanced cases, the teeth loosen and fall out. Periodontal disease in cats has an added dimension: the disease attacks the structure of the teeth, making them so sensitive that the cat may refuse to eat or drink. The cat's teeth can be thoroughly cleaned under anesthesia, but prevention requires brushing the cat's teeth several times each week.

Two Los Angeles dentists work on animals every Wednesday at the Wildlife Waystation in the Los Angeles National Forest. One of the dentists' chores in February of 1987 was root canal work on two fangs belonging to a 550-pound Siberian tiger.

Annually more than 20,000 patients are seen in specialty clinics at the VHUP for orthopedics, neurology, ophthalmology, cardiology, dermatology, internal medicine, and behavior modification. The VHUP was also the first small-animal hospital in the country to offer the services of a social worker to distraught pet owners. Grief counselor, James Quackenbush sees about 700 clients a year.

Wildlife Services

The philosophy of wildlife clinics is different than that of domestic animal clinics because their purpose is to return the animals to the wild. Therefore, the staff refrain from any efforts to make the animals feel at home with humans.

Wildlife clinic veterinarians are apt to have a wide mix of patients at any given moment. In simultaneous recovery the staff and students might have a gull with a surgically patched wing, a snake with blister disease, a possum who tangled with a dog, and an osprey recovering from a gunshot wound. In the TUSVM Wildlife Clinic, an owl that is missing a leg and that could not survive in the wild has a permanent roost in a basement stairwell.

The TUSVM Wildlife Clinic is a federally designated trauma center for nongame and endangered species. It was awarded a grant in 1985 that made possible a series of 12 specialized training programs for veterinarians and other

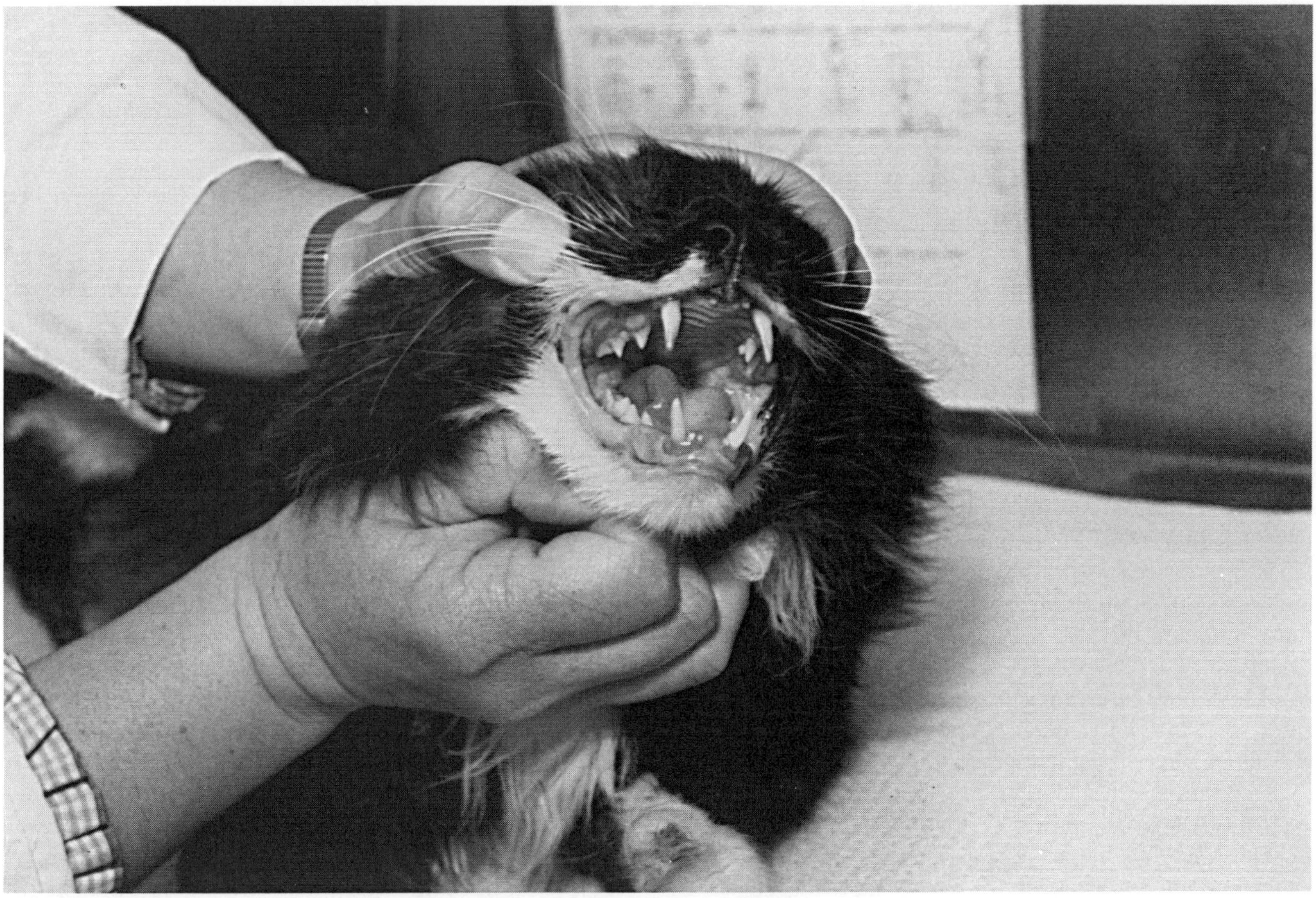

Periodontal disease and tooth loss are common in cats afflicted with FTLV.

Most wildlife in need of medical care must be handled in a way that prevents them from becoming accustomed to living with humans. However, this snowy owl with a missing leg is no longer able to live in the wild and makes its home in the stairwell of TUSVM's Wildlife Clinic.

experts in wildlife rehabilitation. The first was held in 1986, with the rest scheduled over a period of 3 years for the purpose of standardizing wildlife care and rehabilitation.

One evening a week at VHUP, a clinic for exotic pets is held. Owners of rare birds, mustelids, reptiles, amphibians, rodents, rabbits, and monkeys bring in their pets. Exotic animals have to be handled differently than pets. They don't respond to being told to lie down. They must be sedated, which adds to their stress. Birds, a large component of the exotic animal caseload, have very little blood, so blood tests must make do with only a few drops.

A goal of the TUSVM Wildlife Clinic, since its inception in 1983, has been to provide care and rehabilitation for animals that incur injuries as a result of human technology. Many animals, because of the extent of their injuries, cannot be returned to the wild. A problem common to Wildlife Clinics is exotic animals purchased at great expense who turn out to be unsuitable pets. Some of these animals in need of care are turned over to sanctuaries.

The Wildlife Waystation in the San Gabriel mountains north of Los Angeles processes 2,000 animals a year. Open 24 hours a day, the refuge accepts injured, abandoned, or confiscated animals from all over the country. The center, which opened in 1969 on 1 acre, has grown to 160 acres.

The Vermont Raptor Center, a part of the Vermont Institute of Natural Science, has more than 40 birds of prey that have been rehabilitated at the institute's hospital, or at other rehabilitation centers across the country, that could not survive if released.

The birds are housed in flight cages designed by Katherine McKeever, founder and director of the Owl Rehabilitation Research Foundation in Ontario, Canada. The cages are built into the hillsides surrounding the center, with as little disturbance of the woodland environment as possible.

Each cage is designed with a particular species' natural needs in mind. The long-eared owl has hollowed out trees in which to hide during the day. The American kestrel has flight tunnels through which to fly. Ramps are provided for birds whose injuries prevent them from flying.

From its inception in 1972, the Vermont Institute has annually treated more than 200 injured birds, more than half of which have been returned to the wild. The institute has been successful in breeding peregrines to be reintroduced to the East Coast after their extinction there in the 1960s due to pesticides.

A problem with wounded birds that have been rehabilitated is that they lose their ability to eat on their

15

ANIMALS AND PLANTS

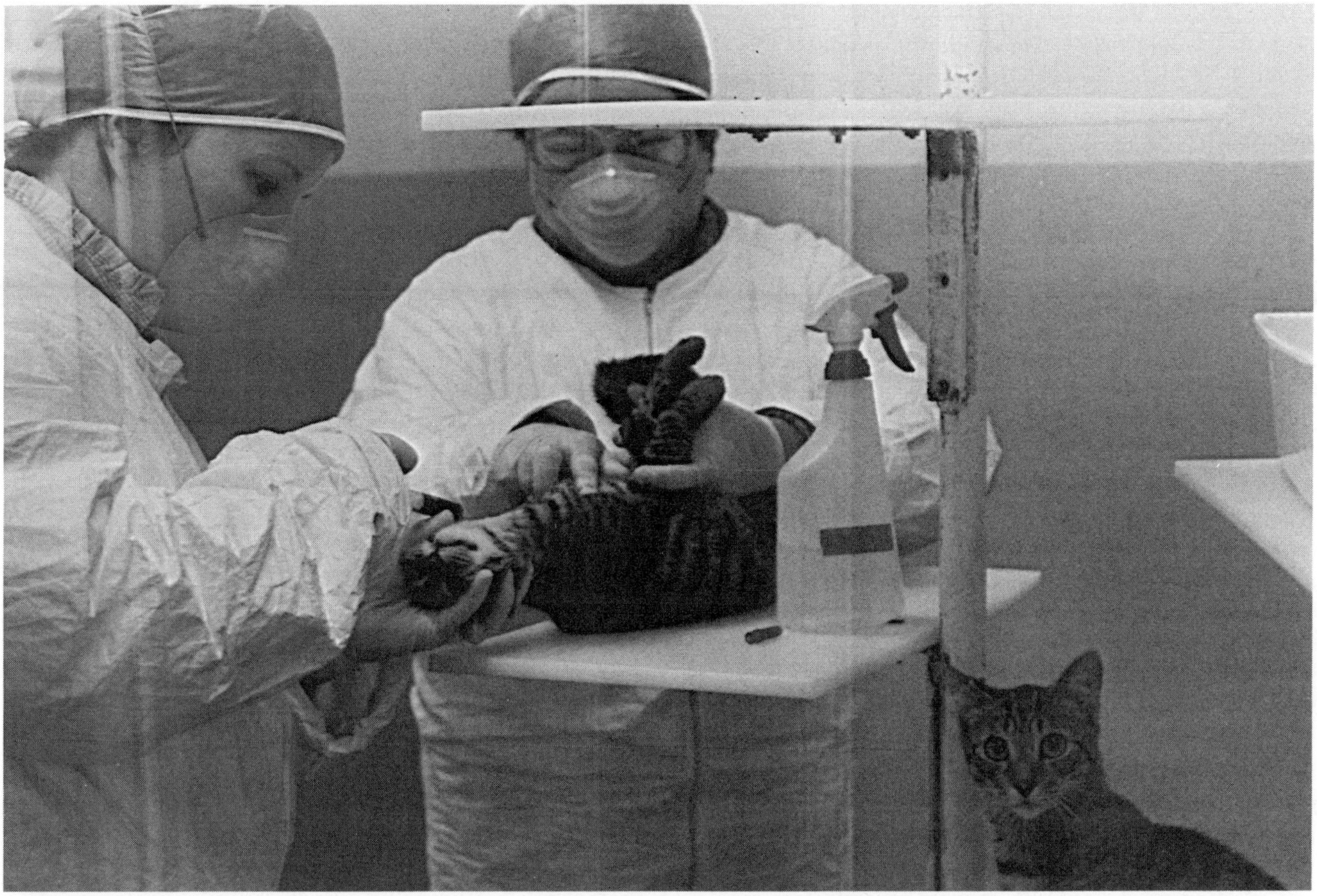

Laboratory technicians in an FTLV isolation chamber at the University of California's School of Veterinary Medicine collect a blood serum sample from a cat infected with FTLV.

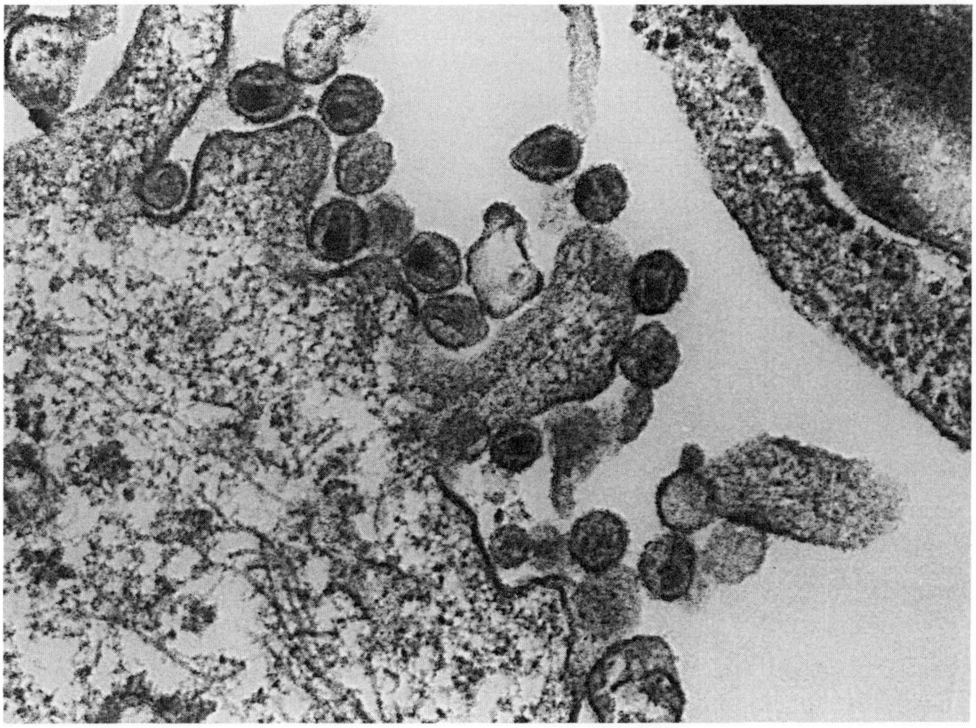

Feline T-Lymphotropic Virus (FTLV) magnified 85,000 times.

own. A wildlife refuge at Mt. Bethel, Pennsylvania, run by the Pennsylvania Raptor and Wildife Association, was co-founded by Hope Carpenter, who has had considerable success in encouraging birds back to normal eating patterns.

A Commitment to Research

In 1987, at the Veterinary Medical Teaching Hospital of the University of California at Davis, (UC Davis) Drs. Niels Pedersen and Janet Yamamoto reported a major research breakthrough: Their discovery involved the recognition, and then the isolation, of Feline T-lymphotropic Lentivirus (FTLV), an AIDS-like virus that may prove valuable for AIDS research in humans. The existence of FTLV was discovered in a Petaluma, California, colony of 43 homeless cats sheltered by a pet owner who had rescued them. The cats, whose ages ranged from kittenhood to 13 years, either lived in the owner's home or were permanently housed in five large open pens designated A through E. During the years 1968 to 1982, the colony suffered few illnesses and few animals died.

Problems began in 1982 with the introduction of a 4-month-old kitten into pen D. Over the next 2 years the cat was persistently sick. Finally, emaciated, ill with chronic infections, and anemic, the cat died. Between 1982 and 1986, 9 other cats from D developed similar illnesses and died. Noticing the similarity between the cats' symptoms and the symptoms of AIDS, the cats' caretaker brought two of the sick animals to the veterinarians at UC Davis. An injection of blood serum from the sick cats into experimental, specific pathogen-free cats quickly produced symptoms showing an inability of the immune system to fight disease. The disease proved to be highly contagious among cats and is spread by intimate and prolonged contact such as biting, scratching, and licking. There is no evidence of cat-to-human or human-to-cat infection.

Laboratory work isolated the FTLV and found it to be genetically different from the AIDS virus but from the same family of retroviruses and related to feline leukemia virus, for which a vaccine has been developed. FTLV could help in the search for AIDS treatments and for an AIDS vaccine. A major barrier in AIDS research has been the lack of a way to cause the disease and test it in laboratory animals. Two viruses can cause AIDS-like symptoms in chimpanzees, but the cat model might prove easier to work with because the feline disease mimics human AIDS more closely.

A second major discovery at UC Davis involved a heart condition called congestive cardiomyopathy, or dilated cardiomyopathy. The disease kills thousands of cats annually. The research at UC Davis recognized the properties of an amino acid called taurine whose absence leads to the disease. As long as a cat is not actually dying, administration of the amino acid corrects and prevents the condition. Upon hearing the news, cat food companies began adding the substance to their products.

At Penn's VHUP, research into hypertension (high blood pressure) in dogs had been going on for several years under the direction of Dr. Kenneth Bovee, chief of the Section of Small Animal Medicine. He has developed a colony of dogs with spontaneously occuring primary hypertension. The only other animal model of hypertension available is 30 generations of rats bred in Japan. A dog model allows researchers to look for new approaches to diagnosis and treatment.

Veterinary epidemiology, or the use of animals to study the causes of disease, is being pursued at VHUP as an alternative to the use of laboratory animals. Pets share an environment with people, and they have many of the same diseases as people, but their shorter life span makes it possible to study the entire course of a disease. Also, pets, in contrast to humans, generally stay at home, don't drink or smoke, and have a relatively constant diet. This reduces many of the variables that complicate studies of humans.

Epidemiologist Lawrence Glickman and his associates have studied the occurrence in dogs of mesothelioma, a lung tumor associated with exposure to asbestos, and tracked the source of the asbestos. The mean age of the dogs with the disease was 8 years, which corresponds to middle age, the period when human asbestos-related diseases are first diagnosed.

The Epidemiology Section is currently conducting a breast cancer study in dogs to examine the risks with nutritional factors, previous hormone use, and drug use. The researchers are collecting data from owners using a questionnaire and a lengthy interview.

Much of veterinary medicine's research has found its way into human medicine and will continue to do so in the future: Just one example is a monumental study begun in the 1960s at Penn's VHUP, in which 10,000 dogs were screened for congenital heart malformations. The researchers were looking for the structural defects that result in oxygen deficient "blue babies," a condition identical in dogs and humans. By breeding litters and removing embryos at various stages of development, the researchers were able to put together a picture that enabled surgeons to operate effectively on human babies who would otherwise have died.

Both human and other animal species gain from the research and treatment of their separate but similar diseases.

URBAN FORESTRY

The Re-Greening of America's Cities

One hundred years ago, the forests of the nation were decimated by harvesting and by forest fires. Citizens alarmed by the loss formed the American Forestry Association and used political leverage and education to help establish the U.S. Forest Service, a federal agency to care for the nation's forests.

Today, the trees that are being decimated are no longer in remote areas, as they were 100 years ago. They are the nation's "urban forest" found in parks, in yards, and on the streets of cities, suburbs, and rural communities.

The nation's urban forest is larger than any national forest. It encompasses 70 million acres of municipal land and innumerable acres in suburbia and in small towns. With continuing development, the forest within urban areas has grown by about 3 million acres during the last decade. Without the excuse of being hidden out of sight in remote areas, the nation's urban forest, nevertheless, is threatened by neglect. But once again, active citizen groups are rallying on behalf of trees.

A 15-Year-Old's Dreams for Future Trees

In 1970, 15-year-old Andy Lipkis was told by a naturalist at summer camp in the San Bernardino mountains that the forest he and his friends were enjoying would be dead from smog in 25 years. Andy's reaction helped to spawn a national and international movement to restore trees to cities.

Andy asked the naturalist what could be done. The naturalist answered that there was not much that could be done about the smog, but there were some trees that would grow in spite of smog. To Andy's question "Why can't we plant them in place of the ones that are dying?" The naturalist said, "You can hardly replant the whole forest."

Before camp ended, however, using camp funds, Andy and his friends planted 20 4-foot-high Coulter pines and incense cedars in the camp's parking lot and ball field. Andy, then spent the next few years learning about smog and trees.

In January of 1973, Andy wrote to the directors of 25 summer camps in the San Bernardino mountains, asking them to join him in a tree-planting project. Twenty agreed to participate. In searching for trees to plant, Andy was met by a daunting lack of interest by the State Division of Forestry. Ultimately, he received help from a state reforestation expert, who in April 1973 presented him with six boxes of seedlings.

If the 8,000 seedlings in the six boxes were to survive until summer planting, each had to be potted in a biodegradable container within 5 days. With the help of scout troops, college students, schoolchildren, and a donation of milk cartons, all the seedlings were potted in time.

During the next 2 months, $10,000 was raised to help with the planting. That fund-raising effort was the beginning of an organization called the California Conservation Project, better known as the "Tree People." Over the summer, the California Air National Guard carried the donated trees to the mountains, and 3,000 campers planted trees. The event became an annual ritual that has renewed the forest at a rate of 150,000 trees every year.

Some years later, in the aftermath of a disaster relief project using volunteers to replace trees destroyed by a forest fire, the Tree People were asked for advice by the city of Los Angeles Planning Department. The department's studies had determined that if 1 million trees were planted in Los Angeles, they would, upon maturity, filter 200 tons of smog from the air every day. Unfortuantely, to plant 1 million trees would take the planning department 20 years and cost the city $200 million.

The Tree People adopted the 1-million-tree-planting goal as a challenge and set the 1984 Summer Olympics as the target completion date. The Tree People pursued a vigorous education and fund-raising campaign, and their three-and-a-half-year effort resulted in the 1 millionth tree being planted 4 days before the start of the Olympics. Andy Lipkis subsequently was made an adviser to the United Nations to work on a plan for a worldwide planting of 1billion trees.

Every year nurseries grow surplus trees to protect themselves against unexpected demand from customers. Usually the surplus is burned to make room for new trees. The Tree People regularly salvage some of that surplus. During the summer of 1986, as part of the Tree People's commitment to worldwide planting, two Tree People volunteers spent 3 months planting 5,000 surplus trees in five countries of Africa. The carefully nurtured 5-year-old, 4-foot-tall apple, plum, pear, almond, pomegranate, and prune trees would bear food within 2 years.

Several years of research, planning, and organizing support within the African countries made the trip possible. The trees were planted in each country to coincide with the rainy season, and to match species with climate and soil conditions.

Trees Atlanta

Andy Lipkis's example has inspired other tree lovers around the country. Atlanta, Georgia, is seriously engaged in trying to protect its urban forest. Atlanta is the most heavily forested city in the United States, with an estimated 62 million trees. Nevertheless, downtown Atlanta offers an impression of mostly asphalt, concrete, and glass.

Between 1977 and 1987, Atlanta lost 15 percent of its trees, as evidenced in photographs taken from the air a decade apart. The loss was due to rapid growth, windstorms, vandalism, disease, and sometimes old age. The city annually loses approximately 4,000 trees from its parks and along its streets. Only about 2,000 trees are replaced each year, creating an escalating loss.

Four Atlantans have battled to turn the tide: Atlanta's city forester, Jay Lowery; Fulton County arborist, Ed Macie; architect-developer John Portman; and the executive director of Trees Atlanta, Marcia Bansley.

Trees Atlanta was founded in 1984. By the end of their Phase I effort, the nonprofit organization raised $106,000 for tree planting; planted 46 large shade trees and 5 large tree planters downtown; obtained $7,000 worth of tree donations for city parks; distributed 3,600 seedlings at both the city's festival of trees and the Historical Society's May Day; donated trees to create the "the Grove of Champions" honoring road race winners; and begun a program to honor "champion trees."

Phase II in 1987 had the goal of raising $150,000 for a targeted street project that would involve planting 63 large willow oaks.

Architect-developer John Portman described some of the special problems of planting city trees. In most central cities, 10 to 12 different owners are found in one city block, most of whom are not convinced they should spend money for trees in front of their property. Portman has been quite successful in persuading owners of the benefits of trees. He believes that the huge scale of downtown buildings calls for 30-to 40-foot-high trees.

Once Atlanta's trees are in the sidewalk, they become the responsibility of City Forester Jay Lowery. He describes a good tree-care program as divided into four parts: (1) planting; (2) maintenance (trimming, mostly); (3) removal; and (4) administration (including surveys and inventories, tree ordinances, and budget battles). His daily problems include concern for drainage, removal of dead limbs, avoidance of hazards to the public, and installation or replacement of tree grates. The needs of a city tree program must be meshed with other needs such as traffic safety and the installation of utility lines.

Fulton County arborist Ed Macie believes trees provide humans with a sense of security, a feeling that home is where trees are. Macie developed 60 pages of administrative guidelines for Fulton County's 1985 tree preservation ordinance. The ordinance says:

> It is the intent of these regulations to provide standards for the preservation of trees as part of the land development and building construction process for the purpose of making unincorporated Fulton County a more attractive place to live, provide a healthy living environment, and to better control of flooding, noise, glare, and soil erosion.

The fact that the ordinance specifically addresses protection and replacement of trees as land is being developed makes it the premier program in the Southeast. Two years after the program had begun, cities in and out of Georgia were looking to it as a guide for their own ordinances.

San Francisco's Friends of the Urban Forest

San Francisco revised its outdated 1959 tree ordinance in July of 1986. The revision also established a salaried urban-forestry position and a Tree Advisory Board to link citizens' concerns for the urban forest with the public agencies responsible for the trees' management.

A San Francisco nonprofit organization, Friends of the Urban Forest (FUF), comparable to the Tree People and Trees Atlanta, was instrumental in the revision of the urban forestry ordinance. An example of a typical community activity involving the FUF took place on the organization's sixth birthday on March 7, 1987. The date coincided with California's Arbor Day. The Arbor Day·birthday celebration was highlighted by a morning of tree planting by students from kindergartens to universities. The catalyst for the project was a group of faculty, parents, and children of the French American International School (FAIS). For almost a year, the FAIS had been "greening" the site of their school, which is leased from the University of California (UC) Extension. As landscape improvements were made, interest grew in the street trees on the exterior sidewalks adjacent to the school.

With help from the FUF, the school organized local residents and organizations to participate with the UC and the FAIS in planting trees around the neighborhood. Volunteers were assisted by workers from the city's Department of Recreation and Parks, who gave up their Saturdays to help plant the trees. The project added more than 60 trees to the neighborhood. The FUF has developed a school program for grades kindergarten through high school, with a curriculum guide and a packet of activities. The step-by-step instructions were tested in 1987 in one elementary, one middle, and one high school. The FUF also works with schools to plant trees on their grounds.

The FUF came into being in response to funding cuts that left no city budget for community tree planting. The responsibility for urban trees in many cities is apt to be divided among a variety of departments and people: for example, the Department of Public Works, Parks and Recreation, Cemetery Boards, and the Port Authority, as well as private owners with trees in their yards. San Francisco departments that had been hard hit by funding cuts drasti-

19

ANIMALS AND PLANTS

Park Place in Atlanta, Georgia. Due to a building boom, parts of downtown Atlanta, the most heavily forested city in the country, have been completely stripped of trees. Tree advocates, in an effort to create a balance between skyscrapers and greenery, are planting 15- to 18-foot trees rather than saplings.

The San Francisco Friends of the Urban Forest have a number of school programs, often helping students to plant trees at their own school or in their neighborhood. One such project was carried out by The Eagle, a community service organization of George Washington High School.

cally reduced tree planting and maintenance. Responsibility for San Francisco's trees was left mostly to property owners. The FUF assumed the task of enlisting private citizens to take on the care of public trees by using a community-organizing approach to engage a four to six block area. To an interested neighborhood, the FUF provides financial assistance; recommends tree species; guides residents through the tree planting permit process; contracts for sidewalk cutting and hole digging; obtains trees, stakes, and ties; provides tools on planting day; teaches workshops on planting; and offers workshops on care and maintenance.

For their part, San Francisco property owners who want street trees are asked to canvass their neighborhood to find other property owners committed to caring for trees and who are willing to pay $95 per tree (approximately half the cost—the FUF pays the rest). A $20 contribution pays for the maintenance education workshops and for a first-year-tree-care visit.

In 1987, the FUF began a yearly maintenance program for both FUF-planted street trees and for non-FUF street trees at about one-third of the cost of a certified arborist. A maintenance call includes pruning, checking supports, cultivating the basin, checking roots, diagnosing problems and recommending treatment, and performing an evaluation of the overall condition of the tree.

The FUF plants about 30 different species of tree. The choice of tree is often dictated by the ''microclimate" in which the tree will be planted. San Francisco's microclimate includes: the coast, with strong winds, salt, fog, and sandy soil; the eastern edge, with more shelter, warmth, and less sand in the soil; and hilltops with rocky soil.

Planned Planting

There is more to planting and protecting trees than digging a hole and dropping a tree into it. The Tree People, the FUF, and Trees Atlanta, all provide substantial technical advice on a local level. In addition, the American Forestry Association provides help on a national level. As a model ordinance, the Fulton County (Georgia) Preservation Ordinance Guidelines cover a wide range of issues such as tree protection, remedial tree care, and standards for selecting replacement stock.

Trees need to be suited to the location in which they are going to be planted. The choice of species depends not only on the microclimate but on neighborhood architecture, constraints such as the width of the sidewalk, and other trees in the area. The wrong kind of root system can damage pipes and tear up the sidewalk. For example, the fig tree family from Australia is suitable for wet areas and attracts certain birds, but needs a wide space such as a public park. For streets, it is usually wise to avoid trees that bear sticky flowers that could make a mess.

When planting a whole area, a variety of trees can be mixed with various options in mind. An area could be in flower all year with a different color each month. Trees could be selected that bear food attractive to particular birds. An area in Australia has eucalyptus trees that attract so many bellbirds that the area is known as Bellbird.

The Function of Trees

Trees do more than provide shelter. They are a major part of the urban watershed. The raindrops trees collect run down their stems into the ground. Without trees and other vegetation, there is erosion, which is a significant problem in many areas of the South. Concrete and asphalt allow only a small percentage of water to soak into the ground; the runoff water is shed into sewer lines, where it causes creeks and rivers to flood.

A mature shade tree cools at the capacity of five room-sized air conditioners running 24 hours a day. With proper placement and species selection, trees form insulation windbreaks in winter. They also absorb glare and dust, reduce the impact of wind, serve as a firebreak, muffle noise, shelter wildlife, and enhance property values.

The Monetary Value of Trees

Unlike trees in remote forests, each tree in the urban forest has a high value. The urban tree is rarely considered for the value of its wood. Instead it is appraised more like real estate. If the street tree is in good condition, its dollar value is about 25 times the value of its remote forest counterpart.

The value of U.S. street trees was calculated in 1982 by James Kielbaso, an urban forestry professor at Michigan State University, to be about $25 billion. Street trees represent only a part of the total urban forest. Park trees may add as much as another $25 billion. More research is needed to determine the census and value of trees on private urban land. However, in the April 1985 issue of *American Forests* feature called "How Valuable Are Your Trees?" Gary Moll provided some "educated guesses" about how to calculate the value of privately owned urban trees. For a 50-year-old tree, he calculated annual values in four areas: air conditioning, $73; erosion and storm-water control, $75; air pollution control, $50; wildlife shelter, $75: Yearly total, $273. Compounded at 5 percent, the tree's lifetime total would amount to $57,151.

The Condition of the Urban Forest

More important than size and value is the condition of the urban forest dispersed over 6,375 urban areas with populations ranging from 2,500 to over 1 million. Urban trees are most healthy during the middle part of their growth cycle—from the time they are about 5 inches in diameter until they are almost 30 years old. The average life span of an urban tree is 32 years.

Once a tree is injured, it invariably becomes infected with microbes and fungi. The tree responds by compartmentalizing the injury to keep the infection from spreading. Isolation of disease is an adaptation of growth processes. The more injuries a tree sustains, the more normal activities are suspended that would otherwise be available for growth. Mature trees contain hundreds, sometimes even thousands, of compartments. When the compartments become too numerous, they can stop the movement of the tree's vital fluids, leading to the death of the tree. Wind, lightning, fire, birds, insects, animals, and pruning are common sources of injury to trees.

The longer trees live, the healthier the condition of the urban forest. The easiest way to extend the average life span of city trees is a good maintenance program, an area likely to be reduced first in budget cuts.

In the North and Central states, trimming cycles should bring maintenance crews to each tree every 5 years. In the South, where trees grow faster, the cycle should be once every 4 years.

Because not enough time and money is spent on maintenance, too much time must be spent on tree removal, which cuts further into the time and money available for planting and maintenance. By extending the life span of its trees to 60 years, the city of Milwaukee, in contrast to other cities, needs to plant only half as many trees to maintain the city's forest.

The Level of Planting Needed to Maintain Current Forest Size

To arrive at the approximate number of trees that should be planted each year, a community can divide the average life span of its trees into the total tree count. For example, New

York City has an inventory of 700,000 trees or locations where trees could be planted. Dividing 32 into 700,000 yields 21,875 trees that New York City should be planting each year. The city's chief forester reported the city planned to plant 9,000 trees in 1987, a substantial increase over previous years, but not even half the number needed.

In 1987, the American Forestry Association reported results of a survey conducted by urban-forest managers of 20 U.S. cities, each of which had been budgeted for tree care for at least the last 10 years. Only 1 city, Lansing, Michigan, was planting as many trees as it removed. A third of the cities plant one tree for every eight removed, and about half replant one-quarter of their losses.

Natural Resource Management

The science of natural resource management in populated areas is gaining in knowledge and skill as specialists in forestry, wildlife, soil science, landscape, and arboriculture interact and exchange information. Recognition also is gaining that an urban tree, if it is to survive, must be able to cope with the hostile environmental conditions of city life.

Although they are more difficult to plant, Trees Atlanta, for example, favors planting mature, majestic trees downtown so that they can be enjoyed almost immediately. Because urban soil is tightly packed, which reduces the oxygen available to the tree, willow oaks and red maples make good replacement trees in Atlanta. Both are native swamp trees used to coping with less oxygen since they live in water. Moreover, willow oaks and red maples cope well with pollution.

For their climate, the Tree People in Los Angeles favor trees that are drought and smog tolerant and they have a Site Inventory Sheet and a Climate Map to help with tree selection. For a paved area where dropping fruit might be a problem, to begin consideration they recommend seven

A worker prepares a site for a tree by breaking up the concrete in order to get at the dirt.

23

ANIMALS AND PLANTS

TREE CARE

WATER

New trees must be given 15 gallons of water per week, which translates to about 20 minutes from a garden hose turned on a low pressure. Adjust the frequency of watering to your particular soil type. If you have sandy or rocky soil, water more frequently but lower the amount so that the tree still gets 15 gallons a week. Clay soil holds water much better, but takes longer to become saturated, so water longer than 20 minutes and less frequently. Check the need for water by feeling for dampness about 2 inches below the surface. For the first six months, the water should be applied only to the surface of the basin. After six months, water half in the basin and half down the gravel watering tube. After one year, the tree can be watered through the gravel column only. This deep watering encourages deep roots and a healthy tree. Watering can be tapered off in 3 or 4 years when the roots become established and ground water supplies its requirements.

ROOTS

Root growth and function are essential for healthy, sturdy trees - but roots can also cause problems with sidewalks and sewer lines. Root pruning can help avoid these problems. A simplified method of root pruning eliminates any roots growing underneath the sidewalk surface. Using a shovel, push the blade into the soil around the edge of the basin to a depth of a least six inches to cut the surface roots. Do this every six months.

SOIL

Cultivate soil regularly. Using a hand spade, loosen the top 1 to 3 inches of soil in the basin so that air and water can reach the roots. Generally, the soil in San Francisco contains the mineral nutrients required by trees, so fertilizer is not usually necessary. If fertilizer is used, FUF recommends a slow-release type such as "Osmocote" that can be sprinkled in the basin and watered into the soil. Be careful when cultivating so that extra soil does not pile up around the trunk. The proper soil level should be at the top of the root crown. If soil builds up around the trunk for an extended time, the tree can be severely injured or killed.

STAKES AND HARDWARE

The small nursery stake that comes with the tree should be removed about one year after the planting. A free-moving trunk develops strength more quickly than one that is tightly bound. The large support stakes, ties, cross-brace and wire mesh provide protection from wind and vandalism. They should be checked regularly for integrity and replaced when broken. Periodic checks should also be made to make sure the tree is not rubbing against the cross-brace. Placing a rubber tie behind the cross-brace will cushion the tree and prevent wounding. Support stakes can be left on until the tree has attained a diameter of 3 inches at four feet above the ground and can support itself.

BASIN

Nothing should be planted in the basin during the first year. Weeds, flowers and groundcovers compete with tree roots for water and nutrients. After the first year, shallow-rooted plants may be put in - although some experts contend that watering them encourages surface roots. Bricks and stones may be placed in the basin one month after planting when the soil has settled. Place them flush with the top of the sidewalk for pedestrian safety. Mulch is also a good basin cover. Mulch is any organic material placed on top of soil to reduce evaporation and weed growth, thereby conserving water. Spread a 2 inch layer of mulch over the surface of the basin each year. Some good mulches are: bark chips, wood chips, leaf mold and compost.

PESTS AND DISEASE

Pests and disease can be checked if they are recognized and treated quickly. Minor attacks can be controlled without pesticides when treated early enough. FUF does not recommend the use of pesticides except in extreme cases. There are some general signs of tree stress to be aware of when checking for pests and disease. Discolored or distorted leaves, abnormal leaf drop, leaves that are chewed or stuck together, cracks and bleeding sap on the trunk, a sooty or white substance on twigs or leaves, and dieback of branches are all indicators of potential problems. Fortunately, most tree species in San Francisco are not especially susceptible to pests or disease, so it's easy to avoid problems with good tree care. A healthy tree is the best defense against attack! The most common pests are aphids, which are easy to control. If aphids are detected, wash the tree with a forceful jet of water. If aphids persist, spray leaves and branches with a mild solution of 1 teaspoon dishsoap dissolved in 1 gallon of water. Repeat three times, each treatment exactly 7 days apart. Spraying your tree is also an effective way to wash off pollution and dust to keep the tree healthier.

**SAN FRANCISCO FRIENDS
OF THE URBAN FOREST**

512 SECOND STREET, FOURTH FLOOR
SAN FRANCISCO, CA 94107
(415) 543-5000

Eventually, this street in Richmond (a section of San Francisco) will be a heavily shaded thoroughfare.

species: the lemon bottlebrush; the weeping bottlebrush; the Australian willow; the Chinese flame tree; the goldenrain tree; the Australian tea tree; and the oleander tree.

Once planted, urban trees need protection from vandalism. Injuries common to street trees are car accidents and nails driven into their trunks to hang up signs.

Urban Forestry on a National Scale

The Director of Programs and Urban Forestry at the American Forestry Association, Gary Moll, describes the condition of the U.S. urban forest as varying by region. The Northeast, from the mid-Atlantic north, with the oldest urban forest, has had to take abuse and neglect for the longest period. On the positive side, a tradition of taking care of trees is older than in other regions, which means that there have been more tree-care programs there. In the Southeast, trees grow too easily to be highly valued, and the region has had fewer, less-effective programs. In the Plains states, on the other hand, where trees are naturally scarce, they have been highly valued. A symbol of their concern is that the National Arbor Day Foundation is located in Nebraska. The urban forest is young in the West, and the traditions of tree care are just now being established. California trees were particularly hurt by tax cuts: Since the early 1980s there has been no state funding for urban tree planting. However, in 1987, a coalition of community and environmental organizations formed to bring a bond issue to the voters in 1988. The bond initiative, called the California Wildlife, Coastal, and Park Land Conservation Act, included $5 million specifically designated for urban forests.

The Broad View Held by Urban Tree-Oriented Groups

The FUF offers guided tours through the urban forest for nature lovers, sightseers, and history buffs. Like the Tree People of Los Angeles, the FUF has enlarged its focus from its own city to include concern for urban forestry on a global basis.

Fulton County arborist Ed Macie in Atlanta, concerns himself with the interrelated systems of the city: wetland habitats, recreational areas, city parks of all sizes, cemeteries where many citizens go jogging, and city landscaping including front yards.

The Tree People have carried their message through workshops and conferences throughout the United States. A result of presentations by Kate and Andy Lipkis in San Francisco and Washington, D.C., was an invitation to help the Smithsonian Institution design an exhibit about the need to save the tropical rainforests. The Smithsonian, in its first advocacy role, committed over a million dollars to the exhibit. The Tree People were to design that part of the exhibit that explores what viewers can do to help save the forests.

The September/October 1987 edition of the Tree People newsletter, *The Seedling News*, announced the fall launching of an urban tree program in England called the "Forest of London." And interest has been expressed in Ireland to establish the "Forest of Dublin," as well as in Scotland for the "Forest of Edinburgh."

Although planting smog-resistant trees is one way of limiting the effects of air pollution on the world's trees, environmentalists feel that this solution, while useful, is simply not a complete answer to the problem. Accordingly, in November of 1987, the American Forestry Association, the oldest citizens' conservation organization in the United States, released a report that asked Congress to move quickly to reauthorize and revitalize the Clean Air Act to control the air pollutants associated with damage to forests.

CONSERVATIONISTS . . . PRESERVATIONISTS . . . ENVIRONMENTALISTS . . . ECOLOGISTS

Are They All the Same People?

Conservationists, preservationists, environmentalists, and ecologists may be—but are not necessarily—the same people. They do share a common goal, the protection of the fragile environments of the world. Where the groups differ is in assigning priorities for protection.

Newspaper, magazine, and television reporters tend to use the terms *conservationist*, *preservationist*, *environmentalist*, and *ecologist* interchangeably. Private citizens who engage in environmental protection activities often use the terms interchangeably, too, and may think of themselves as fitting more than one category. Perhaps the best way to categorize conservationists, preservationists, environmentalists, and ecologists is to look at what each does most frequently.

Conservationists Want to Conserve Threatened Environments

Conservationists are often bent on protecting oceans, waterways, and open spaces to ensure the survival of threatened species in a particular area. The task they set for themselves is frequently called "nature conservation."

Many experts see Madagascar as the world's top priority for nature conservation. Madagascar, officially known as the Malagasy Republic, is a biological treasure in jeopardy.

The fourth-largest island in the world, 1,000 miles wide by 3,000 miles long, Madagascar, located off eastern Africa, evolved in isolation for 30 million years. As a consequence, nature produced plants and animals unique to the

The Ordway Preserve is an open air laboratory for the scientists of the University of Florida.

island. Madagascar is the only home of 142 species of frog, 106 species of birds, more than 6,000 flowering plants, half the world's varieties of chameleon, and more orchid species than all of the African mainland. Ninety-eight of Madagascar's palm tree species, 95 percent of its reptiles, 80 percent of its flowering plants, and 40 percent of its birds are found nowhere else in the world.

The 28 surviving species of lemurs on the island constitute an entire branch of primates. Lemurs are treasured by anthropologists because they provide the closest living approximation of the ancient, squirrel-like ancestors of modern primates, including humans.

Most of the world's experts on lemurs spoke with Malagasy government officials on St. Catherine's Island in Georgia in May of 1987, at a meeting jointly sponsored by St. Catherine's Foundation and the New York Zoological Society. It appears that the government is becoming increasingly committed to conservation. Conservationists hope the beguiling lemurs can become a focus for fund-raising and education. Land set side for lemurs would at the same time maintain the habitat of a multitude of other endangered animals and plants.

The island's biological diversity is crammed into a tiny area, and only about 20 percent of Madagascar remains forested. Its uniqueness survives in fragile habitats: along the eastern coast, a rain forest; in the south, a desert; and along the western coast, an irregular line of deciduous forests. The destruction of a few hundred acres in Madagascar could amount to a greater loss than would the destruction of a much larger area in other parts of the world.

The greatest threat to Madagascar's biological abundance, however, is poverty. Poor farmers slash and burn the forests in order to plant crops. They also use the trees for firewood and eat some of the endangered lemurs.

Madagascar's Spiny Desert.

The crested coua, native to Madagascar, can often be spotted in the dry lowland forests on the northwest side of the island.

Triangular palms found only in an area of several hundred acres in the southern part of Madagascar.

The tree-loving lemurs are small primates found only on Madagascar and a few small islands nearby. Most are cat-sized, ranging down to a few mouse-sized species.

In contrast with other species, the herbivorous, ring-tailed lemur is as much at home on the ground as in the trees. When walking on the ground, the ring-tailed lemur will hold its tail erect in an S shape. Among lemurs, it has the richest vocal repertoire, and appears more likely to bite than other species.

The omniverous mouse lemur is entirely arboreal, leaping from branch to branch through the night, making pinpoint landings. A mouse lemur can be as small as five inches in length.

The white Verreaux's sifaka has a terrier-like muzzle and may have orange, maroon, or black markings. It eats leaves, buds, flowers, fruits, and the bark of large trees. A vertical climber, the sifaka can leap through the cactus-like trees of the spiny forests of south Madagascar without injuring itself.

Another vertical climber, the indri is the largest of the lemurs. Its long back legs create an impression of even greater size. Famous for their eerie howl, a group of indri can be persuaded to howl upon hearing a tape-recording of their own calls.

The last known specimen of giant wild aloe in Madagascar.

The radiated tortoise of Madagascar.

When temperatures become too extreme, this gopher tortoise can find refuge in tunnels beneath the desolate sandhills of Florida. He is on the endangered species list.

The tiny Malagasy tenrec is one of 29 known species of tenrec found on Madagascar. The animal is related to the mole and the shrew.

Not all creatures in need of protection live in Madagascar, or are as appealing as the lemurs.

The Ordway Preserve created from gifts of land to the University of Florida has made it possible for scientists to begin to understand the volatile environment of the Florida sandhills. Shy pocket gophers who endure the fiery summers and bleak freezing winters of the sandhills are tracked into the depths of their burrows using radio transmitters.

Despite their lack of charm, efforts are gaining momentum to save invertebrate (spineless) species in danger of extinction. However, it is difficult to stir up sentiment about snails or horseshoe crabs. The Xerces Society, an organization interested in insects, and the Nature Conservancy, a conservation group, have purchased preserves for invertebrates and have funded research in entomology (the study of insects). A preserve for moths has been created by New Jersey. Entomologists in Japan and New Zealand have successfully moved colonies of wood ants and fist-sized crickets called wetas to safe environments.

Not all creatures to be protected are even living. The Nature Conservancy has purchased a major dinosaur fossil site in Bozeman, Montana. The site, where paleontologist Jack Horner had made some of his most important discoveries, had been closed by the owners because the presence of the scientists and sightseers had interfered with management of the ranch.

Preservationists Try to Preserve Links to the Past

Areas where conservation is practiced are often called "preserves," which serves to blur distinctions between preservation and conservation. As a group, conservationists are likely to be concerned with the future of natural areas and species. Preservationists, on the other hand, are more likely to be concerned with preserving our links to the past.

Salt Lake City preservationists became embroiled in a classic struggle in 1987, when a building listed on the National Register of Historic Places, the Hotel Utah, built in 1911, faced conversion into offices and meeting space. Preservationists were joined by business and government officials in opposition to the plans of the owners of the hotel, the Mormon church. About 73 percent of Utah's 1.7 million residents are members of the Mormon church. The battle to save the Utah ended unsuccessfully on September 1, 1987, when the hotel closed.

Another religious group locked horns with preservationists in Boston. The Church of the Immaculate Conception, whose exterior is listed on the National Register of Historic Places, had its interior partially demolished by its Jesuit owners.

Angry Boston residents and art historians challenged the Jesuits' plan to turn the church's sanctuary into offices and living quarters. The Jesuits explained that they were faced with dwindling congregations and financial problems.

In a move to prevent the demolition, adversaries sought landmark status for the interior of the church. Too late to save the upper sanctuary, the Jesuits agreed to revise their plans and estimated that the new plan would cost them an additional $500,000.

Historical preservation battles are often mounted by local historical societies who raise money through tours, auctions, and sometimes even bake sales. Some more affluent groups are able to raise enough money to buy a historical site, repair it, and sell it under the condition that it will be preserved. With profits from the sale, the groups are often able to buy other endangered sites.

An unusual preservation project involved the purchase by New York State over a period of years of a 250-acre site, 20 miles southeast of Rochester, to be the first Native American State Historic Site. The land surrounds the location of a Seneca village destroyed 300 years ago by French soldiers.

A preservation plan proposed by the National Park Service probably came as a surprise to many Americans, and to visitors from other countries, who assumed a preserve already existed around a historical area in

Spanish moss can be found draped not only on the trees of Ordway, but on trees throughout Florida.

In addition to its desert, from west to east, Ordway has a red-water system of lakes and marshes supporting a variety of life.

The Riviera Theater in Charleston, South Carolina, is caught up in an unresolved debate about its future.

Massachusetts. The plan calls for the restoration of the 4 miles from Merriam's Corner in Concord, past the bloody angle in Lincoln, and on to Fiske Hill in Lexington. These are the 4 miles in which the opening battles of the American Revolution were enacted.

Although there exists a 740-acre Minuteman Park in the area, the actual roadbed where the battles of Lexington and Concord took place belongs to the Commonwealth of Massachusetts, and is concealed beneath blacktop. The plan, proposed 212 years after the battle, is projected to take at least a decade to accomplish. How quickly it is completed will depend on public interest and on Congress. But its fate is up to the lawmakers, who can act under the Historic Sites Act of 1935, which declares, "It is a national policy to preserve for public use historical sites for the inspiration and benefit of the people of the United States."

In Charleston, South Carolina, a city that takes preservation seriously, opponents squared off over a building erected in 1939 on the site of a former music academy. The Riviera Theater, a classic example of Art Deco design, is located on one of the city's most valuable corners. Preservationists hoped to find a developer who would rehabilitate the building as a theater, offering movies, concerts, and plays. The building's owners contended that operation as a theater or a concert hall would be financial suicide. They wanted to remodel the building into offices and shops.

A proposal supported by the owners was rejected by the city's Board of Architectural Review because of proposed exterior changes. Preservationists were unable to find a developer willing to renovate and operate the building at a profit acceptable to the building's owners. The building remained vacant, although everyone wanted it to be preserved.

A preservation project that falls somewhere between preservation and conservation is the Ice Age National Scientific Reserve in Wisconsin. Along 1,000 miles of Ice Age Trail lies a memorial to the passage of the Ice Age in the Pleistocene era. The trail offers a visible record of the last of four ice sheets that melted about 10,000 years ago. Students come from all over the world to study the diversity of landforms in the area.

The reserve was first proposed by Ray Zilmer, Milwaukee lawyer and world explorer, in the 1950s. Zilmer considered the glaciated landscape as an esthetic resource—comparable to seashores, mountains, plains, and deserts. In 1971, Congress established the Ice Age National Scientific Reserve, responding to pleas from Representative Henry Reuss, who demonstrated how our Ice Age heritage had been destroyed in more developed areas. Today, Ray Zilmer's son John carries on his father's concern as director of the National Ice Age Reserve Foundation.

Environmentalists Are Concerned with the Quality of Life

The philosophy of a successful public-interest firm called the Conservation Law Foundation (CLF) highlights a distinction between environmentalists and the other groups. The firm's director, Doug Foy, described his firm's hard-nosed approach in choosing issues in which the attorneys can have an impact. The firm selects areas that affect daily life. Thus, the CLF sued both local and federal agencies to clean up Boston Harbor, the most polluted harbor in the nation. Boston may be the only major city in the country that routinely allows raw sewage to be dumped into its harbor.

In an ongoing case in 1987, the CLF challenged the timber business of the U.S. Forest Service in the White Mountain National Forest in northern New Hampshire and southern Maine. The CLF claimed that the Forest Service lost 43 cents on every taxpayer dollar it spent on the project. In the CLF's opinion, not only did the Forest Service spend money in a waning industry, it jeopardized a quarter-million acres of backcountry whose most valuable use to the local economy was recreation, which brought in visitors.

Environmentalists are concerned with the quality of life, both present and future. An issue of strong concern to environmentalists was addressed with some success in 1987, when the Connecticut Coastal Fishermen's Association sued the cities of Norwalk and Bridgeport, Connecticut.

The suit asserted that the towns were guilty of hundreds of violations of the Federal Clean Water Act. Norwalk agreed to pay $172,500 to an environmental fund established by the group, as well as to pay $45,000 in legal fees.

A federal study scheduled for completion in 1990 had found large amounts of toxic metals, which it traced to discharges into Long Island Sound from sewage-treatment plants. Several of the metals, including copper and cadmium, are known to be ingested by lobsters, crabs, and oysters.

Another environmental action group, the Foundation of Economic Trends, also met with success in 1987. The group, based in Washington, D.C., sued the Department of Defense (DOD). At issue was the DOD's growing research

The EPA has declared that Boston Harbor is the dirtiest in the nation. Inadequate treatment results in the frequent discharge of raw sewage into Boston Harbor.

in biological warfare. The suit claimed that the government was violating the National Environmental Policy Act by not assessing the potential impact of their biological warfare research on the environment.

The DOD agreed to submit its collection of biological warfare research programs to far-reaching environmental impact studies. A compromise between the two parties allowed research to continue while the studies were being conducted.

Ecologists Study the Relationship between Species and Their Environment

One feature that distinguishes ecologists from the other groups is their focus on ecosystems, the interrelations among diverse species and their habitats. Their concerns recently received a substantial boost from the World Bank, the U.S. Agency for International Development. After a 3-year internal review and dogged lobbying by a variety of groups, the World Bank adopted new guidelines, which stipulate that, with few exceptions, the bank will not fund projects that encroach on lands with special concerns, such as those with fragile ecosystems or endangered species. Of particular interest are those areas that support a high diversity of species, such as tropical rain forests, marshes, estuaries, and coral reefs.

In the past, the World Bank has come under sharp criticism for not anticipating the impact of large-scale construction projects in the Third World. Instead of raising the standard of living, critics assert, poor planning had sometimes resulted in environmental catastrophes. For example, they contend that a scheme to raise cattle in Botswana is turning the land into a desert.

The new World Bank policy is expected to encourage countries seeking funding to propose projects that preserve natural resources at the same time they foster economic benefits. Such a project is Bangladesh's shrimp fishery, intended to supplement the current shrimp catch.

Ecologists have seen increased attention to their priorities during the past several years. The Smithsonian Institution and the National Academy of Sciences in Washington, D.C., and the New York Zoological Society in New York, held international conferences that focused on conservation biology. In March of 1987, the U.S. Office of Technology Assessment (OTA) published a report entitled "Technologies to Maintain Biological Diversity."

The stepped-up activity can be attributed to growing recognition that species extinction is being caused by overdevelopment and destruction of natural habitats. Ecologists believe that a diverse environment is more flexible than a homogeneous one. For example, a landscape that includes interspersed woodlands has more diversity than a landscape in which the woodlands have been converted to cropland and grassland. A rangeland with many species of annual and perennial grasses and shrubs has more diversity than the same rangeland after heavy grazing has reduced the number of perennial grass species. An environment that includes both wild and domestic varieties of a crop is more diverse than one that has only domestic plants, because wild plants contain genes not found in today's crop plants.

The OTA report, the result of a 2-year study, was conducted at the request of several congressional committees, including the House Committee on Foreign Affairs. One of the OTA proposals would have a strong impact on private groups concerned with ecology. The proposal called for the establishment of a National Endowment for Biological Diversity, which would have the power to give small grants to expand grassroots efforts.

The report acknowledged how widespread and effective grassroots efforts have been in the United States. Michael Soule, president of the Society for Conservation Biology, based in Washington, D.C., viewed a National Endowment as a critical symbol to underscore the importance of education. In his opinion, the protection and maintenance of biological diversity is as dependent upon widespread education as it is upon developing technologies.

While progress is being made in their various spheres, conservationists, preservationists, environmentalists, and ecologists are wary about the future of the world environment. Many battles continue to be lost, particularly in the areas of illegal smuggling of endangered species, the threat to Africa's elephant herds, the depletion of North American wolf species, and the poisoning of piping plovers and other endangered species of maritime birds as a by-product of a U.S. government program to reduce the population of seagulls on Monmay Islands, Massachusetts.

While conservationists, preservationists, environmentalists, and ecologists focus their activities on slightly different targets, all work toward essentially the same goal of protecting part of the natural or man-made world from an outside threat. Perhaps it could be said that conservationists, preservationists, environmentalists, and ecologists all create a "protection ecosystem." Their separate but similar concerns jostle and jog each other and the rest of us into paying attention to the needs of the planet and to the needs of the creatures on the planet.

2

Health and Medicine

REPRODUCTIVE TECHNOLOGY

The Complexity Grows

Baby craving is the term *Life* magazine has used to describe the urge of otherwise infertile couples to have a child using whatever technology is available. What it means to be infertile depends on the observer's viewpoint. Since 50 percent of all couples having frequent intercourse will achieve pregnancy within 6 months, and 90 percent will be successful within 18 months, one could say that "infertility" begins after 18 months. Other estimates define infertility as the inability to conceive a child after 1 year of unprotected intercourse; under the definition, one out of six American couples are infertile. In 1985, the National Center for Health Statistics estimated that one out of every nine couples either could not achieve a pregnancy or could not carry a pregnancy through to a live birth.

Geneticists and developmental biologists are hard pressed to explain why *all* women are not infertile. A fertilized egg includes "foreign material," the sperm, furnished by the father. Logically, this foreign material should be rejected by the mother's immune system. Thus connections are being made between immunology and reproductive biology. Researchers at Mount Sinai Medical Center in Chicago have shown that in some women, antisperm antibodies do in fact interfere with fertilization.

The Causes of Decreased Fertility

Increased public awareness of infertility is to some extent a result of improved detection of the problem. It is also a reflection of an actual increase in infertility. Statistics from the National Center for Health Statistics recorded a rise among women aged 20 to 24 from 4 percent in 1965 to 11 percent in 1982.

Reasons for the increased inability to have a baby are both environmental and cultural. The environmental sources include exposure to workplace hazards, pollution, and illnesses that damage sperm and ova (eggs). The older a prospective parent is, the more opportunities that parent has had to be exposed to these reproductive risks. Sexually transmitted diseases also contribute to infertility.

The cultural factor that contributes to infertility is postponement of pregnancy. The number of women waiting to have their first child until they are between the ages of 30 and 34 has quadrupled over the last 20 years. The postponement, for whatever reason, reduces the odds for conception and for a successful pregnancy.

A study done by the World Population Council determined that a woman's fertility diminishes slowly until

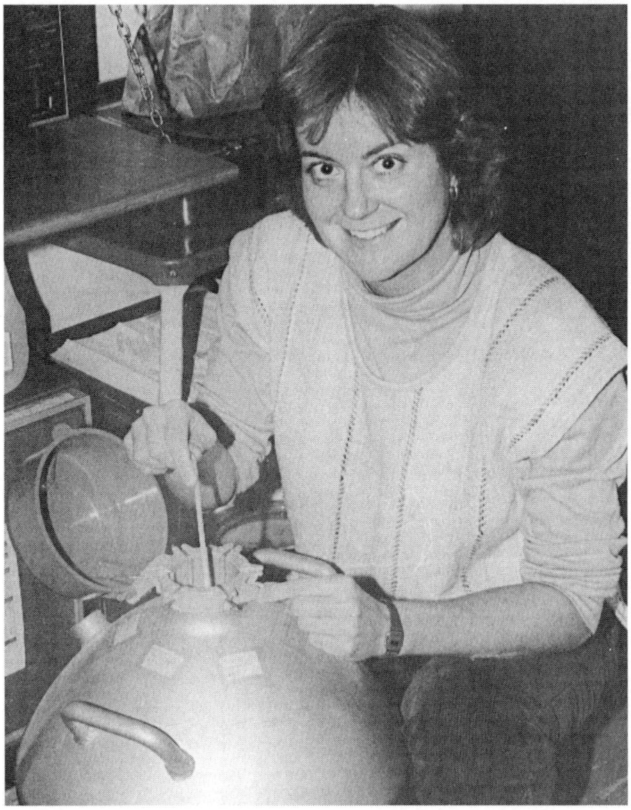

A worker for the Sperm Bank of Northern California is placing vials of sperm into large tanks filled with liquid nitrogen that keep the sperm frozen. The sperm is brought to the storage area in smaller, lighter units that look like thermoses.

age 35, when it drops sharply. The peak of male fertility is reached at about the ages of 18 to 20, after which it decreases. This combination of lowered male and female fertility can make achievement of pregnancy difficult.

Artificial Insemination

Many of the couples who have found themselves infertile have not resigned themselves to the idea. They have turned to reproductive technology or to adoption in order to start their families.

Many of the reproductive technologies have been developed through research by infertility clinics. The best-known technique is probably artificial insemination.

Artificial insemination is a frequent choice when the problem is male infertility. The male may be completely infertile, or the sperm count in his semen may be too low to cause pregnancy. In the latter case, sometimes a simple solution is to concentrate several samples of semen to raise the sperm count to a normal level.

Infertility is not the only reason for artificial insemination. Sometimes the husband may have a transmittable genetic disease, or there might be an Rh incompatibility between the husband's and the wife's blood.

The artificial insemination may use semen from the woman's husband, from an anonymous donor, or from a combination of the two. (Mingling the husband's sperm with that of the donor reduces questions that might ever arise about the child's legitimate status.)

The donor's sperm is commonly purchased from a sperm bank. Increasingly, sperm banks are freezing supplies to enable a couple to return some years later for a second insemination from the same donor, thereby making their children actual siblings. The sperm is kept in vials stored in tanks of liquid nitrogen.

In Vitro Fertilization

In artificial insemination, the sperm is injected into the woman's upper vagina or uterus (womb). In vitro (in glass) fertilization (IVF), sometimes referred to as "test tube fertilization," is more complex than artificial insemination. IVF is most commonly used for women who have blocked fallopian tubes that prevent the mature egg from moving into a position to be fertilized by the sperm.

The woman is first given hormones to increase egg production. Normally one mature egg, ready to be fertilized, is released about once every 28 days. The hormone therapy stimulates the maturation of several eggs at the same time.

When the eggs are ready, the physician inserts a laparoscope (an instrument consisting of a lighted tube with magnifying lenses) through an incision in the woman's abdomen and withdraws them.

The eggs are then fertilized with the husband's sperm in a glass petri dish. After 42 to 78 hours, the fertilized eggs are returned to the uterus where, if all goes well, at least one or more fertilized eggs will become implanted and begin to develop. Since the introduction of the laparoscope into the abdomen carries a certain amount of risk as well as discomfort, to prevent the need for repeated laparoscopies should the hoped-for pregnancy fail, fertilized eggs can be frozen. The freezing technique is called cryopreservation.

The odds of an encounter between a "good egg" and a "good sperm" is subject to a high level of chance, whether the encounter begins "naturally" or "artificially." IVF disappointments are frequent. The nation's oldest in vitro clinic, at the Eastern Verginia Medical School in Norfolk, Virginia, claims a pregnancy success rate of 31 percent. In other words, 69 percent of the center's clients do not achieve a pregnancy. Moreover, some of the pregnancies end in miscarriage. Between 1981 and 1987, IVF produced about 800 babies.

A magnified TV image of the ovum being captured.

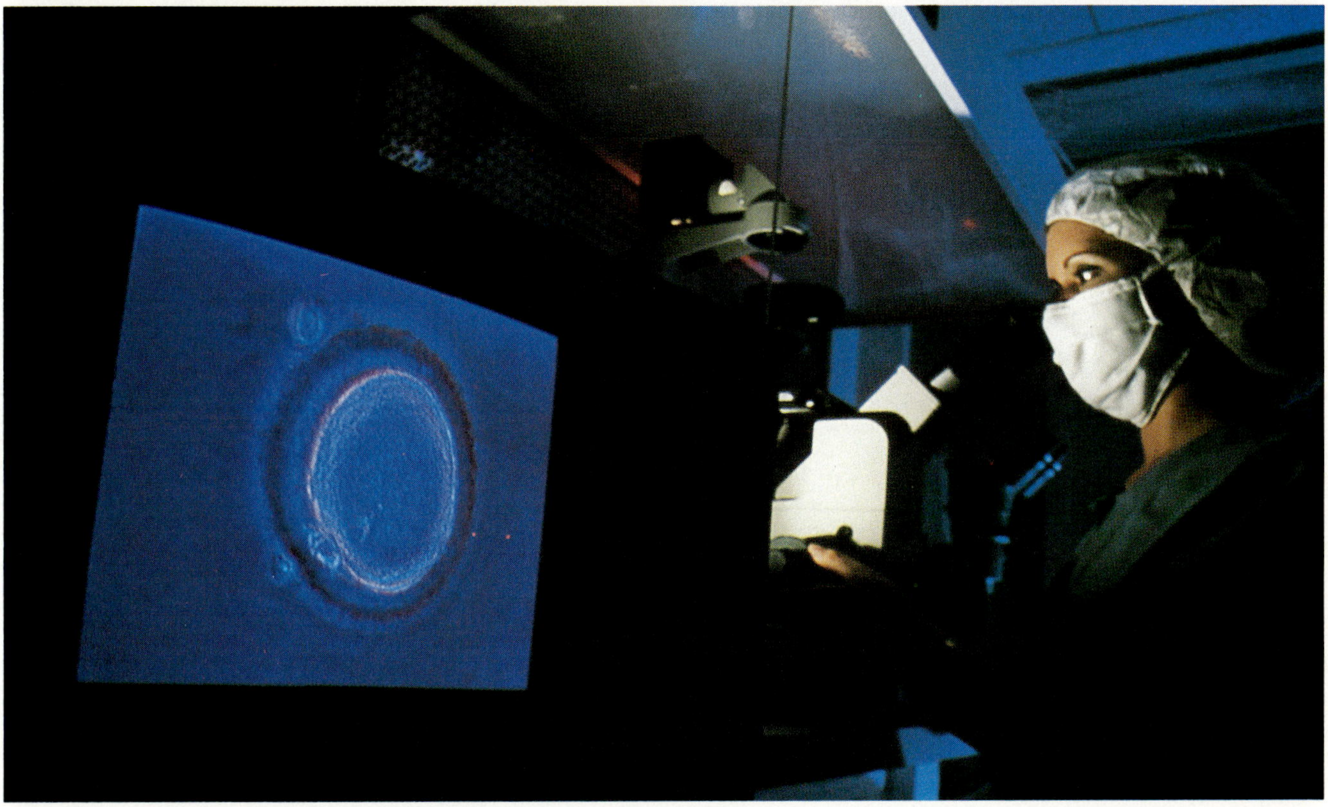

A technician at the Eastern Virginia Medical School in Norfolk looks at an ovum through a microscope to determine if it is mature.

Surrogate Motherhood

There are other options besides IVF that infertile couples can try. If the woman is infertile, or has a health problem that rules out pregnancy, and if her husband is fertile, the couple may use a surrogate mother. This method involves the artificial insemination of another woman with the husband's sperm.

The insemination is preceded by an agreement between the surrogate mother and the couple. The agreement usually calls for the woman to be paid a fee ranging from $10,000 to $25,000. The woman's medical expenses are also usually paid by the couple. Sometimes her living expenses are also paid. In return the surrogate mother agrees to give up all claim to the child.

The practice of surrogate motherhood probably began about 1978. Until 1986, about 600 such arrangements had gone more or less smoothly. In 1986, however, there arose an exception called the Baby M case.

Elizabeth Stern, a professor of pediatrics who had a mild case of multiple sclerosis, and her husband, William, entered into an agreement with surrogate mother Mary Beth Whitehead. However, after the birth of the child, Whitehead did not want to give up the baby, arguing that she had not fully realized the consequences of the agreement when she signed it. The Sterns' position was that William Stern was the father of the child, and that Whitehead had entered into a contract. The case went to court.

Although the idea of surrogate motherhood is not new—there is the biblical story of Sarai, the wife of Abram, who who had her maid bear a child for her—there is no firm body of court cases or customary practices to help determine the outcome of current lawsuits before the courts. One legal view holds that no contract can override the fact that a mother has given birth and is therefore the legal mother. The other legal view holds that a couple's freedom to produce children includes the right to hire a substitute mother. In the case of Mary Beth Whitehead and Baby M, the court awarded the child to the Sterns on March 31, 1987.

While some surrogate mothers perform the service because they need the money, some do it because they enjoy the experience of having babies, and others do it because they like to give the gift of a baby to couples who cannot have one themselves. The sister-in-law of a Massachusetts police officer was inseminated with his sperm so she could carry a baby for her sister, who was unable to bear a child.

A coalition opposing surrogate motherhood, organized by Jeremy Rifkin, president of a small, public policy group called Foundation on Economic Trends, held a news conference in Washington, D.C., on August 31, 1987. At the meeting, Mary Beth Whitehead and several surrogate mothers who wanted their babies returned called on Congress and state governments to outlaw the practice.

Other Help for Infertile Couples

Beside surrogate motherhood, there are still other reproductive technological options. A wife with no eggs of her own but who can otherwise carry a pregnancy to term can receive an egg from an anonymous donor. The donated egg will be fertilized by the sperm of the woman's husband before implantation, then the wife can carry the fetus until birth. In July of 1987, a clinic in Cleveland announced it would recruit women to donate eggs.

There is also a host-womb arrangement. If the woman can produce eggs but cannot carry the baby until birth, she can have one of her eggs fertilized by sperm from her husband and placed in the womb of another woman, where it will be carried to term. The other woman is not necessarily a stranger. In one case, a 48-year-old South African woman, Pat Anthony, was implanted with three embryos belonging to her daughter and son-in-law. She gave birth to two boys and a girl during the fall of 1987. It is even possible for embryos to be fertilized in one uterus, then flushed out and placed in another.

In Washington, surrogate mothers Mary Beth Whitehead (in the foreground) and Patricia Foster (at the podium) added their voices to others asking Congress to ban surrogacy. Foster, unable to finish her speech, was aided by author Gina Corea (center).

In a technique called GIFT (gamete intrafallopian transfer), the egg and the sperm of a husband and wife are placed into the fallopian tube for fertilization to take place in the normal setting. To be successful, GIFT requires that the wife have at least one open fallopian tube.

Avoidance of Pregnancy

In contrast to the many prospective parents who are desperate to have babies, there are many prospective parents who are equally desperate not to have babies. They are looking for methods that will permit sexual intercourse without the risk of a pregnancy. They are looking for a safe method of contraception, more often referred to as birth control.

Birth rates sharply divide the world into two groups. One group limits its population growth to about 0.8 percent annually. The second group has a population growth rate triple that, of approximately 2.5 percent per year.

The second group, consisting of underdeveloped nations, faces a downward spiral in living standards caused by the burden of supporting the additional population. This burden also contributes to the destruction of the environment in these areas. Traditionally, many of these countries have looked to the United States as a model to follow in evaluating new birth control drugs and devices. For many years, the United States was a leader in contraception research and product development, but, according to Elizabeth Cornell, professor of gynecology and obstetrics at Emory University School of Medicine, it no longer is.

Because of the cost of contraceptive research, private industry in the United States has tended to leave most of this work to government agencies or to research projects funded by federal monies. Research for a new contraceptive requires about 15 years, and approximately $45 million in research and development costs, before the product is approved by the Federal Drug Administration (FDA) for sale to the general public.

Now a decline in funding for contraceptive research has stalled the development of new products. The National Institutes of Health (NIH) reduced its annual allocation for contraceptive research from $30 million in 1974 to $7.5 million in 1985. Moreover, most of the money currently being spent on research is for improving present devices rather than developing new techniques.

The number of types of birth control devices available in the United States is shrinking. Lawsuits filed against drug manufacturers have made it difficult for companies to obtain product liability insurance. Lawsuits have also made some birth control products with small profit margins not worth the trouble to produce. Fear of legal action has also led some companies to test and sell new products abroad—some of them thought to be safer and more convenient than products currently in use—without introducing them to the U.S. market.

No birth control method is 100 percent effective or 100 percent free of health risk. Continuing research attempts to raise the level of effectiveness and to reduce the level of risk.

Oral Contraceptives

Oral contraceptives, or birth control pills, first marketed in 1960, supply doses of two hormones, progestin and estrogen, that inhibit release of an egg. Progestin also immobilizes and kills sperm by thickening the mucus of the cervix, through which sperm must pass on the way from the vagina into the uterus.

By 1970, evidence linked oral contraceptives with cardiovascular (heart and blood vessel) problems, and with some types of cancer. Further research found that reduction of the hormones to a fraction of the former amounts drastically reduced the health risks without a loss of effectiveness. However, the birth control pill, once brought into question, never regained its previous popularity. The impact of the adverse publicity continues to make many women fearful of using oral contraceptives.

Barrier Methods

Barrier methods include condoms and diaphragms, which have been in use for thousands of years. A condom is a sheath that covers the erect penis. Originally condoms were made from sheep's gut. Later they were made from rubber. Now they are usually made of thin plastic. Recently condoms have received a great deal of public attention because they provide some, but not complete, protection against AIDS, a lethal sexually transmitted disease (STD).

However, the risk associated with condoms was highlighted by an FDA report in August of 1987 disclosing that among 204 batches of latex condoms tested for water leakage, 41 had a failure rate that exceeded agency standards. In other words, about 1 out of 5 failed the test. Imported brands had an even higher failure rate.

A diaphragm is a cuplike device inserted into the vagina to block sperm from reaching the uterus. Diaphragms are most effective when used with spermicides, chemicals that kill sperm cells.

Spermicides all contain the same active ingredient, nonoxynol-9. They come as jellies, creams, or foams, and can be used either alone or with a diaphragm or condom. Spermicides also come as vaginal sponges, which act as a barrier to cover the cervix, and they come as suppositories and tablets, forms which require a waiting period.

Recently, Ortho Pharmaceutical Corp. launched "Straight Talk,,, the first nationwide classroon sex education program aimed at reducing the number of teen pregnancies. Speaking to the class is obstetrician/ gynecologist Dr. Donald Reisfield.

While not as effective as some other devices, spermicides are used by approximately 3 million women. But as a result of a lawsuit, they may be taken off the market. In a 1985 trial in Atlanta, Georgia, a judge awarded $5.1 million to a woman who claimed that her child's birth defects were the result of a spermicide made by Ortho Pharmaceutical.

The study used by the judge to make the award has been called into question by some doctors. Nevertheless, because spermicides are a low-profit item, manufacturers have little incentive to continue producing them in the face of expensive law suits. Along with spermicides, diaphragms, an even lower-profit item, are also likely to disappear. Ortho Pharmaceutical was the only major U.S. company in the mid-1980s spending significant amounts on the development of contraceptives.

Intrauterine Devices

An adaptation on an old idea, intrauterine devices, or IUDs, were invented in the early 1920s. No one is entirely sure why an IUD, placed inside the uterus, prevents pregnancy. Scientists believe the device inflames the lining of the uterus and prevents the fertilized egg from implanting.

Early IUDs seemed effective and safe. However, as IUDs were used by many women over a long period, adverse effects were discovered. A type of IUD called the Dalkon Shield resulted in hundreds of cases of pelvic inflammatory disease (PID), causing sterility and a number of deaths. At least 12,000 lawsuits, and more then 325,000 claims, were filed against A. H. Robins, the manufacturer. The Dalkon Shield was withdrawn from the market, and the company filed for bankruptcy.

Fears aroused by the Dalkon Shield history may have prompted a number of lawsuits against the widely used Copper-7 IUD, made by G. D. Searle. Most of the suits were decided in favor of the company, but in January of 1986, Searle decided to stop producing both the Copper-7 and another IUD called the Tatum T. With more than 300 lawsuits pending, Searle was unable to obtain product-liability insurance.

IUDs are still worn by 2.3 million American women, but when the devices need to be replaced, most physicians will not have any IUDs on hand. The women will either have to choose another form of contraception or travel to a country where IUDs are still available.

Fertility Awareness

Fertility-awareness methods are also known as "natural family planning," or as the "rhythm method." There are actually three methods, the basal body temperature method, the vaginal mucous method, and the calender method.

The basal body temperature method requires a woman to take her temperature with a thermometer every morning before arising. The sensitive oral thermometer is precise enough to measure tiny changes in body temperature that occur during the normal menstrual cycle.

The temperature drops about 24 hours before ovulation (release of a mature egg), then rises .5 to 1 degree after ovulation. When the temperature has been elevated for 3 full days, it is considered relatively safe to have intercourse. Unsafe days are all the days from the beginning of a woman's menstrual period until the fourth day after the temperature rise.

In the mucous method a woman must pay close attention to the normal changes in the consistency of her vaginal mucus. As ovulation nears, the mucus becomes more abundant, clear, slippery, and stretchable. Ovulation occurs a few days before, or a few days after, maximum "spinnbarkeit," or stretchability, and "peak symptom," when the mucus becomes like the white of an egg.

The calendar method calls for the woman to keep track of the days in the menstrual cycle to try to pinpoint ovulation. The first day of menstruation is counted as Day 1 of a cycle. The last day of the cycle is the day before next month's Day 1. Some cycles are no longer than 21 or 22 days.

Plus or minus 4 days, ovulation occurs 14 days prior to the next Day 1 of the cycle. With a 21-day cycle, ovulation could occur between Day 3 and Day 11. With short menstrual cycles, the method is difficult to regulate.

All three fertility-awareness methods require a substantial number of abstinent days. All three can be rendered unreliable by stress, an illness, jet lag, changes in schedule, or increased or decreased exercise.

Effectiveness of fertility-awareness methods ranges from only 53 percent to 86 percent. However, for women who cannot use other methods, fertility-awareness techniques provide a measure of protection against an unexpected pregnancy. Some advocates suggest that the three methods be used together to increase effectiveness.

In the fall of 1986, researchers at the University of Illinois reported that they might be on the track of an improvement in fertility-awareness methods. They discovered an enzyme in cervical mucus, guaiacol peroxidase, that signals ovulation as much as 6 days beforehand. The enzyme appears to be a gatekeeper that allows sperm to enter only when an egg is present.

Coitus Interruptus

Among the oldest and most unreliable methods of birth control is coitus interruptus. This requires withdrawal of the penis from the vagina before ejaculation, the expulsion of semen. The method is risky for two reasons: Withdrawal is not always achieved on time, and there is always some leakage of sperm even before ejaculation.

Sterilization

The most permanent method of birth control is sterilization. Sterilization for women is called tubal ligation, or tubal sterilization. Using one of five possible approaches through the abdomen or through the vagina, the procedure ties, clips, sews, or seals the fallopian tubes.

Sterilization for men is called vasectomy. In this procedure, one of the ducts through which sperm must travel, the vas deferens, is divided in two, and the ends are tied to prevent the release of sperm.

Both male and female sterilization is almost 100 percent effective. However in a few individuals new channels form around the closed area and restore fertility. As microsurgery techniques improve, the possibility of surgically reversing sterilization increases; however, reversals are expensive and often fail. For these reasons, sterilization should be viewed as permanent by those choosing the method.

Knowledge about and Access to Contraceptives

For several reasons (low profitability, difficulty in getting liability insurance, or public misunderstanding of the product) there are some methods of birth control that are unlikely to become available in the United States. Some of these techniques have already been introduced abroad.

Even without new products, and even with a curtailment of present techniques, there remain available in the United States relatively effective birth control methods. However there also remains widespread lack of knowledge about or lack of access to those methods.

Lack of information and lack of access are worldwide problems. Kenya, which has the world's highest population growth rate, has just borrowed a family-planning education method from Mexico. The well-researched technique uses television soap opera with social messages aimed at altering human behavior.

In Kenya, as in much of the world, awareness is only half of the problem. The other half is access to birth control services. The most recent study in 1984 found that only 48 percent of Kenyan women knew where to get contraceptives, and less than half of those who knew had easy access.

In the United States, many physicians, educators, family planners, and parents attribute the high level of teenage pregnancy to ignorance and to inaccessibility of birth control methods.

Although U.S. teenagers are no more sexually active than their counterparts in other countries, the United States has the highest rate of teenage pregnancy in the developed world. The U.S. rate is 7 times higher than that of the Netherlands, and more than twice as high as that of Canada, Denmark, England, Finland, New Zealand, and Sweden.

Each year, more than 1 million U.S. teenagers become pregnant. Almost half of those pregnancies end in abortion. Given current projected trends, 40 percent of current 14-year-old girls will become pregnant at least once before they reach the age of 20. Some obstetricians believe repeated abortions can lead to later difficulties in carrying a pregnancy to term.

Despite widespread agreement that teenagers are hurt by their ignorance of contraception, there is not much agreement about who should be responsible for providing the information. There is even less agreement about whether teenagers should have access to contraceptives. In 1987, fear of AIDS appeared to be softening resistance to sex-education programs in the schools.

In 1986 the Center for Population Options placed the cost to the public for teenage childbearing at $16.65 billion, not including the cost of housing, day care, or special education. Nor did the Center's figure include the social cost to the teenager who kept her child, thereby curtailing her education and potential adult income. Nor did the figure include the emotional pain to the teenager who chose to have an abortion or to give up her baby to adoptive parents.

The choice to have a baby, or not to have a baby, has never been simple. However in 1987 the situation became more complex than ever before.

AIDS

The Fight Continues

AIDS, acquired immune deficiency syndrome, occupied a prominent position in the news throughout 1987. On national television, and in public forums, the U.S. Surgeon General, C. Everett Koop, in the face of severe criticism, bluntly offered his recommendations for avoiding the disease.

Charged with responsibility for the nation's health, Dr. Koop felt parents and educators were doing too little in the face of the alarming epidemic. He advised parents and educators to provide their children with sex education about the risks of AIDS. Secretary of Education William Bennet differed with Dr. Koop; he argued that school districts should decide for themselves about how to provide information about AIDS to students.

AIDS is a disease spread by the transfer of body fluids such as semen or blood. There is no research evidence that other body fluids, such as saliva or tears, are transmitters. However, on ABC's "Nightline," on June 5, 1987, Dr. Anthony Fauci of the National Institutes of Health (NIH) inserted a qualifying comment about saliva. He said, "What we don't know for sure is whether or not deep heavy kissing, with exchange of substantial amount of saliva, can transmit the virus."

Transfer of the disease is most likely to take place during intercourse, particularly anal intercourse, during childbirth, and by sharing a contaminated needle used for injecting drugs.

A New Definition

Until 1987, a widely accepted definition described people as having AIDS only if they had at least one cancer or one infection known to take advantage of the body's weakened immune system. However, in May of 1987, the Federal Centers for Disease Control (CDC) proposed to a meeting

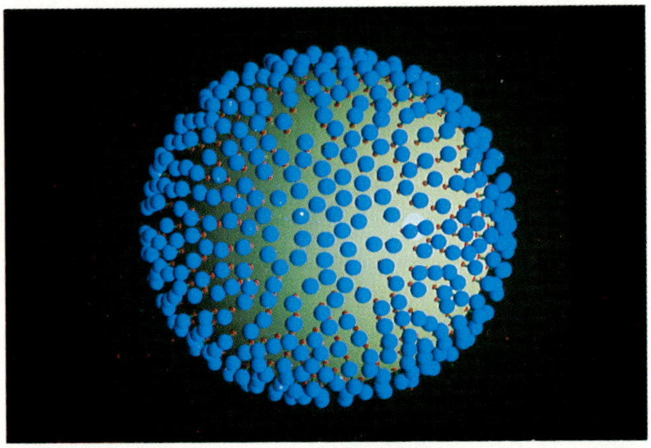

Computer model of HIV, the AIDS virus.

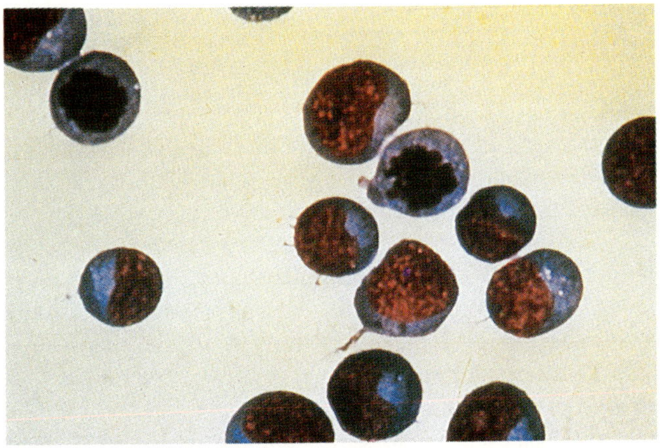

Normal human T cells.

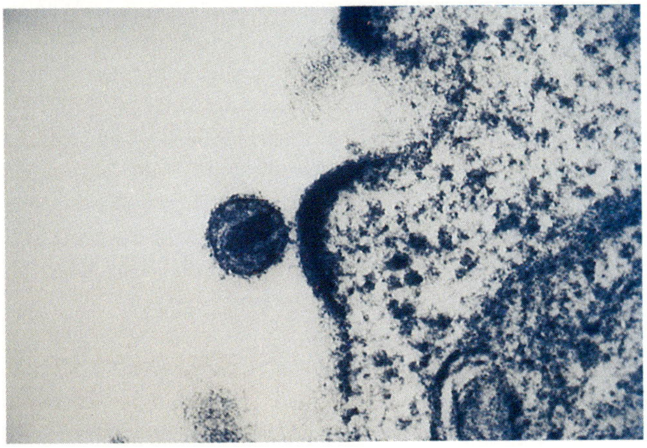

HIV "budding" out of a T cell.

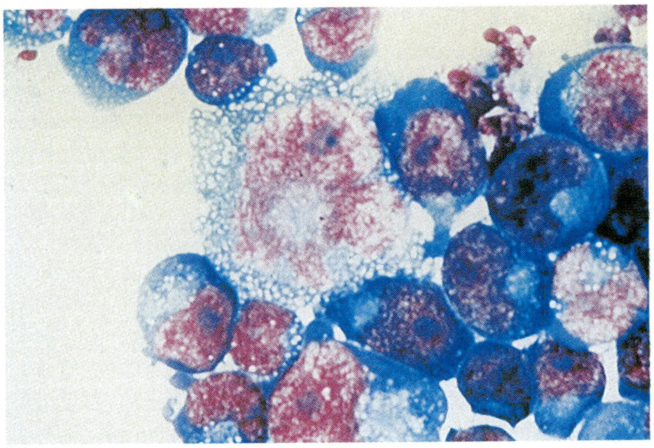

HIV-infected T cells.

of state health officials that the definition of AIDS be broadened to include those who might not have either a cancer or an infection, but who carry the AIDS virus and who suffer from either dementia, a loss of brain function, or from emaciation, a wasting away of the body.

On September 1, 1987, when the nation's AIDS patients stood at 41,366 and the number of deaths from the disease stood at 23, 884, the broadened definition, proposed by the CDC and accepted by state health officials, went into effect. The CDC would henceforth list patients whose physicians presumed they had the disease even if the patients did not meet the CDC's criteria for inclusion.

The new definition makes thousands of additional patients eligible for various programs that could help with some of the social and financial burdens brought on by their illness. The case count with the new inclusions was expected to jump by about 10 to 15 percent.

The Early Fight against AIDS

The exact onset of the AIDS epidemic is not clear. In retrospect, some observers believe that the first case may have been seen as early as 1960.

In the spring of 1981, reports from both the East Coast and the West Coast alerted physicians that otherwise healthy young men were suffering from unexpected illnesses—*pneumocystis carinii* pneumonia (PCP) and Kaposi's sarcoma (KS), a form of skin cancer originally associated with Eastern Europeans. What PCP and KS had in common was that they were both associated with patients who had, for some reason, a suppressed immune system. Kaposi's sarcoma is seen in people who have been given drugs to suppress their immune systems to prevent rejection of a body organ transplant.

It is now known that the AIDS virus is attracted to a particular type of white blood cell known as T-helper cells or T-4 cells. These cells, like all white blood cells, are parts of the immune system, the body's defense against infection. The AIDS virus invades the T-helper cells and in time destroys them.

Under ordinary circumstances, the T-helper cells signal to other immune-system cells that they are needed to do battle against foreign organisms. Once the immune system is suppressed by destruction of the T-helper cells, the body becomes vulnerable to "opportunistic infections," infections that are rebuffed easily by a healthy individual.

Dr. Fauci described the AIDS invasion by saying,

> The genetic material of the virus inserts itself into the genetic material of the cell, but it also has the diabolical capability of just resting there in a way that is hidden from the defenses of the body. . . . The first thing a virus attacks is the very cell that's supposed to protect the body from the virus, so you're essentially wiping out the defense system of the body on the very first day of the war.

The Identification of the AIDS Virus

The pace of AIDS research has been extraordinary. As scientists continued to study the disease, each research advance brought increased awareness of the virus's astonishing complexity. In 1982, only a year after recognition of the disease, experts predicted the virus would be a retrovirus. Many retroviruses were known to infect animals, but only two retroviruses were known at the time to infect humans. AIDS became the third. Retroviruses are so named because of their unusual method of reproduction within the cells that they infect. Their genetic blueprints are in the form of ribonucleic acid, RNA. They carry an enzyme called reverse transcriptase, which commands the infected cell to translate the genetic message of the RNA into deoxyribonucleic acid (DNA), which then instructs the cell to replicate the virus.

In the routine course of genetic functioning, the sequence goes from DNA, the substance of the genes, to RNA, which has several roles in the fabrication of a living cell's products. Since reverse transcriptase reverses the normal sequence, the enzyme has been a target for drugs designed to halt the action of the virus. Success along this line, however, has been limited.

Genes are coded instructions. The cell decodes the message and follows the instructions in order to reproduce itself. Ordinary animal retroviruses have only three genes, which virologists call "pol," the blueprint for the virus's enzymes; "gag," the code for the virus's internal structure; and "env," the gene for the outer coat that determines which kinds of cells the virus can infect.

The AIDS virus has at least eight genes, and probably more. Not all the operations or purposes of the extra five genes are understood. Important among the additional genes that have come under scrutiny is one called "tat." Tat was discovered independently by William Haseltine and his colleagues at Harvard Medical School and Dana Farber Cancer Institute and by Flossie Wong-Staal's research group at the National Cancer Institute. The gene can increase the rate at which a cell can produce new AIDS virus particles by several thousand times. Without tat, the virus cannot be replicated. Therefore, along with reverse transcriptase, tat has become a target for developing drugs to fight the infection.

In its short history, the virus has been known by a variety of names. When Robert Gallo and his colleagues at the National Cancer Institute isolated the first human retrovirus in 1978, they named their discovery "T-cell lymphotropic virus." The virus had an attraction for those white blood

Schematic Diagram of HIV

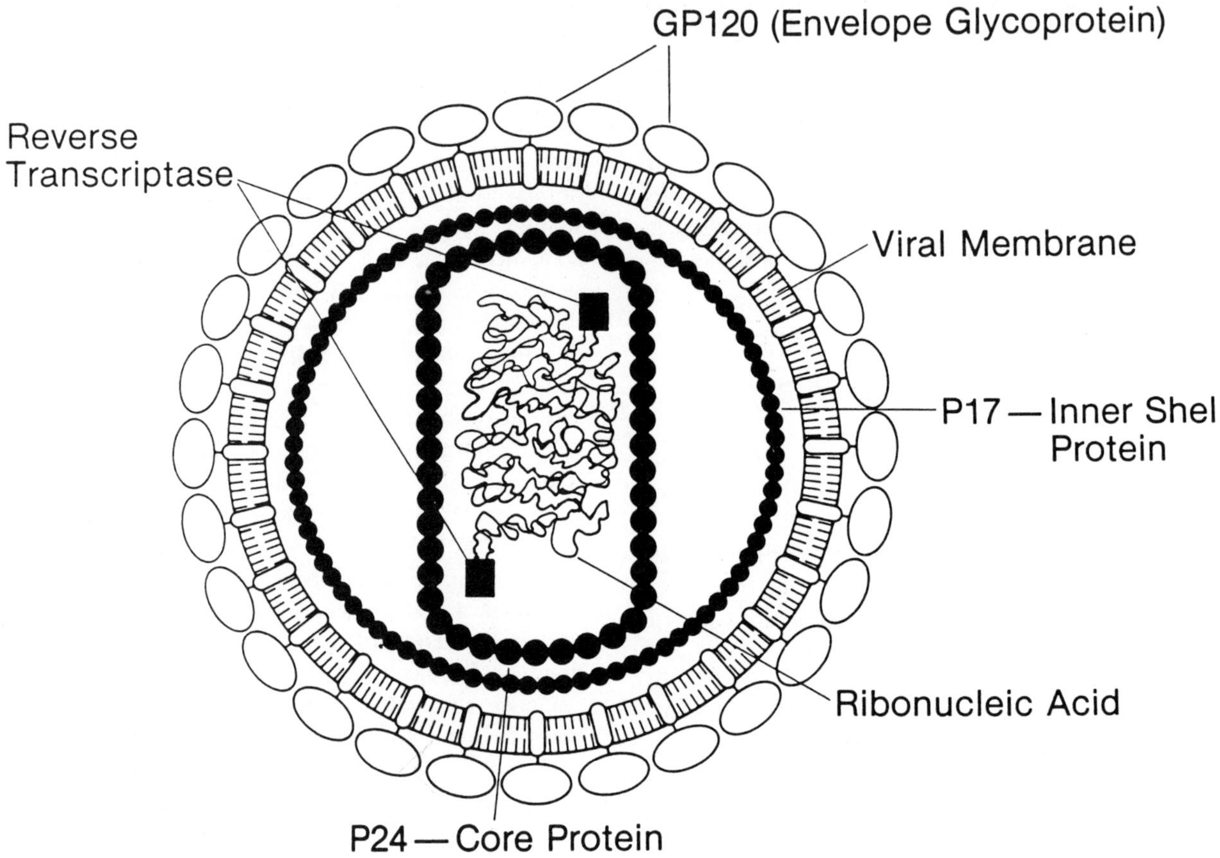

cells that have a crucial role in regulating the immune response. The white blood cells were called "T lymphocytes." The virus led to leukemia.

In 1982, Gallo and his colleagues found a second human retrovirus that also caused leukemia. The first human T-cell lymphotropic virus discovery became known as HTLV-I. The second became known as HTLV-II.

In 1983, researcher Luc Montagnier of the Pasteur Institute in Paris made known to American researchers the results of his work, which led him to believe that AIDS was caused by lymphadenopathy-associated virus, a different but related virus, which he called LAV.

In April 1984, Robert Gallo announced that a variant of the T-lymphotropic retrovirus, which he called HTLV-III, was the probable cause of AIDS. The AIDS virus was ultimately renamed HIV—human immunodeficiency virus. Publications in 1987 tended to use the newer name. Earlier publications were apt to use any one of various terms, HTLV-III, LAV-I, or ARV-I.

Additional research led to a further confusion of names. HTLV-I was later discovered to cause immune deficiency. Luc Montagnier identified among West Africans a retrovirus that he called HIV-2 and that caused disease. Max Essex of the Harvard School of Public Health and his team identified a virus they called HTLV-IV that does not cause disease in humans.

At the Third International Conference on AIDS in Washington, D.C., in June 1987, Robert Gallo announced the discovery of still another, as yet unnamed, retrovirus member of the family that includes AIDS. The new virus was identified among ten patients in Nigeria. Seven of the patients had a disease indistinguishable from AIDS.

In his report at the conference of more than 6,300 scientists and health professionals, Dr. Gallo emphasized that the virus called HIV-I, and known to the public as the AIDS virus, is the principal cause of the global AIDS epidemic.

Dr. Gallo's opinion was that AIDS viruses had infected primates and other animals for millennia, and that many of them periodically had affected humans. Gallo suggested that the infection of a small number of people in rural areas would not be sufficient to continue a chain of human infection for a lengthy period. The infection would die out with the victims it killed. But changes in social mobility have spread people beyond the boundaries of small, isolated groups, where an infection might die out. Changes in sexual attitudes also have increased the potential for widespread infection.

Other scientists disagreed with Gallo's explanation, believing instead that the virus is the result of a more recent mutation of an animal retrovirus.

The Role of T4 Protein

A protein on the surface of T-4 cells has been found to be critical to the cell's interaction with other cells of the immune system—and to the reception of the AIDS virus. The protein has a variety of names: OK T-4, CD-4, and T4.

Researchers believe the AIDS virus attacks cells that have the T4 protein on their surface. William Haseltine, of the Harvard Medical School and the Dana Farber Cancer Institute, believes that the pace at which the AIDS virus kills cells perhaps depends upon the number of T4 proteins that appear on the surface of the infected cell.

Richard Axel and his colleagues at Columbia's College of Physicians and Surgeons transplanted the gene for T4 into human cells that did not normally have that protein. Their experiments found that any human cell with T4 on its surface could be infected with the AIDS virus. They also found that the gene for T4 is active in the human brain.

Edgar Engleman of Stanford University discovered that cells infected with the AIDS virus were changed in a way that increased their likelihood to fuse with nearby uninfected T-4 lymphocytes. By fusing with other cells, the virus could create large, abnormal collections of cells called syncytia. These enormous clusters enable the virus to spread rapidly, killing cells on a large scale.

With continuing research, doubts were raised about whether destruction of the T-4 cells fully explained the impact of AIDS. Evidence of attack by the virus in the brain, as well as in the immune system, was found by Dr. Gallo's team. The virus can also infect monocytes and macrophages (scavenger blood cells that engulf disease-causing invaders).

Scientists were not in agreement about which cells the virus could attack, but the list generally included glial cells (the supporting structure of nervous tissue) of the brain, endothelial cells that line organs and internal body cavities, and possibly cells of the colon. The impact of the virus on other cells suggests that the virus can be sheltered in a variety of cells.

Jeffrey Laurence and his colleagues at Cornell University Medical Center found evidence that in addition to killing T-4 cells, the virus caused the infected cells to produce a protein that reduced the strength of the immune response.

Several groups of scientists in 1985 found that the AIDS virus not only entered the cerebrospinal fluid that bathed the brain and the spinal cord, but that the virus also entered the brain itself. They mounted an effort to discover how the AIDS virus impaired the function of the nervous system.

The neurological symptoms include mild confusion, poor coordination, dementia (psychosis), and an inability to control movement. Researchers were not sure precisely how the AIDS virus damaged the nervous system, but they proposed several hypotheses and began to test them. They reasoned that the intact virus may damage the nervous system either directly or indirectly, that the virus may prompt non-neural cells to secrete toxic substances, or that the virus may act through a combination of ways.

Mark Gurney of the University of Chicago reported that the dementia of AIDS differs from other dementias. In Alzheimer's disease, for example, the cells are dead. With AIDS, they are not. This may mean that AIDS-induced dementia could be reversed.

Difficulties in Developing an AIDS Vaccine

The purpose of a vaccine is to mobilize the immune system against a specific disease. Antibodies are among the body's most effective means of defense against invading viruses and other disease-causing organisms.

Antibodies, made up of protein molecules, recognize and destroy viruses by binding to viral proteins. They thus provoke the immune response. The trigger for this response is called an antigen. A vaccine introduces into the body a harmless form of antigen in order to prepare the body to recognize and respond quickly against a future attack from the actual antigen.

Vaccines in the past have been made with whole viruses that have been killed, or with a viral strain that does not cause the disease. However, researchers are not convinced there are any totally harmless variations of HIV, nor are they assured that an AIDS virus can be rendered irreversibly safe.

Several studies have shown that even the nongenetic component of HIV was sufficient to kill cells. A researcher at Tulane University exposed HIV to ultraviolet radiation, a process that prevents the virus from reproducing itself or from directing the production of new proteins. Yet the virus subjected to radiation killed cells in a culture just as rapidly as did the virus not subjected to radiation.

Whether antibodies to the AIDS virus are sufficient to ward off the disease in humans is also not clear. Some people, in response to the virus, have produced neutralizing antibodies, yet in time have developed full-blown AIDS. Some researchers who have faith in the value of a vaccine speculate that an immune system previously prepared by a vaccine might be in a better position to fight off an attack.

Another significant barrier to the development of an AIDS vaccine is the fact that patients do not recover from the disease. As a consequence, scientists do not fully understand how the virus works, or how the body can successfully defend itself against AIDS. This lack of basic knowledge has resulted in researchers working on a number of different routes toward the development of a vaccine.

A successful vaccine would produce neutralizing antibodies that would bind and kill free viruses, thereby preventing them from infecting cells. A successful vaccine would also incite the body to attack cells that had already been infected. The ability to do battle with already infected cells is critical because HIV can be transmitted within an infected cell as well as being transmitted as a free virus, yet there are no existing vaccines that can neutralize cells that are already infected.

The capacity to destroy infected cells is one part of a larger process called cell-mediated immunity by which T-4 cells instruct a variety of immune cells to perform their tasks. The relative importance of cell-mediated immunity compared with neutralizing antibodies remains unsettled.

Another powerful barrier to the creation of an AIDS vaccine is the variability of the virus. Not only are there variants between people, but viruses even within the same individual have the ability to change. Antibodies developed to recognize the envelope antigens of one variation might not recognize those of another.

A critical question is whether the variations are endless or limited. If the number were limited, a vaccine with a cluster of antigens might be effective. Myron Essex of the Harvard School of Public Health has attempted to analyze the detailed structure of the protein envelope—the shell that encloses the virus's genetic material. Using a detergent that separates proteins, Essex's research team broke down the viral envelope in an effort to learn which protein caused the immune system to make successful antibodies. They were looking for a protein common to all the mutations of the virus that would elicit neutralizing antibodies.

Essex focused on a likely protein candidate called gp120 (glycoprotein, molecular weight 120.0). This molecule sticks out of the virus's envelope like a probe. The probe grabs onto a T-helper cell and enables the virus to penetrate the cell, unless prevented by an antibody locking onto the probe first, like a cork fitting over a pointed object. By generating antibodies to gp120, researchers hoped to disable the virus's capacity to infect T-4 cells.

A physician in Africa sent serum to Essex from many sources, including wild African green monkeys, whose form of the virus was not fatal to either monkeys or to people. Essex suspected that the monkey virus might have mutated in human beings and become HTLV-III, and he thought the monkey virus must have had gp120 or other surface antigens similar to those of HTLV-III. If so, in Essex's view, the manufacture of a vaccine may be possible.

On the other hand, investigators headed by Luc Montagnier of the Pasteur Institute isolated a retrovirus that apparently caused some West Africans to develop AIDS symptoms. The virus was different enough to be undetectable with the standard tests developed for HTLV-III. Montagnier's work thus threw new doubt on the possibility of a vaccine.

At a workshop on AIDS vaccines held in March of 1987, Gerald Quinnan of the Food and Drug Administration predicted there would be initial clinical trials of an AIDS vaccine in the United States during the calendar year. The workshop participants focused on three issues: What is an acceptable end point for an AIDS vaccine trial—protection against infection, or blocking transmission and progression of the disease? How well do preclinical trials predict vaccine results in humans? And which human populations should receive test vaccines?

Even if the search for a vaccine fails, the work accomplished will have an enormous impact on the biological sciences. Particularly significant has been the spirit of cooperation among the researchers.

Predicting AIDS's Incubation Period

For a long while, scientists thought that the less lethal symptoms evident in some AIDS patients might be a milder form of the disease, or perhaps a forerunner of the disease. These less lethal symptoms came to be known by various names, the most common being AIDS-Related Complex (ARC). Estimates place the number of people with ARC as 10 times those diagnosed with full-blown AIDS.

There were hopes that the rates of illness would plateau, or even drop, 5 years or more after the infection. That hope was dashed by data and blood samples gathered in San Francisco beginning in 1977 for a study of hepatitis B. Once a blood test became available in 1985 for detecting HIV antibodies, researchers were able to examine the stored samples and get a rough idea of when some of the persons had become infected.

The San Francisco researchers found that 4 percent of the people who were infected developed the disease within 3

Paul Feorino, PhD, supervisory research microbiologist, uses an ultracentrifuge to search for the agent causing AIDS.

years. After 5 years, the number rose to 14 percent, and after 7 years it climbed to 36 percent. The researchers were unable to identify any factor other than the passage of time that triggered the onset of the illness.

Jeffrey Harris, an economist at the Massachusetts Institute of Technology, an internist at Massachusetts General Hospital, and a member of the Committee on a National Strategy for AIDS, plotted the time elapsed between the original infection and the diagnosis of the illness. Combining results from a study of 83 transfusion recipients, a study of 51 hemophiliacs, and the unpublished CDC study of homosexual men whose blood samples had been collected in San Francisco, Harris developed a composite curve to predict the length of the incubation period. He reported that relatively few subjects developed AIDS during the 3 years following initial infection, although some might have had swollen glands, fever, and other symptoms. After 7 years, many who had been infected still had not developed the disease, but some might have become ill with Aids-Related Complex. Harris predicted that 4 percent of all infected people would have AIDS after 3 years and that 40 percent would have AIDS after 7 and a half years. The median incubation period would be 5 and a half years.

AIDS and Hemophiliacs

Despite the fact that Harris included hemophiliacs in his prediction, an article in *The New York Times* of September 1, 1987, raised questions about whether hemophiliacs fit the norm. More than half of the 20,000 hemophiliacs in the United States are infected with the AIDS virus. Almost all became infected from some of the concentrated clotting factor they received before March of 1985, when blood screening for the AIDS virus was begun. Since a single dose of clotting factor can be derived from 1,000 different blood donors, it is more susceptible to contamination than an ordinary blood transfusion from a single donor. Since 1985, in addition to donor screening, clotting factors have been pasteurized to kill the virus.

Among the approximately 10,000 Americans with severe hemophilia, the CDC has estimated that 70 to 90 percent tested positive for the AIDS virus. Among the remaining 10,000 with mild to moderate hemophilia, the rate of infection was estimated to be 30 to 50 percent.

Despite the high rates of infection, the CDC has reported that only 400 cases of AIDS have been reported among hemophiliacs, 370 in adults and 30 in children. Moreover, the rate of transmission of the AIDS virus to steady sexual partners was considerably lower among hemophiliacs than among other high-risk groups.

Dr. Margaret Hilgartner, chief of the division of pediatric hematology and oncology at New York Hospital, has monitored a group of 200 hemophiliac adults and children since 1979. She suspects that because of the way the clotting-factor concentrates are prepared, hemophiliacs may have received an altered virus that acted like a vaccine against AIDS. Dr. Hilgartner hopes that hemophiliacs might have developed functional antibodies that neutralized the virus. If her suggestion could be proven, it might suggest a route to a vaccine.

National interest turned to hemophiliacs because of a controversy in Arcadia, Florida, over three hemophiliac brothers infected with the AIDS virus. The three boys' ages ranged from 8 to 10.

The local school board barred the children from school, citing them as a hazard to healthy students. When a federal court overruled the school board, the mayor and other parents took their children out of school. There were threats to the family, and their home was burned down under mysterious circumstances. The family eventually left Arcadia to look for a more accepting community.

Dr. Hilgartner points out the absence of grounds for the Arcadia parents' fears. Hemophiliacs are no more likely than anyone else to suffer cuts or to bleed profusely. The hemophiliac's problem is internal bleeding, and the purpose of the clotting factor is to stop bleeding in joints or organs. Thus hemophiliacs do not spread AIDS to others through casual contact.

AIDS's Other Victims

The percentage of AIDS victims in the United States continued to remain higher among gay males than among the population at large, in contrast to Africa, where the AIDS virus strikes down men and women in equal numbers. The ratios among the diagnosed cases in the United States were estimated to be approximately 73 percent for homosexual and bisexual males, 17 percent for IV (intravenous) drug users, 3.8 percent for heterosexuals, 2 percent for blood transfusion recipients, 1 percent for hemophiliacs, and 3 percent undetermined. Many in the undetermined category were counted that way because the patient had died before data could be gathered.

The disease spread so rapidly in Africa that some countries are predicted to lose 25 percent of their populations. The AIDS pandemic (an epidemic over a large region) in Africa threatens world stability.

Some African nations where AIDS is rampant are a source of minerals important to Western economies. Jon Tinker, president of the Panos Institute, a private research and public education organization in London, described preliminary calculations from a study of an unnamed Central African country where AIDS is epidemic. Tinker explained that the net increases in the work force of the country had risen by 3 percent each year for 20 years. He predicted that within 5 to 7 years, the rise would stop and a net decline would begin, even if the current level of 10 to 20 percent among the sexually active who contracted AIDS did not continue to rise.

Many third world governments depend on the military to remain in power. While no firm data are available, anecdotal reports suggest that the military have substantially higher rates of AIDS than does the general population. A rapid turnover in military officers due to illness and death could destabilize some countries.

In 1987, researchers confirmed that AIDS could be passed from women to men—not just from men to men, or men to women. In light of this revelation, efforts to disseminate information about prevention and the reduction of risk were increased. Teenagers were a particular concern in discussions of state-supported AIDS education. Studies indicate that 57 percent of the nation's 25 million young people are sexually active by age 17. Up to one-third of those teenagers do not use contraceptives. Further, teenagers have a higher rate of sexually transmitted diseases than any other age group, which appears to increase their vulnerability to AIDS.

The content of explicit information needed to inform the public about AIDS has created a furor, and the debate showed no signs of tapering off in 1987 as school boards, parents, and health officials battled over dissemination of sex education in schools. Words like *condoms* and phrases like *safe sex* became familiar through repetition on the nightly television news stories and public-service announcements. Debate continued throughout the year over whether heterosexuals who were not members of high-risk groups actually had any reason for alarm.

In August of 1987, the CDC held its first national conference on AIDS and minorities, a population with a disproportionate number of victims. Blacks and Hispanics constitute 19 percent of the nation's population, but they make up 38 percent of all reported cases of AIDS. Among children with AIDS, 80 percent are Black or Hispanic. As of August 24, 1987, there were 563 cases of children with AIDS. The surgeon general predicted there would be 3,000 cases of pediatric AIDS in the next 5 years.

Dennis Bregman (standing) and other CDC staff members are working on AIDS statistics. (Left to right, seated: Paul Pinsky, Kimberly Todd, Richard Rudy, MD, and Liz Cochran.)

Intravenous drug abuse or heterosexual transmission account for 45 percent of Black cases and 39 percent of Hispanic cases. The vast majority of white patients are homosexual or bisexual men.

The Role of Gc Protein

Speculation about behavior contributing to an increased incidence of AIDS continued in 1987. Despite a lack of supporting evidence, sexual promiscuity was widely held to be a causative factor. With a note of surprise, a science news item reported that a woman developed blood signs of viral exposure after only one sexual encounter with her husband, who had acquired AIDS via a transfusion.

A finding by a team of British scientists sheds light on why some victims were vulnerable to even one exposure. The scientists studied blood samples from a group of 375 homosexual men, some of whom were AIDS virus carriers. The scientists found striking differences in susceptibility to AIDS according to the variants of a protein called Gc.

All people have the Gc protein in their blood and on cell surfaces. But the protein is inherited in one of six combinations of three major genetic subgroups. The subgroups the researchers looked at are called "Gc 1 fast"; "Gc 1 slow"; and "Gc 2." All are produced by a gene on chromosome 4. Individuals inherit a combination of subtypes, one from each parent.

The study found that people who had a double Gc 2—they had inherited a Gc 2 from each parent—had a greatly reduced chance of AIDS virus infection even when they had sexual intercourse with partners who were known to be AIDS virus carriers. On the other hand, people who had a double Gc 1 fast—they had inherited a Gc 1 fast from each parent—were far more likely to become infected and to become severely ill. Lesser effects were found in those who had inherited only one Gc 2 or only one Gc 1 fast subtype in combination with some other subtype.

Researchers speculated that variants of Gc might help to explain why AIDS spread rapidly in Africa through heterosexual transmission while in North America and Europe heterosexual transmission had been much slower. In tests done before the discovery of AIDS, 58 percent of 267 Central Africans had at least one Gc 1 fast subtype as compared to only 16 percent among 4,700 Europeans studied.

However, a September news item reported a letter to the *New England Journal of Medicine*, in which scientists at the University of California at Berkeley challenged the British discovery of the Gc gene. The Gc gene was described by the British researchers as able to distinguish those who were vulnerable to AIDS from those who were not. After studying 149 high-risk homosexual men, the Berkeley team concluded there was no link. Clearly, more research is needed in this area.

Other Factors in the Transmission of AIDS

Researchers do not believe that differences in Gc patterns could be the only factor operative in Africa. Research presented at the 1987 International Conference on AIDS in Washington, D.C., shed light on other factors involved in transmission.

Scientists at the University of California at San Francisco presented data from an ongoing study of 513 randomly recruited, heterosexually active women aged 18 or older. The study included about 100 prostitutes. The women were enrolled in the study if they had been engaged in sexual relations during the previous 3 years with a man known to be infected with the AIDS virus, a man in a high-risk group (bisexual, IV drug user, hemophiliac), or at least 5 male sex partners who did not have high-risk factors.

When the study began in 1985, none of the women tested positive for the presence of blood antibodies against the AIDS virus. By the beginning of 1987, 28 had

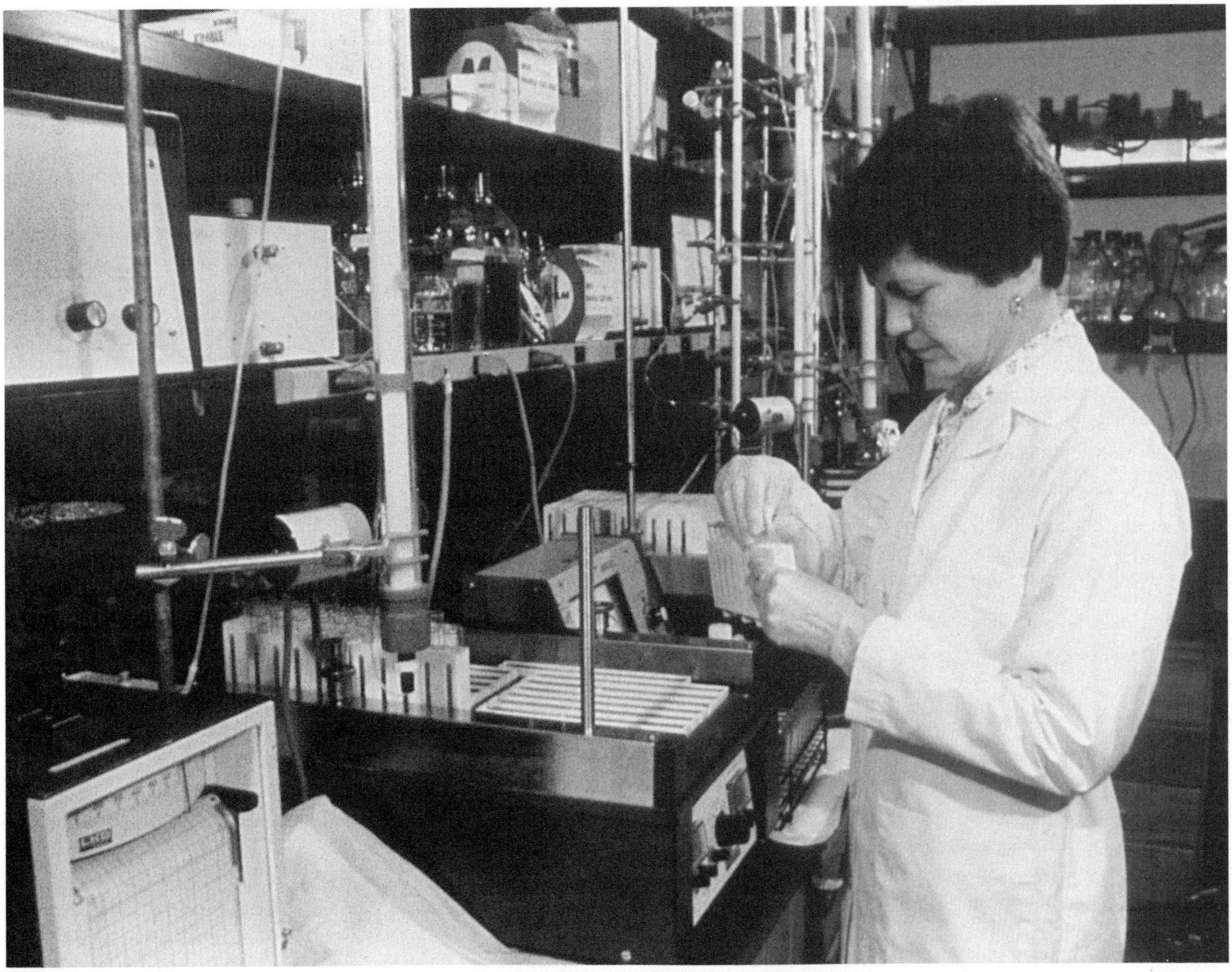

Research chemist Rosemary Ramsey is conducting chromatography of biological fluids from AIDS patients.

"seroconverted" and developed antibodies that indicated infection.

Periodic interviews with the women established patterns of risk. Multiple sex partners who were not from high-risk groups—whether 5 or more than 50 over a 3-year period—did not make a woman more likely than a less sexually active woman to become infected. The risk of infection, however, was doubled through intravenous drug use by the woman, or through sexual intercourse with an intravenous drug user. Having an infected sexual partner carried an even higher risk.

A survey of more than 500 prostitutes in Nairobi by Kenya's Department of Health and by the Institute of Tropical Medicine in Antwerp, Belgium, found that the prevalence of seropositive results increased steadily from 8 percent in 1981 to more than 85 percent in 1987. One significant factor in the Nairobi study seemed to be the presence of other sexually transmitted diseases. Several studies found a strong correlation between increased risk of infection and concurrent venereal disease.

With sexual contact as a principal route of transmission, studies of sexual practices play an important role in predictions about the course of the disease. Researchers at the University of California at Berkeley and at the health departments of San Francisco and California reported a study of 97 female partners of 93 infected men. Researchers found the likelihood of infection increased with the total number of sexual exposures to the infected male partner, and with the practice of anal intercourse.

A study involving patients at sexually transmitted disease clinics in New Mexico found that those not directly confronted with victims of AIDS were less inclined to change their risky sexual behavior.

Treatment of AIDS

On the treatment scene, a drug called azidothymidine (trade name, AZT), began clinical trials in 12 hospitals in February of 1986. Recipients of the drug were AIDS patients who had been stricken with PCP within the previous 4 months. Some patients with ARC who displayed some of the symptoms of full-blown AIDS were also included.

The trials were discontinued in September of 1986 by an independent board sponsored by the National Institutes of Health when preliminary results indicated that among the 145 patients receiving the drug there had been only 1 death, while among the 137 patients receiving a placebo there had been 16 deaths. It was felt, in the light of these findings, that it was no longer ethical to give some of the participants placebos.

AZT stops replication of the AIDS virus, but it does not destroy the nonreplicating virus. The drug can be toxic. In some patients, it suppresses bone marrow production. Since the drug has been tested only on patients with PCP, the effect it will have on children and on adults with other infections or cancer will require further trials. AZT was renamed zidovudine in 1987.

By the spring of 1987, experts in AIDS research were complaining of delays in drug testing caused by technical, ethical, and financial problems; bureaocratic inertia; and lack of cooperation by major drug manufacturers.

The government had planned to license Hoffman-LaRoche to manufacture a promising antiviral drug, DDC (dideoxycytidine), when the plan was challenged by two other drug companies. In spite of apparent industry competition, the president of the Hoffman-LaRoche Exploratory Research Division, when asked why pharmaceutical companies gave a low priority to developing drugs for AIDS, replied "one million people isn't a market that's exciting."

An antiviral drug, AL-721, derived from eggs and developed in Israel, caused such excitement at St. Luke's-Roosevelt Hospital Center in New York that AIDS patients told their doctors they were making the drug at home in their bathtubs. Other promising drugs were slowed by the small size and inexperience of the companies making them.

Advances in hematologic growth factors, hormones that stimulate bone marrow to make red or white cells, offered some promise in the treatment of AIDS patients. When 16 AIDS patients with decreased white cell counts were given granulocyte-macrophage colony-stimulating factor, GM-CSF, the patients' white cell count increased in response. When the treatment with GM-CSF was discontinued, white cell counts returned to low levels. Researchers are hopeful that GM-CSF used in conjunction with zidovudine might alter the fatal course of AIDS.

The majority of cases of AIDS in the United States are clustered in five cities: New York, San Francisco, Los Angeles, Miami, and Newark, New Jersey. The highest per capita concentration of AIDS cases is in a migrant worker's town, Belle Glades, in Palm Beach County, Florida.

The high incidence of AIDS in Belle Glades prompted some observers to suspect that the disease might be transmitted by insects. The CDC, after a brief study, ruled out the insect transmission view, but researchers at the Pasteur Institute in Paris believed insect transmission might be a real possibility.

Caring for AIDS Patients

The concentration of AIDS in urban areas placed financial and staffing burdens upon health care facilities responsible for large AIDS caseloads. Health care staffs in institutions such as Bellevue Hospital in New York daily faced patients whom they knew, despite their best efforts, were going to

In conference are Bruce L. Evatt, MD, director, Division of Host Factors; Steven J. McDougal, MD, chief, Immunology Branch; and Onno van Assendelft, MD, chief, Clinical Medicine Branch.

die. Under those conditions, staffs tended to burn out. Moreover, the fear of being infected remained ever present.

A study of 169 facilities caring for AIDS patients in 1986 by the National Association of Public Hospitals found that hospitals with fewer than 10 percent of the nation's hsopital beds werer caring for 29 percent of all AIDS cases. It cost such hospitals $635 per day to care for AIDS patients, but revenues for the patients averaged only $482 per day.

The surgeon general estimated, in the spring of 1987, that by the year 1991, 145,000 AIDS patients would need health and supportive services at a total cost of $8 to $16 billion.

Services to provide emotional support for AIDS patients, for their families, and for those who treat AIDS patients and families remained scarce. One model therapeutic program is the AIDS Family Therapy Project at the Ackerman Institute on Manhattan's Upper East Side. Another model program that coordinates a variety of services is the Boston AIDS Action Committee. And almost from the beginning of the AIDS epidemic, San Francisco volunteers have created and maintained a wide range of services.

The best of the programs are offered by individuals who have taught themselves the dimensions of the disease, how to raise money for services, and how to provide emotional support for both the dying and those who must learn to live with impending death.

The Future of AIDS

At the end of 1987, experts remained divided in their views of the ultimate fate of HIV-infected people. Many voiced the fear that in time, perhaps two decades or more, every HIV-infected person would develop AIDS. Other experts believe that a significant proportion of the carriers of the virus might never develop AIDS.

During the summer of 1987, the CDC launched a "Long-Term Survivor Study." Twenty-three AIDS-diagnosed patients were enrolled. The project officer, Dr. Ann Hardy, estimated there might eventually be as many as 100 patients included. The earliest date of diagnosis of those enrolled at the outset of the study was 1982.

One long-term survivor, Michael Callen, a singer-songwriter, made a presentation to the annual meeting of the American Public Health Association in 1986. He told the membership that the unthinking repetition of the idea that everyone dies from AIDS contradicted reality and became a self-fulfilling prophecy that made the possibility of survival less likely.

Meanwhile, an eminent historian of science, Barbara Gutman Rosenkrantz, remained unimpressed by projections of the havoc that could be expected from AIDS. She pointed out that AIDS was projected to kill approximately 9,000 victims in 1986 and 54,000 victims in 1991. By comparison, at the turn of the century, tuberculosis killed as many as 150,000 Americans annually. Currently, about 100,000 infants die each year in Latin America from diarrhea.

Whether or not AIDS is an unimpressive disease in the annals of science, it continues to be a disease that not only kills its victims but also stigmatizes their life and death. A reader wrote to a California newspaper, the *Orange County Register*, to ask about an obituary that had reported an individual's cause of death as Kaposi's sarcoma. The reader wondered whether the newspaper were covering up AIDS-related deaths.

The news editor replied to the newspaper's readers, "We can't report it if we're not absolutely sure and if we're not absolutely sure, we shouldn't take the chance of slurring someone's good name after they've gone."

HEMATOLOGIC GROWTH FACTORS

Helping the Body to Produce Blood Cells

In what may be the century's greatest advance against infection, hormones called hematologic growth factors have been developed to stimulate bone marrow (the soft tissue filling spaces in the spongy interior of bone shafts) into making red or white blood cells.

If continuing research is as promising as initial research, then there are many uses to which the hormones may be put. Cancer patients who are given chemotherapeutic drugs that destroy bone marrow are vulnerable to infections while the marrow is growing back. The growth factors could increase the immunity of patients and allow them to safely take higher doses of chemotherapeutic drugs to attack the cancer. In hospital burn units, organ transplant units, and trauma units, patients are more apt to die from infection than from the problem that brought them into care. A wide variety of hospitalized patients would be able to fight infection with the help of the growth factors. In the United States each year, there are an estimated 5,000 bone marrow transplant patients, 200,000 cancer chemotherapy patients, 10,000 to 20,000 burn patients, and more than 20,000 AIDS patients who could benefit from the hemapoietic (blood-producing) growth factors.

Recombinant Erythropoietin and Kidney Dialysis

Stimulation of red blood cell production was the focus of a study at the University of Washington in Seattle by Joseph Eschbach and his colleagues. A substance called recombinant human erythropoietin was administered to 25 anemic patients with chronic kidney failure.

The patients were all undergoing dialysis, a medical procedure in which patients are attached to a machine that filters out elements normally removed from the blood by the kidneys. Anemia, a reduction in oxygen-carrying red blood cells, is a major complication of chronic kidney failure. About 25 percent of patients undergoing dialysis require transfusions of red blood cells.

The mechanisms underlying the dialysis patients' anemia are complex. They include a reduction in the production of erythropoietin, and a shortened survival time for red blood cells. Erythropoietin is a hormone produced mainly in the kidneys in response to low oxygen levels. The hormone controls the production of erythrocytes (red blood

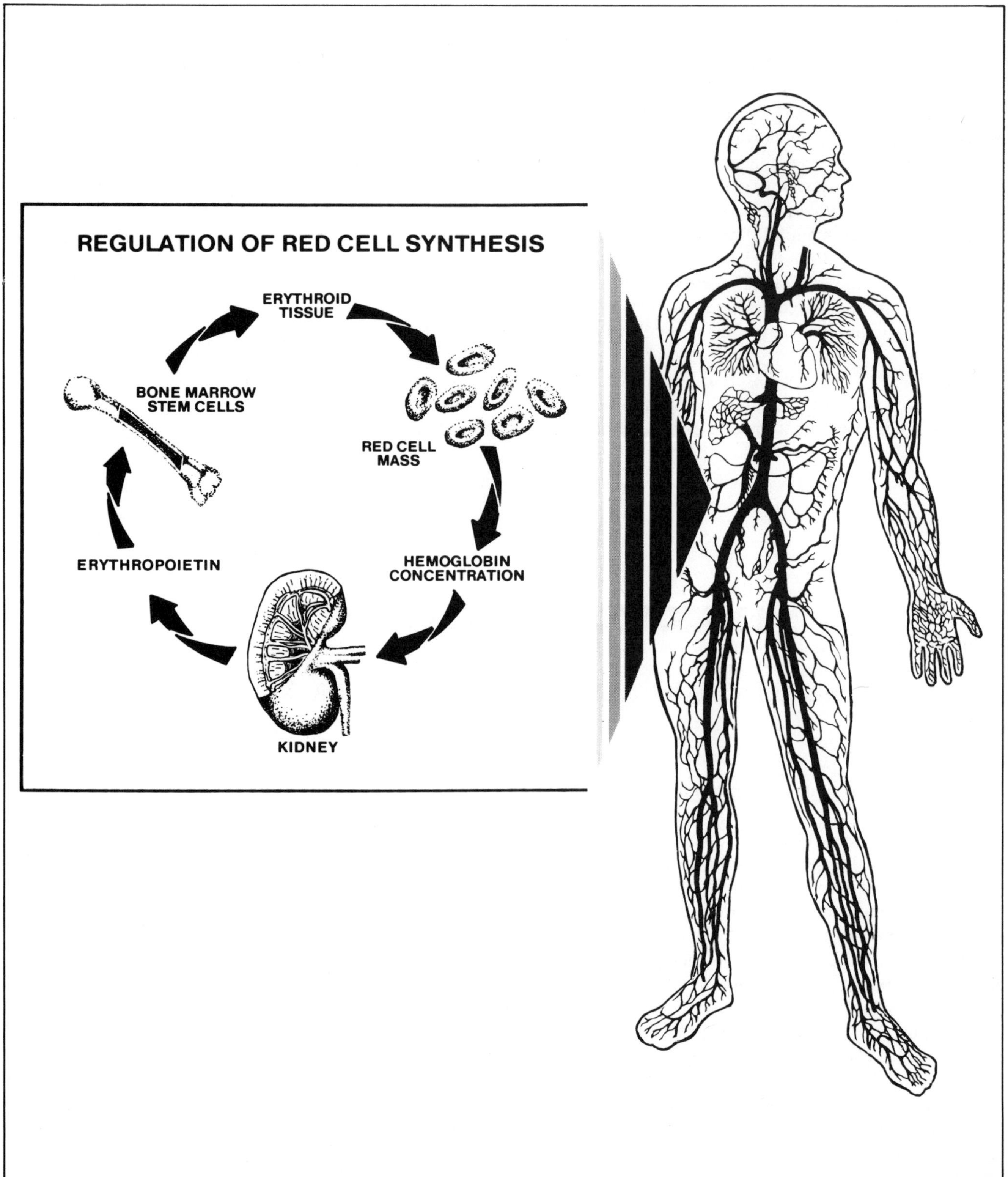

In a normally functioning body the kidneys will produce the hormone erythropoietin, which will then travel to the bone marrow to act upon immature precursor cells (stem cells) causing them to multiply, divide, and differentiate into adult red blood cells. (The stem cells in question can become several different kinds of cells.) The red blood cells will then bring oxygen to tissues and carry away carbon dioxide. The kidneys are triggered to produce more erythropoietin when the hemoglobin concentration falls.

cells), and thus is able to raise the oxygen-carrying capacity of the blood.

With standard care, the anemic dialysis patient has been routinely treated either with blood transfusions or with androgens (male hormones). Treatment with erythropoietin had not been possible in the past because the substance had proven too difficult to purify in large quantities.

The development of recombinant-DNA techniques (in which a DNA molecule is broken into pieces and recombined in a new form) made it possible to produce enough recombinant erythropoietin that the drug could be tested as a treatment method. Varying doses were given to 25 anemic patients, and a response was seen in doses of 50 units per kilogram of body weight or higher. Of 18 patients receiving effective doses of recombinant human erythropoietin, 12 who had required transfusions no longer needed them. In 11 more patients, the number of red cells increased to a level closer to normal.

The elimination of transfusions is a major improvement for anemic patients undergoing dialysis because it removes the risk of iron overload, infection, and the development of antibodies that may prevent an eventual kidney transplant.

The success of the dialysis patient trials at the University of Washington led to multicenter clinical trials with dialysis patients. A similar study was done in Europe. An erythropoietin study was planned for patients not yet in need of dialysis.

The Long Search for Hematologic Growth Factors

Although excitement about the potential of hematologic growth factors is new, study of them has gone on for years. The first reports of a substance like erythropoietin appeared more than 100 years ago, when a French physician, Denis

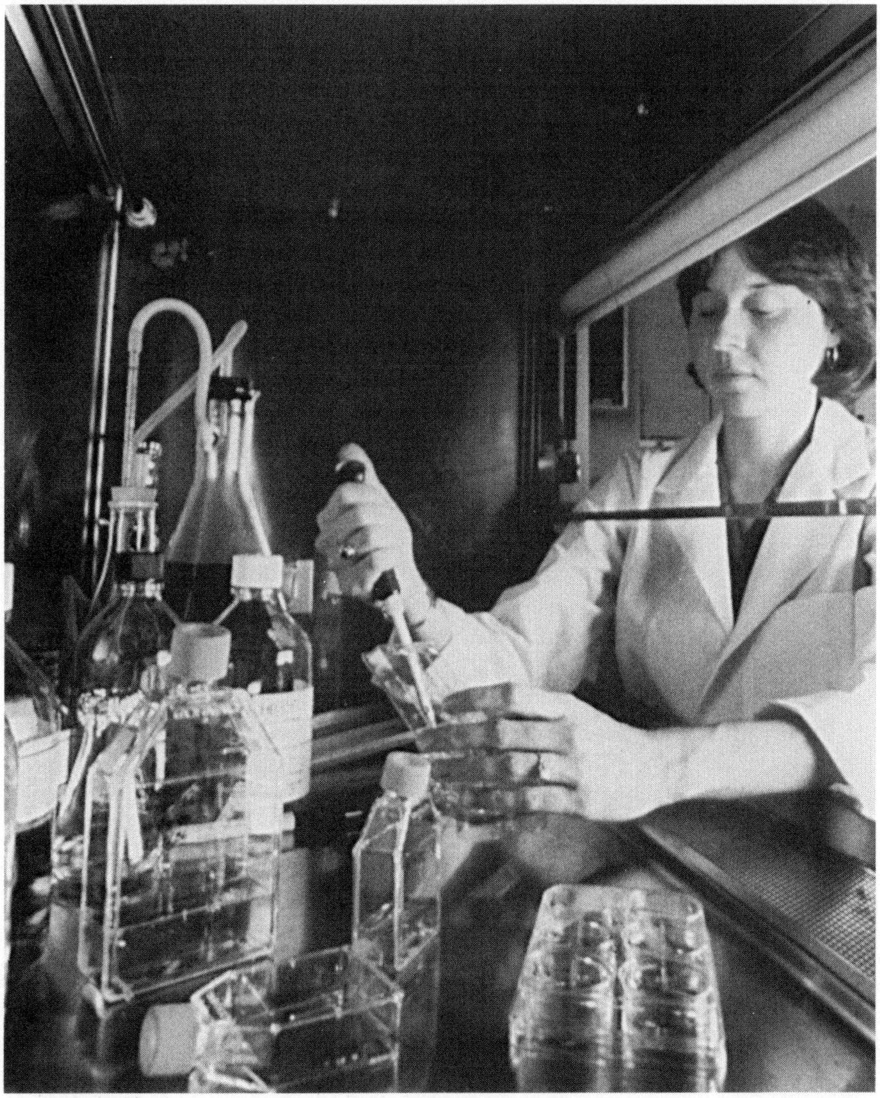

AMGen research scientist Joan Egrie prepares to test a sample of recombinant erythropoietin, which is currently in Phase III testing throughout the United States.

Jourdanet, working with patients who lived in the highlands of Mexico, found they had an increased level of red blood cells.

Early in this century, investigators began a search for a factor that would stimulate the bone marrow's production of red blood cells. In animal research in the 1950s, scientists found an ingredient in the plasma (the watery, colorless liquid part of blood) that could elevate red blood cell production. In 1957, Leon Jacobson of the University of Chicago demonstrated that the ingredient, called erythropoietin, was manufactured by the kidney. In 1985, a researcher at AMGEN, Fu-Kuen Lin, cloned the erythropoietin gene.

The white blood cell·stimulating hormones' history began in the mid-1960s in Australia and in Israel. Donald Metcalfe and his colleagues at the Walter and Eliza Hall Institute of Medical Research at the Royal Melbourne Hospital, and Dov Plusnik and Leo Sachs of the Weitzmann Institute, discovered that the bone marrow of a mouse could be grown in semi-solid agar gel (a gelatin used for cell cultures).

Both red and white blood cells begin in the bone marrow as "stem cells." A stem cell can take several routes as it develops. One direction will result in a white blood cell called a granulocyte, which fights off infections. Another direction will lead to the stem cell becoming a red blood cell.

The researchers found that the marrow cells in culture would grow and become different only if unknown "factors" from body fluids were present. They called these unknown elements colony-stimulating factors.

The unknown factors existed in such tiny amounts that some scientists doubted their existence. The researchers who believed in their reality had to ignore the skepticism of their colleagues while they struggled to purify the substances. Eventually, several researchers, including Donald Metcalfe of Melbourne Hospital in Australia, and David Golde of the UCLA School of Medicine, were able to isolate the colony-stimulating factors. All have since been cloned either by AMGEN of Thousand Oaks, California, or by the Genetics Institute of Cambridge, Massachusetts.

The first trials of hematologic growth factors were performed on monkeys. In one experiment, Karl Welte and his colleagues at the Memorial Sloan-Kettering Cancer Center demonstrated that a white cell-stimulating hormone, granulocyte colony-stimulating factor (G-CSF), had a significant impact.

When the monkeys were given the hormone, their white blood cell count increased from the normal range of 10,000 to as much as 100,000 cells per microliter of blood. Within 24 hours after treatment began, the white cell count began to rise. Within 3 days after treatment had ceased, the effect of G-CSF disappeared.

Welte and his associates next gave to monkeys a drug (cyclophosphamide) that almost destroyed the monkey's bone marrow. The monkeys were then given G-CSF. Instead of the usual 3 to 4 weeks for bone marrow regeneration, the monkeys' marrow was restored in a week.

In still another investigation, Welte and his team extracted and set aside some bone marrow from each monkey. The monkeys were next given dosages of chemotherapeutic drugs that were sufficiently high to eradicate the monkeys' bone marrow.

The marrow extracted earlier was reintroduced into each monkey's body, and the monkey was given G-CSF. Within 10 days, each monkey's marrow had grown back sufficiently for the monkey to have a functioning immune system. Without G-CSF, the restoration of the marrow took 3 weeks.

Human Trials

Following the monkey studies, a human study using G-CSF was done at Sloan-Kettering in New York. The investigation involved patients with genital-urinary tract cancers, mostly bladder cancer. This group of patients was chosen because genital-urinary tract cancer virtually never has an impact on the patient's bone marrow. However, chemotherapy damages the bone marrow and kills the body's cells that make G-CSF. The researchers, Janice Gabrilove and her colleagues at Sloan-Kettering, and Lawrence Souza of AMGEN, the supplier of G-CSF, reasoned that the absence of G-CSF slowed down bone marrow regeneration.

The researchers worked with 16 cancer patients who were receiving chemotherapeutic drugs that are toxic to bone marrow. When the patients were given G-CSF, the response of their bone marrow was comparable to that of the monkeys. The hormone significantly decreased the time it normally took for depleted bone marrow to restore itself.

Another human study by Jerome Groopman of New England Deaconess Hospital in Boston examined a different white cell-stimulating hormone. Working with AIDS patients, Groopman used a recombinant human hormone called granulocyte macrophage colony-stimulating factor, or GM-CSF.

A normal white cell count is 4,000 to 6,000 cells per microliter of blood. The AIDS patients, whose bone marrows had been suppressed as a result of the AIDS infection, had white cell counts as low as 1,600 cells per microliter.

The reasoning underlying the research was the possibility that a GM-CSF deficiency might cause the bone marrow suppression found in the AIDS patients. One proposal was that the GM-CSF might be manufactured by the body's T-cells, which are destroyed by the AIDS virus.

In the collaborative effort, Groopman was joined by David Golde of the UCLA School of Medicine, Dagmar

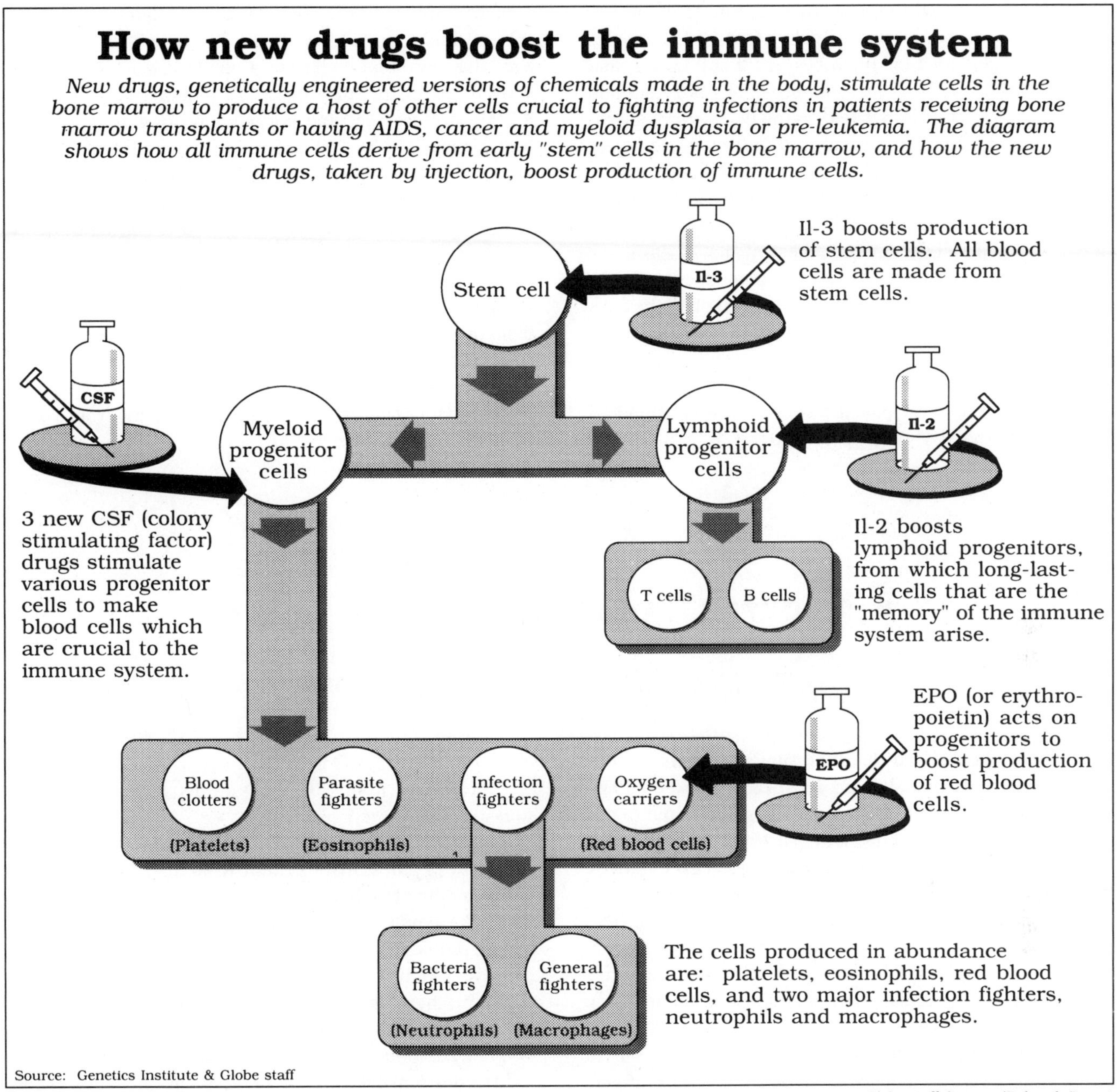

Globe staff diagram/Deborah Perugi

Oette of Sandoz, and Steven Clark and his colleagues at the Genetics Institute. Groopman gave the hormone to 16 AIDS patients. As a consequence of their illness, all the patients had low white cell counts.

The intent of the study was to examine whether the size of the dosage of GM-CSF was related to the size of the increase in the white cell count. It also sought to discover whether there was a maximum tolerated dosage.

Groopman and his colleagues found that increase in white cell counts was directly related to the dosage. They also found that the maximum tolerated dosage was so high that patients at that level produced 50,000 white cells per microliter of blood, approximately 10 times the normal level. The maximum levels were accompanied by minor flulike symptoms.

The white cell counts of AIDS patients on doses of GM-CSF lower than the maximum reached at least a normal white cell range within 10 days of treatment. There were no significant side effects.

A Third Growth Factor

In addition to GM-CSF and G-CSF, a third growth factor called interleukin-3 is also available. GM-CSF, G-CSF, and interleukin-3 all stimulate a different stage in the development of bone marrow cells. GM-CSF activates white blood cells that kill microbes, including viruses and bacteria. G-CSF induces a smaller group of white cells and specifically seems to stimulate the growth of granulocytes, which among other things remove or destroy bacteria and cell debris. G-CSF may also encourage immature white cells to differentiate and mature. Since immature white cells are typically found in patients with leukemia, G-CSF may prove beneficial in the treatment of this disease.

Interleukin-3 acts at the beginning of stem-cell differentiation and is thought to start the growth of all the cells that GM-CSF and G-CSF stimulate, and to also activate T-cell production.

The hematologic growth factors can be expected to be expensive. Their development has taken a long time and therefore has cost a great deal. Robert Kamen of the Genetics Institute estimates that a bone marrow transplant patient might pay $1,000 to $3,000 for GM-CSF. However, the hormone could cut a patient's stay in intensive care by one half. Since intensive care in 1987 could cost $3,000 per day, and the normal stay for a bone marrow transplant might be 18 to 21 days, a reduced hospital stay due to hematologic growth factors could actually result in reduced medical expenses. It could also decrease the patient's exposure to other illnesses that can be acquired while in the hospital.

Reluctant to promise too much, researchers in the area of hematologic growth factors have generally not heralded their findings or sought widespread publicity. Yet, if their results continue to be positive, and if side effects continue to be negligible, hematologic growth factors could create radical changes in the care of patients suffering from a wide range of serious illnesses.

THE EPSTEIN-BARR VIRUS SYNDROME

The So-called Yuppie Disease

A highly publicized and sharply disputed epidemic in the resort community of Lake Tahoe, Nevada, between 1984 and 1986 brought the Epstein-Barr Virus Syndrome to the public's attention. The ailment in question is known under various names—chronic Epstein-Barr virus (EBV) infection, chronic mononucleosis, chronic fatigue syndrome, or sporadic neurasthenia. The illness is believed by some experts to be a growing epidemic and by others to be the latest health hysteria. The syndrome may have existed for some time as isolated cases, but it now appears to be occurring in clusters.

The syndrome has not apparently been fatal, but it wreaks havoc with the lives of its victims. Persistent fatigue is experienced by almost everyone. In some cases the fatigue is so severe that it may become disabling. At the very least, it interferes with work and curtails social life.

Most victims experience low-grade fever, muscle pains, depression, headaches, recurrent sore throats, swollen lymph glands, and allergies. Many victims find it difficult to think clearly or to concentrate. A common description is ''feeling like a Raggedy Ann doll,,, or being caught up in an endless case of the flu coupled with the mental confusion of Alzheimer's disease.

The illness has been referred to as the ''Yuppie Plague,,, or the ''Yuppie Flu,, because of the population it strikes. It seems to disproportionately affect nurses, doctors, and other professionals. Twice as many women as men are affected. And many of the victims have fast-paced, stressful jobs.

Some virus experts are of the opinion that much chronic fatigue is psychosomatic. Eliott Kieff, head of infectious diseases at the Brigham and Women's Hospital in Boston, thinks the syndrome is a disease of younger adults who are having problems at a time of life that is normally difficult. However, Anthony Komaroff, director of general medicine at the Brigham and Women's Hospital, whose group has studied over 500 patients, is convinced that the chronic fatigue syndrome is an organic disease. He believes that the sudden onset of the disease suggests an infectious agent. One day a patient is fine and healthy, and the next day he or she develops something like the flu that never goes away, and may ultimately be left without the strength to lift a comb. Moreover, Komaroff feels that the swollen glands, fever, and sore throats are difficult to attribute to a psychological cause.

An Old Illness by a New Name

Many experts believe the syndrome has been around for many decades, although some accounts do suggest a new illness. The clinical symptoms have appeared in the medi-

One of the country's few experts on the Epstein-Barr virus is Dr. Stephen E. Straus, chief of the medical virology section at the National Institute of Allergy and Infectious Diseases.

cal literature for at least a half a century under such names as encephalitis, Iceland disease, Royal Free disease, and postviral fatigue syndrome. Reports of outbreaks in eight different countries date back to 1934.

Stephen Straus, chief of the medical virology section of the National Institutes of Allergy and Infectious Diseases, is one of the few experts on the illness. He is of the opinion that the symptoms have been described by patients for over a century, and that in each decade a different explanation of the symptoms arises. He sees no evidence that the disease is expanding.

The Extent of the Disease

Accurate estimates of the number of cases are hard to arrive at. The National CEBV (Chronic Epstein-Barr Virus) Syndrome Association has 8,000 dues-paying members, and in 2 years distributed 60,000 brochures to interested people. Gidget Faubion-Jones, president of CEBV, believes that tens of thousands of Americans have the disease. Forty percent of her members are health-care professionals, predominantly nurses; 20 percent are educators; about 10 percent are airline personnel; and the rest fall into other categories.

Investigators at the Brigham and Women's Hospital found during a 6-month period that 20 percent of 500 patients seeking primary care reported they had suffered severe fatigue for at least 6 months, accompanied by chronic sore throat, aching muscles, and headaches. Other scientists are skeptical that 1 out of every 5 medical patients could have suffered from chronic fatigue.

The EBV is known to infect only two different types of cells in the body, white blood cells called B lymphocytes and some salivary gland cells. Saliva is the only bodily fluid that has been proven to contain infectious EBV particles. EBV has been shown to be a herpesvirus, and like all other herpesviruses, once contracted, it persists in the body for life.

One way to confirm that an EBV infection has occurred involves detecting antibodies to some of the virus proteins in the serum of patients. Another test for EBV infection is recovering the virus from the throats of patients. However, finding the virus does not establish how recently the infection began.

The development of specific tests for EBV infection made it possible to test samples from patients with a variety of other conditions of unknown cause. Widespread tests revealed that almost everyone has been exposed to EBV, often during childhood, with little or no apparent effect. Approximately 90 percent of all adult Americans have at some time had contact with the Epstein-Barr virus. The virus lies dormant until the immune system weakens and the virus proliferates.

When exposure to EBV infection is delayed until the teenage and early adult years, about one-third of the cases result in an illness called infectious mononucleosis. It is believed that the symptoms of acute infectious mononucleosis are the result of an excessive response by the body's immune system. Infectious mononucleosis is a syndrome, that is, a clinical collection of signs and symptoms that can result from a variety of causes. EBV is the most common cause of the syndrome, accounting for about 90 percent of all typical cases. The less typical the clinical picture, the less likely that EBV is the cause.

In addition to acute infectious mononucleosis, several rare disorders have been associated with the Epstein-Barr virus. The defense system of patients with some of the rare disorders in which lymphocytes are impaired (immune-deficient patients) may fail to control EBV infections properly. An immune impairment as a result of cancer drugs or as a means to prevent rejection of transplanted organs may have the same effect.

The Source of the Current Flurry of Interest

In January of 1985, the *Annals of Internal Medicine* carried two articles that pointed to the Epstein-Barr virus as a possible cause of chronic fatigue syndrome in the United States. The two articles reported that among 75 patients with persistent fatigue, a sizable majority had high levels of antibodies to the Epstein-Barr virus. The presence of the virus did not necessarily signify that the virus caused the syndrome. The presence of the virus could have been due to some other factor having weakened the immune system.

Publication of the articles was followed by an aggressive mass mailing from a testing company urging physicians to buy an Epstein-Barr evaluation kit. About the same time, the National CEBV Syndrome Association was formed. Physicians were inundated with requests to evaluate chronic fatigue.

Anxiety about the syndrome increased still more when two doctors, Paul Cheney and Daniel Peterson, in Incline Village, Nevada, near Lake Tahoe, diagnosed 150 patients with a chronic mononucleosis-like syndrome between the fall of 1984 and the fall of 1985. Cheney reported that 70 percent had elevated antibody levels for the Epstein-Barr virus.

At the urging of the two Nevada physicians, CDC researchers Gary Holmes and Jon Kaplan went to Lake Tahoe in the fall of 1985 to investigate. As a result of their investigation, Holmes thought that only 15 patients met the case definition. He also felt that there wasn't enough difference between levels of Epstein-Barr antibodies in the case group with levels in a control group to distinguish one group from the other. Moreover, the CDC investigators found that the patients had elevated levels of antibodies against several other viruses, which made the link with the Epstein-Barr virus tenuous. However, Holmes conceded that conversations with patients who had run in marathons and competed in triathlons in the past and now found themselves too weak to brush their teeth made it evident that something was wrong.

Critics of the CDC researchers' report claim that their investigation was conducted too early, when many patients had been ill for only a few months, making it difficult to define the disease clinically and to identify its cause. James Jones of the National Jewish Hospital and Research Center in Denver viewed the CDC study as limited. He advocated a more thorough analysis of possible causes, including the Epstein-Barr virus, in patients who had been ill for a year or more.

Jones is of the opinion that the outbreak was caused by a specific syndrome and that the Epstein-Barr virus is one of the agents that can induce the syndrome. He also points out that many of the patients had classical allergy symptoms, which could signify either an immune system in disarray or a genetic predisposition toward the chronic mononucleosis syndrome.

Robert Gallo, a leading AIDS researcher, and his colleagues at the National Cancer Institute (NCI) found human B-lymphotropic virus (HBLV) rather than Epstein-Barr virus as a common viral denominator in six patients with disorders that affected B-lymphocyte production. Two of the six were also infected with the AIDS virus. The HBLV is a DNA virus that resembles Epstein-Barr virus and other herpes-like viruses in appearance, but differs in several other respects. Before drawing any conclusions, Gallo and his colleagues planned to test a large number of people who did not have the disease to see how many might be infected with HBLV.

A possible connection between HBLV and the chronic mononucleosis-like syndrome led to collaboration between the NCI researchers and physicians like Paul Cheney in Lake Tahoe and other investigators in Boston, New York, Houston, Fort Lauderdale, and Miami, where there had been similar outbreaks of the syndrome. Anthony Komaroff, a member of the collaborative effort, pointed to several possible causes in the New England area. He speculated whether there might be a new variant of the Epstein-Barr virus, or some other virus reactivating a latent Epstein-Barr virus infection, or environmental toxins, or stress as an activator.

Treatment and Prevention

There is no proven treatment for Epstein-Barr virus or any other viral illness. Many physicians simply offer psychological support. Gidget Faubion-Jones is very much at odds with the suggestion of purely psychological help. She feels there are physical symptoms that can benefit from medical treatment.

About 80 percent of CEBV members have vestibular disorders—inner ear and balance problems. Some members have benefited from diet, others from rehabilitation therapy, and others from medication for neurological damage. Dr. Komaroff believes that some symptoms can be treated medically, but until there is a fundamental breakthrough in research, he feels physicians have little to offer.

In hopes of unraveling the mysteries, Congress has ordered the CDC and the National Institutes of Health to study the phenomenon. The CDC began an effort to create a strict definition of chronic fatigue in order to make epidemiological studies feasible.

While EBV is hard to avoid, it is also hard to spread. Only a small percentage of susceptible household contacts

Dr. Anthony Komanoff, director of internal medicine at Brigham and Women's Hospital in Boston, believes that chronic mononucleosis, sometimes called chronic Epstein-Barr virus, "encompasses at least three syndromes." They are true chronic mononucleosis, which "may stem from an immunologic deficiency," the apparently rare severe chronic active EBV infection, and the most common, chronic viral fatigue syndrome.

of those with infectious mononucleosis develop the infection. Nevertheless, contact with the saliva of those infected is not recommended. Patients with the chronic fatigue syndrome that may be associated with EBV also seem unlikely to spread the disease.

The Answers Remain Maybe and Maybe Not

Stephen Straus mused that, normally, more is understood about specific diseases than about their causes; however, with EBV more is known about the biology of the virus than about the diseases it provokes.

There are two reasons to implicate EBV with the chronic fatigue disorder. One, in some cases the chronic fatigue and associated symptoms begin with acute infectious mononucleosis. And two, some of those infected individuals possess levels of antibodies to some EBV proteins in amounts and patterns that suggest recent or active EBV infection.

There are several reasons that argue against EBV as the cause of most chronic fatigue syndrome. The illnesses usually do not begin as acute infectious mononucleosis, and many of the components of that illness are absent. Also, some individuals with symptoms have no antibodies to EBV, and therefore have never been infected with the virus. Finally, some individuals without clinical symptoms of the syndrome carry EBV proteins in amounts and patterns that suggest recent or active EBV infection.

In an editorial published in the *Journal of the American Medical Association* in May of 1987, Stephen Straus wrote,

> It no longer seems appropriate to consider all patients with the chronic fatigue syndrome to be suffering from purely psychoneurotic disorders. On the other hand, we are still struggling to prove an organic basis for this condition. Unfortunately, the present lack of definitive diagnostic and therapeutic tools for assessing and treating individuals with the syndrome leaves both patients and health care providers frustrated.

The Immune System

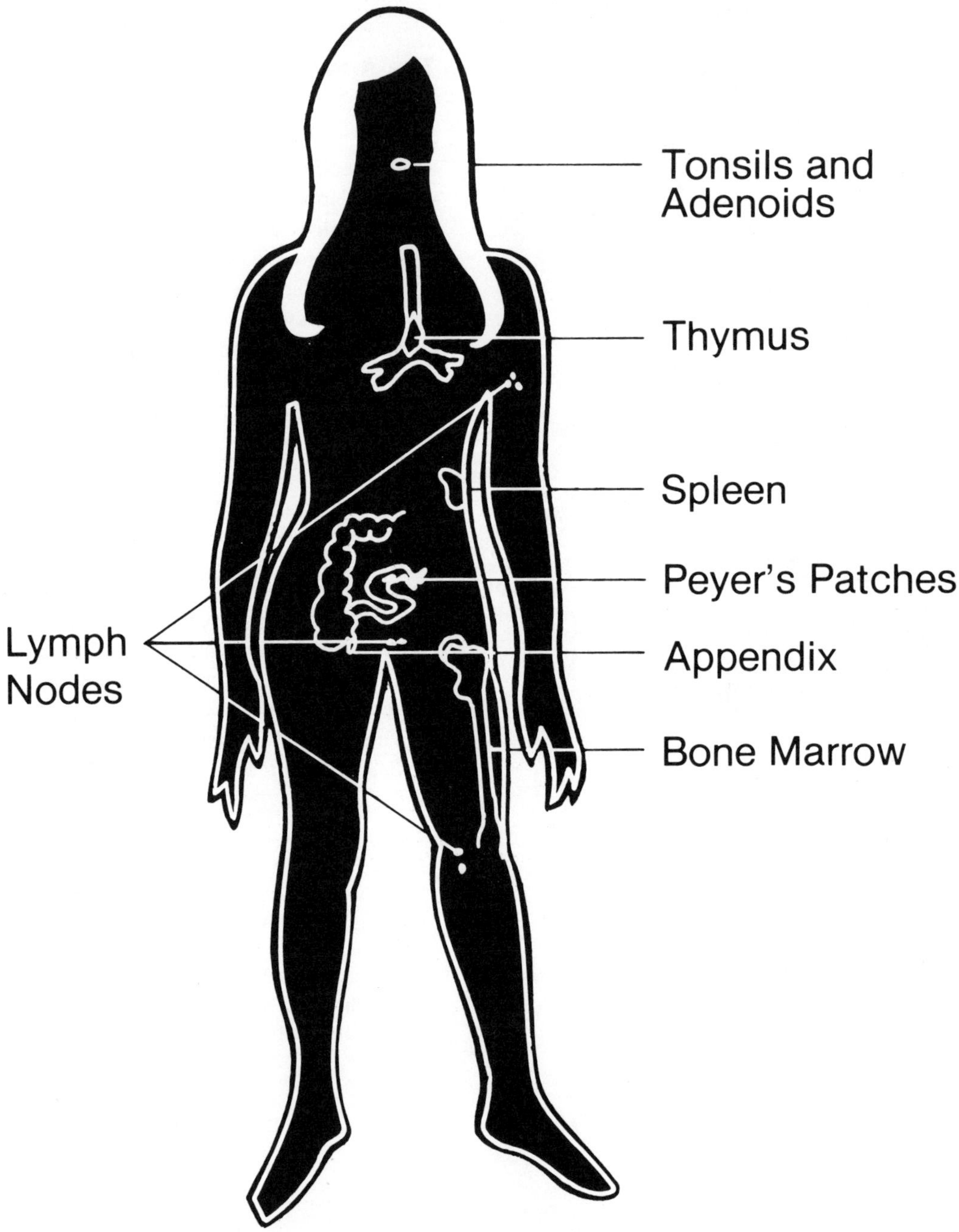

The organs of the immune system, the "lymphoid" organs, are responsible for the growth and destination of lymphocytes, the white blood cells of the immune system. The immune system is able to distinguish between "self" and "nonself," which substances the system encounters in the body actually belong to the body and which don't. The system also remembers previous experiences. E.g., once someone has had the chicken pox, his immune system recognizes the invader and prevents the illnesses from occuring a second time. The purpose of vaccines is to teach the body to recognize a disease without having the disease.

THE SEARCH FOR IMPROVED VACCINES

Tuning Up the Immune System

The effort to "tune up the immune system" is spawning an array of new therapies. Many of the new methods for improving vaccines are based on special proteins called anti-idiotypic antibodies (anti-ids), which are molecules formed by the body when challenged by a foreign cell or protein. Anti-ids are being considered by several biotechnology companies as the basis of new vaccines. The proteins might also be used to treat some forms of cancer as well as some maladies, such as juvenile-onset diabetes, that appear to arise from malfunctions of the immune system.

Formidable obstacles, however, stand in the way of anti-id development. One difficulty is that no one is sure when and how the proteins take part in the immune response. Another limitation is the many different structures found among the billions of antibodies produced during the immune response, and the difficulty of finding in the resulting jumble the antibody with the desired therapeutic property.

Despite the obstacles, anti-id vaccines offer real advantages. Vaccines based on harmless human proteins would not expose patients to the risk of being vaccinated with live organisms. (Even the safest of current vaccines carry a small danger of infection.)

Another advantage of anti-id vaccines is that they could be directed toward precisely selected targets. The vaccines might even be useful for organisms such as the AIDS virus that do not provoke a normal immune response.

A further advantage would be anti-id use in infants that would offer protection at a much earlier age than is now possible. The relatively undeveloped immune system of infants is resistant to conventional vaccines.

Traditional Vaccines and Their Drawbacks

Most vaccines are now prepared in two ways: They are made with dead organisms or with a closely related live strain. A live organism is preferable because it provokes a better immune response. However, harmless strains are often not readily available, so many vaccines use killed pathogens.

To prepare the vaccines using dead organisms, the organism is grown in large batches and then killed with heat or chemicals. One serious drawback to this method is that an organism may survive the efforts to kill it and infect the person vaccinated.

Sometimes dangerous side effects also result from conventional vaccines. For example, the DPT vaccine given to children to protect them against diphtheria, tetanus, and whooping cough frequently provokes fever and acute pain at the injection site. In rare instances, the shot has caused irreversible brain damage, and even death.

In 1984, 73 lawsuits were brought against makers of the DPT vaccine. The average award in 28 suits was $45 million. By 1986, high-liability costs and flat industry sales had driven all but one manufacturer out of the business of making the DPT vaccine.

Side effects are the immediate and easily detected effects of immunization. However, in the view of Robert Mendelsohn, former associate professor of preventive medicine at the University of Illinois and a longtime vaccination critic, there is a growing suspicion that immunizations against childhood diseases may be responsible for a dramatic increase in autoimmune diseases such as rheumatoid arthritis, multiple sclerosis, and AIDS.

Researchers Sybille Muller, H. C. Chang, and Heinz Kohler discovered that repeatedly immunized animals are more susceptible to attack by AIDS. The experiment involved the injection of one breed of mice with cells from a different strain of mice. The presence of foreign cells forced the injected mice to constantly mount an immune response. Following the injection with foreign cells, the scientists next injected the mice with a test antigen (a molecule on the outside of a disease-carrying organism that signals the body's defense system to produce antibodies) and then measured the mice's immune responses. In comparison to a control group, the treated mice produced fewer antibodies. They also had a lower ratio of T-helper cells, which encourage immune response, to T-suppressor cells, which suppress immune response. The suppressed immunity and the altered T-cell ratios are characteristic of AIDS.

The Immune Response Network

The immune system in mammals is divided into two discrete but related networks called the (1) cellular and the (2) humoral. In the cellular network, patrolling cells called macrophages and killer T cells directly attack and destroy foreign bacteria or viruses. The humoral network depends on a bombardment of antibodies, proteins produced by white blood cells called B lymphocytes. These proteins recognize and bind to their corresponding antigens (foreign cells or proteins, or to specific parts of the invaders). The destruction of the antigen by enzymes and other chemicals is signaled by the binding.

Binding is possible because antigens have unique molecular projections called ''epitopes.'' The epitopes may serve as recognition and binding sites for one or more antibodies. Epitopes in some way are memorized by the immune system, creating a lifelong defense against them.

The antigen can be compared to an extended hand with the fingers making up the epitope. As a glove bonds to a hand, an antibody binds to its epitope. The binding takes place only at specialized, diverse portions of the antibody molecule, which are called the idiotype. The remainder of the molecule is left structurally unchanged.

The appeal of anti-id vaccines is that their antigens are not foreign proteins. They are other antibodies. The ''network theory of immunology'' developed by Neils Jerne during the 1970s proposes that the body produces idiotypic antibodies against a foreign protein and also produces anti-idiotypic antibodies against the second antibodies, and so on. Each successive anti-id is the mirror image of its antigenic antibody.

In 1981, American biologist Alfred Nisonoff and British immunologist I. M. Roit pointed out that since each anti-id was in effect an antigen, it could be used in place of natural antigens to trigger an immune response.

Creating an Anti-id Vaccine

To make an anti-id vaccine, lab animals are injected with the antigen under consideration, perhaps an influenza virus. After a week or more, the antiviral antibodies of the animal are purified for injection into another animal. The immune system of the second animal produces anti-id antibodies to the first antibody. The mirror image nature of the process means that some of the anti-ids are structurally similar, perhaps even identical, to the original viral epitopes, and thus should trigger an immune response to the virus.

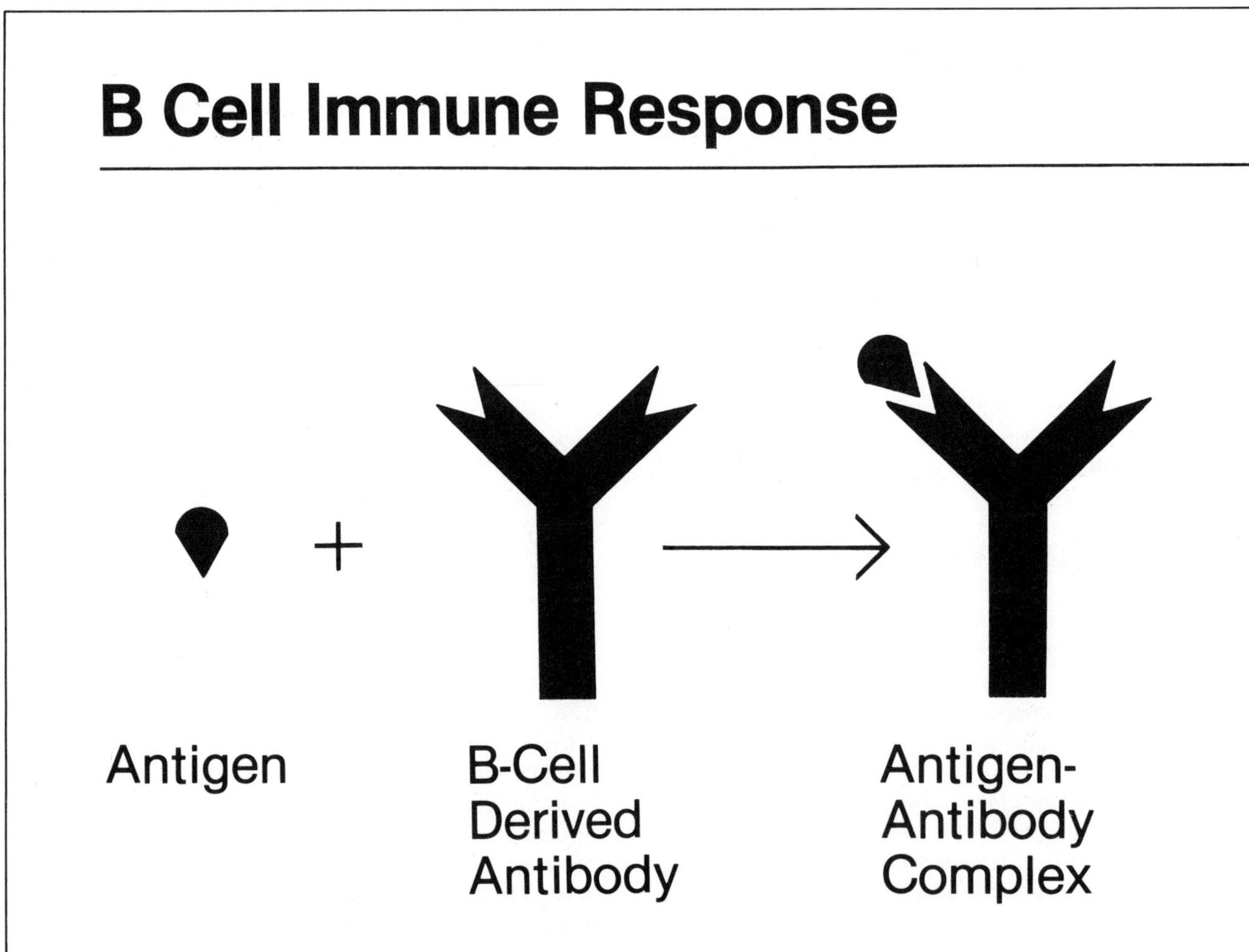

Every B cell is programmed to make only one specific antibody. A vaccine uses the antigen of a disease to activate the immune system against the antigen, thus creating future protection.

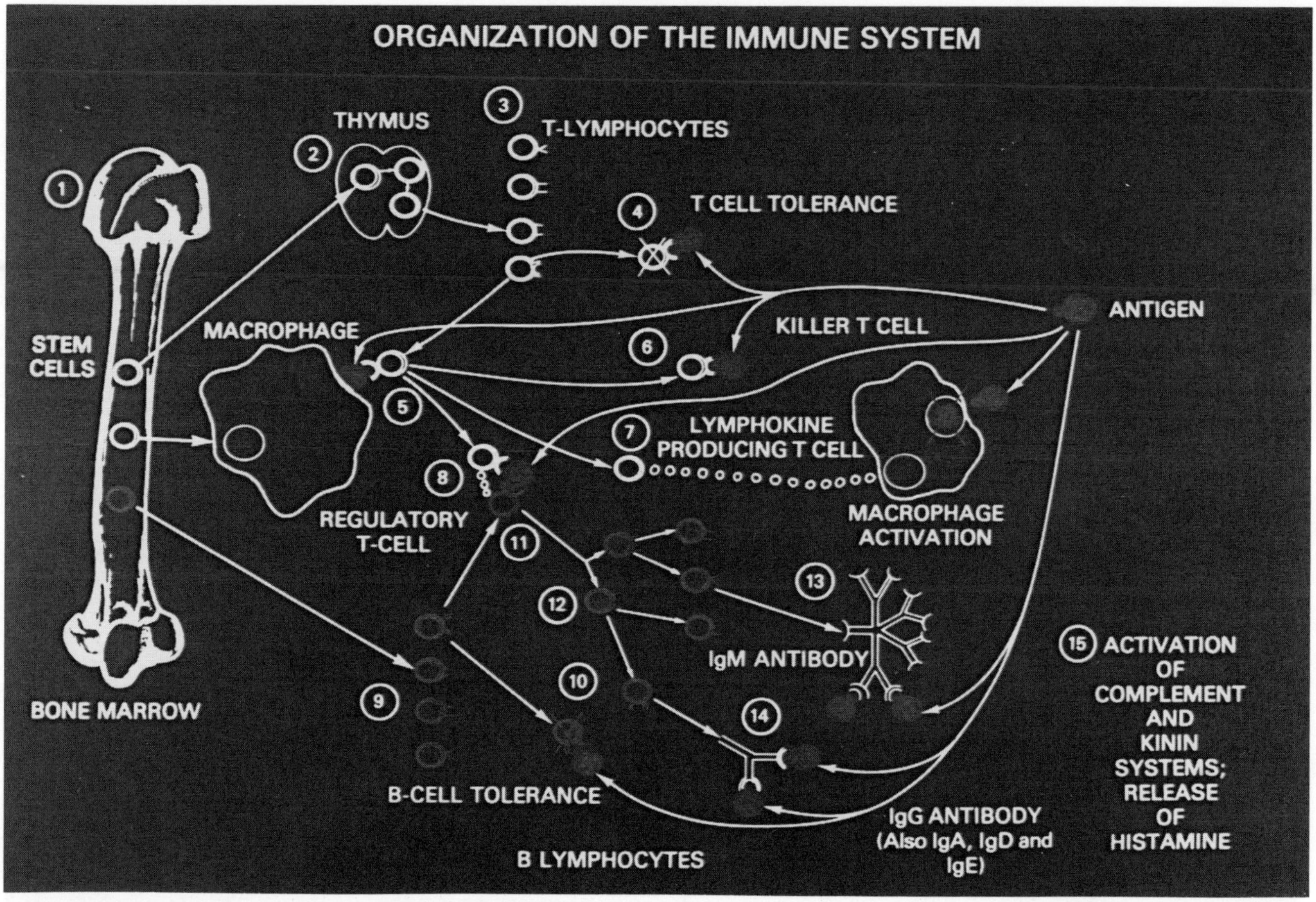

The immune system produces a variety of cells for specific tasks. The antibodies produced by the B cell cannot penetrate living cells, but some can block viruses from entering other cells, some can disable the toxins produced by bacteria, and others can coat the bacteria, making them acceptable to scavenger cells such as macrophages. Various T cells can turn B cells on or off. T lymphocytes, like B cells, will recognize one specific antigen. They can then interlock with the antigen and destroy it.

Against the threat of an invader, the immune system does not manufacture only a single antibody, it constructs hundreds of thousands. Only a very few neutralize the virus by binding to the epitope(s) that actually infect the host cell. The rest attach to viral structures that play minor roles in infection. To identify the one or few neutralizing antibodies requires arduous trial and error. The grueling task involves matching single antibody lines against the organism until a neutralizing line is found. Once found, the B lymphocytes that produce only that antibody species must be cultured.

Immune System Regulators

Another approach to avoiding the risks of current vaccines is the development of vaccines based on synthetic polypeptides (small proteins) and recombinant DNA. The strategy synthesizes only the epitopes needed for an immune response. Substantial information about the epitopes' chemical structure is necessary before the polypeptide can be synthesized. Anti-id vaccines can be made without the voluminous information.

Synthetic vaccines share with current vaccines the problem of effectively immunizing against the whole live pathogen. Some researchers have found that anti-id combined with small doses of synthetic antigen can help to boost the immune response.

More than 60 million people in the United States suffer from autoimmune disorders, such as Type-I diabetes, lupus erythematosus (an inflammatory disease of the skin and connective tissue), and the fatal muscular disorder called myasthenia gravis (which produces progressive muscle weakness and fatigue). Anti-ids might serve as regulators for such disorders.

In autoimmune disorders, antibodies attack the individual's own cells. For instance, the diabetic's insulin-producing beta cells of the pancreas are a target. Some forms of arthritis may be attributable to antibodies attacking the connective tissue of the joints. The isolation of these antagonistic antibodies could make possible the design of anti-ids that would render them harmless or destroy them.

Other Promising Anti-Id Use

Twenty percent of the more than 10,000 kidney transplants performed in a given year are likely to end in rejection, mostly in patients who have tested positive for human lymphocytic antibodies (HLA). Anyone who has ever tested positive for these antibodies is considered a poor risk, even if, as often happens, the antibodies inexplicably disappear.

Surgeons who have performed transplants on patients who formerly tested positive have been frustrated by the fact that some of the transplants are quite successful while others are almost immediately rejected. Recently, researchers have found evidence of a multitiered anti-antibody system that identifies patients for whom the grafts will succeed or fail. Like a series of bigger and bigger gloves fitting over the original hand, the anti-idiotypic antibodies apparently either block or enhance a patient's original HLA antibodies.

A research team led by Elaine Reed of Columbia University College of Physicians and Surgeons in New York City performed retroactive blood tests on 20 kidney patients with a history of antibody sensitization to their donor's HLA antigens. The grafts of 10 patients survived at least 1 year. On those 10 successful patients, 9 showed evidence of anti-antibodies capable of blocking their original HLA antibodies. Moreover, 9 out of 10 of those whose grafts were rejected showed evidence of anti-anti-antibodies, which overwhelmed the anti-antibodies, thereby reinstituting the original immune reaction. Thomas Fuller, a blood-transfer specialist at Massachusetts General Hospital, sees the finding as providing better compatibility testing and leading to methods for inducing antibody-specific immunosuppression in transplant recipients.

Other Promising Vaccines

A genetically engineered vaccine for hepatitis B was recently approved by the FDA. In the development stage, researchers around the country are creating vaccines for certain types of cancer such as melanoma, skin cancer, and colorectal cancer. These vaccines don't prevent the onset of the disease, but they do inhibit the reoccurrence or the worsening of symptoms. The cancer vaccines contain parts of actual cancer cells, which are thought to stimulate the immune system's response to tumor cells.

Clinical trials were going on in 1987 in Australia for a contraceptive vaccine. Administered once a year, the antipregnancy vaccine operates by fabricating antibodies to human chorionic gonadotropin, which stimulates produc-

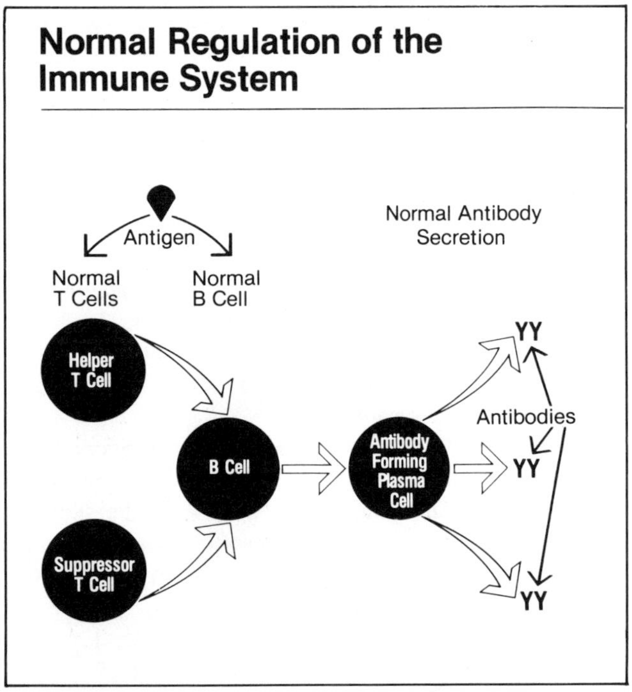

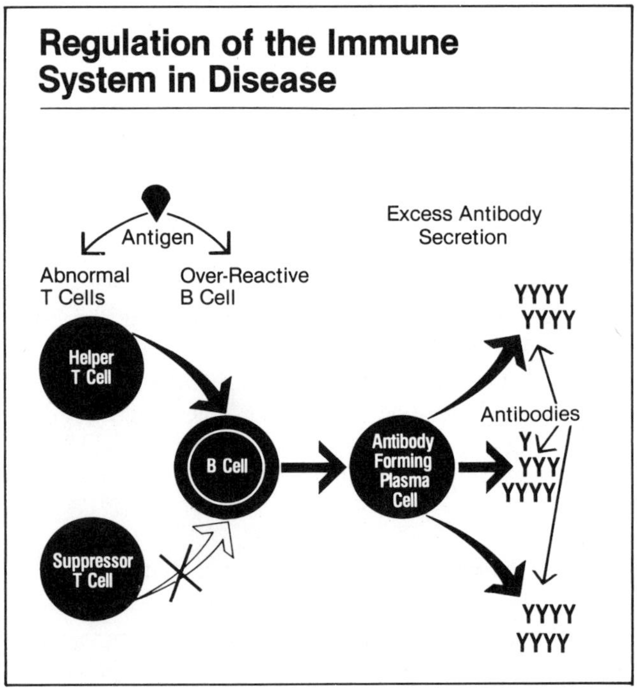

The various cells of the immune system must maintain a proper balance for the system to work. Autoimmune disorders such as lupus erythamatosis develop when suppressor T cells are sluggish. There are hopes that the new anti-ids may serve as immune system regulators for such diseases.

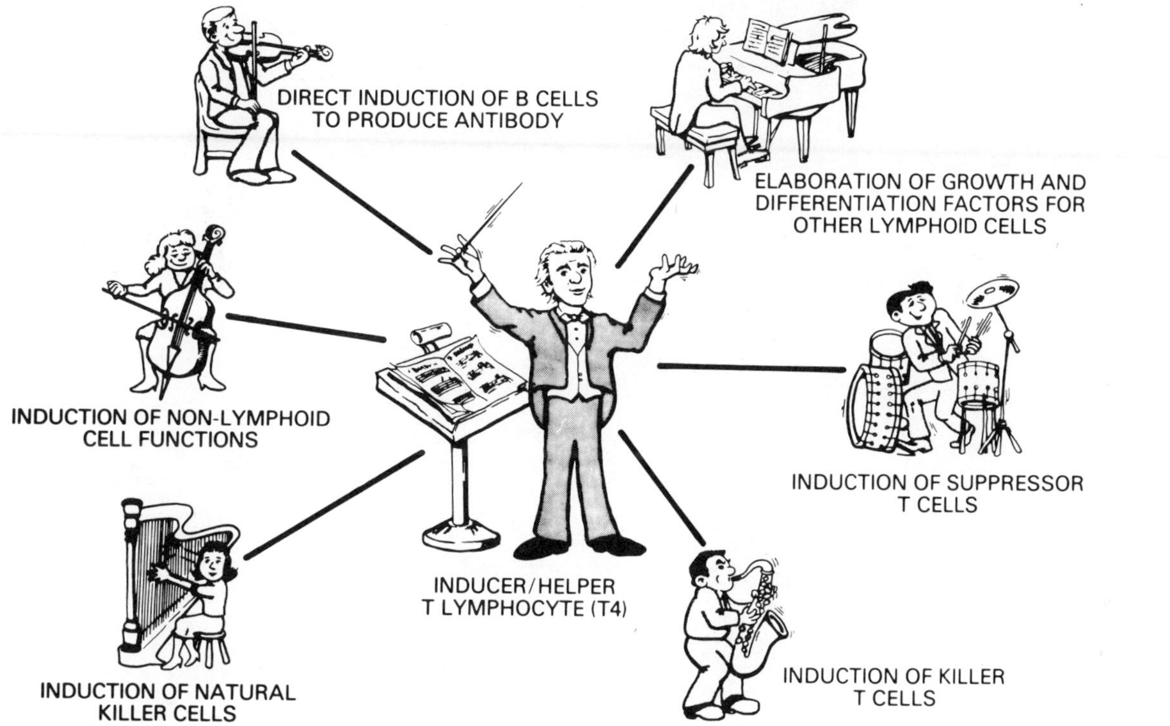

Courtesy, A.S. Fauci, M.D.

tion of progesterone, the hormone needed by the uterus to maintain a pregnancy. The contraceptive injection does not interfere with the menstrual cycle and therefore does not produce the side effects common with birth control pills.

A vaccine was in development for toxoplasmosis, a disease often transmitted to pregnant women by cats or by undercooked meat. The disease causes about 3,000 birth defects annually and infects 2 million people each year. For those with a weakened immune system, the disease can cause brain damage, or even death. The vaccine, which would be administered to cats, may be avilable by the early 1990s.

Several vaccines were in development in 1987 for protection against sexually transmitted diseases. A herpes vaccine was being tested in England and was expected to become available in 1990. Clinical trials for a gonorrhea vaccine were being conducted at the Stanford Medical School.

Malaria Vaccine Disappointments

Each year more than 150 million people suffer with malaria, and at least 1 million children from it. During World War II, U.S. soldiers on active duty developed 500,000 cases of malaria. In the southwest Pacific, it appeared as if the disease would knock out two-thirds of the troops with which General MacArthur hoped to fight the Japanese. During the Vietnam War, the greatest single problem besides the Vietcong was malaria.

Thirty years ago scientists were convinced that malaria would be eradicated by the "wonder drug" chloroquine and the "wonder" pesticide DDT. After eradication in some countries and reduction in others, the disease has returned in many tropical countries to threaten more lives than ever.

Scientists at Walter Reed Army Institute of Research have been working for years on a malaria vaccine. In 1987, they inoculated 15 volunteers with vaccine cloned from the genetic material of the malaria parasite. Six of the volunteers were given booster shots and then were bitten by mosquitos. Two others who had been given no vaccine were also bitten. Seven out of the 8 contracted the disease. At very high doses, antibodies did develop and were able to some extent to offer some protection, which the scientists found encouraging.

Research is concentrating on halting the disease before it reaches the liver. The Walter Reed researchers, working in

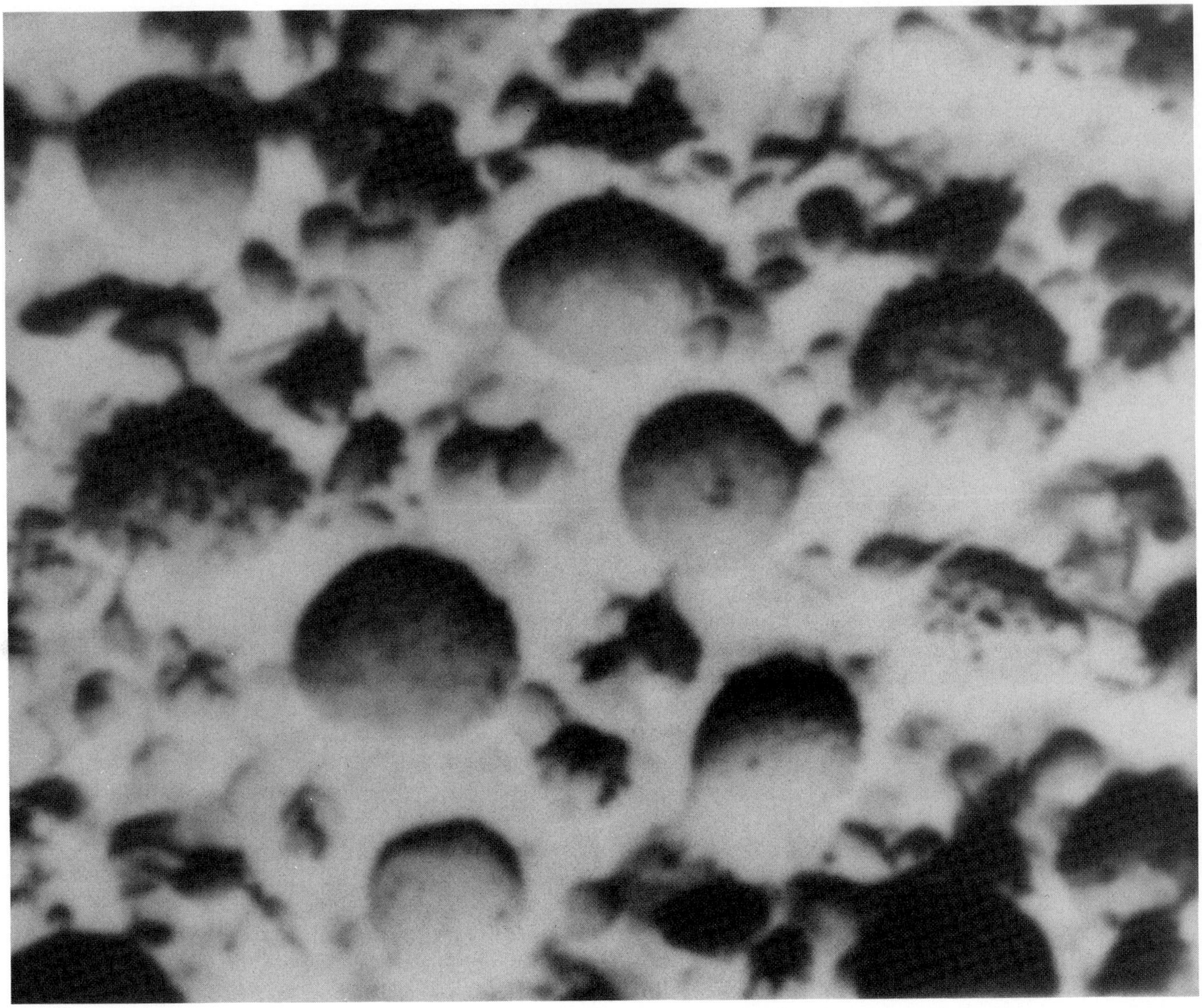

A cluster of immune cells.

collaboration with other groups, say they believe they have identified the correct epitope of the protein. Researcher Carter Diggs of Walter Reed believes they now have to modify their approach so that the epitope will be strong enough to defeat the parasites as they enter the body.

Experiments conducted at a World Health Organization facility in Switzerland and at Stanford University injected mice with a parasite that causes malaria. The mice that developed lethal cerebral malaria had high levels of a protein called tumor necrosis factor (TNF). The blood of the mice with cerebral malaria contained 20 to 25 times the amount of TNF as those without the brain complication. The blood vessels in the brains of the afflicted animals were clogged by red blood cells and by macrophages, the type of blood cell that makes TNF. When malaria-infected mice were treated with an antibody that blocked TNF, they did not develop the brain complications and their brain blood vessels remained unclogged. A scientist involved in the study, Luis Fajardo, a Stanford pathologist and chief of pathology at Veterans Administration Hospital in Palo Alto, California, believes that it is likely that human cerebral malaria occurs in the same manner and thus could be prevented by using antibodies against TNF.

TNF gained its name in 1962 when it was observed that tumors disappeared in mice with high levels of TNF. A belief that the tumors had been destroyed by TNF led to the name tumor necrosis (killing) factor. It is also called cachectin, because it causes cachexia, or the wasting away common in cancer and AIDS patients. Scientists have maintained interest in TNF as an experimental anti-cancer agent and consider it to be involved in a variety of body functions.

The Uncertain Future for Vaccines

The Ninety-ninth Congress passed legislation establishing a no-fault compensation system for vaccine victims. Nevertheless, despite the great strides made in immunization research, more and more parents are deciding against inoculation for their children. Researcher Sybille Muller is concerned that the immune system becomes depressed when pumping out all those antibodies in response to the anti-idiotypic antibody. She believes the evidence suggests that repeated exposure to anti-idiotypic antibodies may make some people more susceptible to the AIDS virus.

Other critics contend that the long-term consequences of immunization have not been fully investigated, and until they are, opponents believe the vaccine revolution should be put on hold.

CDC EPIDEMIOLOGISTS

Scientific Sleuths in Pursuit of Health

The more or less unfamiliar science of epidemiology became familiar during 1987 by reason of the daily news coverage of AIDS. Epidemiologists from the Centers for Disease Control (CDC) in Atlanta were among the first to notice five cases in California during 1981 that signaled the presence of the AIDS in the United States.

The Birth of Epidemiology as a Science

Epidemiology is defined as the study of the occurrence of disease in a human population. The term is derived from three Greek words, *logos*, which means ''a study of,'' *epi*, which means ''on'' or ''upon,'' and *demos* which means ''people.''

The methods of epidemiology were developed during investigations of the great epidemics such as the bubonic plague, cholera, and small pox, which came in surges of widespread illness accompanied by many deaths.

John Snow's studies of cholera in London during the mid-1800s are classics that depict the development of an epidemiologic perspective. Snow's first study was performed during an outbreak of cholera in 1848. The scientist collected information about the residence or workplace of identified cases within an area of London known as the Golden Square.

Using the residence and employment information, Snow developed a ''spot map,'' a map whose dots each indicated a specific number of cases. Water was suspected as a possible source of contamination, so on his map, Snow labeled the Golden Square pumps as A, B, and C. Then he plotted the households of identified cases. Snow's spot map revealed a clustering of cases around Pump A and an absence of clusters around Pumps B and C.

To confirm his suspicions about Pump A as the source of infection, Snow gathered information from the cholera households about their source of water. The residents reported that they avoided Pump B because it was grossly contaminated and they did not use Pump C because it was an inconvenient location. The consumption of water from Pump A was the one factor in common among the cases of disease.

Six years later, in 1854, Snow undertook to study another outbreak of cholera and discovered a definite pattern associated with water supply districts. Residents in districts that had their water supplied exclusively by the Southwark and Vauxhall Company had a risk of death from cholera 5 times higher than residents living in districts exclusively supplied by the Lambeth Company. Populations living in districts supplied by both companies had a death rate somewhere in between. With further investigation, Snow found that Southwark and Vauxhall's water intake was near a major source of contamination and the Lambeth Company's was not.

Snow's studies demonstrated that water could serve as a vehicle for transmitting cholera. He proposed the existence of a microorganism as the causative factor. However, Snow's concept was not accepted until the work of Pasteur and Koch during the period between 1860 and 1890 confirmed the germ theory.

Epidemiology's Conceptual Framework

The process of epidemiology is derived from three interactions: the causative agent, the host, and the environment. Causative agents may be biological agents such as bacteria, viruses, or fungi. They may also be chemical agents such as pesticides, food additives, drugs, or industrial chemicals. Or they may be physical agents such as heat, noise, light, ionizing radiation, vibration, or speeding objects.

The host characteristics include a wide variety of elements. Common factors are: age, sex, ethnic group, socioeconomic status, marital status, previous illness, lifestyle, heredity, and nutrition. Host factors influence the degree of exposure risk to a source of infection. They also influence the degree of susceptibility or resistance to particular diseases or to disease in general.

The single most important host factor related to disease is age. The very old and the very young tend to be most vulnerable. Further, some illnesses are common only within particular age groups. Level of nutrition also is gaining rapidly in importance as a host factor.

A few of the relevant environmental factors are: water, milk, food, plants, animals, housing conditions, weather conditions, and environmental pollutants. The agent, the host, and the environment interrelate in a variety of complex combinations to produce disease in humans.

How an Epidemiologist Might Think

Roger B. Nichols, the director of Boston's Museum of Science, in a Boston Globe interview during May of 1987, used an epidemiologic model to explain the process by which any scientist looks at data. He described the thinking as "a search for symmetries or groupings." By way of an example, Nichols said,

> "I'm a medical epidemiologist and I'm called in to Broken Bow, Okla., and there 350 people are sick. They all came down at once. I go in, and they're from all walks of life—they're young and old and so forth. But I find out that all of these people attended a church supper. Now that's symmetry.
>
> "Are you going to necessarily say that all church suppers are going to make you sick? Well, obviously not.

When looking for the source of a disease, epidemiologists try to discover what the patients have in common. For example, did they eat the same food? Food can be a prime source of infection, particularly if improperly prepared or left unrefrigerated.

Water can be another source of disease-carrying agents, from bacteria to toxic waste.

"So you go out, and you take the next cut at it. One thousand people attended the church supper, and only 350 of them got sick.

"Did you eat the roast beef? Did you eat the turkey? The potato salad? The ice cream?

"A vast majority of the people who got sick had potato salad—not all but most of them. So in the particular individual, you cannot arrive at some conclusion. . . . You can say there might be something in that potato salad that wasn't good for you.

"Now you go back one more step—when did you make the salad dressing?
Did it ever sit out? You track this thing backward."

Common Epidemiologic Symmetries

To find the symmetries that Nichols suggests are in data, an epidemiologist looking for an infectious disease would examine the interaction of agent, host, and environment. He or she would analyze six components that are sometimes called "the chain of infection."

The components of the chain of infection are:

1. The causative agent;
2. The reservoir of the agent (that is the habitat in which the infectious agent lives, multiplies, and/or grows);
3. The portal of exit of the agent from the host (Is it sneezed out, defecated, sexually transmitted?);
4. The mode of transmission of the agent into the new host (Is it carried in air, in soil, in animals or mosquitoes?);
5. Portal of entry into the new host (Is it breathed in, ingested with food, admitted through a break in the skin?);
6. Host susceptibility (Preexisting ill health, natural or acquired immunity, predisposing genetic factors, etc.).

In the process of collecting data, epidemiologists have found it helpful to organize data around time, person, and place. In an outbreak of rubella from a common source,

The headquarters of the Centers for Disease Control in Atlanta. The CDC is the national center for tracking the course of disease in the United States.

time may be used to pinpoint the initial exposure to the source of infection and to mark the point at which the disease became evident. In order to pinpoint questions to ask the identified patients about where they were and with whom they had contact around the suspected date, knowing the incubation period for an illness, the epidemiologist can graph the cases by working backward from the peak of an epidemic.

Time as a piece of evidence is a critical factor in diseases that have seasonal variations. Some diseases have cycles longer than a year. For example, viral hepatitis had been observed to have cycles as long as 7 years.

Place as an organizing factor can be as specific as a street address. However, more often place breaks data down into dichotomies: rural verus urban; resident versus nonresident; or institutional (such as a hospital, school, or jail) versus noninstitutional. In general, disease spreads more rapidly in urban areas. However, diseases transmitted from animal to humans are more likely in rural areas. Socioeconomic factors are also related to *place*. People who have similar economic resources tend to live near each other. As socioeconomic status improves, the immediate environment tends to improve, and individual immunity is likely to be higher. In general, the incidence of death and disease is greater in poorer neighborhoods.

Person as a device to reveal order can be used to sort data in accordance with inherent factors such as age, sex, race, or by acquired characteristics such as level of immunity and marital status. Another assortment using *person* might look at activities such as type of work, play, religious practices, and ethnic customs. Still another arrangement might look at daily living conditions such as housing with toilet facilities and heat, sufficient income to purchase food and clothing, and environmental factors such as the presence of parasites or toxic waste.

The Centers for Disease Control: A Wellspring of Epidemiology

The impetus for much of the work in epidemiology in the United States comes from the Federal Centers for Disease Control (CDC). In 1987, the CDC celebrated its forty-first birthday as a scientific detective agency for the United States and for the rest of the world.

The CDC is the only major federal agency headquartered outside metropolitan Washington, D.C. The agency began its mission as the offspring of a World War II agency, Malaria Control in War Areas (MCWA), based in Atlanta, Georgia, because, at the time, malaria was a problem in the Southeast. The agency had two tasks. It was charged with protecting from malaria troops training the the southeastern United States. And the agency had nationwide responsibility for training state and local health personnel to diagnose tropical diseases such as yellow fever or dengue fever that might be brought home by returning military personnel.

All during World War II, MCWA's entomologists studied mosquitoes in the laboratory and in the field. Throughout the South, hundreds of miles of drainage ditches were dug, and thousands of acres were sprayed with new insect-killing pesticides. By war's end, malaria in the United States was almost under control. However, many diseases with impact upon the whole nation remained. Polio killed and disabled thousands of Americans. Children suffered through a half million cases of measles each year. Tuberculosis and diphtheria were an ever-present threat.

A visionary officer of the U.S. Public Health Service, James Mountin, believed that the nation's public health problems could be brought under control as had been malaria. He proposed establishment of a "center of excellence." Dr. Mountin's vision of a center of excellence became the Communicable Disease Center, which took over the facilities and staff of the disbanded MCWA on July 1, 1946.

In 1970, the Communicable Disease Center's name was changed to Center for Disease Control. In 1973, the CDC was incorporated into the Public Health Service and was given an expanded role: prevention of unnecessary illness and death and the enhancement of the health of the American people.

In 1980, the CDC was reorganized as the Centers for Disease Control with six operational units. The units are:

1. The Center for Environmental Health;
2. The Center for Health Promotion and Education;
3. The Center for Prevention Services;
4. The Center for Professional Development and Training;
5. The Center for Infectious Diseases;
6. The National Institute for Occupational Safety and Health.

A major focus of the CDC continues to be tracking the incidence and trends of disease. As an outgrowth of the CDC's original mandate to work with state and local health departments, the agency is heavily involved in developing and operating control programs for venereal disease, childhood immunizations, childhood lead-poising prevention, and community water fluoridation.

The CDC provides laboratory diagnostic services for unusual problems, and rare vaccines, immunoglobulins, and therapeutic drugs not otherwise obtainable are stocked by the agency to prevent or treat unusual diseases.

Training is a significant activity of the agency. Among many other programs, the CDC has a self-help program that, with local arrangements for monitored testing, can be completed through the mail. Annually, the agency trains 20,000 health workers and assists state health departments in investigating 1,500 outbreaks of disease. The investigation of Legionnaires' disease in Philadelphia during the summer of 1976 and the identification of the emerging epidemic of AIDS in California in 1981 were examples of cooperative investigations between state health officers and the CDC.

At any given moment, approximately 50 percent of the CDC's 4,300 staff are based in Atlanta, Georgia. The rest are scattered around the country and around the world. Some may be working on projects with state and local health departments. Some may be stationed abroad to work on special surveys or programs. Some may be sent overseas on short-term assignments to deal with a health emergency or an epidemic.

The Disease Detectives

A unique service of the CDC may have led to the increasing use of terms like *disease detective* or *medical detective* to describe the activities of epidemiologists. This service, called the Epidemic Intelligence Service (EIS), emerged as the result of a dispute.

When the CDC was launched as an agency at the beginning of the atomic era, controversy rocketed between the medical community and the military over the issue of biological warfare. Discussions were cloaked in secrecy. Alexander Langmuir, who became the CDC's Chief epidemiologist in the summer of 1949, argued that the existing need for scarce epidemiologists for ordinary civilian needs would become even more acute in the advent of biological warfare. During discussions that eventually led to a program for recruiting and training epidemiologists, Dr. James Mountin, the physician who originally envisioned the CDC as a center of excellence, blurted out that an epidemic intelligence service was needed. The Epidemic Intelligence Service (EIS), appropriately enough, became the name of the new program.

The EIS began in July of 1951 with 22 physicians and 1 sanitary engineer. The bulk of the graduates over the years has been physicians, but graduates have included veterinarians, dentists, statisticians, nurses, behavioral and social scientists, and other professionals. More than 1,300 graduates have emerged from the program. Armed with their new skills, they have dispersed around the country and around the world. Most return to Atlanta, Georgia, in April each year for a week-long conference that is conducted along the lines of an open scientific meeting. The EIS officers report on work in progress.

The EIS is a 2-year program that begins with attendance at the April conference, when the location of assignments is determined. In July, the incoming officers report to Atlanta, Georgia, for a 3 to 4-week training program in the principles of epidemiology and biostatistics. The new officers of the Public Health Service Commissioned Corps then move out into their assignments. Some EIS officers are assigned to units of the CDC in Atlanta or at field stations. Others are assigned to health departments around the country. CDC assignments are usually related to specific disease or program categories. Health department assignments are likely to involve a broad range of public health problems. No matter what the assignment, the officers learn and practice epidemiology under the supervision of experienced epidemiologists. They maintain close telephone and computer contact with Atlanta staff.

EIS officers were involved with the dramatic tracking of Legionnaires' disease, AIDS, and toxic shock syndrome. But not all of their work progresses to that level of significance. Sometimes it simply nips a local problem in the bud. Such a case was the report of an outbreak of salmonella poisoning in a small Midwestern town.

Salmonella is an illness characterized by diarrhea, nausea, abdominal pain, and headache that can be fatal to the elderly or to the very young. The illness is usually associated with the processing of food.

The EIS investigators called in to track down the source of the salmonella outbreak concentrated their initial attention on food, which proved to be a dead end. There was no peak level of cases to signal a common source such as a church supper. Instead the cases trickled in.

Next the investigators looked at water—another dead end. Then they turned to age. They found the bulk of the cases were either between ages 12 and 35, or under 5. The parents of the children all were in the age range of 19 to 20. The investigators focused their attention on the characteristics of the young adults. They fell into two distinct groups: high school students and mill workers. They had nothing in common socially and did not hang out in the same locations.

A casual remark by the wife of one of the investigators tipped the balance. She mentioned drugs as a possible link, and the investigators secured local marijuana samples. They found them to be heavily contaminated with salmonella. They speculated that the marijuana may have become tainted through the use of contaminated animal manure used as fertilizer. The children's illness could be explained by the inhalation of their parent's smoke.

The Weekly *Morbidity and Mortality Report*

Every week, the CDC publishes a brisk, lucid, small magazine called *Morbidity and Mortality Report* (MMWR). The magazine carries health news to more than 50,000 subscribers, most of whom are physicians, around the world.

The news includes tables and charts noting such items as death by cause for selected cities and the incidence of specific diseases. Each issue carries 3 or 4 feature articles that identify geographic location and carry intriguing title such as "Niacin Intoxication from Pumpernickel Bagels," and "Contamination of Potable Water by Phenol from a Solar Water Tank Liner." The editors solicit from their readers accounts of noteworthy cases, outbreaks, environmental hazards, and various public health problems.

Global CDC Services

Almost since its inception, the CDC has provided technical help to other countries in crises. During the Biafran War in Nigeria, many epidemiologists began to serve temporary assignments in West Africa in 1968 to carry out nutrition and disease assessments and to assist with the health problems created by the civil war. Since 1973, the CDC has documented, almost every year, the geographic distribution and prevalence of protein-energy malnutrition in drought-stricken sub-Saharan Africa.

The CDC relentlessly pursued global eradication of smallpox. During an international smallpox campaign, mobile units called "White Whales" roamed Africa carrying supplies and smallpox and measles vaccine to field-workers. The last endemic case of smallpox occurred in Somalia in October of 1977—more than a decade ago.

A CDC activity that links foreign and domestic problems involves the agency's concern with refugees. Since 1975, more than 1 million refugees, mostly from Southeast Asia, have entered the United States. The Refugee Act of 1980 delegated responsibility to the CDC for refugee health care. That accountability includes: overseas monitoring of medical examinations; visual inspection of refugees at point of entry into the country; notification of state and local officials of resettlement destinations; resettlement health assessments soon after arrival; and follow-up on refugee health needs.

Violent Injury and Death: An American Epidemic

In 1981 William Foege, then director of the CDC, ordered a study to document the most serious health problems in the

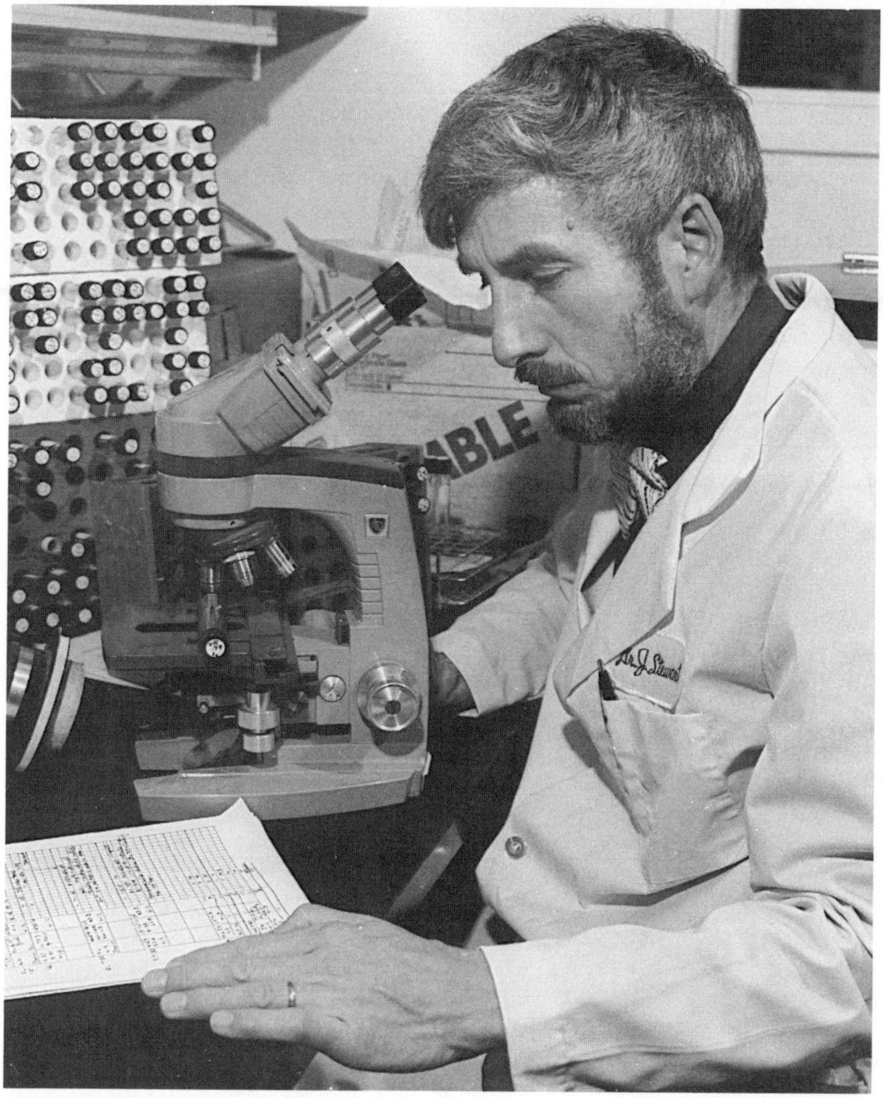

Dr. John A. Stewart, a research medical officer with the CDC, is attempting to isolate viruses in cell cultures.

United States. High on the list of problems uncovered, along with heart disease and cancer, was violence. The study's report prompted formation of the violence epidemiology section in 1983 to apply epidemiologic techniques to the problems of homicide, child abuse, and suicide.

In 1985, the CDC created an injury epidemiology and control division. The violence epidemiology section became a part of the injury and control division in 1986. Also in 1986, the CDC was charged by Congress with establishing a national injury prevention research center. The center was given a $10 million appropriation to implement the findings of a National Academy of Sciences report called *Injury in America*. The Center for Environmental Health was given responsibility for directing an expanded effort to examine intentional and unintentional injuries.

Homicide is the fourth leading cause of early death for Americans. According to a study released in August of 1987, 19,796 Americans were killed and 29,286 Americans committed suicide in 1984.

The chief of the CDC's violence section, Mark Rosenberg, compared the prevalence of violence with the medical model of disease. He pointed out that death rates from tuberculosis began to fall 100 years before there was a vaccine because there was recognition that nutrition and sanitation were contributing factors. Before violence can be cured, researchers need to understand violent behavior as well as they do simple infections.

Acts of violence are not randomly distributed. The United States has the highest murder rate in the industrialized world. During the last 20 years, the homicide rate in the United States has more than doubled to greater than 10 murders per 100,000 people—10 times the rate in the world's other 19 most developed nations.

Murder rates are highest in the South. White men have the highest death rate from suicide. Black men have the highest death rate from homicide. Accidents, suicide, and homicide are the major killers of teenagers and young adults. Suicides, especially among teenagers, often occur in clusters.

A question raised by research into violence is the role of "contagion,,, which is one way of describing imitation. Given a cluster of suicides among teenagers who know one another—some may have served as pallbearers at the funerals of friends—the effect of contagion is easily inferred. A more difficult task is to make a direct connection between an event such as a violent movie, or a murder in the next block, with other specific acts of violence.

In a violence-related study reported in the *Journal of the American Medical Association*, CDC researchers compared postservice mortality rates for 9,324 Vietnam veterans with those of 8,989 veterans who served elsewhere. The researchers found a 45 percent higher death rate among Vietnam veterans in the 5 years after discharge.

In addition, the Vietnam group had 72 percent more suicides, 93 percent more automobile fatalities, and 69 percent more poisoning deaths, mostly from drug overdoses. By the end of the study in 1983, deaths among Vietnam veterans remained 17 percent higher than among other veterans.

The obvious conclusion might seem that the excess deaths among Vietnam veterans were due to stress endured while stationed in a hostile war zone. However, as with many studies of violent behavior, the nature of the data cannot rule out factors such as exposure to Agent Orange or lack of social support upon returning home.

Among the CDC's ongoing projects related to intentional injuries is the evaluation of laws banning concealed firearms. The CDC is not alone in its concern about violent injury and death. Epidemiologists at the Unviersity of Tennessee, Arthur Kellerman and Donald Reay, wondered whether guns really did fight crime and provide protection for their owners. The two scientists reviewed all gunshot deaths that occurred in homes in King County, Washington, between 1978 and 1983. Of 743 firearm-related deaths, 398 occurred in the home of the gun owner. Of those 398 deaths, 333 were suicides, 50 were homicides, 12 were accidents, and 3 were undetermined. Kellerman and Reay

In 1983 the CDC began applying epidemiologic techniques to the study of violence, including risk-taking behavior. For that reason accidents, which are often the result of risk taking, are examined. In addition, accidents are sometimes a covert method of suicide.

found that King County gun owners killed a member of their household 18 times more often than they killed a stranger. For every self-protection homicide, there were 37 suicides, 4.6 homicides, and 1.3 accidental deaths.

In a violence-related study presented at a meeting of the American Academy of Neurology, George Locke and his colleagues at the King/Drew Medical Center in Los Angeles reported the results of a study of 638 children up to age 18 treated for head injuries. (The number represented about 75 percent of the pediatric head injuries treated during the year at King/Drew.) Parents or guardians were interviewed about the circumstances of the injuries and the cases were then sorted into accidental or nonaccidental. Nonaccidental cases encompassed known or suspected child abuse, injuries inflicted by children or adults outside the family, and injuries attributed to neglect or careless supervision. Nearly 30 percent of the pediatric head injuries were qualified as nonaccidental. Locke's research also revealed that even mild head injuries can result in permanent intellectual impairment.

Risk-Taking Behavior as a Source of Injury and Death

The study of violence is not unrelated to the study of risk-taking behavior. In 1981, the CDC began a Behavioral Risk Factor Surveillance System to assist states in conducting telephone surveys to determine prevalence of major behavioral risks in adult populations. Among the immediate concerns of the survey were issues such as smoking, excess body weight, drinking and driving, nonuse of seatbelts, and lack of exercise.

By 1987, public health officials had become concerned with the risk-taking behaviors of unprotected sex and intravenous drug use as a factor in the spread of AIDS. They also were concerned with the chilling statistics that show adolescence as the only age group in which mortality has risen since 1960. Three-quarters of adolescent deaths are caused by accidents, homicide, and suicide, with accidents alone accounting for 60 percent of the deaths.

A conference called "Self-Regulation and Risk-Taking Behavior," sponsored by the National Institute of Mental Health (NIMH), brought together psychologists, sociologists, brain scientists, and others to pool their understanding of risk-taking behavior. The conference discussed the spectrum from scuba diving and skateboard acrobatics to drunk driving and murder. The participants concluded that some degree of fearlessness is admirable, but the American culture was in the midst of an epidemic of violent and self-destructive risk-taking behavior.

Among the most controversial explanations about risk-taking behavior is the biochemical theory that certain people are biologically predisposed "sensation seekers." Marvin Zuckerman, a psychologist at the University of Delaware in Newark, has devised a four-part sensation-seeking scale which measures: "thrill and adventure seeking" (activities with physical risk); "experience seeking" (nonconforming life-style and travel); "disinhibition" (drinking, partying, sexual variety); and "boredom susceptibility." Zuckerman found strong neurophysiological and biochemical correlations among people who scored high on the scale.

Zuckerman's biochemical model is not universally accepted, but it holds an appeal for scientists trying to sort out an ill-defined behavioral phenomenon. Several psychological models relate risk taking to the concept of *akrasia*, or lack of control.

Akrasia is an ancient Greek idea that implies that some people succumb to risky behavior even though safer alternatives are obviously available. Some psychologists attribute the lapse to "modular cognitive separation," or relegation of selected bits of information to a mental Siberia because they do not fit with older experiences or because they thwart unrecognized wishes.

A psychiatrist at Langley Porter Psychiatric Institute at the University of California at San Francisco asserts that some risks are taken to affirm a sense of control, to inflict pain on loved ones, or to harm oneself as a punishment.

Many explanations presume that all possibilities are weighed before behavior that appears to make the most sense is taken. However, many studies have shown that information is not processed in consistent, logical ways. Newer information is given disproportionate weight, and people generally overestimate their base knowledge. Other studies show that people prefer voluntary risks, even if more dangerous, than risks forced on them.

Real understanding of risk-taking behavior can only come with understanding of decision making, a complex, integrative function that is barely understood. On a cultural level, social scientists agree that Americans are ambivalent about risk-taking behavior. On the one hand, we have high expectations for personal and public health, and at the same time risk-taking heroes are praised.

Given the CDC's success as a solver of health problems and epidemiology's effectiveness as a scientific method, both can be expected to flourish in the distant future. John Snow, had he lived in the twentieth century, would probably have been pleased to work at the CDC.

3

Biology

GENETIC MARKERS

Boon to Medicine or Threat to Privacy?

Nineteen eighty-seven saw the continuation of the recent, unprecedented series of discoveries in the area of genetic research. The current advances, made possible by two techniques first envisioned several years ago, involve the use of "genetic markers" to determine an individual's hereditary susceptibility to a given disease.

The first technique is the use of "restriction enzymes" to cut pieces of DNA (deoxyribonucleic acid) into fragments, allowing the segments to be sorted and identified. The second technique, called "pulsed gel electrophoresis," uses pulses of electricity to sort DNA fragments according to their size.

The nucleus of every healthy human cell (except human sex cells and red blood cells) contains 46 threadlike strands of genetic material called chromosomes, each of which consists of a double strand of thousands of genes.

DNA is the critical chemical of genes, the blueprint of heredity. It resembles a spiral staircase, with each step consisting of a pair of chemicals, called nucleotide bases, which lock into one another. The precise sequence of nucleotides determines a gene. The possible sequences total in the millions.

DNA's long, twisted strands consist of four fundamental subunits, adenine, guanine, cytosine, and thymine. For brevity's sake, they are called A, G, C, and T. In a variety of repetitions, the subunits of A, G, C, and T create a chemical map of biological inheritance. An arrangement of three subunits provides a signal for the production of one or another of 20 different amino acids needed to build proteins, the main ingredients of living cells.

Dr. David Botstein of the Massachusetts Institute of Technology (MIT) conceived the idea of restriction enzymes. The enzymes behave as biological scissors for the subunits. Each enzyme has a different series of subunits to which it is sensitive, and a particular enzyme will make a cut whenever it finds a specific sequence of subunits in a strand of DNA. The resulting chunks created by the restriction enzymes are called "restriction fragments" or "restriction fragment length polymorphisms" (RFLPs). They provide a pattern of normal variations. Any shift in a subunit pattern will cause the enzyme not to make the cut, leaving behind a gene fragment of an odd length.

Dr. Charles Cantor of Columbia University pioneered the technique of pulsed gel electrophoresis, which uses pulses of electricity to sort out fragments of DNA according

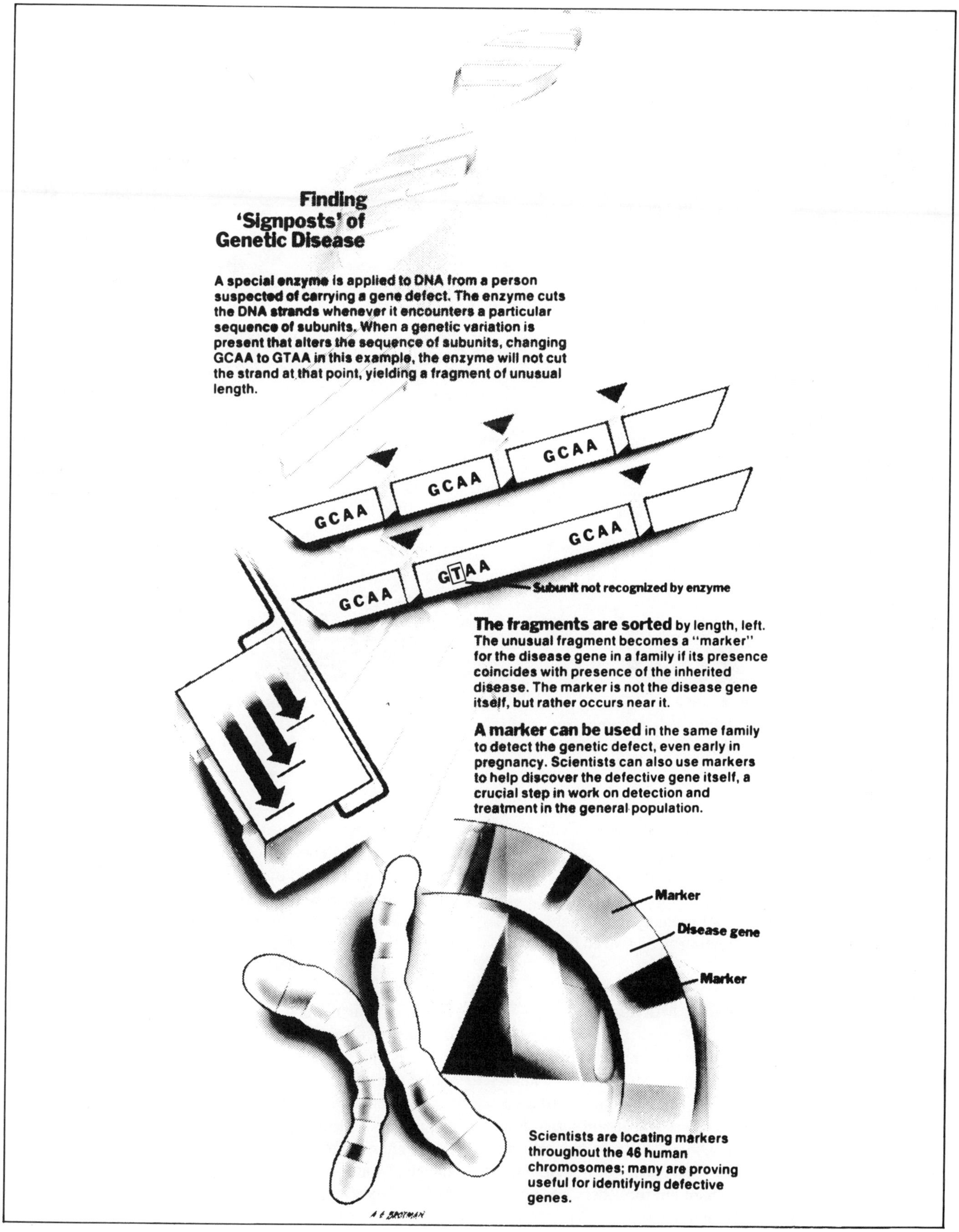
Finding
'Signposts' of
Genetic Disease
A special enzyme is applied to DNA from a person suspected of carrying a gene defect. The enzyme cuts the DNA strands whenever it encounters a particular sequence of subunits. When a genetic variation is present that alters the sequence of subunits, changing GCAA to GTAA in this example, the enzyme will not cut the strand at that point, yielding a fragment of unusual length.
GCAA
GCAA
GCAA
GCAA
GCAA
GTAA
Subunit not recognized by enzyme
The fragments are sorted by length, left. The unusual fragment becomes a "marker" for the disease gene in a family if its presence coincides with presence of the inherited disease. The marker is not the disease gene itself, but rather occurs near it.
A marker can be used in the same family to detect the genetic defect, even early in pregnancy. Scientists can also use markers to help discover the defective gene itself, a crucial step in work on detection and treatment in the general population.
Marker
Disease gene
Marker
Scientists are locating markers throughout the 46 human chromosomes; many are proving useful for identifying defective genes.

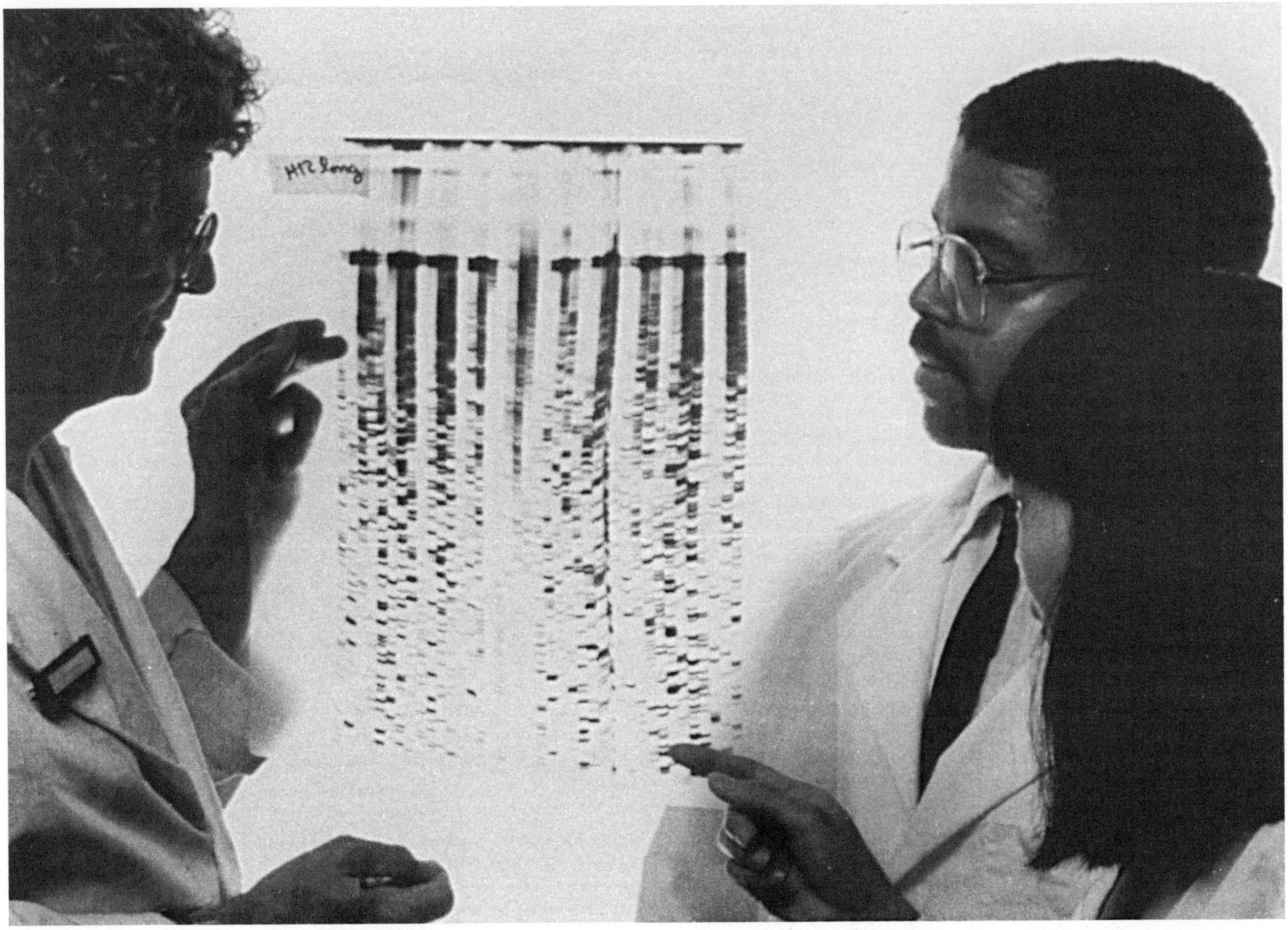

Pulsed gel electrophoresis. A gel made out of acrylamide is poured between two sheets of plastic. Samples of DNA are placed on the gel. An electrical field is then run through the gel for several hours, causing base pairs of the DNA to migrate. How they migrate depends on their size. Next, dye is applied so the different bands will show up, and a picture is taken of the final product.

to length. This grouping by size facilitates identification of significant sections of the genetic material.

When an individual is suspected of carrying a gene defect, a specific enzyme is applied to DNA from that individual. Where a genetic variation changes a sequence, the enzyme fails to make a cut, creating an odd-sized fragment.

What Are Genetic Markers?

Chromosomes are inherited in pairs, one from the father and one from the mother. Segments of DNA in paired chromosomes are often identical. However, sometimes a definite dissimilarity occurs. One such dissimilarity is a single based polymorphism where one base pair of the chain of subunits that makeup DNA will not match. Two varieties of such a polymorphism are the "deletion type" and the "insertion type." The deletion type has a portion of DNA missing. The insertion type has an extra portion of DNA inserted. The systematic inheritance of variations, such as deletions and insertions, in a family with a history of disease serves as markers for the disease. In most cases, the marker is not the faulty gene itself. Instead, it is located nearby the problem gene. As a close neighbor, the marker is almost always inherited with the defective gene and thus "marks" the location of that gene. Study of the gene may then lead to an understanding of the problem underlying the disease. At the moment, RFLPs are useful only with families that have a documented history of a particular genetic disease.

Another approach used by scientists to study genes is sometimes called "reverse genetics." This method involves using knowledge of the chemistry of the disease to look for the gene that is contributing to the disease, or for one that is failing to perform its role and thereby creating the condition for the disease.

Finding a Genetic Marker

Fragments of DNA, or genetic material, in paired chromosomes are often identical, or homozygous. But sometimes a recognizable difference in the pattern appears. Two variations are the insertion type and the deletion type. In the deletion type, a piece of DNA is absent; in the insertion type there is an extra piece of DNA in the fragment. When variations of these kinds are systematically inherited along with a genetic disease in a family, they can be used as genetic markers to signal the presence of a defect — even though they are not the defect itself. Chromosomes are inherited in pairs, one from the father and one from the mother.

DNA in Paired Chromosomes

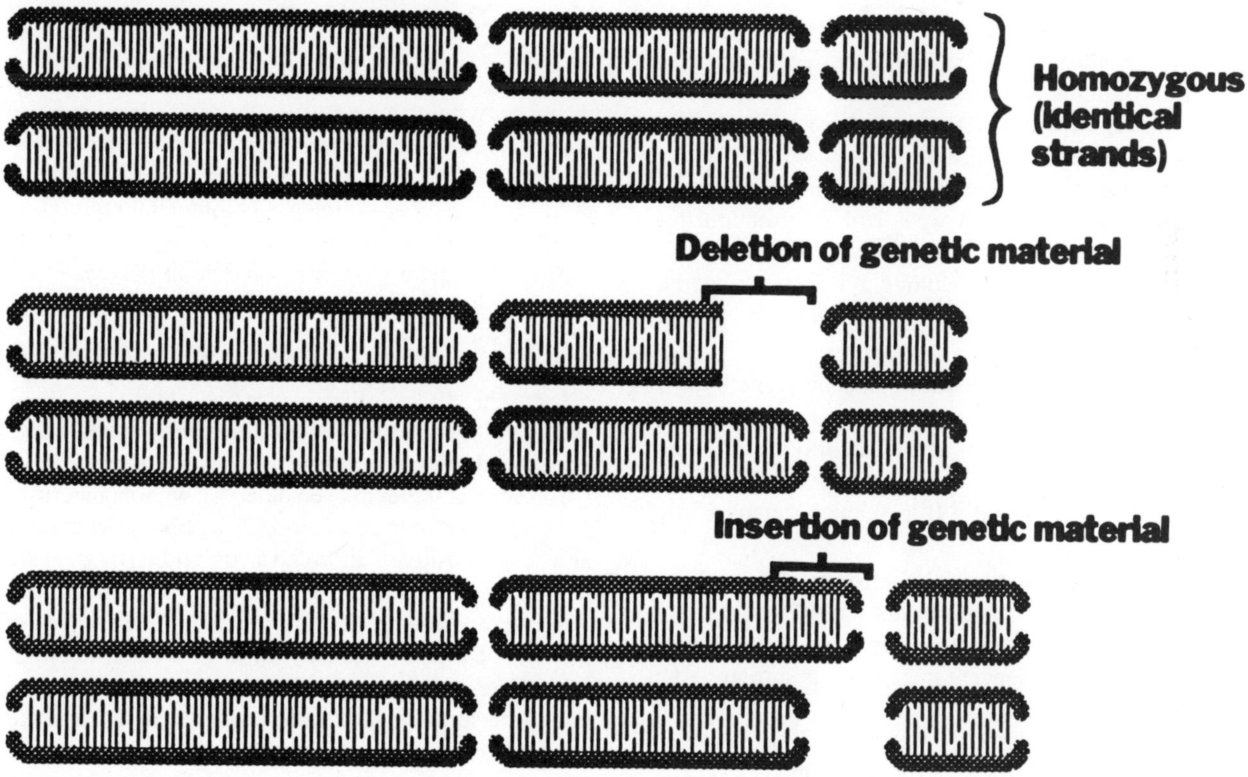

Recent discoveries have found markers for genes associated with Alzheimer's disease; cleft palate; manic depression; von Recklinghausen neurofibromatosis (NF), the Elephant Man's disease; cystic fibrosis; muscular dystrophy; schizophrenia; phenylketonuria (PKU); Gaucher's disease, a potentially fatal enzyme deficiency in infants; retinoblastoma, a rare eye cancer; colon cancer; and a pattern of inherited cell proteins that may explain why only some people exposed to AIDS virus get the disease.

Cataloguing Genetic Markers

Genetic research is moving swiftly: In the course of ongoing research directed toward the genetics of particular diseases, scientists create a catalogue, or map, of genetic markers. Primary maps have been made for most of the human chromosomes.

Strenuous debate has gone on among scientists about the priorities of "sequencing the genome" (creating a map of every human gene). Such a map would include information about 50,000 to 100,000 human genes and would document in proper order the sequence of an estimated 3 billion genetic subunits.

A complete genome sequence map would serve a variety of purposes: It would help scientists to identify the genes, to locate their exact position, and would probably aid in understanding the purpose of the substantial amount of DNA in human cells that does not seem to function as codes for any of the genes.

A workshop on the probable cost of genome sequencing was held by the congressional Office of Technology Assessment in August of 1987. The cost of an entire genomic map might be in the billions. The estimated expenditure for a workable genetic marker map would be about $11 million.

Some scientists believe that a map of the entire genome should be undertaken as a special national project. One man sharing this opinion is Daniel Koshland, the editor of *Science*, the magazine of the American Association for the Advancement of Science. In Koshland's opinion, such a map would advance our understanding of human biology, since human subjects offer a wealth of information not duplicated by other species. In addition, Koshland feels that development of a methodology for sequencing the human genome would also accelerate our understanding of other species.

Other scientists favor the current piecemeal method of pursuing specific diseases and developing a map of signposts by filling in portions as they are discovered. One of the fears these scientists have of a massive project concerns what researchers call "Big Science versus Little Science."

The Big Science/Little Science controversy involves the expectation that a massive research program would drain financial support and attention away from a myriad of smaller programs. The concern in genetics is similar to the anxiety of scientists in other disciplines who are upset about the potential loss of funding of small research programs to the massive Strategic Defense Initiative ("Star Wars") and to the colossal Superconducting Supercollider.

Opponents of a massive project point out that a map of genetic signposts is a step on the road to a record of the entire genome. On the way, a workable genetic linkage map would include a record of a set of recognized DNA segments. The segments would be mostly those that are found in families known to have a pattern of a particular genetic disease.

About 1,000 genetic markers have been detected over the past 5 years or so. Another approximately 700 useful markers would be necessary. To be useful, they would need to be relatively evenly spaced over the 23 pairs of human chromosomes.

Completion of a workable map is expected sometime in 1988 or 1989. Even after a usable map is completed, additional information will continue to be entered into the map as discoveries are made.

In the United States, two independent teams are working to compile genetic marker maps. One is headed by Dr. Helen Donis-Keller of Collaborative Research, a biotechnology company in Massachusetts. The other is led by Dr. Raymond White of the Howard Hughes Institute of Medical Research at the University of Utah. The two teams do not collaborate directly, but they do each contribute to an international research program coordinated by Dr. Jean Dausset of the Center for the Study of Human Polymorphisms in Paris.

The Uses for Genetic Marking

If extensive mapping were available, it would be possible to diagnose, within a few weeks after conception, many of the approximately 3,000 diseases associated with a defect in a single gene. Only a few of the more common single-gene diseases have received intense commercial research attention. The common diseases in this category include cystic fibrosis, muscular dystrophy, and adult polycystic kidney disease, which is responsible for as many as one-third of the kidney failures in the United States.

A map would also shed light on some widespread, catastrophic diseases that may be traceable to more than one gene. Among these illnesses are diabetes, heart disease, high blood pressure, arthritis, and many forms of cancer.

Because a marker may be inherited without inheriting the gene, any test for the marker is susceptible to what is known as a "false positive," in which an individual might test positive for the disease-causing gene when in fact he or she does not have it. Another limitation is that the discovery of the general location of a faulty gene or genes does not imply an immediate treatment for the problem. However, it may allow the individual to take certain actions to make the onset of the disease less likely.

Even in the face of the limited information now available, genetic tests are already being incorporated into "wellness" programs. The 1,000 employees of the Chesapeake & Potomac Telephone Company are already offered such a program. Family histories of volunteer participants are analyzed by computer and the participant's blood undergoes 32 tests for 14 diseases. The results are reviewed with the patient by a "health advocate." The patient signs a "personal health action plan" of anticipated preventive actions that he or she expects to take.

Proponents of genetic testing believe its use will be widespread by the year 2000. They argue that knowledge of genetic risks to health will encourage individuals to make appropriate life-style changes.

In the area of heart disease, there are already discoveries that promote life-style changes—if the victim chooses to use the knowledge. In 1983, geneticists at the University of Texas Health Science Center in Dallas located genetic mutations related to the premature onset of atherosclerosis. The presence of this defect results in an inability to rid the body of low-density lipoproteins (LDLs), which are a combination of cholesterol and protein and which contribute to heart disease. The mutant gene is widespread, in about 1 in 500 individuals. The first apparent symptom for carriers is apt to be a heart attack as early as age 30.

This work led to identification of several other genes that are implicated in heart disease. At Tufts University, a different defective gene was found to be associated with heart attacks that occur after age 40. This gene interferes with the production of high-density lipoproteins (HDLs), which transport cholesterol out of the bloodstream. This defective gene, carried by 1 in 25 people, is the most common genetic cause of cardiovascular disease. Among patients with confirmed heart disease, almost one-third carry the gene.

Research in oncogenes, or cancer-causing genes, highlights the promise of genetic mapping. Dr. Jorge Yunis of the University of Minnesota Medical School has developed innovative techniques for studying detailed structures of chromosomes. Yunis has found that 70 percent of oncogenes are positioned close to inherited frail sites on chromosomes. These weak points are areas where the genetic molecule is predisposed to break or rearrange. If a chromosome cracks close to an oncogene, the ordinary genetic control mechanisms break down and the conditions are ready for the development of cancer.

Yunis's work leads in the direction of understanding the interlocking mechanisms of internal and external factors that contribute to the onset of various cancers. For example, investigators have found that petroleum-based products, such as pesticides and insecticides, damage specific sites on chromosomes 5 and 7, 2 of the 23 pairs of human chromosomes. Farmers with frail sites at those locations, in theory, have an increased potential for leukemia when they are exposed to petroleum-based chemicals. However, at least 10 or more years of clinical trials would be needed to establish whether knowledge of such a risk might be used to prevent the cancer.

A team of AIDS researchers led by Lesley-Jane Eagles of St. Mary's Hospital Medical School in London has examined six varieties of an inherited protein found on all human cell surfaces. The scientists found that one protein variation makes the people who carry it resistant to AIDS, while another makes them highly vulnerable. The remaining four variations fall somewhere in between. No one is entirely resistant. This research may help to explain why AIDS is spreading so rapidly among heterosexuals in Central Africa, where Blacks carry the most susceptible protein 10 times more often than whites.

Encouraged by discoveries of genetic markers for dyslexia, Alzheimer's disease, and manic depression, geneticists are becoming interested in the study of mental illness and behavioral problems. The usefulness of testing for vulnerability to illnesses such as alcoholism, Huntington's chorea, and Alzheimer's depends whether genes are a major cause of the problem. For example, Huntington's disease is always caused by a defective gene, but because only 10 percent of Alzheimer's cases are traced to heredity, testing for Alzheimer's would be practical only in families with a history of the disease.

Research into mental illness is made particularly difficult because a diagnostic label may be used to cover a variety of

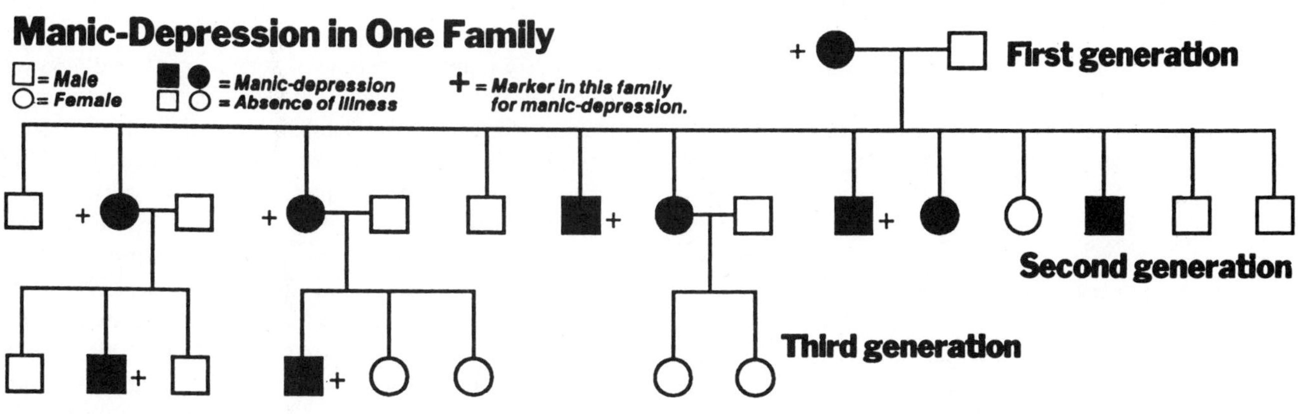

In one Jerusalem family the gene for color-blindness was found to be often inherited along with a tendency to develop manic-depression. Hence in this family, but not necessarily others, that gene is a marker for an inherited predisposition to the mental disease. There is no biological link between color-blindness and the illness, but the finding should help scientists pinpoint the location of a gene for manic-depression and lead to an improved ability to diagnose the disease.

biochemical anomalies. Thus, in a study of a large Israeli family with a history of manic depression, a faulty gene was found on the X chromosome, the female sex chromosome. In a similar study of a Pennsylvania Amish family, the defective gene was found on chromosome 11.

A gene that may lead to a better understanding of schizophrenia was located due to the chance comment of the mother of a student who was schizophrenic. The mother remarked that her son looked like her own brother, who was also schizophrenic. The two men had many physical similarities, and they each had a portion of chromosome 5 duplicated and inserted into chromosome 1. Thus the men had three copies of a portion of chromosome 5. The mother had the same segment inserted into chromosome 1, but it was absent in one of her pairs of chromosome 5.

A third copy of a gene, or of a portion of a gene, is known to cause other genetic problems, among them Down's syndrome, which is associated with a third copy of chromosome 21.

Problems Posed by Genetic Testing

The value of genetic mapping and genetic testing as a diagnostic tool is clear. What is not as clear are the uses to which the additional information might be put. Because current genetic tests find only markers rather than a specific defective gene, they are indirect, expensive, time consuming, and possibly misleading. Therefore, their use is not yet widespread. But by the mid-1990s they are expected to be perfected into a one-step test that would dramatically cut the cost of screening.

The first widespread use is likely to be the screening of fetuses, which will probably increase the number of abortions. Fetuses are currently aborted because they are likely to be born with a birth defect. In the future, expectant parents may be faced with deciding whether to abort the fetus because it has a genetic predisposition toward alcoholism, or heart disease, or Alzheimer's disease.

A predisposition to an illness is not a guarantee of onset. It is an estimate based on probabilities. Thus, fetuses may be aborted and other decisions may be made based on risks that never become a reality. Genetic counselors have already seen couples who have abandoned plans for marriage on the basis of minor genetic defects.

Another problem is that genetic testing, like most testing, has a potential for discrimination. Companies may make genetic testing a job requirement, then use the test results to pass over a candidate who has a gene for a particular disease. The company can argue that they cannot afford to spend money training an employee who might get sick. Not too many years ago, a similar argument was used to pass over women as job candidates, because firms did not want to spend money on women who might get pregnant. Some job candidates with a genetic defect may never get sick, just as some women never become pregnant.

Genetic testing is hailed as a blessing to preschoolers, who can be screened for dyslexia. Early recognition can be used to begin remedial training. However, it could be used to "track" youngsters out of challenging programs and into ones that might not let them fully develop what abilities they do possess. Similar tracking could be used in institutions such as the military and government service to keep individuals from moving up in the ranks of their profession.

Some diseases affect one sex more than the other, or appear more often in a particular ethnic group. Thus, genetic-risk profiles could become a way to reinstitute old prejudices under a new guise. The health insurance industry could use genetic-risk data to raise the premiums of certain individuals. Industry spokespersons claim that genetic testing coupled with preventive health care should reduce rates. As an example, they point to the past 15 years of the fitness movement, which has resulted in a 25 percent drop in smoking, a 35 percent drop in heart attacks, and a 50 percent reduction in deaths due to strokes. Proponents of genetic testing also suggest that increased awareness of genetic risk would increase individual attention to environmental factors, which are thought to cause 20 percent of the premature deaths in the United States.

Opponents to genetic testing worry about the ever-present risk with any medical information, a breach of confidentiality. The possibility of breach of confidentiality will depend on who has access to the information and how they treat that information.

Huntington's Disease: A Case in Point

If cures for genetic diseases could keep pace with discovery of the causes of the illnesses, apprehension over possible misuse of genetic testing might be lessened. Huntington's chorea is a graphic example of such a lag. The illness was described in the medical literature over 100 years ago, yet scientists still do not understand how the gene, present at birth, is able to kill the bearer three or four decades later. About 25,000 Americans have Huntington's disease, and approximately 125,000 are at risk of getting it. Its most famous victim was folk singer Woody Guthrie.

The early symptoms of the disease are irritability, clumsiness, and depression. These progress to uncontrolled movement, known as chorea: staggering gait, slurred speech, facial grimaces, compulsive fist clenching, and flailing of arms and legs. Gradually the victim loses his or her ability to talk, to swallow, or to remember recent events. Fifteen or 20 years pass before he or she dies, mute and unaware of what has happened to him or her.

As a result of the work of molecular geneticist James Gusella and his colleagues, it is possible to determine with

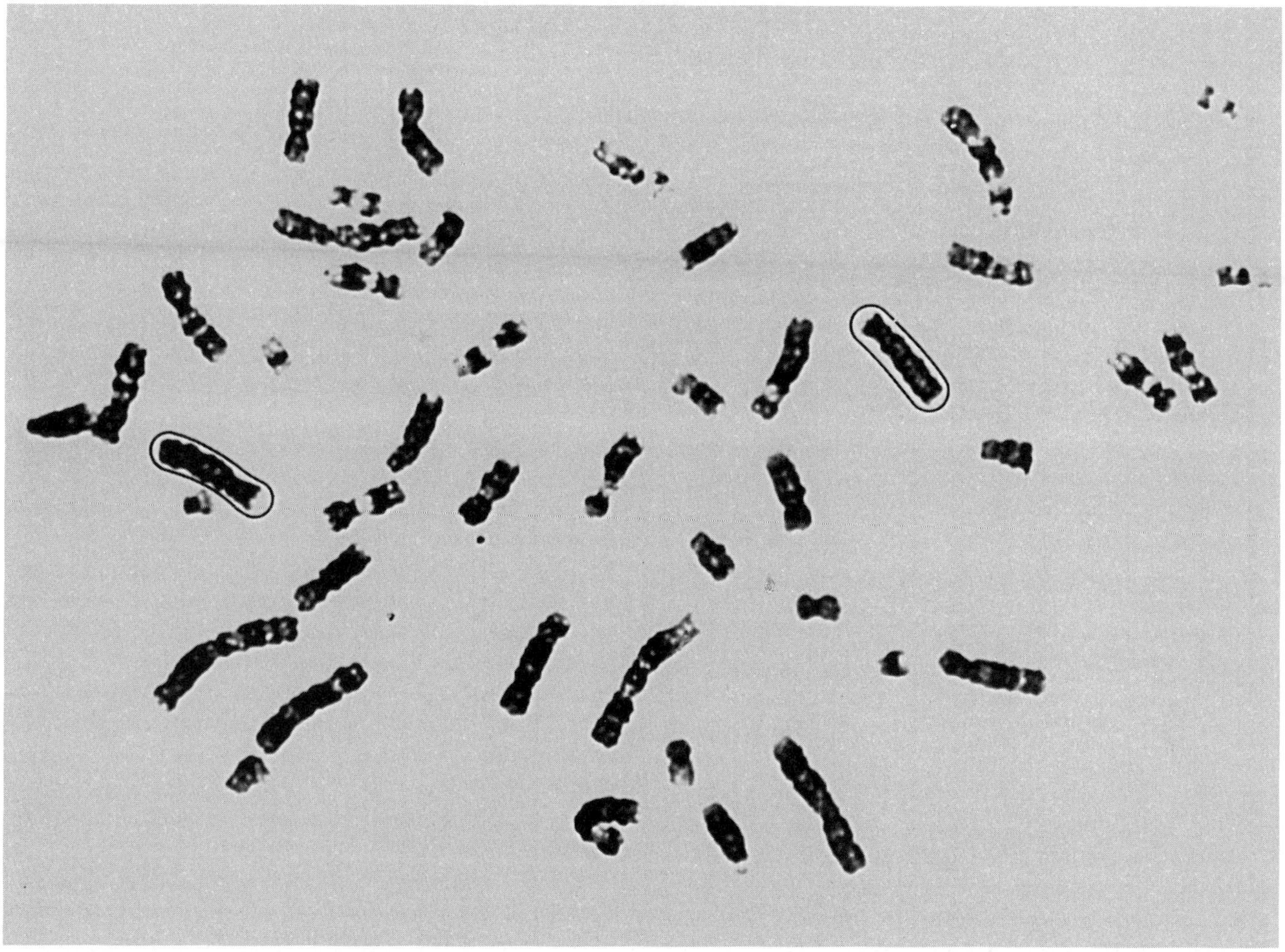

Chromosome 4 (circled) is the site of a marker gene for Huntington's chorea, a fatal inherited nervous system disorder affecting movement and mental ability.

96 percent certainty whether a particular individual carries the gene for Huntington's disease. Surveys taken before the test was developed found that 60 to 80 percent of those at risk expressed a wish to know their chances of developing the disease. However, once the test was available, only 10 of 350 people at risk signed up at Johns Hopkins Hospital in Baltimore to ascertain their risk. At Massachusetts General Hospital in Boston, among 1,500 at risk in New England—many of whom knew about the test through their local Huntington's Disease Society—only 32 appeared for preliminary counseling.

Being at risk of developing a life-threatening illness affects every part of an individual's life—career, marriage, having children, even having a future. Without a cure on the horizon, many individuals have concluded that ignorance of their risk is the only way for them to continue to live their lives.

Proponents who argue in favor of a massive national effort to map the entire genome claim that such a catalogue would enable scientists to understand the role of genetics in health and disease from the embryo stage to old age. Even scientists who have reservations about such a "Big Science" effort will welcome the genome catalogue when it becomes available. Yet, for individuals in whom the genome map discovers an increased risk for a genetic disease, the new knowledge may be a mixed blessing.

BRAIN RESEARCH

From Minor Role to Center Stage

The Neurobiology of Memory

A melody heard for the first time can be recognized if it is repeated during the same performance, or if it is repeated days or even decades later. The melody somehow is impressed upon the listener. In 1950, Karl Lashley, one of the most esteemed neuroscientists of his era, described the melody's memory trace as an engram, a permanent change produced by a stimulus that becomes part of the brain. The question thus far unanswered is how the permanent change, the memory, is made.

The brain, to most neuroscientists, is a vast network of tens of billions of neurons that communicate with one another using electrical impulses. Through its dendrite, a structure with thousands of tiny branches, a neuron recieves signals funneled from sensory organs or from other neurons.

Once a neuron amasses a strong enough signal, it fires. The neuron's electrical impulse is sent down a stalk called an axon, which, through connections called synapses, directs the impulse into the dendrites of other cells. Thus a neuron can receive signals from thousands of neurons and in turn can convey signals to thousands more.

When a signal reaches a terminal, the end of an axon's branches, molecules called neurotransmitters transport the signal across a space called the synaptic gap. On the opposite side of the synapse, a bump on the next neuron contains receptors that recognize the incoming neurotransmitters. If there are sufficient neurotransmitter molecules, the receiving neuron fires, sending on another electrical impulse.

Although the communication process of neurons has become better understood, how they store information is still not clear. Researchers assume that when the brain records a new experience—an image or a sound—an individual pattern of neurons is energized. The new neural configuration might be retained by creating new synapses between neurons or by strengthening already existing synapses. Either way, what we call memory would be the reactivation of the circuit.

This theory proposes that something that produces a neural pattern similar to the one in storage would result in recognition. A neural circuit that had preserved overlapping characteristics of hundreds of encounters with dogs might create a concept of *dog* when faced with a particular breed never before experienced.

The Biochemistry of Memory

Some memory researchers are primarily concerned with looking at anatomy, i.e., where memories are stored in the brain; others such as Gary Lynch of the University of California at Irvine are more concerned with the biochemistry of memory.

Lynch began with an interest in "sprouting," which for a time was viewed as a possible cure for brain damage. Neurons, unlike other cells, are not replaced when they die. However, sometimes when the connections between neurons—the dendrites, axons, and synapses—are damaged they sprout back. Lynch decided to see if this phenomenon, which had been observed in the spinal cord and primitive lower brain, might occur in a more complex region of the brain called the hippocampus that had been shown to be important in the formation of memories.

Lynch and a colleague, Carl W. Coltman, designed a sprouting experiment that in time resulted in newly grown synapses. Lynch wondered whether sprouting might be a mechanism for growing circuits that store memories. It would not be enough for Lynch to show that sprouting occures in the hippocampus; he needed to demonstrate actual changes in the brain in response to information.

Since nerves use electrical impulses to transmit data, Lynch set up an experiment to stimulate hippocampal tissue to produce as many neural pathways as possible. It took a year of tedious work to find the synapses he was looking for.

If Lynch were right, an electrical impulse that lasted but a fraction of a second could within minutes create synapses. If electrical signals within the brain created the same effect, then the encoding of a memory, be it of a birthday or a baseball score, could leave its engram or memory trace.

Lynch reasoned that if the brain were growing new synapses, it would have to produce more receptors to detect the presence of the neurotransmitter. With a colleague, Michel Baudry, a neurochemist from Paris, Lynch performed an experiment that seemed to indicate that electrically stimulating the brain could make more receptors. Additional experiments showed that the mineral calcium was responsibile for setting off the reaction.

The question in Lynch's mind was, how could a cell change as quickly? The wall of a cell is flexible, but it is held in place by protein scaffolding called cytoskeleton. Looking elsewhere in the body for a clue to sudden

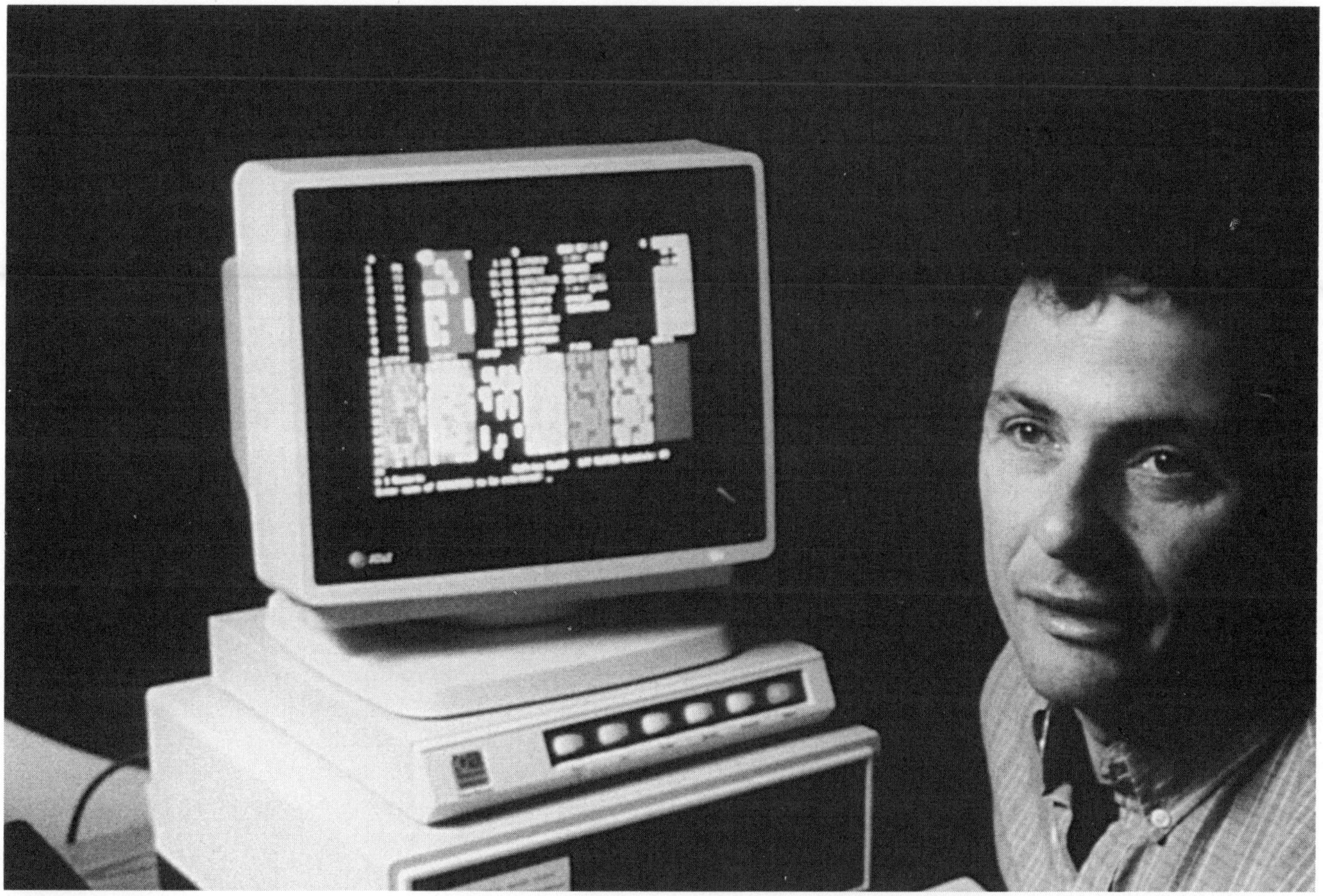

Researchers at the University of California at Irvine, in studying how the brain learns and remembers, are attempting to electronically duplicate certain brain functions on a computer by simulating their circuitry. Here Dr. Gary Lynch runs a program simulating the neural pathways of the olfactory cortex. Smells represented by data concerning the chemical components of each aroma are entered into the computer. The simulation automatically creates and sorts the smells into categories as the human brain would, although programmers did not intend to give the simulation that ability.

structural change, he found that calcium plays a part when blood platelets hook together to quickly seal a wound.

Lynch speculated that platelets' shapes are modified when a calcium-activated enzyme, calpain, cuts through the cells' skeleton. He theorized that a memory might occur when an electrical signal prompts channels to open in the dendritic spine, letting calcium flood in. The enzyme calpain, activated by the calcium, would eat through the cytoskeleton, allowing receptors hidden deeper in the membrane to pop out. The dendrite would become more sensitive to the neurotransmitter, and the neurons on either side of the synapse would be linked in a circuit. (Lynch later proposed that a memory trace could be left without the appearance of the hidden receptors).

Repeated stimulation might promote more radical effects. Groups of newly exposed receptors might change locations and form new clusters of new synapses. The processes of strengthening existing memories and growing new ones could, Lynch believes, account for short-term and long-term memory. To explore Lynch's theory, his colleague, Ursala Staubi, infused a rat's brains with a chemical that inhibits calpain activity. The chemical interfered with the rat's ability to learn.

Lynch and Baudry published their findings in 1984 in the journal *Science*. Refined and publicized in the intervening years, the hypothesis by 1987 had become a leading contender in the experimental struggle to explain memory.

However, there are other biochemical models of memory. Aryeh Routtenberg at Northwestern University believes that an enzyme called protein kinase C, not calpain, may be the significant factor.

Frontiers of Brain Surgery

Increased knowledge about the human brain has made it possible to transplant nerve cells into the brain. Using this procedure, scientists in the United States, Sweden, and China have cured animals of symptoms of Parkinson's disease.

Most animal experiments transplant brain cells from aborted animal fetuses. In several countries, experiments in humans are under way, or are being planned, that use human fetal brain cells. Since abortions, whether spontaneous, medically required, or elective, are likely to be the largest source of fetal tissue, the experiments are controversial.

After 100 years of failure, researchers are surprised by their own success. The change has come about through the convergence of various lines of research. Scientists now know that human adult brains regardless of age are remarkably plastic. Throughout life, cells migrate, make connections, and stimulate targets, including transplanted cells.

In contrast to brain cells transplanted in the past, transplanted fetal cells continue to grow. Moreover, scientists have learned—without understanding why—that a transplanted substance can influence chemical reactions in part of the brain distant from the transplant site.

Earlier strategies of making point-to-point connections between existing and transplanted cells have changed. The new strategy is to implant cells that excrete chemicals in the precise location where they are normally produced, and thus to promote functional rather than anatomical change.

Brain cell implants appear to tap into the brain's own nerve growth factors. Recently discovered, nerve growth factors are substances manufactured in the brain that help nerve cells survive, grow, and make new connections. Five kinds of cells are under investigation for transplantation:

1. Human fetal cells. These give the best results. When placed into a host brain, fetal cells follow the proper genetic sequence for making connections and for secreting chemicals. The cells integrate themselves without being rejected.
2. Animal fetal cells. Research is under way to make the animal tissue immunologically acceptable by humans.
3. Human fetal cells grown in test tubes. Banks of artificially propagated nerves cells may one day be available.
4. Human cancer cells. Some cells release needed brain chemicals. While they can be kept alive in test tubes, the cells stop producing chemicals after implantation. Before they can become feasible for implant, a mechanism has to be found to prevent the cells from producing cancer.
5. Cells from the adrenal gland. The glands produce a chemical comparable to one missing in the brains of patients with Parkinson's disease. An adrenal gland rests on top of each kidney.

The surgical procedure to retrieve adrenal tissue destroys the gland, but as long as the patient's second gland is healthy, this shouldn't be a problem. Rejection is not an issue since the tissue is the patient's own. On the negative side, adrenal cells are not true nerve cells, and their introduction into the brain could have unknown long-range consequences.

Despite their limitations, adrenal gland implants have been moved out of the laboratory and into the operating room. By July of 1987, 43 patients worldwide had undergone such surgery. Nineteen adrenal gland implants had been done by a team headed by Ignacio Madrazo Navarro, chairman of the department of neurosurgery at La Raza Medical Center in Mexico City. The implant seems to do more than just halt degeneration. It appears to induce regeneration of the diseased areas.

The Search for Physical Evidence of Mental Illness

Research into schizophrenia has made tremendous strides in recent years to alleviate the suffering of the 1 percent of Americans who have the disease. On any given day, the afflicted fill 100,000 hospital beds, and thousands more wander the streets among the homeless. Until relatively recently the disease was viewed as a psychological problem brought on by the victim's upbringing.

A major site of research into schizophrenia is a brain bank in McLean Hospital in Boston that receives brains donated by the families of mental patients who have died. The donated brains are weighed, measured, sliced, stained for microscopic examination, chemically analyzed, and stored in a large freezer. Any one of 75 areas of each brain can be examined by a scientist, along with the deceased patient's medical chart.

Computer-imaging techniques have revealed that the brains of many schizophrenics show damage, underdevelopment, or abnormal biochemical function. A consistent pattern, however, has not been found. In any event, the abnormalities themselves are not sufficient to bring on the disease. If they were, the damage would not lie dormant until age 15 or 20, when schizophrenia is most likely to be first diagnosed.

A promising research finding at McLean Hospital is the discovery that the majority of schizophrenics, and about half of their relatives, have a subtle but distinctive problem in tracking a moving target with their eyes. The researchers, Steven Matthysse, a psychobiologist, and Philip Holzman, a psychologist, speculate that the defect may be passed on in families in the way that diseases caused by a single gene are passed on.

A genetic link is less obvious in schizophrenia than it is in many other diseases. About 80 percent of schizophrenics do not have an affected parent. Critics of the single-gene hypothesis argue that schizophrenia's inheritance pattern resembles diseases such as cancer and diabetes, which are likely to involve several variant genes that produce a genetic predisposition that then interacts with environmental factors to trigger the onset of the disease.

The only real breakthrough in treatment of schizophrenia came 30 years ago with the development of antipsychotic drugs that calmed the most flagrant of the symptoms, allowing many patients to live outside the hospital. The drugs blocked the action of the brain chemical dopamine. A major part of subsequent research has gone into trying to understand what dopamine does in various parts of the brain.

A researcher at Johns Hopkins University, Dean Wong, found that schizophrenia patients had more dopamine receptors than did normal persons. It had long been suspected that excessive activity of dopamine in schizophrenic brains might be due to an excess of receptors.

A successful new drug, Clozapine, that blocks dopamine has strengthened the evidence implicating dopamine. An increasing focus of schizophrenic research is a part of the brain called the dorso-lateral prefrontal cortex, to which dopamine pathways connect. This area is the site of judgment. Knowledge learned from experience, abstract reasoning, conformance with social norms, and sustained attention—all areas seriously disturbed by schizophrenia.

Mapping the Brain's Magnetic Fields

The brain's changing magnetic fields make it possible to pinpoint and to measure sites of neural activity. The techniques of neuromagnetism, both new and experimental, enable researchers, using a variety of discriminating sensors placed over the head, to produce images of the brain's functioning. During one set of trials, researchers played tones of different pitches and tracked the electrical

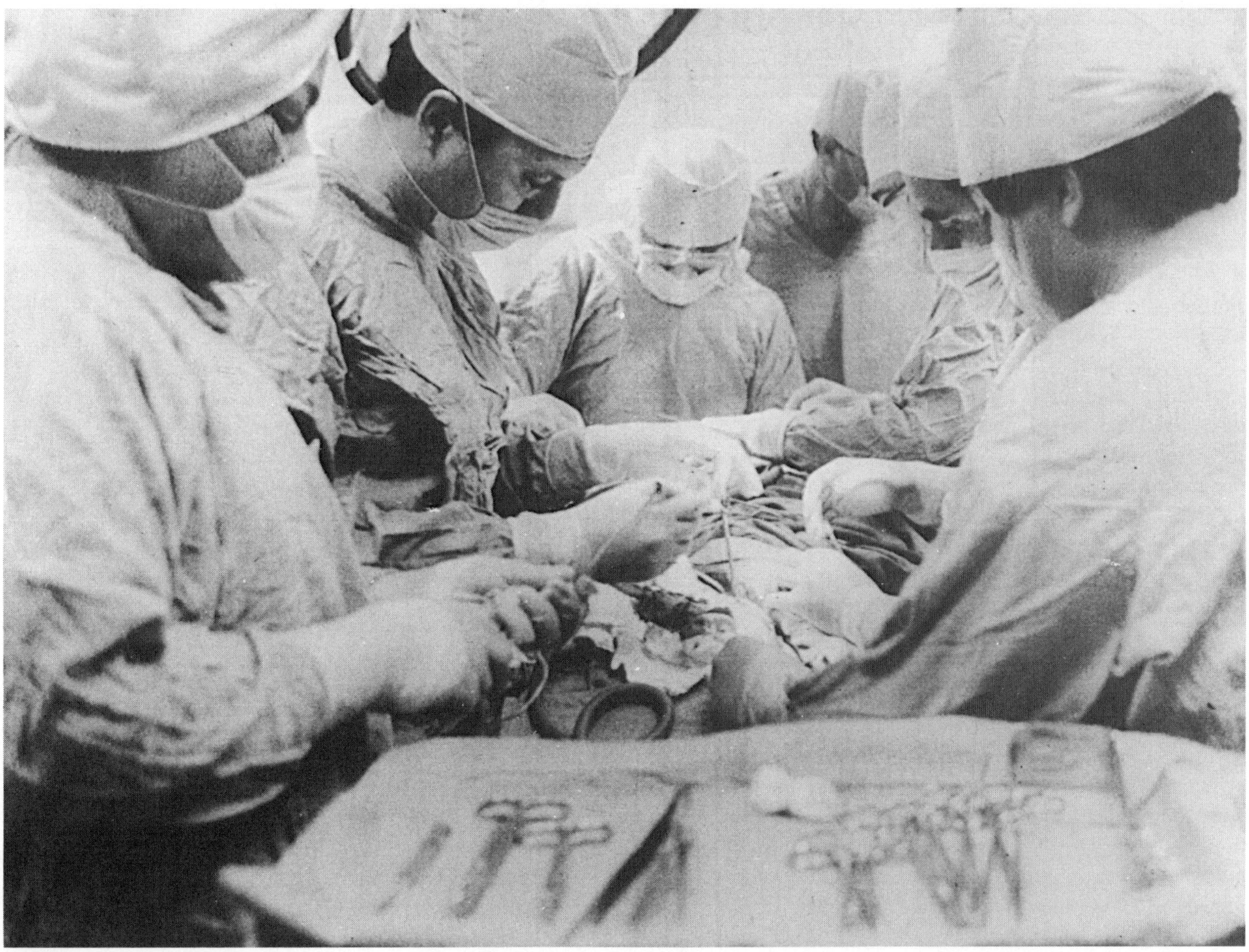

Doctors performing pioneering brain implant surgery to treat symptoms of Parkinson's disease, at the La Raza Medical Center in Mexico City.

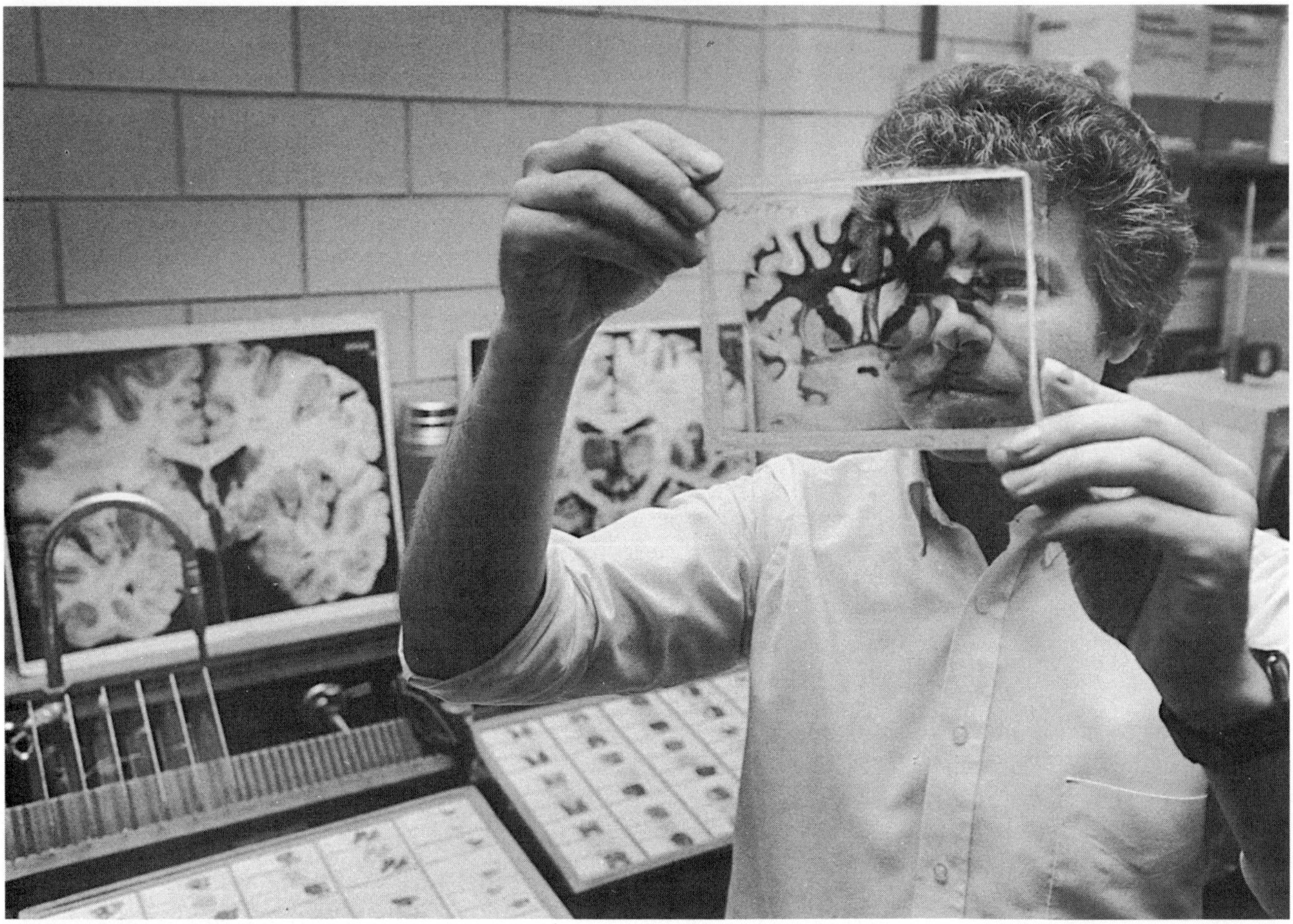

Tim Wheelock, a histologist at McLean Hospital in Belmont, Mass., holding a slide section of the human brain.

signals in the auditory center of the brain. With changes in tone, the locale of brain activity changed.

Any electrical current, including the currents that move muscle cells and energize the brain's neurons, creates a magnetic field. Until two decades ago the fields generated by the body's currents could hardly be detected. Superconducting quantum interference devices, or "squids," have made it possible to measure magnetic fields at a level of precision that allows computers to pinpoint the location of the original signal. Squids are sensitive enough to measure fields a billionth of the strength of the earth's own magnetic field.

Superconductors carry electric currents with perfect efficiency, which makes it possible for the sensors to detect very weak magnetic fields. However, the present generation of squids are cumbersome and expensive because superconductivity requires extreme cold. Researchers look forward to flexible squid-studded helmets suitable for heads of a variety of sizes.

The skull has long been a source of frustration in brain research. The protection the skull provides the brain also shields it from observation. EEGs, electroencephalograms, which measure voltage at the surface of the skull, offer only a crude picture of underlying activity. The skull dampens current, but with the use of magnetism, the skull becomes transparent.

In electromagnetism laboratories at New York University (NYU), at the University of Rome, and at the Helsinki Institute of Technology, scientists pick out signals from the brain's complex magnetic haze. They conduct experiments in how sights and sounds are perceived, how muscles provide feedback, and how "attention" is focused.

During one experiment at NYU, while two different tunes were played, subjects were asked to pay attention to only one or the other. One tune was high-pitched and the other low-pitched, which enabled the researchers to track the magnetic signals corresponding to the pitch. The scientists discovered that the conscious act of paying attention turned up the amplitude of one signal and turned down the amplitude of its competitor.

Thus far the neuromagnetic techniques are best suited to brain functions associated with specific locations. Higher level activities, such as thought and memory, distributed over wide areas involving millions or billions of neurons, must await a higher lever of understanding of complex processes.

The first neuromagnetic clinical research efforts and successes have come in the treatment of epilepsy. Scientists at the University of California at Los Angeles and at the National Institutes of Health in Bethesda, Maryland, are conducting basic neuromagnetic research into epilepsy and are screening patients who may be candidates for surgery.

At the Johns Hopkins University Applied Physics Laboratory in Laurel, Maryland, researchers have performed animal experiments to locate the site of epileptic seizures. Traditional approaches to pinpointing the site of hard-to-locate seizure sites have included drilling holes in the skull to insert wires in the brain.

The Johns Hopkins researchers are also using neuromagnetism to monitor brain swelling. Continuous monitoring of brain swelling currently calls for pressure sensors implanted beneath the patient's skull. The other option for continuous monitoring is the use of scans using radiation, which entails a risk of overexposure.

Other research using the brain's magnetic field is being conducted at the University of California at Los Angeles's (UCLA) Human Neurophysiology Laboratory, with a computer-based technology called magnetoencephalography (MEG).

MEG's subject lies down on a table or sits in a chair. A neuromagnetometer is placed near the subject's head, where it acts like an antenna. MEG senses magnetic-field patterns produced by brain cells, locates the field's source, and takes a picture one thousand times per second. UCLA researcher Jack Beatty describes the goal of MEG research as the acquisition of a map of normal brain events, i.e., the physiology of thought. Edward Flynn, a physicist at Los Alamos national laboratory in New Mexico, views his goal as a four-dimensional picture of the functioning brain.

Still another device for mapping the brain's functions is an X-ray machine about 7 to 10 years away from being built by computer scientist Alan Gevins. At EEG Systems Laboratory (EEGSL) in San Francisco, Gevins and his colleagues have brought together a combination of biomedical engineering, neuroscience, and computer graphics to study a few microseconds of intense brain activity. The goal is to study how different areas of the brain interact with one another, and how the brain prepares itself to act. The initial work took 4 and a half years, cost $2 million dollars, and required a trillion computer operations.

Subjects were chosen for their ability to concentrate. Prior to playing a simple video game called a Finger Pressure Test, the outside of each subject's brain was mapped by running a sensor-equipped robotic arm over the subject's head. From coordinates fed into a computer, a three-dimensional image was made of each head.

Next, cross-sectional pictures of each subject's brain were made using a magnetic resonance imaging system (MRI). The MRI image slices were stacked to create a three-dimensional model of the brain. During game play, each player wore a cap embedded with 64 electrodes that relayed brain waves to a computer to be recorded.

The game requires the player to respond to a number from one to nine flashed on a screen by pressing a button with an appropriate level of pressure. On average the players were accurate 6 out of every 10 tries.

Using a pattern recognition program developed by electrical engineer Nelson Morgan, the scientists were able to edit out brain signals not involved in the game play. They discovered that a distinct pattern of waves they called "preparation set"—which appeared prior to the brain's reaction signal—was sent to the body. The brain constantly tuned and retuned itself in response to anticipated environmental changes. In time, the scientists could tell how players would respond milliseconds before they responded. Moreover, the scientists could identify patterns associated with accurate and inaccurate responses. During inaccurate plays, players' attention lapses. They lose their concentration.

Another kind of brain-imaging machine is being used to detect mental disorders in the Department of Psychiatry's Brain Imaging Center at the University of California at Irvine (UCI). The scanner is called a positron emission tomography (PET) machine. The patient is injected with radioactive glucose, which when absorbed by the brain provides a "color-enhanced blueprint" of the organ. During an hour-long scan, nine separate slices are photographed.

By mid-1987, psychiatry professor Monte Buchsbaum had performed almost 200 scans over a 3-year span. One result from the research has been a challenge to the long-held opinion that autism is a childhood form of schizophrenia. The UCI team has consistently found a high metabolic rate in the left frontal lobes of recovered autistics. In contrast, they have found that schizophrenics exhibit low metabolic rates in their frontal lobes.

Behavioral Medicine: The Mind/Body Connection

An area in which long-held views of the mind are having to give way in the face of new findings is the field of behavioral medicine, the linkage between mind and body. Pioneering work in biofeedback done by Neal Miller at Rockefeller University in New York gave the field its first clinical credibility. In 1977, Robert Adler, now director of the division of behavioral and psychosocial medicine at the University of Rochester's medical school, demonstrated that a rat could be conditioned to suppress an antibody response to the taste of saccharine. By 1987, approximately 400 universities offered some training in behavioral medicine.

The volume of research being done has led to a new discipline, psychoneuroimmunology (PNI). The name of the new discipline is not yet settled. Sometimes it's called behavioral medicine, in reference to clinical studies, and sometimes it is called neuroimmunomodulation, in reference to laboratory work with underlying mechanisms.

PNI combines science with the concept of holistic medicine. Instead of talking about how the *mind* heals the *body*, PNI researchers investigate how the *brain* affects the *immune cells*. The immune system and the nervous system have been known to be linked since the turn of the century, but immunology was not taken seriously until the 1960s. In turn, immunologists did not take seriously the brain's role in immunology until the early 1980s.

At the forefront of the research has been Candace Pert, neuropharmacologist at the National Institute of Mental Health. Pert has devoted herself to studying neuropeptides, small protein-like chemicals (including endorphins, the body's own morphine-like chemical) made by cells in the brain. The effects of neuropeptides are often mimicked by psychoactive drugs, and they all seem to exist in high concentrations in the limbic system, a primitive part of the brain that exercises control over emotions and physical drives. In Pert's view, neuropeptides are biochemical units of emotion.

Along with immunologist Michael Ruff, Pert has studied the macrophage, the big, amoeba-like cell that oozes around a site of infection, where it rebuilds damaged tissues and devours bacteria and viruses. Almost every neuropeptide Pert and Ruff have studied was able to latch onto macrophages and affect the speed and direction of the macrophages' movement. Pert reasoned that if each neuropeptide influenced macrophage movement, then moods could influence the battle macrophages made with disease.

In one study done by Pert and Ruff, test subjects were made to feel helpless by being exposed to a loud noise that prevented them from concentrating on a puzzle. The subject's macrophages were discovered to move more slowly.

Psychoneuroimmunologist Gerard Renoux of the University of Tours in France believes that the brain's cortex plays as important a part in regulating the immune system as that played by the more primitive areas of the brain. He destroyed an area of a mouse's cortex that has no significant effect upon the mouse's behavior. When Renoux damaged a section on the left side of the cortex, the number of white blood cells in the mouse's spleen dropped and the remaining ones became less efficient. When he

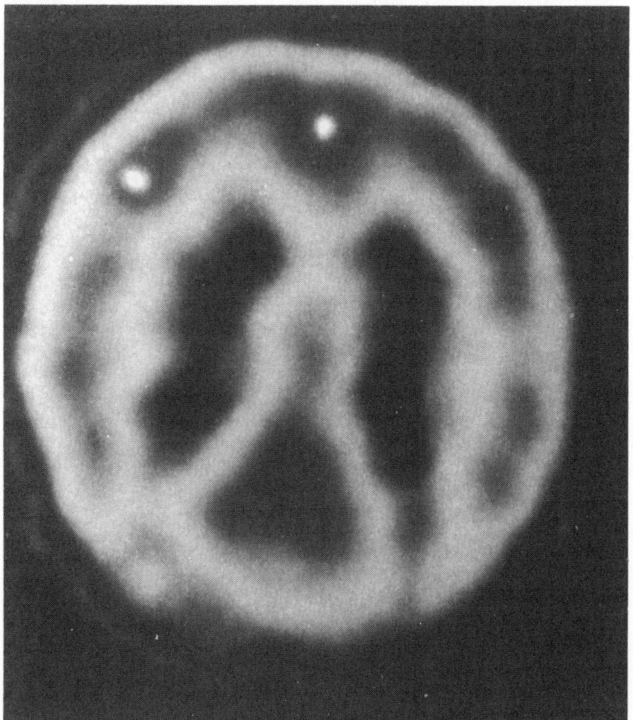

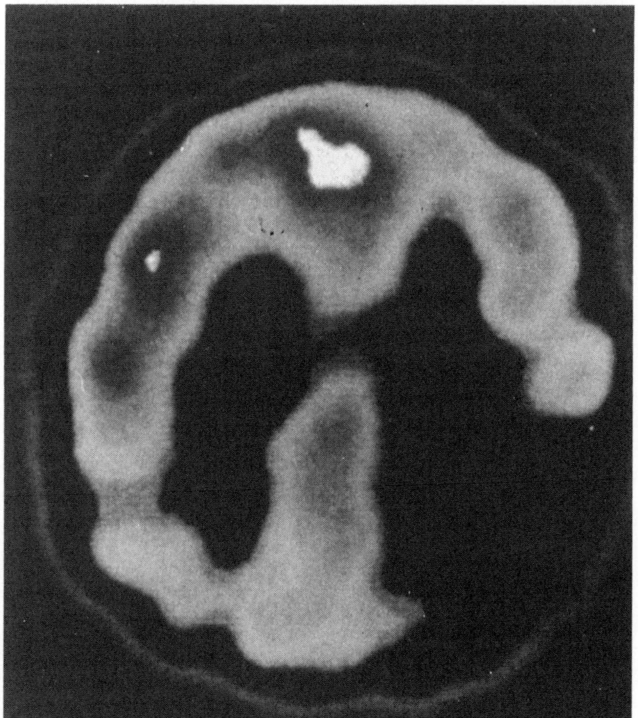

On the left is a PET scan of a normal brain. On the right is the PET scan of the brain of a 65-year-old housewife suffering from Alzheimer's disease. The scan shows loss of activity in the right side of the brain, the visual-spatial side.

damaged a section on the right side, the white blood cells became slightly more aggressive. Renoux concluded that the right and left sides must cooperate, with the left side stimulating the immune system and the right side suppressing it.

Holistic cancer treatments, which have supplemented medical treatment by attempting to change the patient's mood as a way of mobilizing the immune system, have been a target of critics. Skeptics have pointed out that instead of depression exacerbating a patient's cancer, the fact of having cancer has depressed patients. Nevertheless, PNI researchers believe there is a physiological connection. If the brain can influence the immune system, the patient's mood can have an effect on bodily processes. If in turn the immune system can affect the brain, it can affect the patient's mood.

In the early 1970s Hugo Besedovsky, who is now at the Swiss Research Institute in Davos-Platz, Switzerland, looked for feedback from the immune system to the brain. With immunologist Ernst Sorkin and biochemist Adriana del Rey, he implanted electrodes in the brains of rats and then injected foreign cells that stirred the immune system into action. With the introduction of the foreign cells, electrical activity in the rat's brain increased and the levels of important brain chemicals temporarily dropped, an indication that the brain was aware of what the immune system was doing.

In a series of experiments that began in 1979, Ed Blalock, an immunologist at the University of Alabama, has demonstrated that the immune cells can speak to the brain in the same way that brain and glands speak to the immune system—in the language of hormones. While studying interferons, the chemicals from white blood cells that fight off viruses and tumors, Blalock noticed that interferons sometimes mimicked the activity of some hormones. Moreover, when he put immune cells into a petri dish and stimulated them to make interferons, he found hormones. With further work, he found they could produce endorphins, ACTH (adrenocorticotropic hormone), growth hormone, thyroid-stimulating hormone, and reproductive hormones. Recent work in Blalock's lab suggests that the growth and survival of embryos may be dependent on hormones produced by a mother's immune system in response to the foreign tissue that is the embryo.

After researchers at Johns Hopkins reported that cancer patients with a "fighting spirit" lived longer than those who were passive, Sandra Levy, associate professor of psychiatry and medicine at the University of Pittsburg School of Medicine, undertook a study of 36 women diagnosed as having advanced breast cancer. After the first year, Dr. Levy found that the significant survival factor was not anger but a sense of joy with life. In fact, joy was a more statistically significant indicator of survival than the number of sites to which the cancer had spread.

Only within the past 5 years have PNI researchers seen their work achieve a measure of respect and had their submissions to journals accepted, even sought after. Funding for PNI research has begun to grow. In 1983, the National Institutes of Health set up a grant program under the auspices of its immunology and neuroscience branches. In 1987, $11 million was allocated by the National Institute of Mental Health (NIMH) for PNI, most of it for studying the behavioral aspects of AIDS.

There is also a growing literature on the subject by professionals with solid scientific credentials. In *Hypnosis and Behavioral Medicine*, Daniel Brown of Cambridge Hospital and Ericka Fromm of the University of Chicago reviewed recent research and reported that a variety of largely interchangeable methods—muscle relaxation, hypnosis, meditation, controlled breathing, and biofeedback—have helped in the treatment of some types of allergies, asthma, hypertension, migraine and tension headaches, herpes lesions, irritable-bowel syndrome, and peptic ulcer.

However, the practice of behavioral medicine appears to lack a unifying theory to explain why becoming deeply relaxed should seem to relieve symptoms for so many patients with medical disorders. One promising theory had been offered by Herbert Benson of Harvard, director of a behavioral medicine program at Boston's Deaconess Hospital, and George Everly, a Harvard clinical psychologist. They suggest the disorders that benefit from relaxation are "disorders of arousal" in which the limbic circuitry of the brain has become hypersensitive. Relaxation may dampen the adrenergic catecholamines, brain chemicals that stimulate the limbic system.

After a long history of playing only a minor role, brain research at last has taken center stage. The neurobiology of memory, transplant surgery, the search for physical evidence of psychosis, the mapping of the brain's magnetic field, and behavioral medicine are only a few examples of a vigorously growing area of research.

FORENSIC SCIENCE

Sherlock Holmes's Modern Counterpart

The television series "Quincy," about a colorful big-city chief medical examiner, provided the general public with an introduction to forensic medicine, the application of medical science to resolve legal issues. Dr. Quincy's cases for the most part involved traumatic deaths, such as accidents, suicides, and homicides. Real-life medical examiners' services and procedures vary significantly from state to state, but generally these professionals become involved in cases in which the cause of death is in question.

At the Scene of the Crime

The body is only one part of a criminal investigation. The gathering of physical evidence does not wait for the results of an autopsy. The process begins immediately with the discovery that a crime has been committed. Despite the fact that murders often occur in awkward places—bathrooms, swimming pools, wooded groves, back roads, and busy street corners—the gathering of evidence proceeds in an orderly fashion, in keeping with the tradition of the scientific method.

The crime scene must be cordoned off immediately to prevent bystanders—curious neighbors, children at play, stray dogs, and the first wave of crime investigators—from inadvertently destroying evidence or from innocently contributing misleading evidence. Photographs and sketches of the crime scene give investigators a base on which to reconstruct the crime. The quality of these visual recordings is critical because crimes such as murder cannot be reproduced in a laboratory.

A medical examiner has the responsibility of identifying a dead body. To establish that identification, the medical examiner will make use of personal identification by friends or relatives, fingerprints, teeth, scars, evidence of past medical or surgical procedures, tattoos, body shape and size, congenital malformations, comparison of X rays, identification of clothing and its contents, and photographs. Some of these methods are more certain than others. For example, both identification of clothing and its contents and identification of a badly decomposed or mutilated body by relatives or friends are obviously subject to substantial error. They are also subject to deliberate deception.

Dental Records

Teeth are useful in the identification of a victim because they are resistant to the changes undergone by more vulnerable parts of the body. Also, no two sets of teeth are exactly alike. Some distinguishing factors examined by forensic odontologists (dentists) are size, shape, position (tilted or rotated), restorations (fillings, crowns, bridges, root canals), spaces between teeth, ridges on the edges of teeth, and grooves on the front or back of the teeth. Teeth are also useful in determining the age of a body because teeth undergo predictable changes at various life stages.

Teeth are not only important in identifying the victim, but may also be useful in identifying the criminal. Criminals have left behind identifiable bite marks on surfaces such as chewing gum, cheese, fruit, chocolate, and butter. They also frequently leave behind bite marks on the victim. In fact, bite marks on victims are common enough that the yearly meeting of the American Academy of Forensic Sciences includes a "Bite Mark Breakfast" at which information is shared among police, medical examiners, and forensic researchers. Bite marks provide not only a pattern of the attacker's teeth, but may also provide a specimen of saliva, which can be used to determine the blood type of the attacker.

Fingerprints

In the case of homicide, an important purpose of physical evidence is to establish the identity of both the victim and the offender. Perhaps the most significant turning point in forensics was the discovery that fingerprints are unique, that no two individuals have exactly the same pattern. However, until recently, fingerprints were used to solve crimes much more in fiction than in everyday police work. The procedure of comparing a suspect's fingerprints with many other prints was too time consuming to be practical for local police departments. Until prints were computerized, the match had to be done laboriously by hand. The chances of finding a match with only a single print were slim. Moreover, the suspect's prints had to be in the particular data bank being searched.

A major breakthrough has been the Automated Fingerprint Identification System (AFIS), which can rapidly analyze and classify fingerprints. The system's computer scans the prints, makes maps of the ridge patterns, and translates the information into a digital code, which it compares with other prints on file at a rate of 500 to 600 per second. Prints that are closely matched by the computer are verified by a trained technician for a final identification.

During the first few months that the AFIS was in use in Baltimore, Maryland, the system identified 525 previously

Dr. William Maples of the University of Florida excavates around a body found in Cross City, along with an investigator from the Florida Department of Law Enforcement.

arrested men and women who were using aliases. In California, where the AFIS was introduced in 1984, the police have used it to solve hundreds of cases, including the Los Angeles "Night Stalker."

In its first year of use in San Francisco, the AFIS processed 5,514 fingerprints, made 1,001 identifications, and helped clear 816 cases, including 52 homicides, one of which dated back 25 years.

"Sherlock," the $2.6-million AFIS leased in Massachusetts in 1987, was predicted to solve at least 10 percent of the 17,000 unsolved cases in which latent prints were on file. Officials believe that the success of Sherlock will encourage local police departments to put a greater emphasis on searching for prints at crime scenes. Sherlock normally provides five ranked possibilities from its bank. If the comparison scores fall below a set minimum, they are perceived as unfeasible.

Local fingerprint data banks will eventually be merged into statewide systems, which in turn will be combined into regional or national networks. Today, the delay in widespread use of fingerprints is not due to a lack of existing technology, but to a lack of funds to make the larger systems possible.

Even with larger systems, the suspect's prints still must be in the system before they can be matched. They are likely to be there only if he or she were fingerprinted during a criminal investigation, as a member of the military, or as an employee in a government-related job.

All types of prints that feature friction ridges—including the palm of the hand and the sole of the foot—provide information that can be matched.

To commit a crime without leaving prints is difficult. Good sources of prints are windows and doors through which the criminal entered. As the crime progresses, criminals tend to become careless about leaving prints on areas such as light switches and liquor bottles.

Prints can be divided into three categories: plastic prints, which are left when an impression is made on a soft surface such as gum, soap, or wax; visible prints, which occur when the ridges have become covered with a substance such as flour, ink, or dust before touching a clean surface; and latent prints, which occur when grease or dirt is mixed with

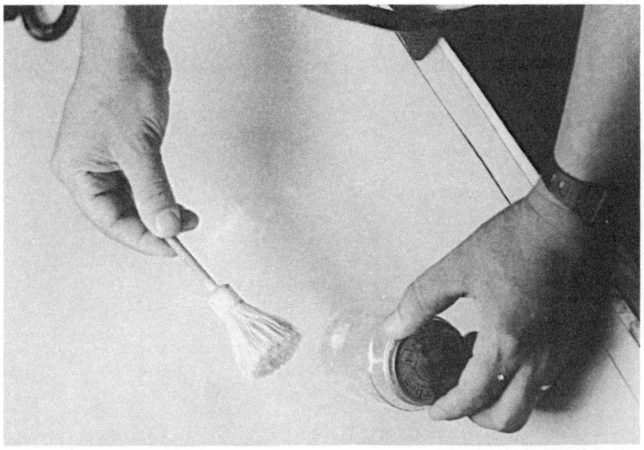

An object is dusted for prints.

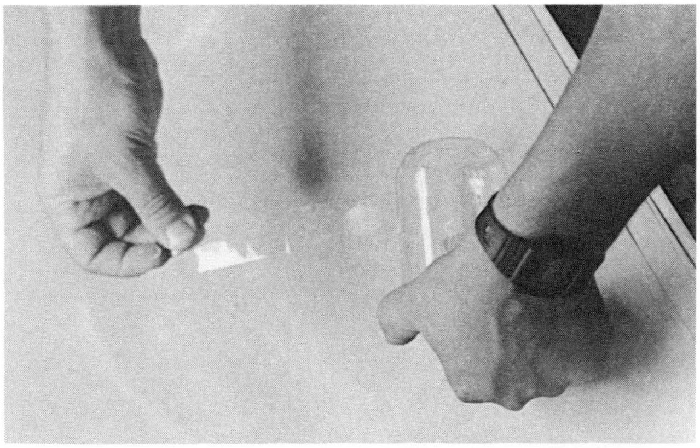

If a latent print is found, it is "lifted" off with tape. The tape is similar to Scotch tape but is more transparent.

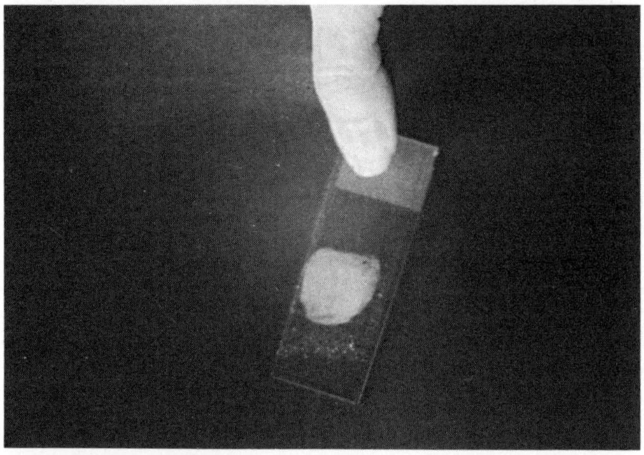

The tape is then afixed to a glass microscope slide.

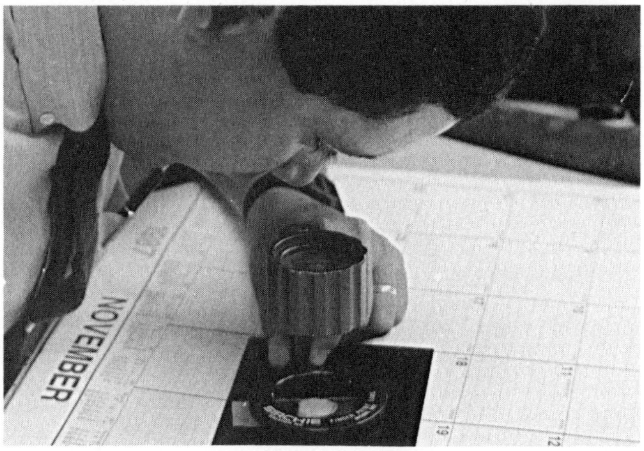

The slide can then be examined with a magnifying glass.

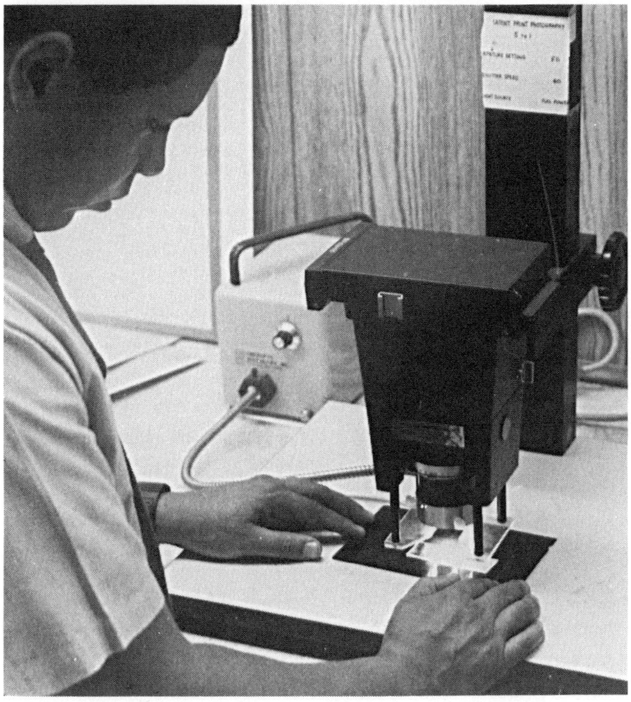

Or the image can be enlarged by being photographed.

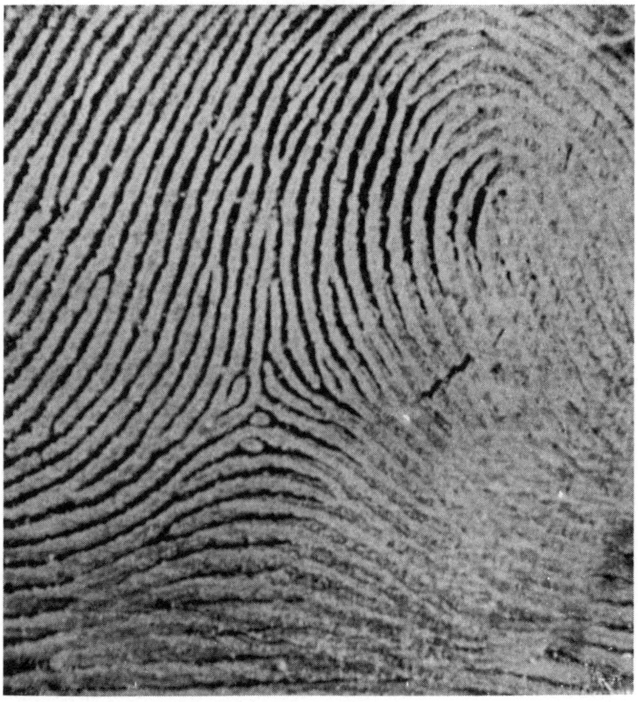

An enlargement of a latent print.

the natural skin secretions such as perspiration and which are only partly visible or are visible only after they have been chemically treated.

Latent prints are the most difficult for investigators to find, but now a combination of laser and image-processing methods are increasing the recovery of latent prints. Although lasers were introduced into police work in 1976, by 1985 only about 15 percent of North American crime laboratories were using them. The lag may have been due in part to funding problems, but more likely, to the fact that lasers are most effective only when used in conjunction with other visualization techniques. New image-processing methods have increased the visibility of prints that until recently had been inadequate for identification.

In image processing, latent prints are examined with a video camera. The video signal is fed into a computer that can distinguish hundreds of shades of grey. The greys show up as various densities. The image-processing technique is particularly effective with prints on a textured surface, which are otherwise difficult to capture. Lasers even make it possible to try to find prints on the bodies of victims, especially on the skin of children and women. Ideally investigators stabilize prints on a body with chemicals at the crime scene, then check them with a portable laser before the body is moved.

Fingerprint-gathering techniques are still developing and are expected to improve and become more routine in the future. The proliferation of relatively inexpensive microcomputers has finally placed the necessary technology within the budgets of many police laboratories.

DNA Mapping

In the future, a method expected to rival fingerprints in importance is the developing method of DNA

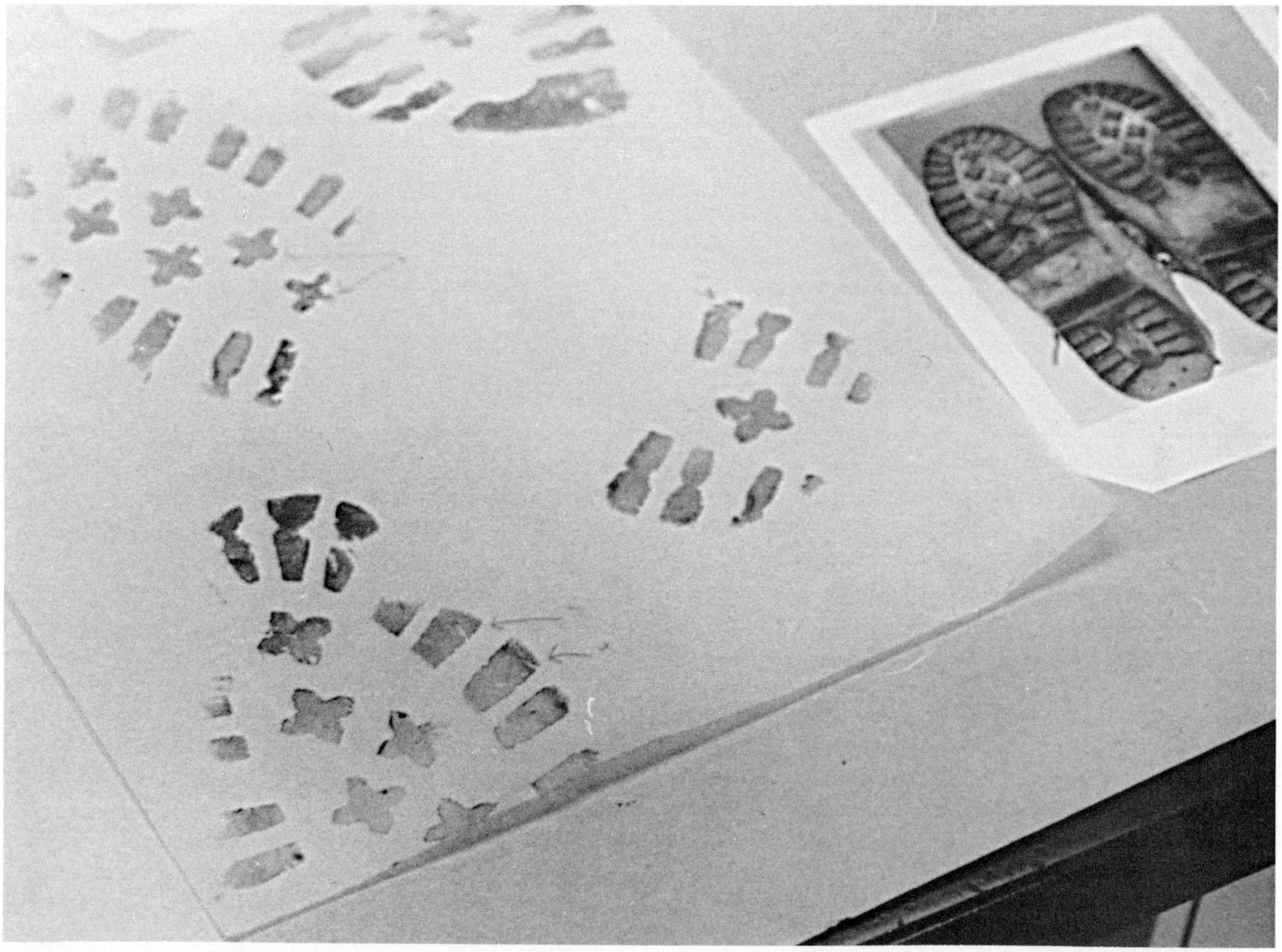

Clothes can help identify people or place them at the scene of a crime. Left are shoe prints to be examined by the Chemical Laboratory of the Mass. State Police. Although shoes are a mass-produced item, the tread of every shoe made is different, particularly once the shoe has been worn. A person's weight and gait will wear the tread in particular areas, and the tread will acquire scuff and cut marks that can be matched up and identified.

Dr. William Maples examing X-rays of vertebrae to determine cause of death.

(deoxyribonucleic acid) mapping of blood and other body fluids and tissues. In this technique, bits of DNA are purified, chemically separated, subjected to a process called electrophoresis, then spread out by size on a sheet of special paper. The resulting pattern is always the same for an individual—a DNA "fingerprint."

Technicians apply several DNA probes—radioactively labeled bits of DNA—to seek specific complementary pieces of DNA in the sample and bind them. When the sheet of paper containing the DNA pattern is sealed in a cassette with X-ray film, the radioactivity exposes the film, leaving behind an image of the DNA fragments. When the fragments from two samples match, probability tables are used to compute the odds of such a match occurring by chance. By combining the odds for different probes, investigators can sharply limit the chances of a false match.

With continuing refinements, researchers expect to be able to use almost any body cell, including hair, for identification. In time, scientists anticipate, they will be able to say with absolute certainty that a given DNA pattern belongs to a specific individual; now they can only say that the pattern occurs in perhaps one out of a million people in the population.

Aside from its use in criminal investigations, DNA typing is also used to settle maternity and paternity questions. The technique has even been extended to nonprimates, where making fine distinctions of parentage has often been difficult. For example, the technique was applied to wild sparrows at the University of Leicester in Great Britain, where it unraveled complex genealogies.

Some scientists expect DNA typing to become as commonplace as fingerprinting. Others express doubts over the immediate future of the technique, suggesting that concern about personal privacy may prevent or postpone routine use.

Anthropologists Aid Crime Investigations

Forensic anthropologists specialize in identification of the deceased through the examination of their bones as well as other factors. They use many bits of evidence to glean clues to the identity of bones under their scrutiny. For example, the skull and pelvis of men and women are quite different. The demarcation of growing areas on a child's long bones provide clues to age as do ridges on the upper edge of the pelvis (they smooth with age). The Caucasian face tends to be narrow, and the profile is almost flat from forehead to chin. Blacks tend to have a broader nose bridge. Native American skulls have a squarer shape, and certain of their teeth have a distinctive appearance.

Michael Charney, a forensic anthropologist at Colorado State University, was contacted several years ago by the widow of an American serviceman missing in action. The army identification lab had recently "positively" identified her husband, but the widow was skeptical that so much could be deduced from a few bone fragments gathered at a site where there were also found the remains of other soldiers. Charney agreed, and now the case is likely to evolve into a lawsuit.

Forensic anthropoligist William Maples, director of the C. A. Pound Human Identification Laboratory at the University of Florida, serves as a resource for medical examiners all over the state. The area's warm climate, abundance of insects, and varied ethnic populations can render the identification of bodies quite difficult. When all else fails, Dr. Maples can often turn failure into success.

When the crime scene is a burial site, forensic anthropologists are often called in. They are also consulted when the police need to know the best way to excavate a suspected grave site. These experts can be particularly helpful in providing information about the effect on bodies of burial, burning, or major disaster.

A device that uses proton magnetometers to detect changes in the earth's magnetic field is now in use by archeologists to look for ancient burial sites. The device is expected to become common among law enforcement officers searching for buried bodies.

In spite of the importance "time of death" plays in fictional detection, in routine police investigations the exact time of death is not so easily established. Generally, within the first 3 days after death, medical examiners can make accurate calculations, but beyond 3 days, research on which estimates can be based has been limited.

A unique research program is the University of Tennessee Anthropology Research Facility, known simply as the "decay facility." At the decay facility, newly dead, unembalmed bodies are monitored to record the details of decomposition. William Bass, a renowned forensic scientist and chairman of the anthropology department, works with the aid of his graduate students to provide facts where there now are none.

The dearth of research about time of death is due in part to the many difficult-to-control variables, including climate, weather, animals and insect activity, injuries, and individual physiology (fat bodies decay faster than thin ones).

Another factor contributing to the lack of research is the distasteful nature of the work. The research at the University of Tennessee's decay facility, for example, involves charting the day-by-day advance of insects and collecting and measuring specimens of maggots and flies. One precise measurement that has emerged from the research is that the millimeter length of the largest maggot, plus two, will equal the number of days the victim has been dead.

Bodies are not just exposed to the weather at the decay facility; some are buried to determine the effects both on the body and the soil above it. One study found that plant

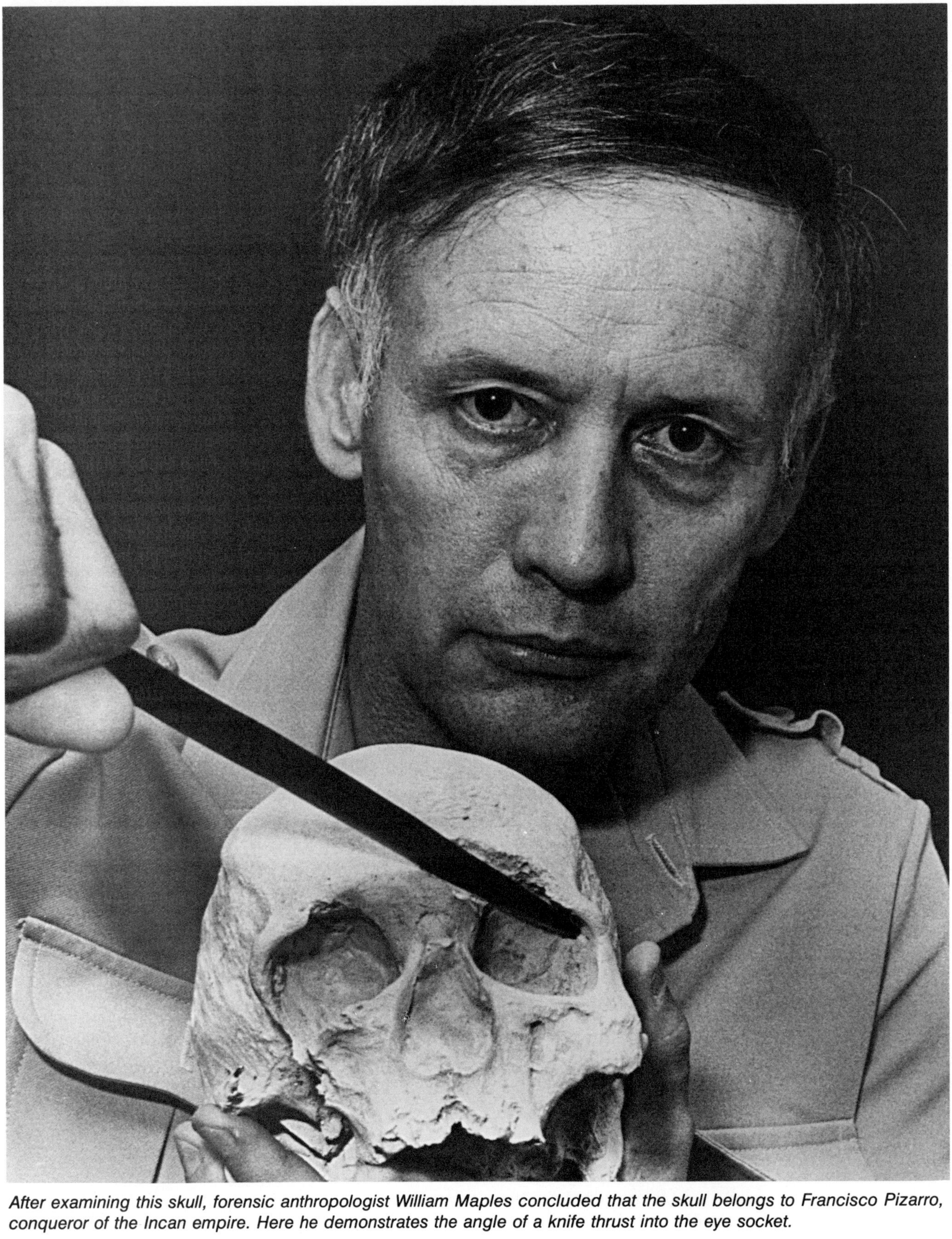

After examining this skull, forensic anthropologist William Maples concluded that the skull belongs to Francisco Pizarro, conqueror of the Incan empire. Here he demonstrates the angle of a knife thrust into the eye socket.

growth accelerated rapidly over shallow graves, and that soil settling after a burial leaves a noticeable depression.

Skeletal remains found in remote woods cause difficulties for investigators, because bears, coyotes, and dogs are apt to scatter the bones as far as a mile away from the original site.

Clues from Entomology

Henry Ryan, chief medical examiner for the State of Maine, has also used a method of estimating the date of death of a decomposed body that involves insects. Flies gather almost immediately on a body and lay their eggs, which begin developing. Ryan gathers some of the maggots and sends them to John Burger, an entomologist at the University of New Hampshire in Durham. The entire life cycle of the fly from egg to adult is thirty days. Thus, if the collected maggots take 25 days to reach maturity, then the investigators can conclude that the person died 5 days before being found.

Facial Reconstruction: A Combination of Anthropology and Art

When bodies have decomposed to a point where only the skeleton remains and there are no external clues to identification, establishing the identity of the body becomes difficult. In the best-selling novel *Gorky Park*, a body is identified by a painstaking sculpting of a face dictated by the shape of the skull. An easier version of the sculpting technique is used by Lewis Sadler, an associate professor at the University of Texas Health Science Center in Dallas. A medical illustrator, Sadler places markers that specify how deep the tissue should be at 60 locations on a skull. After photographing the skull, Sadler uses the markers as a guide to draw the face that belonged with the skull.

Graphics computers are expected eventually to reconstruct in short order what it now takes artists days to produce. A physical anthropologist at Louisiana State University, Douglas Owsley, is working with a graphics computer to try to match the skulls of skeletons with photographs of missing persons.

A Panorama of Skills

Fingerprinting, DNA mapping, judging time of death, facial reconstruction, and examination of dental records are only a few of the ways that scientists are helping police investigators do their work. Invaluable assistance also comes from experts in explosives, arson, ballistics, human psychology, and other specialists.

4

The Changing Environment

TECHNOLOGY ON BEHALF OF THE DISABLED

Helping with the Daily Struggle

Five out of every six currently disabled individuals became impaired during their working or retirement lives, some temporarily, others permanently. But regardless of whether a disability is temporary or permanent, mild or severe, accommodations must be made to cope with daily living. Technology is becoming an important source of help.

Tallies of the Disabled

Among a population of 240 million Americans, estimates of the number of disabled vary between 25 million and 50 million. The variance is so wide because those making the estimates include or exclude different groups. Even the high end of the estimates obviously does not include some groups: For example, the estimated 43 million persons with heart conditions are usually not included. And while there is a standard definition for being legally blind, there is no definition for what it means to be legally deaf.

The following are conservative estimates of the number of disabled persons in the United States. An estimated 8 million Americans have learning disabilities, including dyslexia. (Undiagnosed dyslexia is a major contributing factor to adult illiteracy.) Approximately 6.5 million have restricted motion in their arms and/or legs, frequently due to arthritis. About 5 million people are mentally retarded. An estimated 3.5 million are affected by central nervous system disorders, including cerebral palsy, muscular dystrophy, multiple sclerosis, paraplegia, and quadriplegia. Some 2 million suffer from severe mental illness. Just under 1.7 million have poor vision or are legally blind. About 1 million have epileptic conditions that cause periodic seizures.

The hearing-impaired are not included in the above list because the estimates are confounded by several factors. Gallaudet University, whose mission is the education of the deaf and hearing-impaired, defines deaf as "unable to identify spoken speech with or without a hearing aid."

The most recent national health survey that asked questions about the presence of deaf persons in the household was performed by the National Center for Health Statistics in 1977. From that survey, Gallaudet's researchers estimate that about 346,000 Americans are deaf.

A frequently quoted statistic is 2 million deaf Americans. This figure is extrapolated from a widely used 1974 book called *The Deaf Population of the United States* by Schein and Delk, whose assumptions have been called into question. Another frequently quoted statistic claims that there are 17 to 22 million hearing-impaired Americans. This figure takes into account any loss of hearing, even of a few decibels. Perhaps the best that can be said is that there are approximately 346,000 Americans who are deaf and possibly as many as 22 million who suffer some hearing loss, however mild.

A common assumption is that the wheelchair-bound are the largest disability group. While their numbers are substantial—500,000 adults and 150,000 school-age children—they are small when compared with the other groups. However, their numbers are growing at a rate of 10,000 per year as a result of head and neck injuries sustained in automobile accidents.

Recent Rapid Change in Living Conditions for the Disabled

Until the 1970s many disabled lived in institutions but by 1987 only about 2 million did. The trend away from institutionalization was the result of the disabled's demands to become part of the mainstream society on the one hand, and on soaring institutional costs on the other. (Costs now average about $85,000 per patient per year.)

Because the disabled lived in institutions for so long, the architects of houses, buildings, and cities never had to take them into consideration. The Rehabilitation Act of 1973 began to change that inattention. The act required that all federal buildings be made accessible to the disabled. In 1977, the requirements were extended to all structures built with federal grant money.

The structural changes were opposed by some architects who thought the requirements would detract from the beauty of their designs, by some builders who cited higher construction costs, and by some universities and other institutions who claimed they could not afford to modify existing buildings.

However, the changes made in response to the economic pressure brought to bear by the federal government have made accessible buildings so convenient that architects are hard pressed to explain why they were not built for convenience earlier. Ramps are not used just by the disabled. They are used by parents pushing strollers, by vendors

Due to improvements in treating spinal and neck injuries, more people are surviving devastating accidents to try to cope with living as paraplegics or quadraplegics.

making deliveries, by bicycle riders and skateboarders, and by those who find it easier to walk up a ramp than climb stairs.

For universities that complied, sagging enrollments have been boosted by the earlier untapped population of disabled students. Approximately 7.4 percent of the nation's 1.6 million college freshmen in 1987 were diabled, up from 2.6 percent in 1976. As a direct result of increased accessibility, a half million disabled students were enrolled at all levels in colleges and universities in 1987.

Designing Computers for Wide Access

Just as buildings and cities had not been designed for the disabled, computers were not designed with nonprogrammers in mind, disabled or not. It was not until 1980 and 1981, when the personal computers Apple IIe and the IBM PC were introduced, that the idea of "user friendly" computers began to blossom.

Some people with disabilities quickly recognized the capacity personal computers (PCs) offered to help with their everyday obstacles. All over the country, individuals created solutions—called "patches" in computerese—to make their personal computers fit their needs. Only a few of those patches have become widely available.

Frank Bowe in an article called "Making Computers Accessible to Disabled People," written for *Technology Review* in January of 1987, used three concepts to describe what is needed to make computers easier to use for everyone, disabled or not. The concepts are "transparency," "redundancy," and easy physical access to the machines.

Transparency involves designing the parts of the personal computer to work without the need for adaptations. A transparent personal computer would not distinguish between input from a keyboard or joystick, or any other device. Nor would the computer need to know that the output was being expressed by a voice synthesizer rather than a screen.

Redundancy concerns designing the hardware and the software to permit simultaneous output. At the user's option, both the screen and synthetic speech might be activated, or a pictorial symbol might be accompanied by a text that could remain hidden unless asked for by a blind or dyslexic user.

Ease of physical access is concerned with such issues as the awkward location of on and off switches at the rear of personal computers and the need to hold down two keys for some commands. Both of these are easy design changes.

For most current models, personal computer users with limited finger mobility can use a light pen, joystick, or large keyboard to give commands to the computer; however the substitution is limited to only a few commercially available programs. In addition, the computer must be made to think that the input is coming from the standard keyboard using an "emulator" attached between the keyboard and the operating system. Each emulator must be custom designed for each personal computer model, even those manufactured by the same company. Adaptations for someone with cerebral palsy may cost as much as $20,000.

Speaker Recognition Systems

Companies developing computers that respond to the spoken word did not start out with the disabled in mind. They were concerned with the scarcity of secretaries coupled with the reluctance of executives to use a keyboard, and with workers on assembly lines whose hands were otherwise occupied.

Speaker independent systems are not predicted to be widely available for 5 or 10 years. However, vocabulary speech recognition has been in existence for several years. The small-vocabulary system records samples of the way a given user pronounces each word and then uses the recording to make comparisons with incoming words with distinct sounds.

Large-vocabularly speech recognition works quite differently. IBM's system uses a statistical data base compiled from 25 million words of computer-industry letters and memos. When a new word arrives, the system scans the data base to find which words most often follow the last word identified.

Kurzweil Applied Intelligence Company of Cambridge, Massachusetts, has designed a system with 6,000 words to work with an IBM PC. Using half a dozen programs, the system analyzes English syntax, determines the words most likely to appear, and identifies them by sound.

Another Massachusetts company, Dragon Systems of Newton, founded by James Baker, a mathematician and expert in stochastic processing, and by Janet Baker, a biophysicist, has used a variety of methods to develop what they call "the first natural-language speech-recognition package." Their product, called Voice-scribe-1000, recognizes 1,000 words that can be tailored to meet the needs of the user. The company licenses the product to IBM and to Apricot Ltd. of England. In speech-recognition systems that are governed by probability, when the system hears a word it is unsure of, it must calculate the most probable choice.

Biophysics is not as obvious a component of speech recognition as probability is. Knowledge of how humans and other organisms receive and send signals is still limited. Nevertheless, Dragon Systems has utilized research on how neurons in the ear process sound signals.

Computers that can recognize the speech of different people will make revolutionary changes in the lives of many

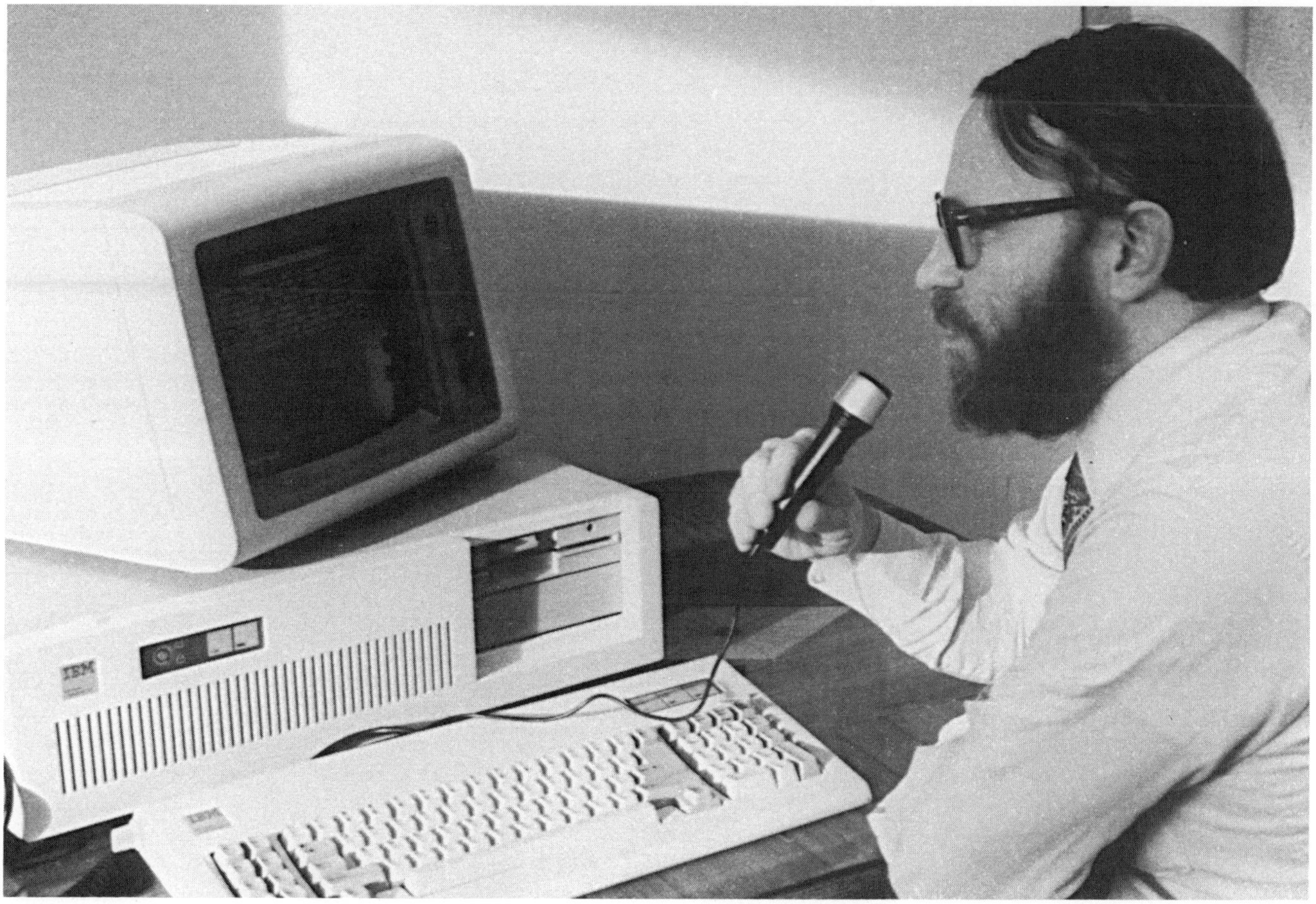

Dragon Systems' speech recognition bypasses the keyboard for fast data entry and limited dictation.

disabled persons. The machines will probably use chips that offer extensive amounts of memory to allow the computer to run several software programs simultaneously. The chips are expected to make possible software that understands thousands of words, and to enable desktop computers to print what they hear as they hear it, and to enable deaf people to talk on the telephone.

Voices for the Silent: Computer-aided Speech

A computer-aided speech system in use at the Model Secondary School for the Deaf at Gallaudet University was never intended for the handicapped. The system, developed for musicians, uses an Apple McIntosh computer, an Emulator II synthesizer, and software called Sound Design by DigiDesign, a Palo Alto, California, company. The sound quality of the system is quite good and the software was immediately usable without modification.

The system allows sound to be visualized in wave form on the computer in either two or three dimensions. The sound is presented in terms of its frequency and amplitude, and measured over time. Teachers record phrases and sentences using a computer to store them and play them back. Then a student or teacher can retrieve a stored sound by hitting a particular key on the synthesizer's keyboard. For example, Gallaudet speech therapist Maureen Nichols might play back a sentence such as "I will order a pizza" over and over with slightly different intonations until her student is able to mimic her production. The staff working with a student can pinpoint a frequency such as the high-frequency sound of *z* in pizza and let a student practice the sound.

An audio engineer at the model school, Howard Schlieper, who is a musician, made the staff aware of the system, which was developed to allow musicians to produce precise sounds. The computer provides a visual display of peaks and valleys that represent different sounds. The graphic representation on the computer screen is as close as the program's students have ever come to hearing the sound. In addition to speech, the students can record environmental sounds and music.

Using the environmental noises, audiologist Leslie Page will ask a student if they can identify or describe the sound. Trying to progress from detection to comprehension with

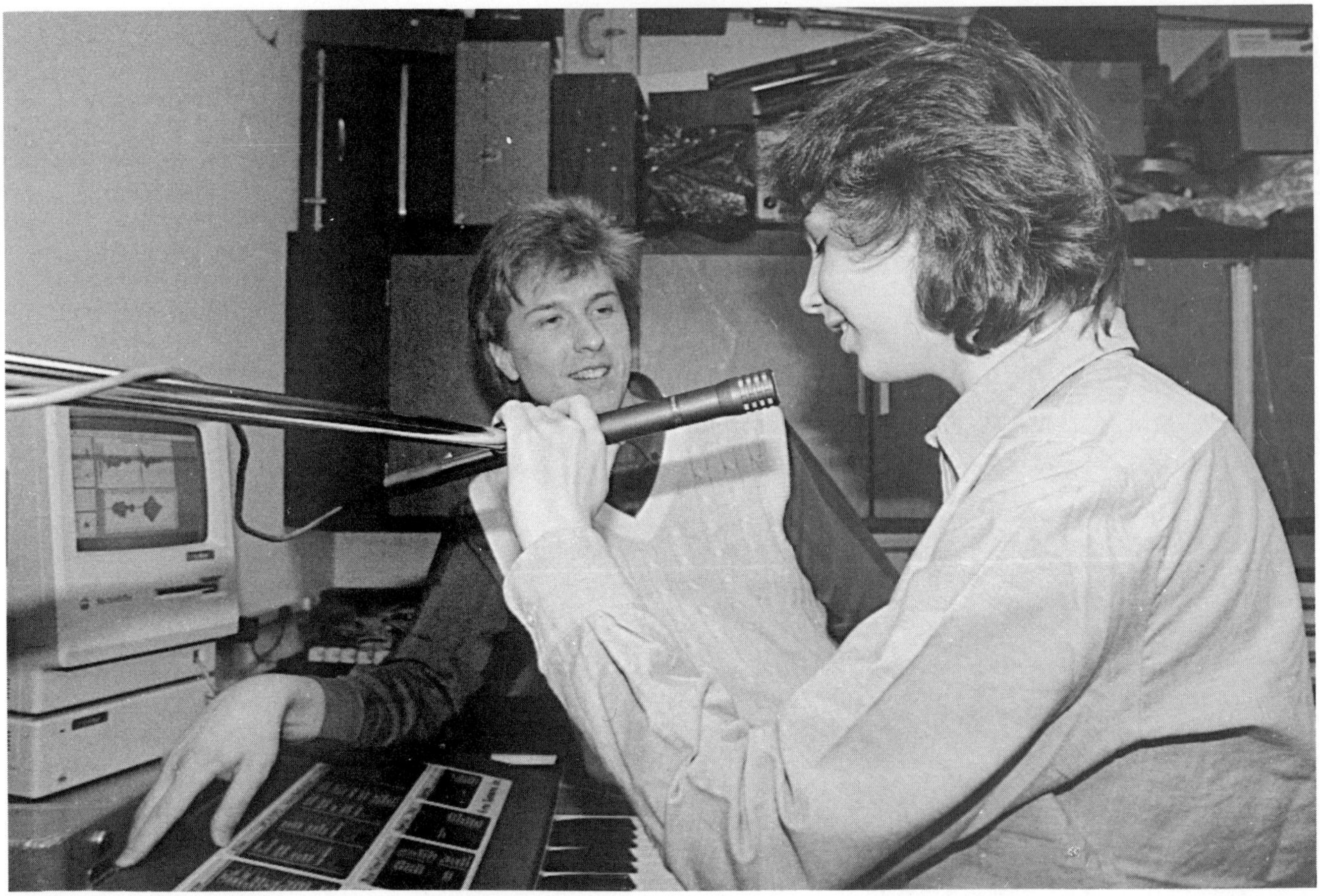

Howard Schlieper, an audio engineer, and Karla Anderson, a student at the Model Secondary School for the Deaf (MSSD), experiment with the Emulator II's recording capacity.

both environmental and speech sounds, the student and staff member will work on words, phrases, and paragraphs.

To participate in the program, a student must have some residual hearing and wear a hearing aid. (Absolute deafness is rare.) By their teenage years, many deaf students have stopped wearing hearing aids and are bored after years of auditory and speech therapy. Being able to see sound, to see syllabificiation and stress, has motivated many to begin wearing hearing aids in order to enter the program. The Model School's pilot project is the only one like it in the country.

Another kind of computer-aided speech was developed by Matsushita Electric Company of Secaucus, New Jersey. The speech therapy system displays syllables that the student tries to duplicate. Sensors attached to a child's nose and throat evaluate how well the child actually makes the sounds. The data gathered are used to graphically display the proper position of the tongue for better pronunciation. The instant feedback permits the child to constantly modify his or her speech to match the desired sound.

Being able to hear speech and to understand how it is produced are not the only blocks to the production of sound. People who are severely disabled by congenital or degenerative illnesses such as muscular dystrophy, multiple sclerosis, or cerebral palsy are often unable to speak clearly or to use sign language because of muscle incoordination. An associate professor of electrical and computer engineering at Northeastern University, John Deller, has worked on a device to make the garbled speech intelligible.

Deller's speech recognition system listens to what the disabled person says and then guesses the message. The guessed elements are transferred to a video screen and the subject is asked if the guesses are correct. Incorrect guesses are eliminated.

Deller has his subjects read aloud 16 words at least 20 times to provide a sample of words against which a specialized program can compare future messages. Because the number and quality of reliable sounds will be different for each person, the machine has to be trained with each individual to recognize their particular patterns.

Non-verbal people are apt to have trouble in getting a message started and then lose their momentum toward the end of their delivery. Therefore, the middle of the message

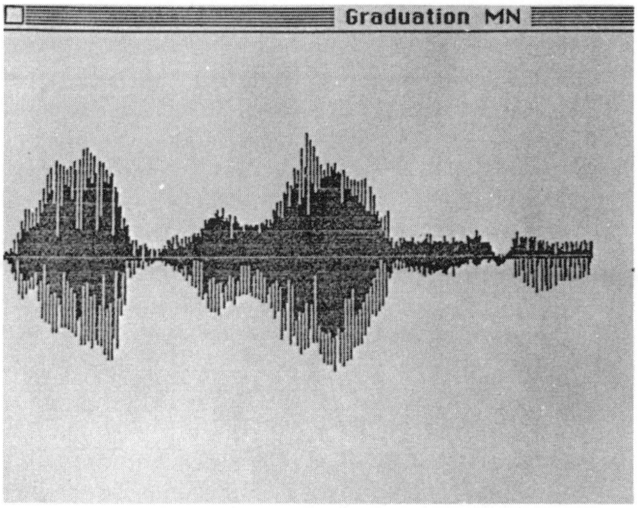

A visual representation of MSSD speech pathologist Maureen Nichols saying "graduation."

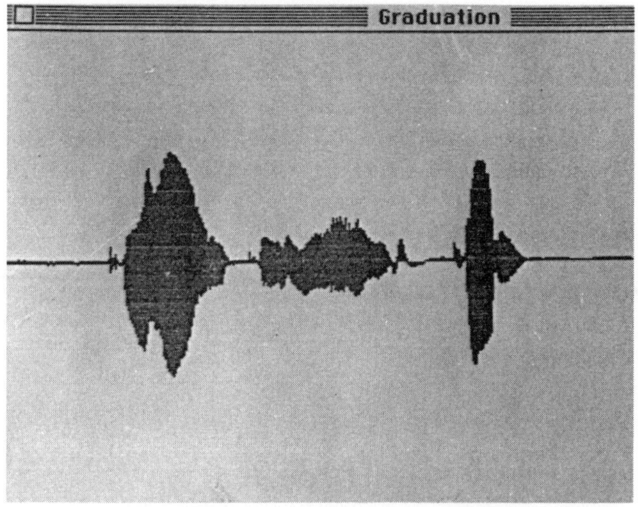

A visual representation of a student saying "graduation." Using "Sound Designer" software, the students can isolate each syllable to listen and to see. See below.

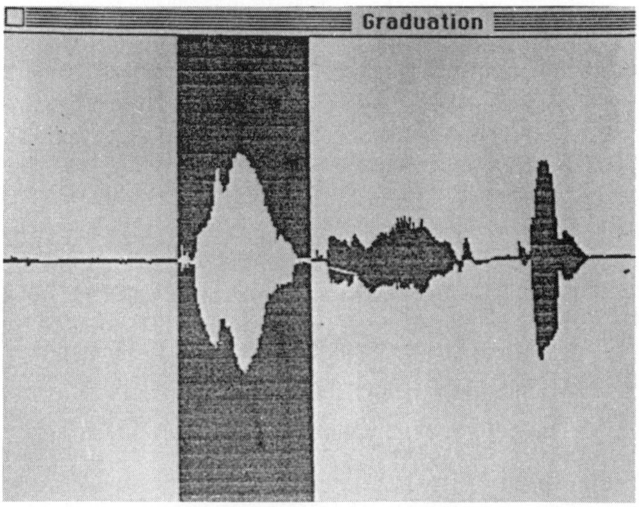

The shaded area represents the first syllable "grad"

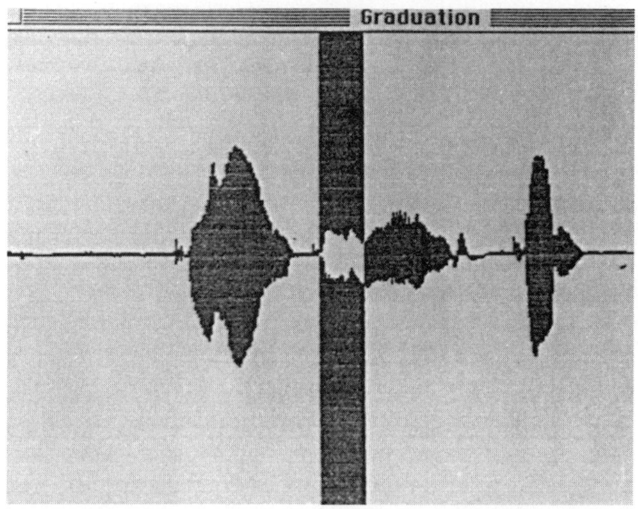

Second syllable "u"

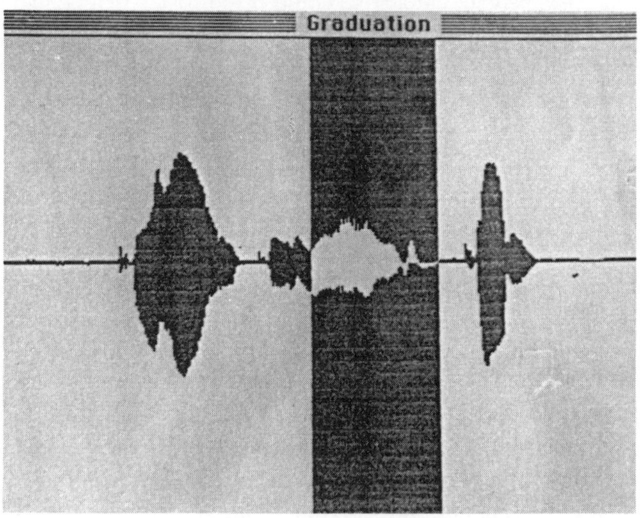

"a"

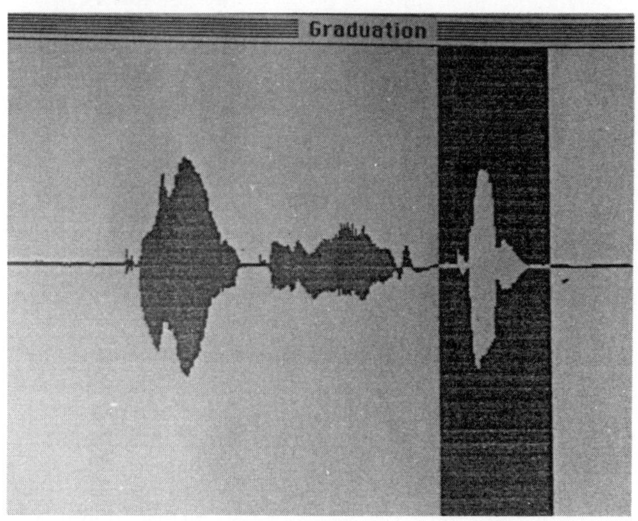

"tion"

conveys the most coherent information. Deller has used graph theorem work done by Northeastern University mathematicians Margaret Cozzeus and C. G. Venkatesh to focus system attention on the middle of the message.

By combining the data gathered from subjects with advances in signal processing and artificial intelligence, Deller expects to develop a model microprocessor that could operate from the arm of a wheelchair. Deller hopes to have a relatively sophisticated lab prototype completed within 3 years.

Phones for the Deaf

Teletype machines are used as substitutes for phones by about 70,000 deaf Americans, but they are expensive and awkward. George Sperling, a psychology professor at New York University, and a scientist who worked for 26 years at AT&T Bell Laboratories, has specialized in how people perceive visual signals. He is particularly interested in how the deaf use American Sign Language (ASL) and in the problem of building an efficient video telephone.

While Sperling was with Bell Labs, engineers developed Picturephone, which was a technological success but a commercial failure. The crystal-clear image required a communications line with a bandwidth capacity of about 1 million hertz, whereas standard telephone lines can carry only about 3,000 hertz. The modifications needed to make a picturephone work would make it terribly expensive.

Sperling had the idea that if a standard telephone line could carry an image that was fuzzy but intelligible, a useable videophone could be developed for about the price of a VCR. With National Science Foundation funding, Sperling and colleagues built a computer-imaging system that produced moving pictures of varying clarity. Using a simulation of the quality obtainable on a bandwidth of 2,800 hertz, they filmed a deaf person signing ASL.

To the scientists the images appeared quite blurred, yet when the movie was shown to deaf users of ASL, their comprehension rate was 86 percent. Sperling also simulated the image obtainable using the digital transmission capacity (4,800 bits per second) of the phone line. The stark black and white outlines were also intelligible to ASL users.

Hearing Assistance

Compared with other electronics, advances in hearing aids have been slow. Only about 3.9 million people use hearing aids but new technology may change that. The obstacle has been in getting sound quality and performance in a package the size of a thumbnail.

A major difficulty for hearing-aid users is an inability to discriminate conversation from background noise. A new automatic signal processing may fix that. Special microchips also have been developed to act as filters in hearing aids to screen unwanted noise.

The approximately 20 percent of hearing-impaired people whose hearing loss is due to faulty conduction caused by infection or malfunction of the inner ear may be helped by a hearing device cleared by the U.S. Food and Drug Administration (FDA) in 1987. First a tiny magnet is implanted in the skull behind the ear, next an external, detachable, sound-processing unit is held in place by the magnet. Sound converted into vibrations is transmitted directly to the magnet, and then to the inner ear for a clearer sound than other types of hearing aids.

A wireless transmitting device called the infrared system, often nicknamed "binoculars for the hearing impaired" makes it possible for those with diminished hearing to attend public performances. The user wears a headset that receives sound from emitters installed throughout the auditorium. First installed in Broadway theaters in 1980, systems have since been installed in 20,000 regional theaters, auditoriums, sports arenas, and houses of worship.

Independent Living

Architect Ronald Mace, whose parents were advised to institutionalize him after he was left paralyzed by childhood polio, is the president of a Raleigh, North Carolina, company called Barrier Free Environments. Mace designs homes and products such as showers, tubs, telephones, drinking fountains, hardware, and transportation equipment.

In 1987, Mace was one of 150 representatives from government, industry, and various rehabilitation fields who met at Roosevelt Warm Springs Institute for a conference on what private enterprise could do to foster independent living for the disabled and the elderly. The main question of the conference was whether it was possible for business to make profits by increasing sales of products useful for the disabled.

Whirlpool, one of the participants, already provides an information service and appliance experts to customize kitchens and make them barrier free. Kits are available to change standard appliance controls to Braille. One display featured a Whirlpool washing machine and dryer with simplified instructions in larger print designed for low-vision customers. Given the number of people who find small print troublesome, the design is expected to increase general sales.

The possibility of technology transfer, that is, the wider use of products invented for a special purpose, is the key to gaining the attention of private industry and government. An often-cited example is Velcro, invented by NASA, which is a boon for fastening the clothes and shoes of the disabled and of children.

The Roosevelt Institute plans to raise $10 million to build and equip a building where, in collaboration with the Georgia Institute of Technology, new rehabilitation products could be tested or built.

Private Initiative; Volunteers for Medical Engineering

Not everyone is willing to wait for industry or government to become interested in the needs of the disabled. At the Westinghouse Defense and Electronics Center near Baltimore, Maryland, where engineers work on sophisticated electromechanical systems for F-16 fighter planes, the B-1B bomber, and other weapons, a group called Volunteers for Medical Engineering (VME) was started in 1981 by John Staehlin, a radar antenna engineer.

More than 200 engineers and technicians are members of the nonprofit group, which by 1987 had four chapters around the country, with six new chapters in the planning stages. The focus of VME is practical, low-cost solutions to real problems faced by individuals and by medical and rehabilitation services. Needs are defined on a case-by-case basis. Once a need is identified, VME looks for the engineering talent to invent an appropriate solution.

Among the solutions already developed is the "Servo-Driven Orthosis" for an individual who, as a result of a spinal injury, cannot open and close the fingers of his or her hand. An electronic patch on the shoulder sends a signal that activates a tiny electric motor attached to a flexible brace on the hand.

Another VME solution is the "Blinkwriter," which provides the power to communicate to an individual who, except for the ability to blink, is totally paralyzed. The individual wears glasses that use a switch to detect eye blinks. The reflection of the closed eye directs the computer's cursor to select from a menu a computer screen. With appropriate interfacing equipment, the individual can also control some aspects of his or her environment. The computer system can be used with a variety of input devices of which the eye-blink sensor is only one.

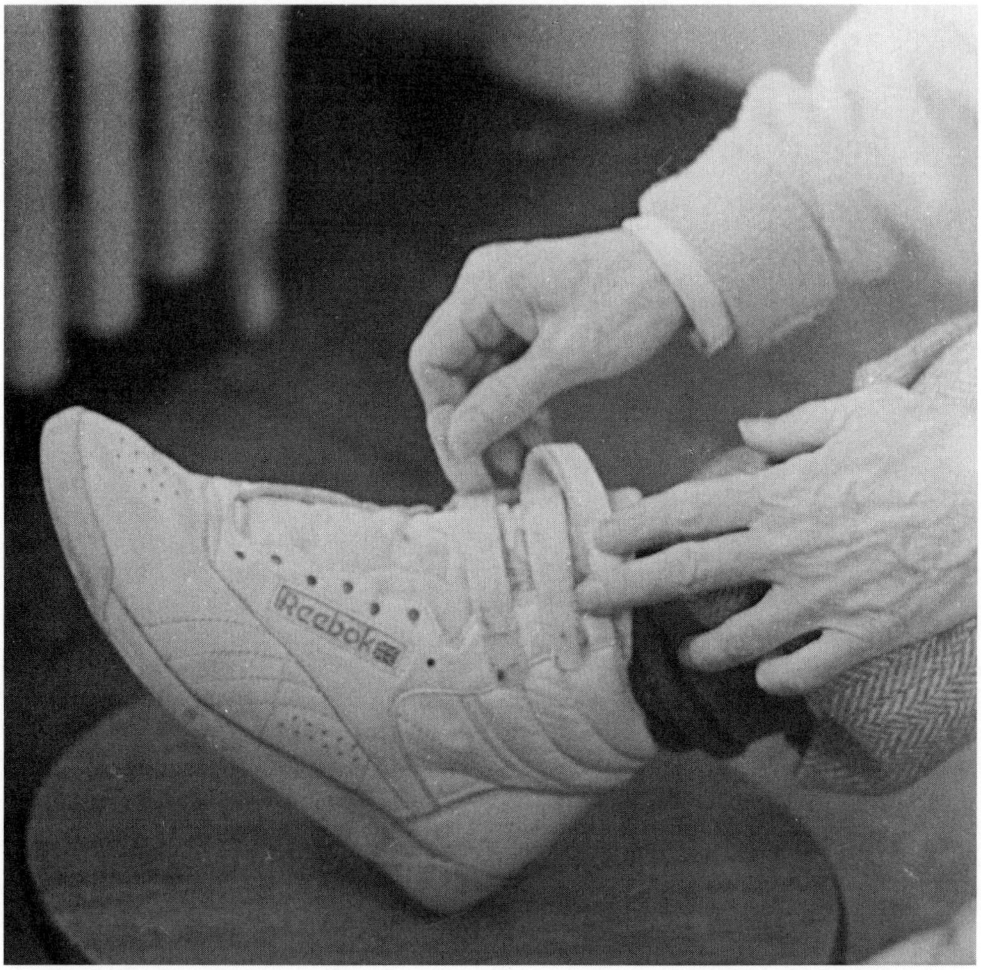

Velcro, which was invented by NASA, is useful for people lacking full use of their hands, but it is also purchased for other reasons. In the theater, costume designers sew Velcro fasteners into clothes for actors who must make quick changes.

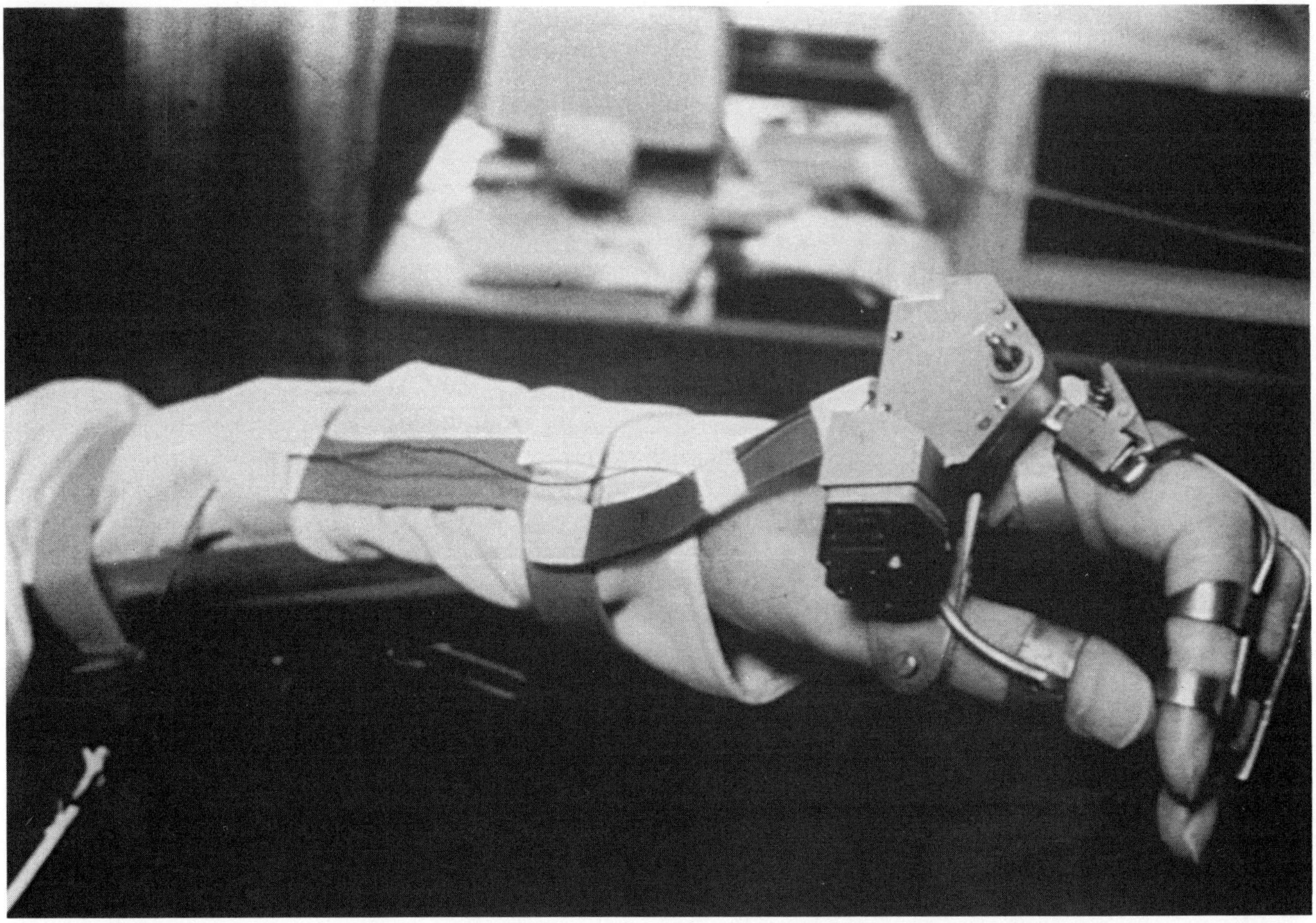

When the nervous system can no longer operate a hand from within, the "Servo-Driven Orthosis" can open and close the hand from without.

Still another VME solution is the Mobile Standing Frame. The device is a "standing wheelchair." The user stands on a platform and uses arm-level wheels to move floor-level wheels. The Mobile Standing Frame allows the user to interact with others at their eye level rather than suffer the constant disadvantage of being seated. Standing also offers internal organs an opportunity to be uncramped for periods of time, and reduces muscle atrophy.

One more VME solution is the Overhead Rail Adaptation for individuals who have difficulty getting from their bed to their wheelchair. The adaptation involves an aluminum wall bracket on one wall, an overhead I Beam between the walls, and an option of various hoists and trolleys. The individual is hoisted in a sling and moved electronically in response to pressure on a button.

A VME project in the very early stages of development is the "artificial muscle." VME scientists noticed that two polymers had characteristics similar to muscle. Working with two scientists at the National Institutes of Health, they have experimented with putting the polymers into a chemical solution and then electrifying the solution. A resulting change in the PH balance of the solution causes the polymers to contract just as muscle contracts. One of the next steps is to develop bundles to mimic normal muscle bundles.

A private solution for the disabled that did not emanate from VME came instead from a class project of four Stanford University mechanical engineering students. For almost 15,000 deaf-blind Americans, the use of hand-to-hand finger-spelling with a friend, relative, or professional interpreter is their only means of communication. Finger-spelling uses hand and finger configurations for each letter of the alphabet.

To make this form of communication easier to use and understand, the students developed Dexter, a sophisticated mechanical hand powered by compressed air that functions at the command of a microcomputer. Dexter finger-spells with four jointed aluminum fingers and a thumb. A finger-spelling glove is also being developed to allow the deaf-blind to send messages via computer. Unlike human hands, Dexter never gets tired, and the robot hand's uniform signals are helpful for people trying to learn finger-spelling.

The Service Industry for the Disabled

Despite the lack of solutions for a multitude of problems, many companies of varying sizes make products for the disabled, although most are not readily available. They usually must be purchased directly from the manufacturer. IBM's Awareness Programs has compiled an extensive data base of resources that are compatible with an IBM PC. Suzanne Lunt in the *Handbook for the Disabled: Ideas and Inventions for Easier Living* describes many products and provides addresses for manufacturers.

For people with limited vision, the characters on a computer screen and the print in a book cannot be seen clearly, a serious problem for partially sighted students who are "mainstreamed" into regular classrooms, and for elderly people who have to give up reading. FDR, a closed circuit TV system manufactured by Optelec of Harvard, Massachusetts, magnifies images from books and documents up to 45 times their normal size onto a TV screen. Using a swiveling device, a child can also read from a classroom blackboard.

For the hearing-impaired who live alone, the ringing of alarm clocks, doorbells, phones, and oven timers is apt to go unheeded. An array of listening and alerting devices have become available, ranging in cost from expensive to do-it-yourself options. A wake-up call may come from a

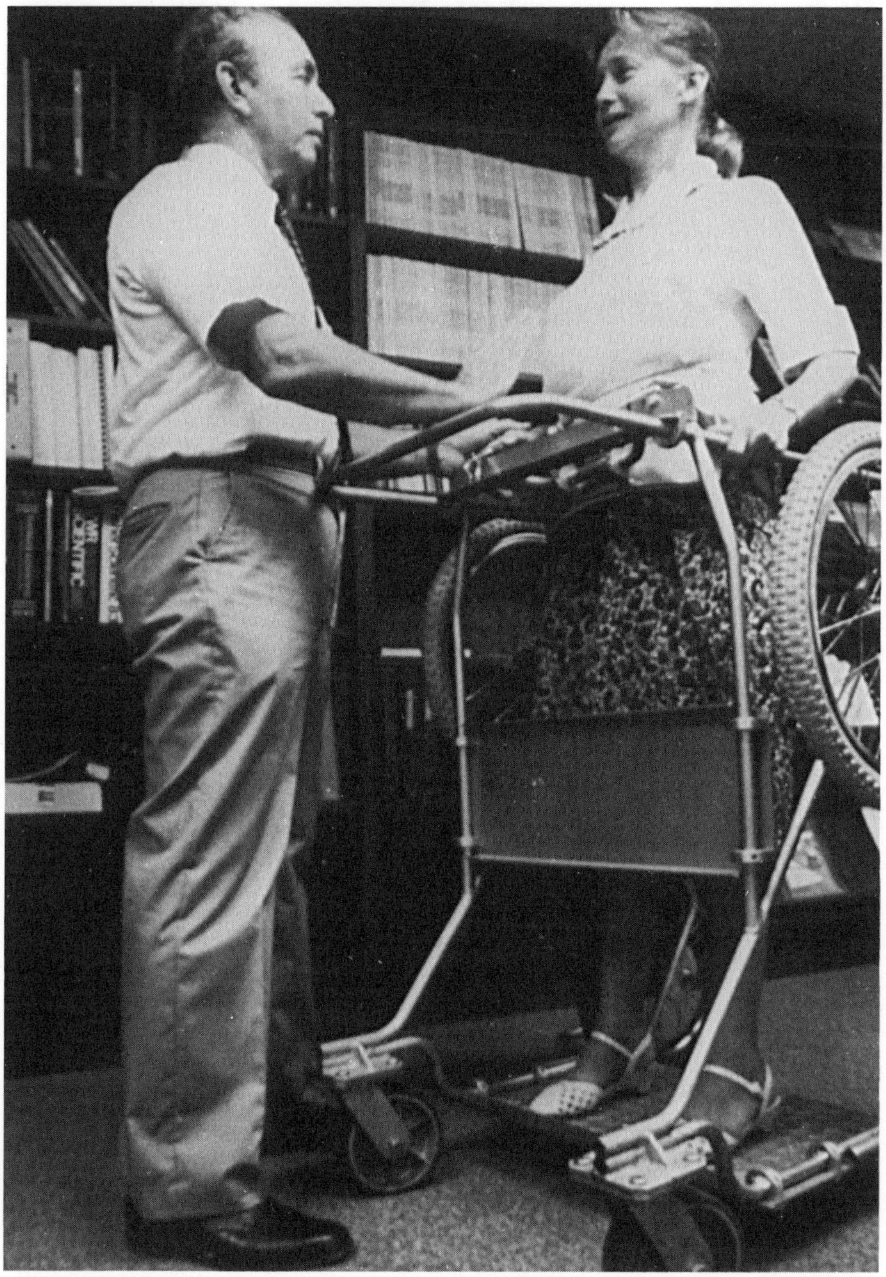

The Mobile Standing Frame allows a wheelchair user to stand for awhile. The user is strapped in place. He or she leans his or her weight on the front bar of the frame. The individual must possess some dexterity to use the frame.

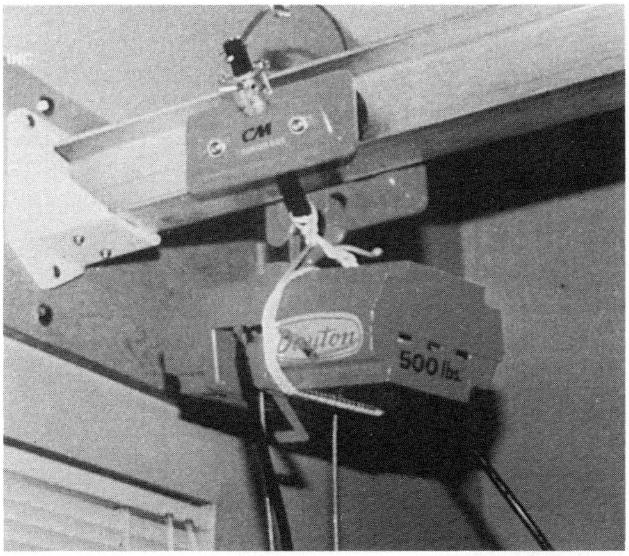

With the Overhead Rail Adaptation a paraplegic can swing himself out of bed with a sling. The Volunteers for Medical Engineering invented this system for a man whose wife had injured her back and could no longer help him in and out of bed. Above is a close-up of the mechanism.

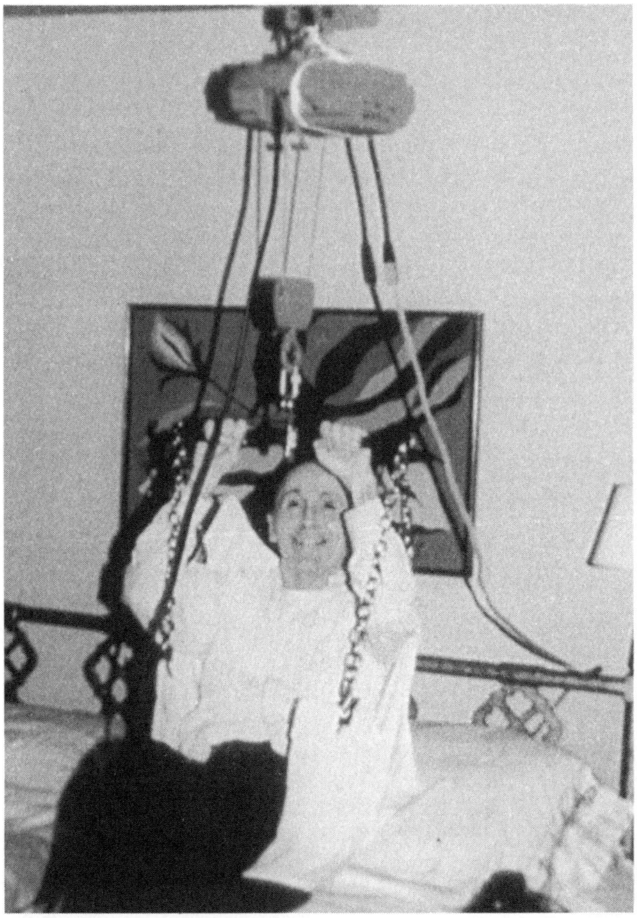

vibrating mattress or pillow. The doorbell or the phone may turn lights on and off or turn on a fan. A more complicated and expensive device is a vibrotactile wristwatch/pager that is connected to appliances. When a timer bell on the over sounds, the watch vibrates.

The Consumer Impact on the Wheelchair Industry

Improvements in wheelchairs are a recent phenomenon. As the pool of wheelchair users has grown, their numbers have included veterans and athletes unwilling to settle for the unwieldy options available. Old wheelchairs featured weighty, chrome-plated frames with hard rubber tires, heavy wire spokes, and small front wheels that fluttered like those on a shopping cart. Seats were uncomfortable Naugahyde slings. The wheelchairs weighed as much as 70 pounds.

A chair that now weighs more than 30 pounds has become unacceptable. Bicycle-type tires are mounted on lightweight spokes, making the chairs easier to push. To prevent the wobble caused by dirt, front wheel casters have been sealed. Materials such as Kevlar developed by NASA have been incorporated into the frames. Better braking, propulsion, and gear systems have improved maneuverability. Durable upholstery and nylon padding have made the seats more comfortable.

Frederick Colson started wheelchair racing shortly after being paralyzed in a truck accident. He found he could cover 10 kilometers in 45 to 50 minutes. In order to improve his time, he took his chair apart: To deliver more power to each stroke and reach the hand rims more easily, he raised the back wheels. He removed the armrests and drilled holes in the footrests. The chair's weight was reduced by 10 pounds, and Colson's racing time was reduced by 15 minutes. Nine years after his original experiment, Colson plays basketball in a 13-pound chair.

Not only have design innovations developed by veterans and wheelchair athletes been adopted by wheelchair companies, but some users have founded their own companies. Ten years ago there were only three or four manufacturers; today there are more than a dozen.

George Murray and Chris Peterson founded Top End to produce racing wheelchairs. Customers who are able to travel to the company's Florida site can have their chairs custom made. While Peterson builds the chair, the customer has the option to train with Murray, who was the first wheelchair athlete to become a "Wheaties Champion." Also available from Top End is a stationary training device that simulates road conditions and can be used for speeds up to 20 miles per hour.

Wheelchair Travel

The tourist industry has discovered the disabled. Coverage of travel routes and facilities has become a regular feature in major newspapers. Ann Levitt, the editor of *The Physically Challenged*, a monthly newspaper published in Rockville Centre, New York, claims that European countries have made more accommodations to make travel easier for the disabled than has the United States.

One device that makes travel easier is collapsible ramps manufactured by Mobility Systems of Berkeley, California. The ramps are 6 inches wide, 80 inches at full length, and each weigh 12 pounds. They divide into four 20-inch sections that fit into each other. The ramps are carried on a vinyl case made to hang from the back handles of a wheelchair. They can be used for getting into and out of a van or to span two or three steps of a building, and one section can be used on each side of a door without a flat threshold.

Without a ramp, obstacles as small as 8-inch sidewalk curbs can stymie a wheelchair user. But a device that would make wheelchair travel easier anywhere may never become available in the United States. The invention, called the Rollsteiger, was developed in West Germany by the Bjorn Steiger Foundation. The electric wheelchair cannot only clear curbs, it can ascend and descend stairs, crawl like a tank through sand and gravel, and even climb hills.

The Rollsteiger rides on ordinary front wheels and fixed-cog rear wheels at speeds of up to 5 miles per hour on level hard surfaces. Faced with a flight of stairs as steep as 35 degrees, or a steep hill, the wheelchair's occupant switches to lugged tracks similar to those on a bulldozer. Made of vulcanized rubber, the tracks are laminated with steel bands.

The Rollsteiger can climb a simple ramp into a van, eliminating the need for an expensive motorized lift. As the wheelchair backs up an incline, the wheelchair's occupant adjusts the seat angle to remain level. Should the joystick be released while on the stairs, the chair will safely creep down by itself.

The president of the Dory Corporation of Aurora, Colorado, Frank Guttierez, planned to import the wheelchairs from West Germany, but was forced to abandon the plan when he discovered that liability insurance to protect against accidents would cost his company $150,000 per year.

Increasing Awareness Will Benefit All Consumers

Some architects and architecture students view compliance with codes that require handicapped accessibility as a nuisance rather than a factor contributing to design. To increase their consciousness, Bruce Carell, a teacher at the Boston Architectural Center, required his students to spend a day in September of 1987 in wheelchairs, attempting to negotiate Boston's Faneuil Hall marketplace. The rule for the day was that under no circumstance could a student leave his or her wheelchair. Steep ramps, quick-shutting elevator doors, and inaccessible toilets became major obstacles sensitizing the 15 architectural students.

Industry has begun to recognize that products designed to meet the needs of disabled consumers, by reason of their flexibility, become more attractive to all customers. The problem of physical access was highlighted when IBM and Xerox tried to sell their large copier in Japan. For the small-statured Japanese, the controls were too high. Instead of lowering the control panel, the U.S. companies suggested the use of stools.

Similarly, the concept of transparency has appeal for nondisabled users who want to link up hardware and software from different vendors, particularly in offices with computers, printers, and other devices that need to work together. Steven Wozniak, co-founder of Apple Computer, and now president of another company called Cloud Nine, is working on building transparency into remote control devices that would be able to function with any television, stereo, or compact disc player.

Given the ever-increasing size of the aged population—by the year 2033 1 out of every 5 people in the United States will be elderly—many products originally designed to aid the disabled are gaining wider appeal and are being reported more often in the popular press.

THE IMPACT OF LEAD ON HEALTH

How Low Is Low Enough?

The Environmental Protection Agency (EPA) and the Environmental Defense Fund (EDF) are apparently not in agreement with the Centers for Disease Control (CDC) about the risk of high levels of lead to children. In 1985, the CDC revised downward its definition of "an excessive absorption of lead" by children from 30 to 25 micrograms of lead per deciliter of blood. The EPA and a panel of outside investigators have recommended reducing the acceptable level of lead by another 60 percent.

Based on a range of new studies, an internal EPA staff report proposed that the CDC consider blood levels above 10 micrograms per deciliter as excessive. One study published in the March 1986 issue of *Pediatrics* found a linear relationship between diminished height and an elevated blood level beginning at 7 micrograms of lead per decilitier of blood.

Another study correlated lower birth weight and slower childhood neuromoter development with blood-lead levels less than 10 to 15 micrograms per deciliter. Other studies have shown IQ deficits for children whose blood-lead levels were less than 20 micrograms per deciliter.

The EPA felt justified in calling for new guidelines based on research done by EPA staff, and based on information from the most recent National Health and Nutrition Examination Survey. Using data gathered from 3,000 youths between ages 4 to 19, the EPA scientists correlated blood-lead levels with hearing loss at pitches between 500 and 4,000 hertz, a range that covers most speech. As blood-lead levels increased from 10 to approximately 30 or 35 micrograms per deciliter, there was a hearing loss of about 10 decibels. Deficits could be linked with levels as low as 12 micrograms per deciliter.

Although most audiologists would not consider 5 to 10 decibel losses as "clinically" significant, the EPA researchers believe the slight impairment could contribute to learning disabilities, even speech impairment, that could go unnoticed among preschoolers.

Ellen Silbergeld, an EDF toxicologist specializing in lead, explained that a change in the CDC's definition would shift the percentage of U.S. children currently carrying an excess of lead from 25 percent to 88 percent. Moreover, 77 percent of adults would fit the excess lead criteria if the acceptable level were lowered. A study by the U.S. Public Health Service and Harvard University found an increase in blood pressure among men with blood-lead level increases from 10 to 20 micrograms per deciliter.

Officials at the CDC, an agency that issues lead guidelines independently of any other agency, were unconvinced that the new studies proved a clear adverse health hazard below 25 micrograms per deciliter. By the fall of 1987, approximately a year after the EPA requested the change, the CDC still had no plans to issue new guidelines.

Evidence continued to accumulate in 1987 that would suggest that new guidelines might be appropriate. Research reported finding effects in the development of infants and toddlers at levels as low as 8 to 10 micrograms of lead per deciliter of blood.

A Scottish study of 501 Edinburgh schoolchildren aged 6 to 9 suggested that any body burden of metal carried a risk of diminishing intellectual ability and learning skills in children. The mean blood-lead level of the children in the study was 10.4 micrograms per deciliter, roughly half the level the CDC views as excessive.

After accounting for 33 possible confounding variables, the study found a 5.8-point differential in score results between the most-and the least-exposed children on the British Ability Scales, a test measuring mental ability and educational attainment. University of Edinburgh epidemiologist Mary Fulton, one of the study's authors, described the statistically significant effect as extending down to the lowest-exposure group and as a larger effect than other studies have found.

How Low Is Low Enough?

While the EPA and the EDF agreed that the CDC should lower the standard for the acceptable level of lead in children, they were not in agreement about how to reach that goal. The EPA proposed to reduce the permissible amount of lead in drinking water from 50 parts per billion to 20 parts per billion. The EDF's senior scientist, Dr. Ellen Silbergeld, criticized the EPA's proposed standard as too high. She felt the reduction should be to 10 rather than 20 parts per billion in order to make a dent in the "lead epidemic."

Silbergeld's objection to the EPA's standard was that it reduced the body burden of lead in Americans to just above toxicity levels, that is, levels associated with increased blood pressure and pre- and neonatal toxicity to the nervous system. Also, the standard reflects an average water consumption, and thus offers no protection for those who consume greater amounts of water, such as infants who are fed with formulas made with water. Silbergeld believes a prudent standard of protection calls for blood-lead levels in the United States to be less than 10 micrograms per deciliter of blood.

Many reductions in sources of lead have been accomplished through controls placed on lead in new paint and gasoline, and on the use of solders in cans. Old, flaking paint and tap water remain the major sources.

Lead Contamination in Water

Lead rarely occurs naturally in water. High concentrations of lead are apt to be found in water transported in lead pipes, or stored in lead storage tanks, or where lead solder has been used to seal pipes. The disintegration of pipes into the water that flows through them is the major source of lead in drinking water. The amount of lead that leaches from pipes and soldered joints depends on the corrosiveness of the water and on the length of time the water is in contact with the plumbing. (Water standing overnight in pipes will have a higher lead content than water drawn frequently during the day.)

The Safe Drinking Water Act Amendments of 1986 addressed the issue of lead in the drinking water and many provisions are scheduled to go into effect on June 19, 1988. Some of the new requirements include:

1. The immediate prohibition in public water systems, and in plumbing connected to public water systems, of lead solder, flux, and pipes that exceed 0.2 percent lead content.
2. Notification of consumers by public water systems about contamination.

Recently it has been discovered that electronically controlled water fountains can be a source of lead in water. Lead rarely ever occurs in water naturally.

Lead was used in paint for many years. Young children often eat flaking paint chips containing lead, and fine dust from disintegrating lead paint can be inhaled by anyone nearby.

3. Enforcement mechanisms to be in place by June 19, 1988.
4. Enforcement failures to carry the threat of holding back as much as 5 percent of a State's Public Water System funds.
5. A prohibition against the issuance of mortgage insurance or property assistance by the Department of Housing and Urban Development and the Veterans Administration where limits are exceeded.
6. A prominent warning label against use in drinking water systems to be displayed on solder with a lead content in excess of 0.2 percent.

The new amendments do not address the problem of existing plumbing. The best, though expensive, solution would be to replace existing plumbing, provided lead solder was not used in the replacement pipes.

Lead Paint Contamination

The removal of lead paint from homes and public buildings and from the soil that surrounds them poses a problem equally as difficult as the removal of lead from the nation's water supply. In the fall of 1987, the Massachusetts legislature had under consideration a bill that would give the state the most stringent anti-lead laws in the country. The bill called for the removal of contaminated soil; regulation of lead paint removal; mandatory testing of children; and a system of loans, grants, and tax credits to assist property owners in removing lead paint.

In the spring of 1988, the state's capital, Boston, was scheduled to begin a pilot project funded with EPA Superfunds to remove soil contaminated by flaking paint in 28 high-incidence neighborhoods. The pilot project called for the removal of the top 3 to 6 inches of soil. Although the individual areas to be treated each comprise an average of less than three blocks, they have been the source of 30 percent of the city's lead-poisoning cases over a 5-year period. From 10 to 50 percent of the children who live in the contaminated neighborhoods have been poisoned. Soil samples reveal lead levels 4 to 10 times above a level likely to contribute to lead poisoning.

One of the provisions of the Massachusetts bill calls for the identification of "Emergency Lead Areas" throughout the state to increase removal in high-contamination areas. With millions of homes and yards lead-contaminated, the size of the task overwhelms officials.

An example of the logistical problems involved is evident in a Massachusetts city called Lynn. With a population of 80,000, the city has the highest rate of lead-paint poisoning in the state. Nearly 28,000 rental units in Lynn are likely to contain lead paint.

The city has three health inspectors who together can test two apartments per day. Working 7 days a week, presuming no one moved in or out, it would take almost 37 years to test every rental unit in the city.

The city also has a severe housing shortage. Under existing law, if inspectors find lead, the landlord cannot rent to families with children. De-leading costs about $500 per room. Strict enforcement would make the city's housing shortage more acute. Many parents who are aware of the risks feel they have no other economic choice but to go on living in a lead-painted apartment.

The Outlook for Treatment

While prevention of poisoning offered formidable obstacles, strategies for treatment looked promising in 1987. One study pursuing strategies for limiting toxicity found that the impact of lead upon those at highest risk—inner city children in low-income families—could be reduced by the addition of sufficient iron into the diets of the children.

For years, scientists have known that two people, both carrying the same high burden in their body of a toxic susbtance, like inorganic lead, would not necessarily suffer equally. Scientists have sought some type of indicator to predict which victim would be most harmed. For certain classes of metals, porphyrins provide an answer.

Porphyrins are small, ring-shaped chemicals that participate in the body's multistage synthesis of heme, the iron-carrying component of hemoglobin in red blood cells. Heme synthesis takes place in almost all tissues, and plays a part in many bodily functions.

During the synthesis of heme, enzymes that transform one porphyrin to the next are, as a group, sensitive to chemically induced disturbances. When an enzyme in a process is blocked, almost immediately the porphyrin upon which it was to have acted begins to accumulate in the blood or urine.

Michael Moore of the Gardiner Institute of the University of Glasgow in Scotland described inorganic lead as having the capacity to interrupt three heme-cycle enzymes. Bruce Fowler, a toxicologist with the National Institute of Environmental Health in Research Triangle, North Carolina, pointed out the diagnostic value of the interruption in the heme cycle: An excess of one or more porphyrins in blood or urine and a shortage of porphyrins that normally follow the one in excess indicate which enzymes are being inhibited by a toxic chemical. In this way the porphyrins not only flag a chemical's enzymatic site, they may serve as an early warning signal for ongoing low-dose toxicity.

Fowler's preliminary animal studies suggest that porphyrin ratios may offer a subtle signal of toxic exposure. Moreover, the porphyrin "fingerprint" of the effect of lead differs from the fingerprint of the effect of arsenic. The effect of the two metals combined yields still another fingerprint, and the addition of another metal results in still another fingerprint.

Fowler speculates that it may become possible to ferret out the source of an individual's toxicity by the body levels of various porphyrins compared with a map of ratios typical for specific chemicals or mixes of chemicals. It might even become possible to estimate the dose of the toxic substance by measuring the strength of the fingerprint.

Blood screening for an abnormal ratio of porphyrins has replaced blood-lead measurements, especially in children. In 1972, Sergio Piomelli and his colleagues at Columbia University in New York City developed what has become the standard porphyrin-based finger-prick test to screen children for high-lead levels.

Ten years later, Piomelli and his team verified in children that lead's harmful effects on one porphyrin begin at blood-lead levels as low as 14 to 17 micrograms per deciliter. In other words, they found that profound alterations of the heme-biosynthetic pathway took place long before clinical symptoms of lead poisoning became apparent.

New research by Piomelli's group in 1987 indicated that one way lead changes the heme system is by hindering the last enzyme in the heme building pathway. The scientists described iron and lead as being in competition for a binding site on the enzyme. When the site is properly filled with iron, the enzyme is less susceptible to being rendered inactive by lead. However when lead, rather than iron, binds to the enzyme the heme-building process is damaged.

Piomelli's studies have examined blood porphyrin levels in several thousand New York City children. The research confirms that porphyrin changes indicating onset of adverse lead effects begin at lower blood-lead levels in those children who are most iron-deficient. That is to say, the frequency of lead poisoning and iron deficiency is highest

Another source of lead is exhaust from automobiles.

among the youngest and poorest children. Supplementing the children's diet with iron could limit toxicity in such populations.

Porphyrin Research

Over the past decade, interest has grown in the use of porphyrin ratios as potential indicators of toxic exposures. To identify progress in this small, esoteric field, toxicologists Ellen Silbergeld and Bruce Fowler convened an international conference in Rye, New York, under the auspices of the New York Academy of Sciences. The results of the meeting established that porphyrinopathy (abnormal levels of porphyrins) may eventually prove more useful as an index of exposure and of developing toxicity than any currenly existing gauge.

Evidence is accumulating that porphyrinopathies might serve as biomarkers of toxic exposure. In Brussels, Alfred Bernard and his colleagues at the University of Louvain found in cultured cells and in animals that copper, mercury, silver, zinc, and cadmium can each reduce or obstruct the performance of the porphyrin-building enzyme called ALAD.

Bernard also found that ALAD activity in people undergoing dialysis is inhibited by aluminum. Aluminum hydroxide is an ordinary antacid given to dialysis patients to control their body phosphate levels. The porphyrinopathy uncovered by Bernard's research may be the source for—and thus a biomarker of—developing anemia, which is a frequent problem among dialysis patients.

Some of the porphyrinopathy research has almost immediate application. George Drummond at Rockefeller University in New York City has been examining factors that alter the effectiveness of the enzyme that breaks down heme. The rate of heme production can be altered either by interference with heme production or by allowing its degeneration.

Drummond's research found that several non-iron-based metal porphyrins—particularly tin protoporphyrin—can check the heme-breakdown enzyme action. This discovery offers a potential treatment for infants faced with brain damage from a toxic buildup of bilirubin, a product in the blood of heme-breakdown.

Another by-product of porphyrin research is the identification of a genetic factor in humans that signals increased susceptibility to lead toxicity. Robert Desnick of the Mount Sinai School of Medicine in New York City has identified a structural gene mutation. The mutation, coding for ALAD systhesis, may make the ALAD enzyme—and thus the porphyrin pathway—more vulnerable to lead.

Desnick's findings can be interpreted to mean that some individuals carry a genetic predisposition to lead poisoning. If Desnick's preliminary finds hold up, industry may someday be able to prevent workplace incidences of lead poisoning by screening employees to avoid using in high-risk areas those who are especially susceptible.

Porphyrinopathies may in time serve as regulation standards for exposure to toxic chemicals: Government regulators are more comfortable with clear-cut evidence of the level of exposure at which toxicity can be demonstrated, and porphyrins will allow detection of precisely when and where harmful changes begin.

Another source of lead poisoning was recently recognized by a professor of pediatrics, Robert Guthrie, at the State University of New York in Buffalo. Guthrie pointed out that the black eyeliner used on infants and children by parents who have emigrated from countries such as Kuwait, India, and Pakistan frequently contains galena, a glittery substance that is a form of lead. Blood screening of infants and children under Dr. Guthrie's care showed seriously elevated lead levels.

Changing a cultural practice such as the decorative use of eyeliner would require a significant public education effort among parents. The other alternative would be to require manufacturers to change the ingredients in eyeliner.

Prospects for the End of Lead Poisoning

Given the disagreements about acceptable lead levels, and given the difficult tasks involved in ridding water of lead and in removing traces of old paint, the near future does not look too hopeful. On the other hand, many Americans have become involved in the effort.

Lead poisoning is a cultural problem whose solution cannot be postponed for too long. Some scientists suspect that the fall of the Roman Empire was due to the use of lead sugar (lead acetate) as a sweetner. Chemist John Emsley of King's College in London speculates that "Mad King George," whose behavior prompted the American colonies to break away from Britain, suffered from the effects of lead leached by two of his favorite foods, lemomade and sauerkraut, from lead-glazed pottery.

THE FIGHT FOR OPEN SPACE

Local Citizens Become Involved in Land Development

The disappearance of open spaces as a result of condominium and commercial development has alarmed many local citizens throughout North America. In some communities that alarm has been expressed by the formation of committees appointed to oversee conservation of wetlands, waterfront acreage, and other property.

Land Banks

The threads of many issues are interwoven around the idea of open space. Among some citizens, there is a desire to preserve the beauty of the land and natural bodies of water. Others are concerned about potential damage to the environment. Many citizens simply feel too crowded. However, the desire to preserve open land comes into direct conflict with the need for new housing and businesses. Both of these conflicting needs become acute in densely populated areas.

In the United States, there are 550 land trusts, whose purpose is to preserve land from development. More than half of them are in densely populated New England.

In an article called "Locking Up the Landscape," Daniel Okrent in the March 1987 issue of *New England Monthly* suggested that placing land in a conservation trust drove up the cost of existing land and housing. Okrent pointed to the fact that many people who work in the service economy of New England cannot afford to live within 30 miles of where they work. This includes fishermen who must drive from inland areas—where they can afford housing—to the water's edge where they put out to sea.

The relationship between land preservation and new housing is further complicated by many factors: For example, people tend to want to live in certain areas, particularly areas close to the water, which also drives up the cost of housing in those locations.

Fashions change in what is considered desirable housing. Dilapidated shanties where fishermen once lived at the water's edge, and run-down buildings where the poor once lived downtown, are now targets for restoration by the more affluent. Conversions of moderate-income housing to high-income condominiums have progressed so rapidly that officials in some areas have put moratoriums (legal delays) on such conversions. Thus, even if land presently tied up in preservation trusts were put back into the housing market, the more affluent could continue to outbid the less affluent for currently desirable locations. In an effort to mediate the conflicting needs for open space and continued development, some local governments and state governments have developed the concept of land banks.

One land bank approach is to levy a tax whenever real estate is sold. The tax derived from these real estate trans-

A seacoast village home being refurbished and thus made too expensive for local fishermen.

fers can then be used to purchase land to keep or to create open space.

Land banks are not always devoted solely to creating open spaces. Some take on the additional task of developing affordable housing. The Massachusetts Land Bank was created in 1973 to develop three closed military bases, bringing business, jobs, and affordable housing to distressed areas of the state.

The Effects of Real Estate Development

An example of an active, effective local citizen's group fighting new development is the Old Greenwich Association, which represents 577 households in Old Greenwich, Connecticut. Old Greenwich is a village wedged between development in neighboring Stamford and Greenwich. Complaining that their neighborhood of colonial and Victorian homes had become traffic routes for workers and residents of the nearby developments, Old Greenwich residents raised money for a court action against expansion of a company's corporate headquarters. They appear regularly at public hearings in both Stamford and Greenwich, where they are vocal about their concerns.

The impact of real estate development money on the seashore recently became clear in Boston, Massachusetts, and Portland, Maine.

For years, Boston lobstermen were bounced from pier to pier by real estate developers who refused to have fishing boats moored on their property. In response to the wishes of the late cardinal of Boston, Umberto Medeiros, who came from a family of fishermen, his successor, Cardinal Law, lobbied the state legislature for money to build a lobster boat pier for the Boston lobstermen.

In Portland, a referendum to ban nonmarine development on the city's waterfront passed by a substantial majority. Proponents argued that booming condominium and office developments threatened the continued existence of fishermen. Opponents claimed there was not enough marine-related industry to sustain the waterfront without other types of development.

Threatened Wetlands

The impact of development has not only crowded human beings, it has also crowded wildlife. Wetlands have been particularly vulnerable to encroachment. Wetlands, occupying an interface between land and water, provide habitats, nursery grounds, and food sources for a great variety of plant and animal species. Most commercially valuable fish and shellfish depend on thc wetlands, and the Atlantic Coast wetland-estuary is capable of producing 125 pounds of commercial fish per acre. Concerned communities have begun to add wetlands as an issue to be examined by their planning boards and conservation boards.

Let the Sun Shine In

Citizen concern is not confined to small cities and towns. Urban residents are also alarmed about runaway development. In New York City, planners have begun to grapple with questions about sunlight. How much sunlight is the public entitled to? Are the growing number of massive towers robbing citizens of access to the sun? In a battle over a tiny park on Manhattan's East 51st Street between Second and Third avenues, preservationists, including the urban analyst William Whyte, were able to block a three-story addition to a building by demonstrating that the extra height would leave the miniature Greenacre Park in the dark.

New York is not alone in its concern over sunlight. A number of locales, both in the United States and abroad, have taken steps to guarantee solar access. San Francisco,

Greenacre Park in New York City.

for example, severely limits new structures that would block the sun from public parks.

Rural Development

Not all battles for space take place in cities or at the water's edge. As employment figures in New Jersey have grown from 2 million workers in 1970 to an expected 3.4 million in 1988, some parts of the scenic central part of the state have become the settings for bumper-to-bumper traffic. The towns of Lawrence, Princeton, and Montgomery have started "downzoning" areas intended for office parks, trying to direct growth toward already urbanized areas and away from environmentally or esthetically sensitive open country and wetlands.

Greenways: Access to the Land

Concern for open space was addressed differently in Brooklyn and Queens, New York, where a nonprofit group called the Open Space Coalitions proposed an ambitious plan for a greenway. Greenways are usually natural corridors such as railroad right-of-ways and stream beds that allow wildlife to migrate. However, the Brooklyn-Queens Greenway would be for people. The plan calls for a 40-mile bicycle and pedestrian path that would link parks, museums, cultural centers, and recreational space in the area. In March 1987, the President's Commission on Americans Outdoors recommended that the policies of the nation's parks focus on creating a system of greenways to connect parks and open spaces across the country.

One of the underlying concerns about open space, whether it be a waterfront or a pedestrian walkway, is access. In the past, when large tracts of waterfront or other scenic land were purchased by wealthy individuals or by hotels, that land was closed to the public. On Miami Beach, for example, the closeness of many hotels leaves pedestrians with only a sliver of ocean view between buildings. Beaches in front of the hotels are used by the out-of-town tourists who stay at the hotels.

Reclaiming Neglected Space

Once public access has been lost, efforts to regain it are often fruitless or result in a prolonged court battle. But

Local involvement in the fate of land and water may sometimes mean physically going out and cleaning up an area. The finds on these expeditions can be surprising.

A boy involved in the Massachusetts Adopt-a-Stream program.

development is not the only reason the public loses access to open space. Sometimes it is lost to neglect. All over the United States, there is a resurgent interest in reclaiming these neglected spaces.

In New York City, nature-loving citizens have over the years defended wildlife and natural environments against urban intrusion. They found an ally in Parks Commissioner Henry Stern, who created a division within the Parks Department called the Natural Resources Group. The group uses scientifically planned restoration in combination with "benign neglect" to foster environments suitable for wild plants and wild animals.

Of New York City's 26,000 acres of parklands, 7,000 are predominantly natural: meadow, freshwater and saltwater wetlands, woodlands and forests. Long-absent wildlife are returning to the city's parks.

Public Purchase of Land

In Massachusetts, beginning in 1968, one dollar of the cost of a hunting or fishing license was applied toward the purchase of wildlife lands and habitats. By 1986, the Division of Fisheries and Wildlife had acquired 49,878 acres in wildlife habitats. However, the program faced severe pressures as the state's booming economy put the division in competition with private-sector developers for the limited land available for purchase.

As a way to preserve natural open space, the division placed an emphasis on riparian lands (those along rivers and streams), which provide important breeding grounds, sources of food, and means of mobility for wildlife. Among the programs to improve the rivers and streams, the division started an "Adopt-a-Stream" program to support citizen groups with an interest in a portion of a particular river or creek.

An area in which open space is being lost all over the country is farmland. As the economics of farming and the burden of heavy debts force many farmers to give up their occupation, their land is often sold to developers. On Cape Cod, where farming, like fishing, has been a tradition, the value of real estate to a developer far exceeds its value as farmland. On nearby Martha's Vineyard, residents spent

$1.4 million to purchase a 28-acre farm, which four farmers now lease from the town.

In the face of a current development rate of 1,200 to 1,500 acres in that state each year, a Connecticut panel recommended that the state acquire another 100,000 acres by the year 2000. To preserve the diminishing supply of open land for ecological and recreational purposes, the panel pointed out, only a long-term program could preserve and maintain open space.

Urban Gardens

Another approach to promoting attractive open space is the concept of urban gardens. A program in New York City called Greenthumb, and one in Boston called GreenSpace, are some of several intended to improve the local environment.

Urban garden programs take over vacant lots, have them cleared, help plan a garden, and provide local groups with training, lumber, plants, and seeds to make the garden a reality. Some gardens produce food. Others are devoted to flowers. Many are on rundown streets where they are the only oasis.

A Bitter Battle in Hollywood

Not all fights against development have taken place on the East Coast of the United States. In California in November of 1986, Los Angeles and San Francisco passed sweeping laws limiting the construction of commercial buildings. In June of 1987, faced with 44 percent growth in 17 years, San Diego limited the building of new housing units to 8,000 each year, becoming the largest city in the country ever to take action to limit its population.

A bitter battle over a $922 million redevelopment plan in Hollywood, California, was scheduled to go to court in late 1987. The *Los Angeles Times* spent 6 months investigating the history of the plan. At the same time a small number of property owners were buying up land in the center of Hollywood, according to the *Times* report, they were pushing through a redevelopment plan that would double the value of their land.

Under California state law, publicly supported redevelopment can be used in an urban area worthy of being saved when financial support cannot be found elsewhere. Direct public assistance can be made to private builders for certain projects; such aid might include government-financed parking garages, and government-backed construction loans.

Hollywood property owners urged the city of Los Angeles Community Redevelopment Agency (CRA) to pursue urban renewal for Hollywood, which needed a "face lift." The CRA worked through the Hollywood Chamber of Commerce and a citizen's committee was chosen to draft the original plan. Although demographic reports showed that business interests were in a minority in the area, the Hollywood redevelopment committee became the only one out of half a dozen similar committees in the Los Angeles area on which business interests held more seats than residents.

The plan adopted in 1986 by the CRA and by the Los Angeles City Council set a direction toward large-scale growth. Incentives were included for building high-rise office and hotel towers. Also included was the authority to remove existing smaller structures, even over the wishes of the occupants. Hollywood was designated as a "regional center" exempt from stricter building limits enforced in other areas of the city. The plan did not mirror the "slow-growth" movement reflected elsewhere in Los Angeles. The redevelopment zone was planned to move across an area that housed 37,000 people. How many of those residents would have to move was not known.

The extent of the Chamber of Commerce's representation on the redevelopment committee prompted residents to file suit in 1986. Opposition to the plan was slow in growing, but over time it became a volatile political issue. Supporting the suit were residents, small merchants, and the large Federation of Hillside and Canyon Associations, which represents Hollywood Hills homeowners. They claimed that the law intended to shield Hollywood citizens from redevelopment not only failed to protect them but actually rewarded the developers.

Prince Charles Steps In

Ordinary citizens were not the only ones upset with development in their neighborhoods in 1987. Prince Charles, heir to the British throne, annoyed British architects and town planners with his interference in plans to redevelop part of London. The disagreement arose over a scheme for Pasternoster Square, which adjoins St. Paul's Cathedral, the masterpiece of Britain's most famous architect, Sir Christopher Wren (1632-1723). The zone around St. Paul's was virtually leveled during World War II, and during the 1960s, the area was rebuilt with concrete office towers. The towers blocked some views of the cathedral.

Plans are now under way to replace the towers with something more attractive. Developers of the site announced a competition for the best design. The results of the competition were to be made public on July 2, 1987, but the announcement was postponed when Prince Charles asked to see the designs. The prince had concerns over the impact of the new buildings on the cathedral, and the developers agreed to take the prince's concerns into

St. Paul's Cathedral in London. Prince Charles is concerned about the catherdral's potential architectural neighbors.

account. He, in turn, agreed not to make his views public until after a master plan was completed.

Three years earlier, the prince had attacked a plan for extensive development of the residence of the lord mayor. That project became stalled indefinitely due to wrangling over alternative plans.

A Setback for Open Spaces

Despite their recent gains, the open-space movement received a serious setback from the Supreme Court in July of 1987. A group of Cranston, Rhode Island, investors alleged that their rights had been compromised by an ordinance that increased the minimum size of house lots from 30,000 square feet to 200,000 square feet. The group claimed the change cut the value of their 4-acre lots by 50 percent. In a case that will be viewed as an important precedent by every municipality and developer across the country, the Supreme Court ruled the group was entitled to compensation when government regulation denied them "all use" of their property. This ruling will make it more difficult for local governments to regulate growth in their jurisdiction.

As the economy and population expand in the coming years, the conflict between the need for more offices, stores, and houses on the one hand and for preserving open spaces for people, plants, and animals on the other will continue to occupy the front pages of newspapers all across the continent.

5

Archeology

URBAN ARCHEOLOGY

Scientists Race Against the Bulldozers

Boston's City Archeology Program

Armed with dustpans and trowels, a group of 50 volunteers under the direction of city of Boston archeologist Steven Pendery are digging beneath Boston Common, the nation's oldest public park. Unlike New York's Central Park, Boston Common has been left largely intact since 1634, when John Winthrop and his neighbors raised $150 to buy land to be used for public grazing. By 1675, the land was described as "a small but pleasant Common where the Gallants a little before Sunset walk." When the park became a recreational area in 1830, livestock were banned and tree-lined walkways were extended. The park became a setting for public monuments and public meetings.

The undertaking called "Archaeology of the Boston Common" is conducted by Boston's City Archaeology Program. The effort began out of concern for possible destruction of the park's historical record by construction projects such as subway renovations and utility installations.

At the outset of the Common operation in 1986, the archeologists identified 100 possible sites for digging. By mid-1987, they had narrowed their work to 4 fruitful locations chosen for their degree of preservation and for what was found in test digs on the sites.

The Boston Common archeologists are looking for prehistoric and colonial artifacts. They have found ceramics and lithics (instruments made of stone). They have also found shell deposits, testimony to the fact that much of current downtown Boston was once under water.

The refuse recovered from beneath the Common reaches back through the American Revolution to the founding of the Massachusetts Bay Colony. Horse bridles, military uniforms, and military decorations verify that the park was used as a British encampment before the American Revolution. Large numbers of ceramic, glass, and metal artifacts, including children's toys, have been found to document the increasing use of the park for recreation during the nineteenth century. Some other treasures that have been uncovered give a look further into the past. Stone tools and weapons dating back 8,000 years have been found.

The archeologists' daily routine on the Common has settled down to digging a 1-meter-square hole each day. At the end of the day, the hole is refilled to keep intruders from tampering with the site or from falling in. Digging at a location continues downward until no further artifacts are

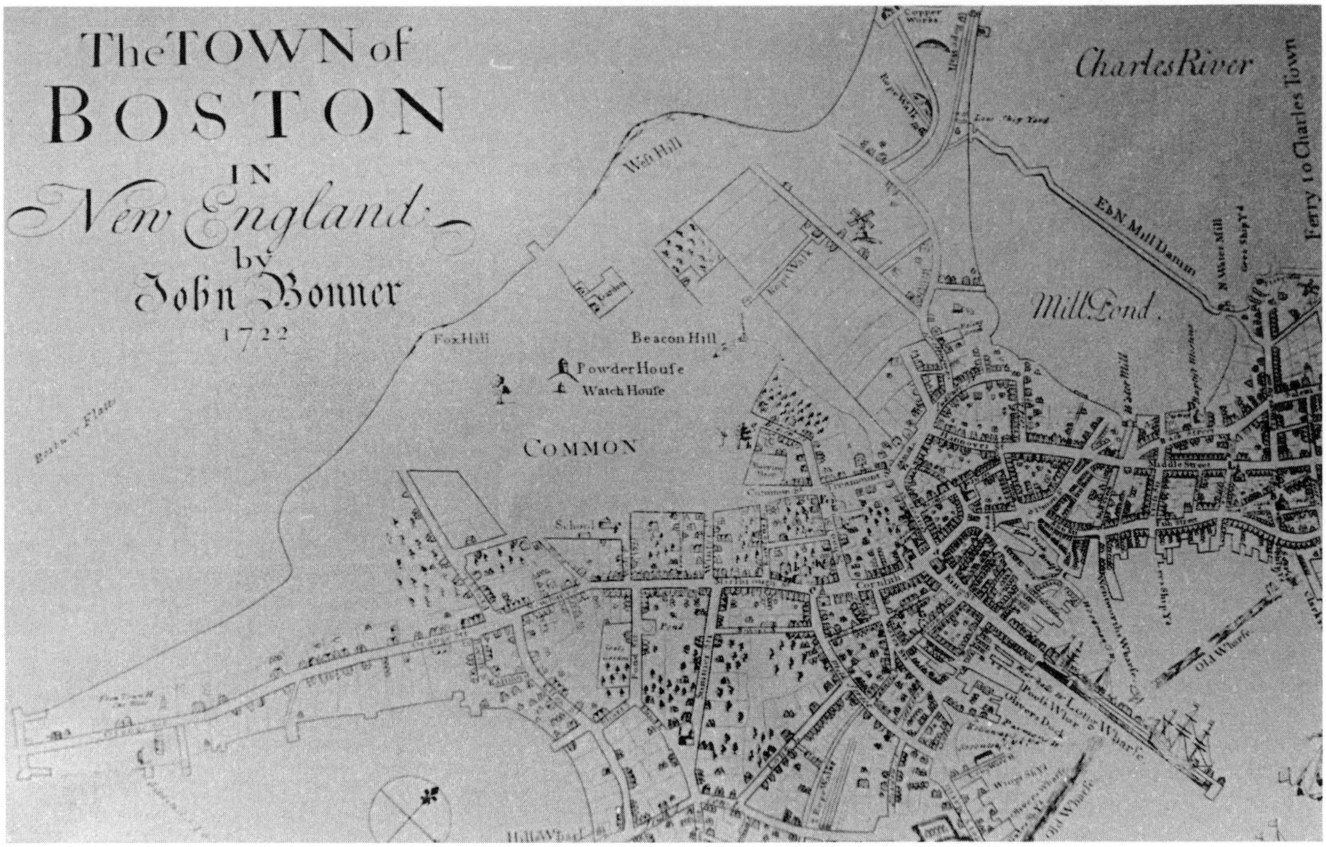

found. When the crew is finished with a site, the grass is sprayed with red paint to remind the archeologists of where they have been and to let utility workers know they are free to proceed in that area.

Besides the work being done on the Common, the Boston City Archaeology Program is active at several other sites. At Long Island Head, an island that has often been the site of military fortifications, the program attempts to locate and identify prehistoric sites, as it does on other islands in the city.

A short distance from the Common, Boston's downtown building boom has provided urban archeologists and historians with their best opportunity in a century to poke around in an earlier society's trash. One location, on State Street, has proved particularly worthwhile: The construction site marks the original shoreline of the Shawmut Peninsula where Native Americans once fished and hunted, and where English settlers built the center of commercial Boston. As buildings have been demolished in a 1.37-acre wedge of land where State and Kilby streets intersect, archeologists have discovered old cellars, pilings (long heavy timbers driven into the ground, sometimes under water, to support a bridge or dock), remnants of old wharves, and an abandoned sewer line.

On the State Street site, records, maps, deeds, and other public documents provided some prior knowledge of what might be found beneath. Most of the site was once under water, but by the middle of the 1700s, the area had been filled in and wharves built out from it. Later in the century, fires periodically devastated the wharves. Once the burned-out ruins were knocked down, the process of rebuilding began with landfill brought in from all over the city. The landfill confuses the historical picture, but archeologists still find it worth sifting through.

For the next several years, Boston is likely to keep urban archeologists busy. A major highway construction program called the Central Artery is under way, and the Department of Public Works has introduced archeologists early into the process.

London Discoveries

In London, another city likely to keep archeologists occupied for a long time to come, archeological research has been continuing since 1973. About 100 archeologists have worked in the square mile of the City of London. Beginning in 1983, another team of about the same size has been working in Greater London.

Archeologists, working with some assistance from developers, have begun to put together plausible theories about the founding of the British capital. Early theories proposed that London had been continuously occupied from prehistoric times, but those theories have not stood up to scrutiny. It now appears that the city's development was not continuous and that there were long periods of decline. The city was even abandoned when the Romans withdrew before the Saxon invasion.

In the view of Brian Hobley, chief urban archeologist of the Museum of London, archeologists can be perceived as students of urban renewal intent on studying urban change. The progress of urban change, a plan to erect an office building, gave Hobley a rare opportunity to dig at the site of London's earliest-known building. With a year's grace and financial help from the Legal and General Society, the archeologist had a chance to examine the traces of important Roman buildings in London. The site included a huge basilica built by the Romans about A.D. 120 as the seat of local government, justice, and finance. The basilica, and its associated forum, or marketplace, covered 8 acres. Estimated to have been 40 feet high, 165 feet wide, and 555 feet long, it was the largest Roman building north of the Alps. Moreover, the area's street patterns, and the decisions made about the design of the city at the time the basilica was built persist in today's London. The district continues to be the core of London's financial quarter, having remained a business center century after century.

The archeologists did not stop their search at the level of the basilica. They continued down to natural ground surface as the deadline neared for the office-building construction to begin. Beneath the basilica, they found timber dwellings, each with a hearth, up to 17 feet square. To one side of the basilica was a large garbage dump and deep holes thought to be quarries for earth used to make bricks.

The quarries offered an explanation for one of the major discoveries at the site. Large cracks ran through the basilica's foundation walls, probably due to the sinking of earth beneath. In Roman times, the basilica must have been unstable, with cracks in the upper stories comparable to those in the foundation that may have curtailed the building's life. These cracks may have been caused by the quarries beneath.

The Boston City Archaeology Program is now working alternately at four sites on the Boston Common. Each evening the workers must fill in their hole and re-dig it the next day.

London was an international port in about A.D. 60, when there was a native revolt. When Roman Londinium was rebuilt, it assumed some of the functions of the original provincial capital, Camulodunum. The town was probably near the height of its development by A.D. 100. The last half of the century saw prosperity crumble. The archeologists found many shops and houses of the first century covered by extensive deposits of dark earth, which represents open, cultivated spaces.

The basilica may have collapsed about that time and, the town's life moved to the waterfront. Using some stones that seem to have come from ruined buildings and monuments, a 2-mile city wall was built to the north. A similar riverside wall was built about 270. Economic decline continued through most of the fourth century. The Saxon incursions increased. The Romans withdrew in 410, and there is evidence of a Roman-British enclave living in the walled city about 457.

Profoundly suspicious of cities, the Anglo-Saxons settled outside the crumbling walls of Londinium. Archeological findings indicate no evidence of Anglo-Saxon occupation inside the city until the seventh century, and no structures before the eighth. Not until King Alfred led them to reoccupy the city—after the Vikings' resumed sacking of the open settlements on the Strand—did the Anglo-Saxons use the walled city extensively.

By 1200, the city dominated the unifying England and had a population of 25,000. Before the plague struck in 1348, the population numbered 100,000. The plague preceded a 150-year decline.

But by 1500, the population had increased to 40,000. By 1600, it was 200,000. And by 1700, 575,000 people lived in London.

For its tenth anniversary, in the fall of 1986, the Museum of London opened an exhibit devoted to archeological findings about Roman, Saxon, and medieval London discovered by archeologists over the previous 15 years, during which about $11 million in private and public funds were spent on the more than 200 sites.

Pensacola, Florida

Excavations for underground wiring at the Pensacola, Florida, Naval Air Station in February of 1987, uncovered what archeologists believe may be part of the remains of the first European settlement in the United States, a seventeenth-century Spanish fort. The archeologists found hand-forged nails, hand-painted Spanish ceramics, brass buttons and buckles, and musketballs. But the most significant find at the Naval Air Station is the building foundation. Composed of oyster and clam shells combined

Volunteer Monika Bolino sifts every spoonful of dirt through a screen in order to obtain bits of treasure such as the piece of broken pottery.

Stone projectile points found on the Boston Common.

with lime and sand, the mixture made a crude form of cement. An archeologist for the Army Corps of Engineers, Neil Robison, theorized that the find could be the foundation for Fort San Carlos de Austria, built in 1698. The dig did not deter the electrical installation. The archeologists' task was to stay ahead of the electricians.

During a 1986 excavation by the city of Pensacola for a downtown sidewalk and street-repair project, artifacts from the original downtown settlement were found. The site, containing shards of china, straight pins, beef bones, and wine bottles, was probably an eighteenth-century trash heap.

Plymouth Plantation

In Plymouth Plantation, Massachusetts, rumors of an Indian burial ground concerned developers David Myers and Phillip Cronin. They had heard that a 5.5-acre parcel included within 25 acres on which they planned to build houses was thought to be a sacred site for Native Americans.

The developers contacted the Public Archeology Laboratory of Providence, Rhode Island, for advice. A team of archeologists spent 5 weeks at the wooded site near the center of town.

The site appears to have been periodically inhabited, first as a hunting camp, and later as a village, from approximately 4000 B.C. to approximately A.D. 1600. Native Americans spent time at the site not long before the Pilgrims arrived.

Although Indian sites have been excavated in southern New England that date back to 10,000 B.C., all have been essentially hunting sites. The unique feature of the Plymouth Plantation site is that it marks a permanent village dating back 1,000 years.

Given the new information, the developers redesigned their construction plans. Instead of building 28 single-family homes, they elected to build 12 two-family homes and to leave the archeological site protected.

New York City

A less ancient archeological site came to light when Harry and Arlene Nance decided to build an addition onto the kitchen of their home in Greenwich Village, on the southern part of Manhattan Island. When the builders excavated the cistern, they found refuse dating back 140 years.

Cisterns were used during the middle of the nineteenth century to collect rainwater for domestic use. When they were made obsolete by indoor plumbing, cisterns were often filled with trash, then covered over with dirt, and forgotten.

The couple had seen an article in *The Villager*, a weekly community newspaper, about a local archeology project. They called New York University (NYU), and soon the Greenwich Village Archeology project had its first backyard site.

A group of volunteers led by Dr. Bert Salwen, an anthropology professor at NYU, set up camp in the Nances' backyard. The process involved sifting through the cistern, tagging each find, and bagging the find to be sent off to laboratories for closer examination.

Since garbage can be a particularly useful record of how people lived, cistern trash provides a record of family life. Public life of the nineteenth century is well recorded, but relatively little is known about private life.

The Greenwich Village cistern discards are expected to yield a variety of information. From the scratches on the silverware, and the labels on the medicine bottles, to the number of liquor bottles, the finds can shed light on the social history, health care, migration patterns, and class differences of the period.

Besides expanding knowledge of what life was like in earlier periods, urban archeological projects allow nonprofessional volunteers to participate in the research.

Although some volunteers who dig in sites like the Boston Common are graduate students in archeology, many volunteers help out simply because they like the challenge and excitement of uncovering the remnants of a lost past. In contrast to field projects, where volunteers may use their 2 weeks of vacation to work at remote sites, many urban archeological digs allow volunteers to work on one project for an extended period. Urban archeology offers those volunteers, and their professional supervisors, the enjoyment of doing valuable fieldwork without the discomfort of leaving home.

CANNIBALISM

A New Look at an Old Practice

Although interest in cannibalism has waxed and waned, recently interest has risen once again as social scientists have recognized that phenomena such as cannibalism are significant to theories about human behavior.

Has Cannibalism Truly Existed?

One reason cannibalism has not remained a continuing interest is the difficulty in documenting the practice. In his 1979 book *The Man-Eating Myth*, William Arens criticized existing evidence for cannibalism. In Arens' opinion, the evidence is based on one of three sources: accusations by others, usually neighboring groups; statements that one's ancestors were cannibals; or travelers' tales gleaned from a language with which they weren't familiar. In Arens's view, the accusation of cannibalism was a method of saying that the alleged cannibals were less than human.

Many anthropologists, particularly those who have worked in South America and the Pacific, disagree with Arens's skepticism. They report that cannibalism is well known and well documented among groups with whom they are familiar.

Anthropologist Peggy Reeves Sanday is among those who believe that cannibalism is a real phenomenon. In her book *Divine Hunger: Cannibalism as a Cultural System*, Sanday examines a sample of 156 well-known, well-described cultures ranging in time from 1750 B.C. to the late 1960s. Sanday asserts that besides the sources Arens mentions, descriptions of cannibalism also come from interviews with eyewitnesses; written accounts left by witnesses, such as missionaries and travelers; and from accounts of tribal traditions. Most reports come from North America and the Pacific Islands.

Paleontologist Pat Shipman, in an article called "The Myth and Perturbing Realities of Cannibalism" in *Discover* magazine, recounted her favorite report on cannibalism. The story was told by Richard Meinertzhagen—explorer, soldier, naturalist, and hunter—who, in 1905, described his personal encounter with cannibalism while struggling to "pacify" the Nandi tribe of western Kenya. One of Meinertzhagen's native corporals returned from patrol with five hands stuck in his belt. Until Meinertzhagen interfered, the corporal had planned to have the hands for his supper.

Researchers who have accepted the existence of cannibalism have tended to explain the practice from one of three different perspectives. A psychological explanation has seen cannibalism as an expression of a deep psychic need. A utilitarian explanation has described cannibalism as a response to hunger, or to a protein deficiency. A broad cultural explanation has envisioned cannibalism as part of a society's effort to interpret life and death. Sanday believes all three perspectives help to clarify the behavior.

During excavation this cluster of human bones was discovered in one of the pits at the Fontbrégoua Cave in southeastern France.

Aztec Cannibalism

One of the societies that Sanday examined is the Aztecs, who ruled central Mexico for centuries. It is thought that by the fifteenth century, about 1 percent of the Aztec's population of approximately 250,000—or 2,500 people—served as human sacrifices each year.

It appears that a protein shortage may have played a role in the Aztec's cannibalism. The Aztec nobility and merchant class ate substantial protein in the form of wild game. Commoners, who did not have access to much protein, were allowed to consume human flesh and wild game after single-handedly taking three enemy captives. In this way, commoners were rewarded with scarce protein in exchange for participation in military operations. However, since almost all the societies that Sanday examined experienced routine hunger, or periodic famines or protein shortages, and more than half the cultures showed no evidence of cannibalism, nutritional needs alone could not explain cannibalism, or fully explain the Aztec sacrifices.

The Aztecs believed that eating their victim transmitted divine power from the gods, who accepted the sacrifice, to the person who offered up his claim on the prisoner. Without the nourishment of sacrifices, the gods could not be expected to work on behalf of humans. The sky could be expected to fall, and the universe to return to a state of chaos. Thus the ritual value of enemies lay in the spiritual power they brought into Aztec society.

Cannibalism among the Iroquois and Hurons

The Iroquois were reported to be eating war victims as late as 1756. An account of how Iroquois tortured and cannibalized a Jesuit priest in a Huron village was obtained from Christian Hurons who were present.

The flesh was stripped from the priest's thighs, legs, and arms to be roasted and eaten. The priest's heart was cut out to be also roasted and eaten. The Indians who drank the priest's blood commented on his courage in the face of pain. They expected his blood to make them courageous like him.

An Iroquois and Huron practice called second burial may also shed some light on their cannibalism. The Iroquois and Huron tribes had elaborate and lengthy burial rites to help

The cut-marks on this child's clavicle found at Fontbrégoua were done with a stone knife while dismembering the body.

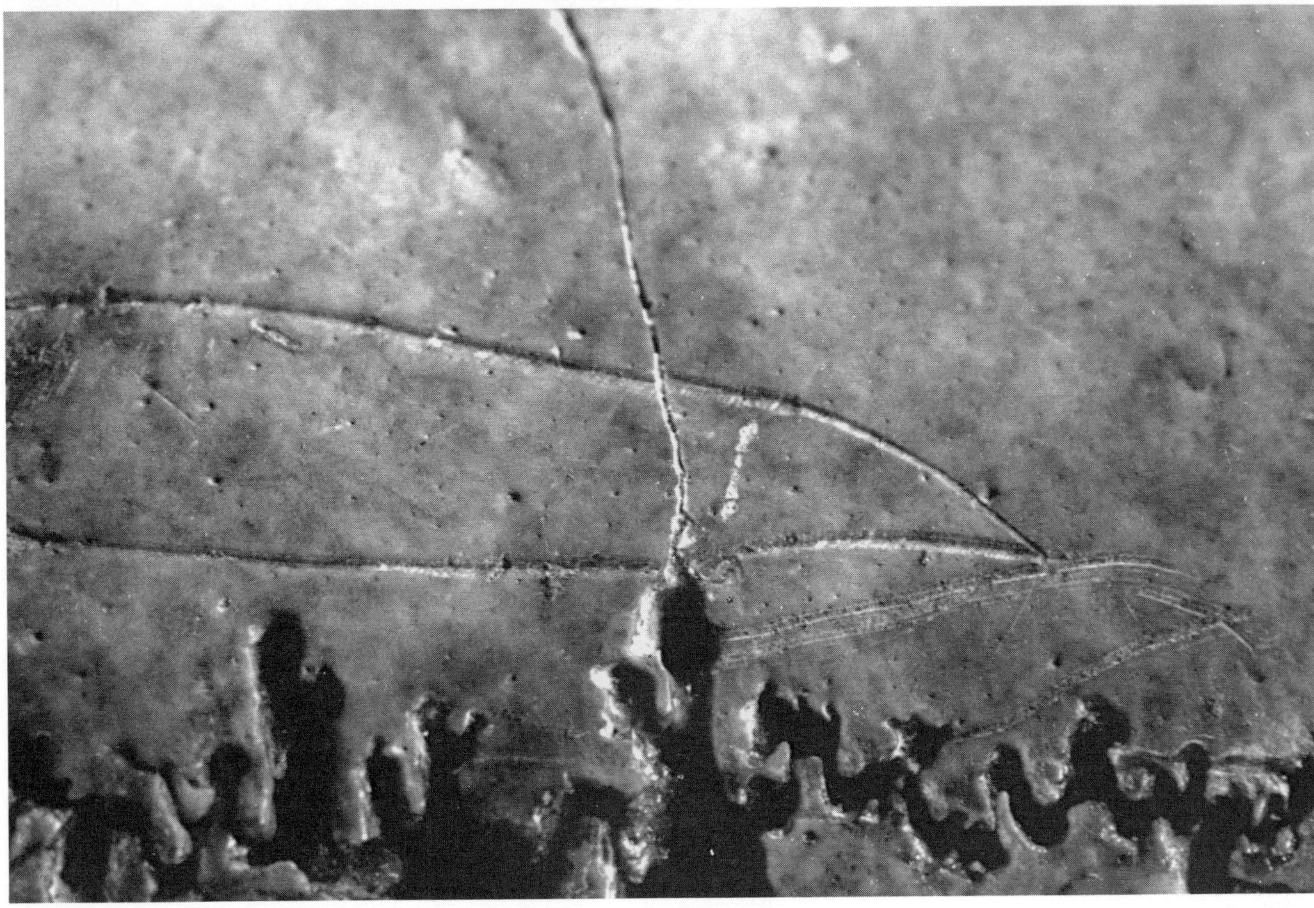

The long lines seen on this child (or adolescent) skull are skimming marks.

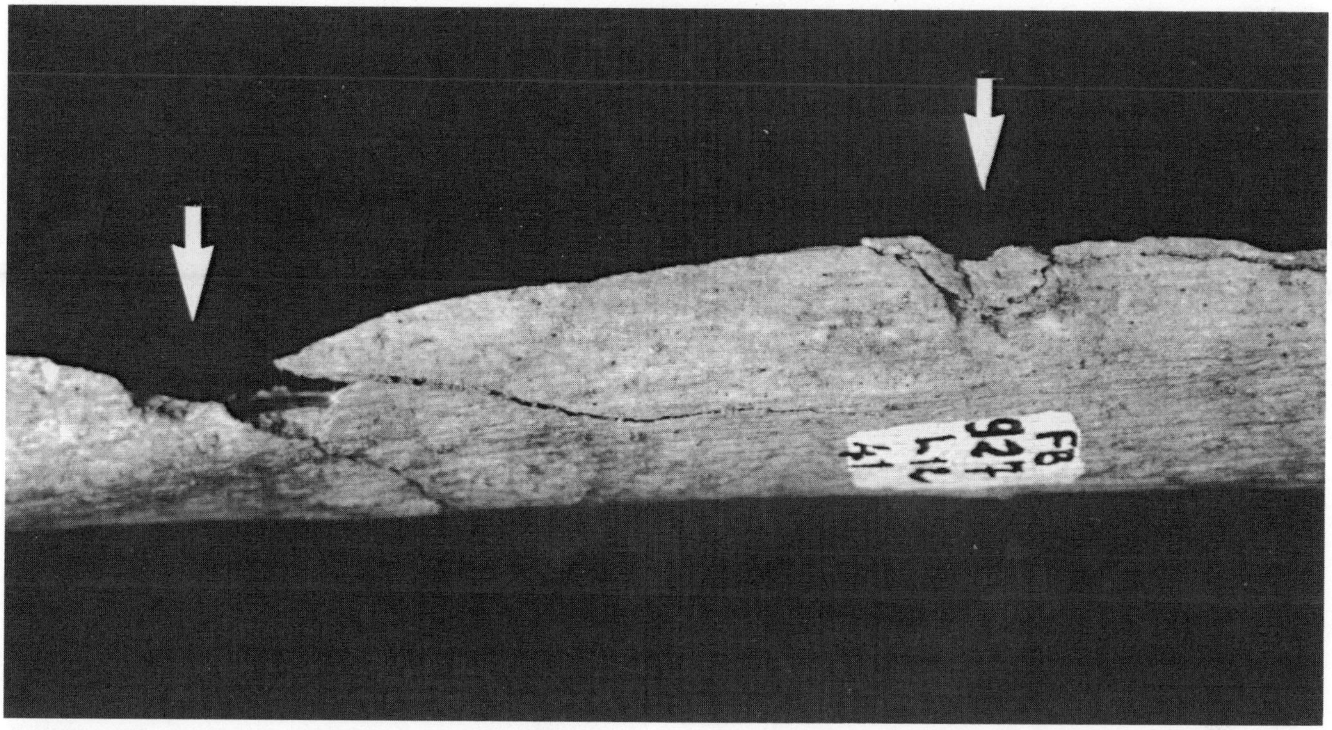

the bereaved sever their relationship with the deceased. As death approached, the dying held a feast to which friends were invited. After death, the bereaved spent great effort clothing the dead and providing gifts for funeral guests. Intense mourning lasted for 10 days, and to a lesser extent for a year afterward.

At the time of the Feast of the Dead, each family would exhume the remains of those relatives buried since the last feast. After exhumation, the bones would be cleaned of remaining flesh, adorned with new clothing and garlands, and transported to a central meeting place.

The collection of the bones in one place united friends and relatives in harmony. At the same time, it helped the living to sever their emotional attachment to the dead.

However, a Huron who died in battle was not reburied at the Feast of the Dead because the Hurons believed that those who had died in war had no communication in the afterlife with other souls. Therefore, a kinsman lost in battle was lost to more than just death: The warrior's kin had no way of handling their grief. The Huron solution was to find someone who could fill this gap. The substitute, an enemy captive, could be allowed to live as the dead warrior, or he could be tortured and killed. If the second way was chosen, at the final feast for the victim, the victim's body provided the food.

Neolithic Cannibalism

Second burial has been, and still is, common around the world. Indirectly, the custom may shed some light on cannibalism that even Arens might not reject. The case in-

The photo and the drawing show the same human tibia that was broken apart in order to extract bone marrow. The indicating arrows on the photo, and at fragment 5 on the drawing, point to impact scars made by blows of a stone. The drawing gives an idea of the degree of fragmentation of these bones. On the right hand side of the drawing is the reconstructed tibia.

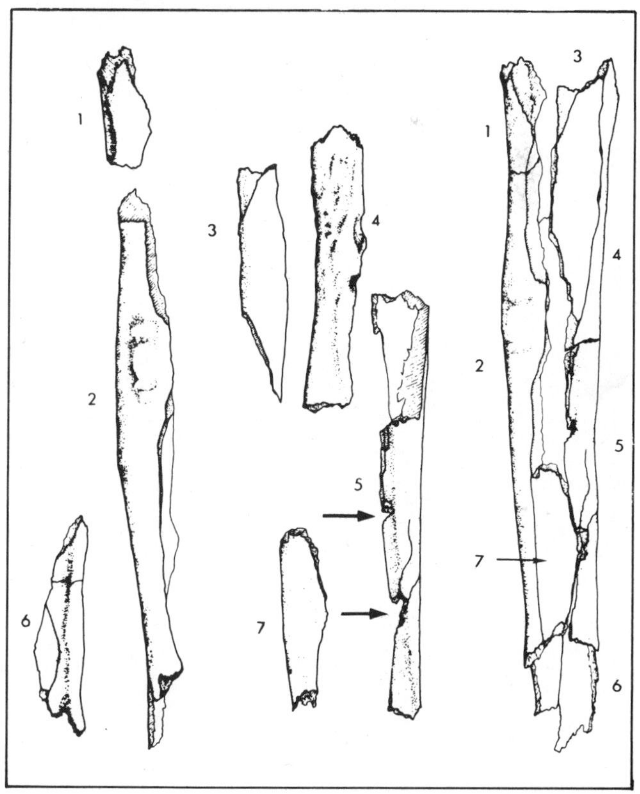

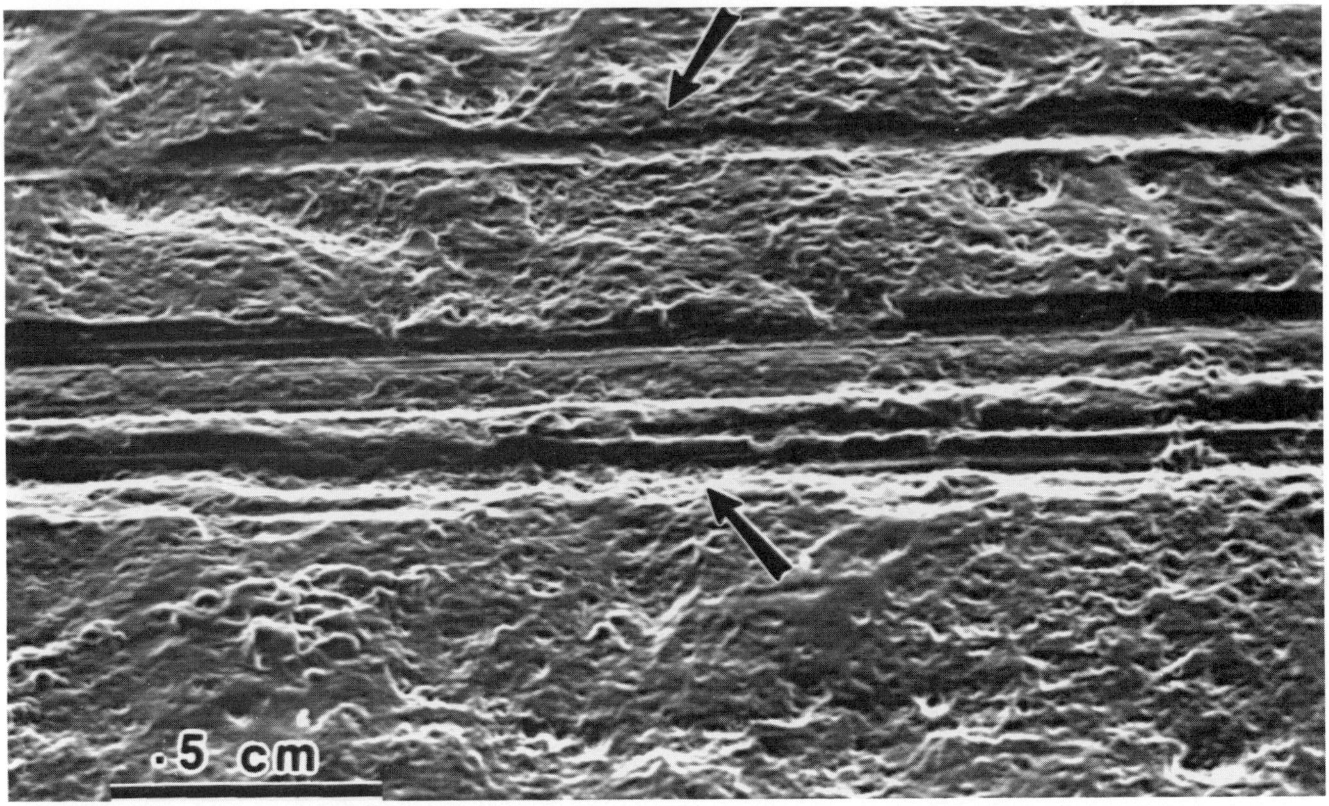

The bones from Fontbrégoua were examined under a scanning electron microscope. All the bones, both animal and human, showed signs of immediate processing. The arrows point to cut-marks on a human frontal skull bone.

The cutmarks found on the mandible (jaw) of this sheep or goat are consistent with the findings on the human bones. They indicate immediate processing.

volves a 6000-year-old Neolithic cave inhabited repeatedly during the fourth and fifth millennia B.C. in southeastern France, at a site called Fontbrégoua. The research effort was led by Paola Villa of the University of Colorado.

The cave includes a series of pits dug in the sandy floor that can be construed as Neolithic garbage dumps. In many of the pits were found clusters of bones. The clusters probably represent separate incidents when food was butchered. Animal bones bear cut marks in similar locations on the bones, which suggests that the animals were butchered in a consistent, systematic manner.

Besides the animal bones, three pits were excavated containing the bones of 13 or 14 humans. Some of the human bones bore marks and breakage patterns similar to those of the animal bones. Marrow bones were broken into small pieces, and they bore the scars of having been struck. Large carnivores can produce a similar type of breakage, but only one bone bore carnivore tooth marks.

Some of the bones, along with high-fidelity casts of marks on other bones, were dispatched to paleontologist Pat Shipman for inspection using the scanning electron microscope.

Under the microscope, the cut marks appeared extraordinarily fresh. Shipman speculated either that the bones were unusually well preserved, or that the marks had been made after the flesh had rotted off. If the latter were true, then the Fontbrégoua bones might have been subjected to second burial rather than to cannibalism.

Shipman enlarged her sample to include animal bones from the pits, since it was unlikely that animals might have been given second burials. However, the marks on the animal bones were identical to those on the human bones, suggesting that both had been processed for food.

A colleague of Shipman's, Mary Russell, set up a blind test to see if Shipman could distinguish immediate processing for food from delayed processing for secondary burial. She experimentally cut a series of fresh and aged bones, some of which bore cut marks from some years earlier.

Bone surfaces and cut marks weather and age over time. A fresh cut on a fresh bone, or an old cut on an old bone, signifies immediate processing. A fresh cut on an old bone signifies delayed processing. Shipman was able to distinguish all of the experimental sample easily.

Shipman undertook to reanalyze all of the Fontbrégoua bones previously examined, both animal and human. They all showed the features of immediate processing, which ruled out secondary burial and made a case for cannibalism.

It is impossible to tell whether the three pits with human bones represent three closely spaced episodes or were made by three different groups who inhabited the cave at different times. If the three episodes were simultaneous, perhaps the group was trapped in the cave and ate some members for survival. However, the meat obtained from 13 or 14 people—especially when added to the animal remains that date from the same period—amounts to a great deal of food. The quantity makes it difficult to argue that the cave's inhabitants might have been on the edge of starvation.

Shipman believes the bones are evidence of a practice by people who simply saw no difference between sheep, goats, wild boars, deer, and humans. If Shipman's view is accurate, then the Fontbrégoua remains represent an example of dietary cannibalism. More research is in progress that may expand understanding of how common cannibalism has been practiced throughout human history and what purpose it served for those who favored it.

Part Two

Earth and Space Science

EVENTS AND TRENDS IN EARTH AND SPACE SCIENCE

From fertilizing with rocks, to examining the interior of the Earth with a CAT scan, to the painstaking removal of a cylinder a mile and a half long from an Arctic icecap to document 160,000 years of the earth's climate, 1987 was a fruitful year for earth and space science.

The Earth and Its Oceans

The coelacanth (pronounced see-la-kanth) was known to science for a long time as a fossil that appeared in 70-million-year-old rocks. It is a member of a family of fishes that flourished when fins and gills were evolving into feet. The coelacanth stopped being viewed as extinct in 1938 when one was caught by a fisherman in the Indian Ocean off the coast of Africa. A second specimen of the elusive fish was not caught until 1952.

Some scientists believe that coelacanths are the only remaining examples of crossopterygians, an ancient line of fish that may have spawned the first tetrapods, or four-legged land animals.

The first observations of a living coelacanth were reported by Jacques Millot, the director of the Madagascar Institute of Scientific Research. The fish was caught on a line and released into a tank. It sought the darkest corners of the tank and within hours was dead. Coelacanths caught subsequently and released for study at the surface of the ocean died within days. The fish's normal habitat is at depths of 200 meters.

West German scientists from the Max Planck Institute in Seewiesen and the Zoological Institute of the University of Saarland in Saarbrücken set out to study coelacanths in their native habitat. They made 40 dives near the Comoro Islands to the northwest of Madagascar, during which they observed six coelacanths. Eighty hours of the sometimes inexplicable behavior of the creatures were captured in still photographs, videotape, and film.

Coelacanths swim backward, drift upside down, and perform their own version of a headstand. Scientists hope the coelacanths will aid in understanding vertebrate transition from water to land. Fleshy lobes, thought to be evolutionary forerunners of limbs, connect the fins to the body.

Scientists had speculated that coelacanths might use a pair of pectoral fins and a pair of pelvic fins to crawl along the ocean bottom. However, the West Germans found that the paired fins were not used for crawling or stalking. But they did find that opposite pectoral and pelvic fins sometimes moved in synchrony, a pattern common to horses and other tetrapods. The West German scientists speculate that such coordination might be a preadaptation that could have facilitated the transition to locomotion on land. Critics question the relevance of the observed behavior, contending that the coelacanths are only distantly related to tetrapods, if at all.

Other kinds of rare sea life were uncovered in a research effort intended to examine underwater petroleum leaks. Oceanographer Mahlon Kennicutt of Texas A&M University's Geochemical and Environmental Research Group in College Station was examining oil seepage as an indicator of good sites for drilling. In 2,000-foot-deep water, at vents where petroleum seeps out of natural underwater reservoirs on the floor of Mexico, Kennicutt found thriving colonies of undersea life, including three-foot-long tubeworms, limpets, mussels, and clams. Similar organisms have been found at deep-ocean hydrothermal vents in the Pacific Ocean and at other underwater sites.

The dispersion of these unusual organisms, which depend on chemicals rather than on sunlight for energy, raises the question of whether they may play a larger role in global ecology than had previously been thought.

Weather and Climate

Lightning kills or injures several hundred Americans each year. During their fifth summer of research, in 1987, 30 scientists working in a NASA-sponsored program sent up small rockets trailing wires into thunderclouds to precipitate lighting strikes. Cameras, remote sensors, radio receivers, and other instruments recorded and measured the electrical surge that traveled to the ground.

NASA's interest in protection against lightning has been sparked by such events as a lightning bolt, shortly after liftoff on March 26, 1987, scrambling the electronics of an unmanned Atlas-Centaur rocket tumbling the $160 million vehicle out of control. Ground control was forced to destroy the rocket.

Scientists are still trying to understand the physical properties of lightning. Following that, they want to discover how lightning begins and forms. An improved ability to predict lightning is dependent on determining electrical conditions in storm clouds prior to the lightning strike.

The NASA research program goes into alert conditions when ground detectors register an electric potential in the atmosphere of a negative or positive charge of 1,000 volts per meter. (A fair-weather electrical field averages no more than 200 volts.) A rocket is then loaded into a metal cylinder on a platform. A diesel generator is switched on to protect the recording instruments from the power of the storm. As soon as meters register a negative atmospheric charge of 3,000 to 4,000 volts—a "triggerable field"—a 10-second countdown begins.

More often than not, the launched rocket creates a bolt of lightning. A massive flow of electricity is drawn down the wire when the rocket enters the lower layers of a thundercloud, an area of concentrated negative charge. The strong current vaporizes the wire. The crackling flash of the thunderbolt takes place when the downward negative current connects with the positive current propagated from the ground.

Scientists hope to determine the precise source of lightning activity in order to develop a method that would predict lightning at least 20 minutes before the event.

Earth in the Past

When early plants first left oceans and lakes to take up life on land, they were assaulted by a harsh environment of dryness and ultraviolet radiation and by problems with nutrition. One theory holds that the earliest land plants survived by having a symbiotic relationship with fungi, a relationship common among present-day plants.

In modern symbiosis, fungi live in or around a plant's roots. The fungi assist the plant in the uptake of nitrogen and phosphorus, and in return receive carbohydrates. Evidence in support of the early fungi-plant symbiosis has been sketchy.

Paleobotanist Sara Stubblefield of Ohio State University and her colleagues reported in 1987 some supporting evidence for the early relationship. They found for the first time fossilized arbuscules, fungal organs that allow the exchange of nutrients between fungus and plant. These fossils, which date back 220 million years, strengthen the argument that symbiosis was occurring at that time.

Stars and the Universe

Relics from the recent past are a risk to space missions. Inside a hollowed-out mountain near Colorado Springs, the United States Space Command tracks almost 7,000 objects the size of a baseball or larger that are orbiting Earth. Using sensitive telescopes, NASA scientists have estimated that 35,000 man-made objects as small as marbles are orbiting the earth. Since the outset of the space age, the amount of orbiting litter has grown steadily. The numbers of objects escalated in 1981 with the explosion of an American Delta rocket in January and the breakup of a Soviet satellite in July. Some experts suspect that rocket debris may have collided with the Soviet satellite.

The debris includes operating and dead satellites, an astronaut's wrench, used-up rocket engines, and thousands of fragments spawned by the accidental breakup of more than 90 satellites and rockets. In the midst of the jumble that can be tracked may hide millions of small bits. A fast-moving fragment no bigger than a pea has the potential to shatter a $100 million satellite.

Engineers have modified rocket designs to lower the potential for engine explosion from a chance encounter. The altitude of Strategic Defense Initiative ("Star Wars") antimissile tests have been limited to speed up the reentry of fragments into the atmosphere.

The orbiting junkyard is a problem for astronomers. A recent astronomical discovery proved to be the flash of sunlight off debris. Photographs of distant stars are regularly disfigured by orbiting leftovers.

Experts warn that a continued increase in space debris will drastically elevate the risk of collisions that could destroy satellites and manned spacecraft. At worst, the breakup of one satellite could touch off other breakups in a cascade.

Knowing the exact orbit of debris is important so that when it eventually falls to the Earth it can be differentiated from enemy warheads and can be kept from collisions with spacecraft. NASA's greatest concern is the $1 billion Space Telescope to be lofted by the shuttle in the next few years, followed by the multibillion-dollar space station scheduled for launch during the 1990s.

The time has passed when protection could be built into the Space Telescope, for which planning began in the 1970s. At best, scientists at the Marshall Space Flight Center are trying to develop shielding for the space station.

6

The Earth and Its Oceans

OCEAN TRACKING

Solutions to Problems Old and New

Bubble Cloud Tracking

A new method for monitoring the mixing process that takes place in upper layers of the ocean was reported during 1987. The technique uses sonar and thermistors (electric thermometers) to track the movement of clouds of bubbles. Breaking waves at the ocean's surface create bubble clouds. Sonar emits and receives sound waves reflected off changes in the water, including bubbles, and are recorded when they return to the sonar.

The research revealed a downward movement of relatively warm near-surface water into colder, deeper water where bubbles are normally absent. As the bubbles descend and are subject to increased pressure, they shrink until they disappear. The gases carried in the bubbles are then transferred into the ocean. Thus the ocean provides a sink for important gases such as carbon dioxide.

The uppermost layer of the ocean exchanges heat, momentum, and gases with the atmosphere in a process that drives the ocean currents, influences short-term weather, and affects gradual shifts in the global climate. Scientists know that the subsurface mixing of water is an important link between the atmosphere and the deep ocean, yet the processes are hardly known and are essentially unmeasured.

The slow vertical flows are easily obscured by the turbulence of ocean waves. The scientists who devised the method for tracking cloud bubbles, S. A. Thorpe of the University of Southampton and A. J. Hall of the Institute of Oceanographic Sciences in Surrey, England, towed a catamaran that had sonar and thermistors hung at various depths beneath the vessel. The catamaran is a vessel that can ride the waves without disturbing the subsurface waters. During trials in the seas east of Iceland, the scientists were able to monitor the top 8.5 meters of ocean.

Acoustic Tomography

Oceanographers have begun to use an observation method called ocean acoustic tomography, analogous to scanning methods used in medicine, to study the seas. The technique will provide global views of ocean circulation and temperature patterns. Contrary to the widely held idea that oceans have smoothly flowing circulations, oceans behave much like the constantly changing atmosphere, except that while the oceans' time scale is measured in weeks, months, and years, the atmosphere operates on a time scale of minutes, hours, and days.

The ocean tomography technique was developed primarily by Walter Munk of the Scripps Institution of Oceanography in La Jolla, California, and by Carl Wunsch of the Massachusetts Institute of Technology. The method had been tried on a small scale successfully in the Atlantic, and was being tested in the Pacific in 1987. With the new technique, the heretofore hidden movements in the ocean are revealed to be at least as complex as the movements in the atmosphere. The tomography technique has found that ocean areas operate as independently moving bodies of water.

An assumption long held by scientists has been that the enormous heat storage capacity of the oceans prevented sudden drastic changes in climate. However, recent evidence suggests that the oceans contribute to rather than prevent swift change.

The ocean acoustic tomography technique sends sonar pulses, or pings, between moored buoys. A pulse moving in the same direction as the water travels faster than a pulse moving against the water flow. Thus travel time signals water direction. Travel times can also establish temperature, because warm water transmits sound faster than cold water.

An exchange between three stations could detect a mid-ocean eddy. The technique was being tested in 1987 north of Hawaii, in water 2 miles deep. Three buoys formed a triangle 600 miles on each side. To each mooring, a transmitter of sonic pulses and a receiver were attached. The ping sent out from one buoy moves in various directions before it reaches a receiving buoy. The multiple arrivals of the pulses provide data for an analysis of water conditions at many depths, allowing for a three-dimensional map.

A full-scale operation would include dozens of buoys and hundreds of travel paths. With the aid of computers, it could make possible the mapping of water motions and temperatures throughout an ocean basin. The challenge is to develop inexpensive, reliable transmitter-receiver stations to make a full-scale system feasible.

The director of the Woods Hole Oceanographic Institution in Massachusetts, John Steele, believes enough has already been learned to recognize that current textbook descriptions of ocean circulation are in error or are substantially incomplete. Surface currents have been mapped, but deep currents, even major ones, may remain as yet undiscovered.

The experiments with ocean acoustic tomography are a preliminary to the World Ocean Circulation Experiment planned for the years 1990 to 1995. The program, involving almost all the world's maritime nations, will use satellites, ships, and buoys, both moored and drifting. Some of the buoys will be submerged at fixed depths to trace deep currents. Once independently moving bodies are identified and tracked, data on them can be fed into computer models to forecast climate changes.

Following the Gulf Stream

The river of water known as the Gulf Stream flows northeast from the Straits of Florida up the Atlantic to east of Newfoundland where it slowly splinters into rivulets that have been tracked by buoys to the Azores, west of Portugal. For the body of water it transports, it is the world's fastest major ocean current.

Benjamin Franklin was co-author of the first chart to outline the dimensions of the Gulf Stream. Franklin was the deputy postmaster for the American colonies. He learned that British customs officials were complaining because fast transatlantic mail ships took at least 2 weeks longer to arrive at New York than did plodding merchant ships that docked by nearby Providence, Rhode Island.

By asking questions on the docks of London and on the docks of Falmouth, Massachusetts, Franklin found a reason for the difference. On the advice of American whaling ship crews, merchant skippers were bypassing a strong mid-ocean current. The haughtier mail packet captains were above accepting counsel from fishermen. They chose the more direct course across the Atlantic that for much of their voyage placed them in opposition to currents of up to 4 miles an hour.

Franklin elected to study the waters himself during the course of his many Atlantic crossings. He dropped thermometers off the ships on which he traveled. The thrust of Franklin's chart of the Gulf Stream was accurate; however, given the limited technology of his day, many details were substantially inaccurate.

The English had no interest in Franklin's chart. However, after the American Revolution broke out and Franklin was sent to France, America's ally was interested enough in the map to have it printed and to use it to dispatch guns to America. Although the chart may not have won the war, it certainly was an asset.

The Gulf Stream has a significant impact on the world's climate. Europe's food production depends on the warmth carried from the equator by the current. A recent discovery has found that an immense flow of highly saline (salty) water runs beneath the Gulf Stream in the opposite direction. This salty current is a critical factor in the behavior of the Gulf Stream.

The circulation of the Gulf Stream was greatly affected by the last Ice Age, which ended 10,000 years ago. After a considerable amount of the world's water became frozen in ice sheets, sea levels dropped about 300 feet. The circulation that drew the Gulf Stream far north was diminished.

Temperatures in Europe dropped 16 to 20 degrees while in other parts of the world at similar latitudes the drop in temperature was only 8 degrees.

The northerly flow of the Gulf Stream is largely dependent on the deep return of the saline water flowing beneath it. The pull of the earth's rotation keeps the southward travel of the saline flow and the northward travel of the Gulf Stream hugging the western edge of the Atlantic basin.

As the Gulf Stream travels into the North Atlantic, it becomes saltier and heavier due to evaporation. In the area near Iceland, the saltier water cools and sinks and flows back to the south. The warmer Gulf Stream water continues to flow northward and the cycle continues.

Scientists believe that the fall of 300 feet during the Ice Age prevented the salty water from flowing in large volume over the region made shallow between Greenland, Iceland, and Norway. Without the push of the return flow, the Gulf Stream was no longer drawn that far north, and the temperatures fell.

Oceanographers predict that any global warming would occur at high latitudes, which would reduce the difference in temperature between the tropics and the Arctic. This temperature difference is the generator of winds and ocean currents. A reduction in temperature could have the effect of changing the route of the Gulf Stream, thereby cooling the lands bordering the North Atlantic.

An oceanographer with the National Weather Service, Jenifer Clark, has interpreted infrared satellite images of the Gulf Stream for various institutions for 15 years. A Navy-funded project called the Harvard Gulfcasting Program begun in the spring of 1986 combines Clark's infrared analysis with other techniques to keep close track of the Gulf Stream.

An Air Deployable Expendable Bathythermo (AXBT). This device is dropped into the Gulf Stream, where it takes temperature readings of the water and radios them back to research scientists.

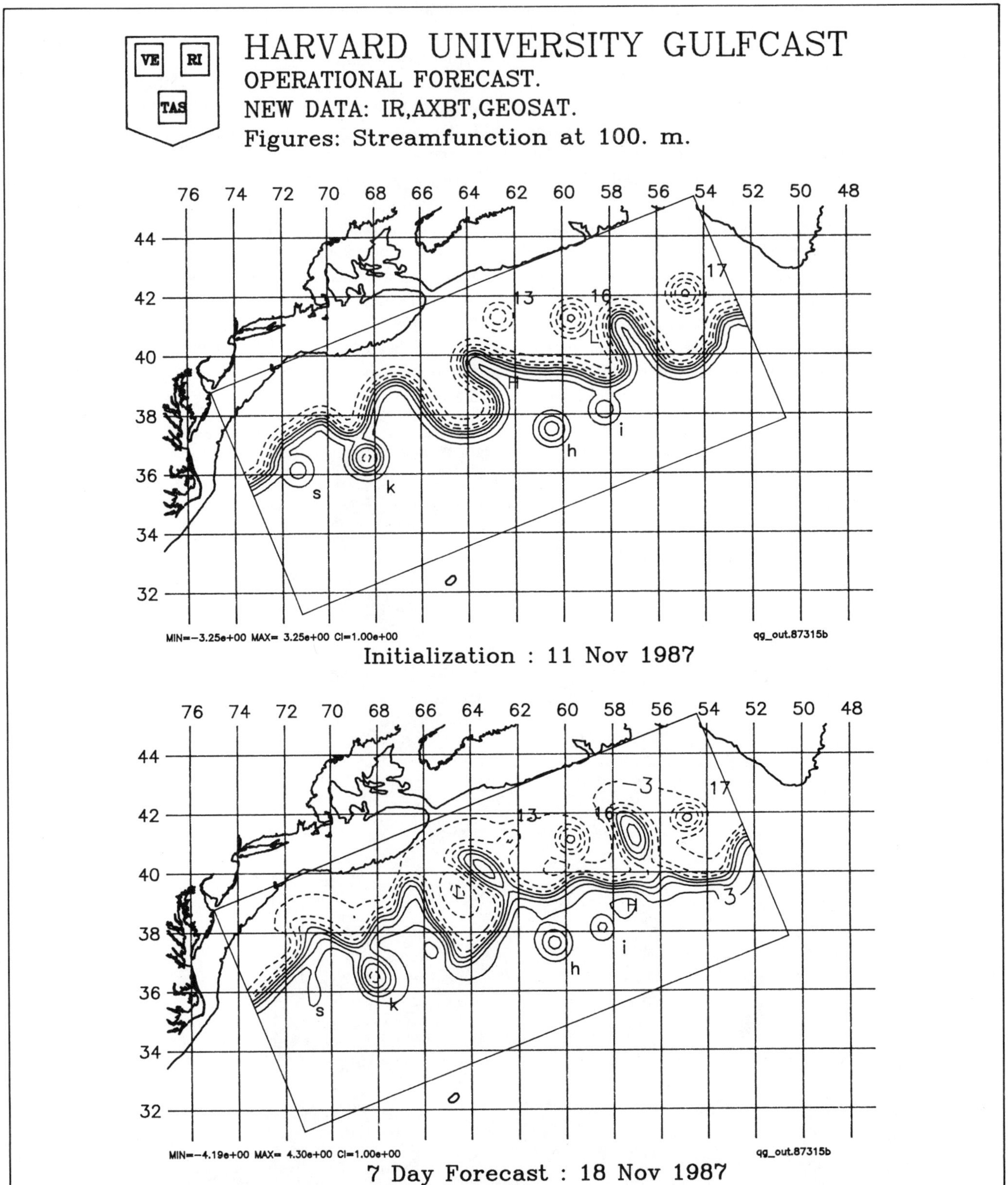

From Harvard University's Gulfcasting Program, the top graph shows the actual position of the Gulf Stream on November 11, 1987; the bottom graph shows the Gulf Stream's projected position seven days hence. Harvard divides the depth of the water into six strata. The graphs illustrate the top stratum, the first 100 meters (328 ft., 1 in.). The circles on the coastal side of the stream (indicated by numbers 13, 16, and 17) are warm core rings. Circles to the opposite side of the stream (indicated by lower-case letters) are cold core rings.

The Gulfcasting scientists use a complex computer model of oceanographic dynamics developed by Harvard oceanographer Allan Robinson. They also use a weekly survey of temperature readings from thermometers dropped from aircraft, as well as data collected from infrared satellite images. Each week, Harvard's Gulfcasting scientists assess Gulf Stream locations and predict where they will be 7 days later. The computer model of the Gulf Stream dynamics combines wind, water, and earth movement.

George Milkowski of the University of Rhode Island Graduate School of Oceanography describes the Gulf Stream as a river within the ocean that transports warm water from the south to the north. It can have strong surface currents with speeds up to 80 inches per second.

The Gulf Stream flows between the Sargasso Sea on its right and the "north slope water" (the ocean area between the eastern seaboard and the Continental Shelf) on its left. A constant high-pressure weather system above the North Atlantic pushes the wind around the perimeter of the ocean, mixing the surface water beneath.

The Gulf Stream's most narrow, straight, and rapid course is off the coast of Florida, where the water is funneled at 6 miles per hour through the 60-mile channel between the mainland and Grand Bahama Island. Like the water in a river's hairpin curve, the water piles up while waiting to pass through the opening.

By the time the Gulf Stream reaches the Carolinas, the flow has widened to about 90 miles and slowed to 4 miles per hour. Caught between two forces, the Gulf Stream begins to meander.

One force tugging the Gulf Stream is the Sargasso Sea, which is about 3 feet higher than the north slope water, creating a gravity pull northward. The second force is the Earth's spin, which creates the Coriolis effect that pushes surface water in the Northern Hemisphere in an easterly direction. Here the Gulf Stream takes on a resemblance to a snake.

Some loops swing so far they circle back on themselves, creating a well of water as much as 100 miles wide. A loop on the north will isolate cold northern water to spin it clockwise as the Gulf Stream straightens and continues north. A loop to the south will isolate warm Sargasso Sea water to spin it counterclockwise.

As many as a dozen eddies may be spinning to the left and right of the Gulf Stream. The Coriolis effect causes the eddies to move in a direction opposite to the Gulf Stream. A strong eddy may make one complete revolution in a week as it moves down the coast at about 6 miles an hour, taking as long as 2 years for the journey. The movement of warm core eddies filled with Sargasso Sea and Gulf Stream water explains why divers from the New England Aquarium can often collect Caribbean fish larvae off the Rhode Island coast or off Cape Cod.

Along the boundary of an eddy, the temperature may vary as much as 18 degrees. A thermal wall is thus created that colder-sea marine life prefer not to pass. Cold-water organisms pile up against the wall and become food for warm-water dolphin, swordfish, mako shark, and tuna that ride the Gulf Stream or circle one of the eddies.

The Gulf Stream has long been credited with the virtual absence of snow in London. On the other hand, the large eddies 200 miles southeast off Nantucket are suspected of creating thermal convections that create sudden winter storms to batter New England.

An 18-month study called the Gale Project by the National Weather Service and university meteorologists documented the formation of violent storms east of the Carolinas over the Gulf Stream. During the winter of 1987, Carl Kreitzberg, a meteorologist at Drexel University in Philadelphia, with a team of scientists, was scheduled to explore several theories as a follow-up to the federally funded Gale Project.

The precision with which the course of the Gulf Stream can now be plotted has a variety of uses. Shipping companies can ride a current to save fuel costs. Fishermen can be helped in their search for rich fishing grounds. And the Navy can hide submarines behind the Gulf Stream's sonar-bending walls.

Tracking with Remote Sensing

A remote color-sensing photograph of the eastern seaboard of the United States as seen from space displays the Gulf Stream as molten orange and red "ribbon candy" flowing northward. As it flows, it is flanked on either side by swirls and whirlpools, some cool blue or green, and others in warm yellow, red, or orange. A comparable photograph in black and white displays the Gulf Stream's behavior in varying shades of gray.

The photograph is a pictorial summation of data collected by a space satellite and beamed back to Earth as coded radio signals. The radio signals are decoded and transformed into scientific English and then transformed once more into a photograph.

Remote sensing, the ability to acquire oceanographic information with the aid of satellite technology, is becoming increasingly commonplace. However, in the opinion of Otis Brown, director of the Remote Sensing Group at the Unviersity of Miami Rosentiel School of Marine and Atmospheric Science (RSMAS), the technique is still an art, which scientists are attempting to turn into a science.

Beginning in the 1960s, remote sensors in space satellites have provided the first scientific glimpses of the Earth as a whole. They have done this by collecting

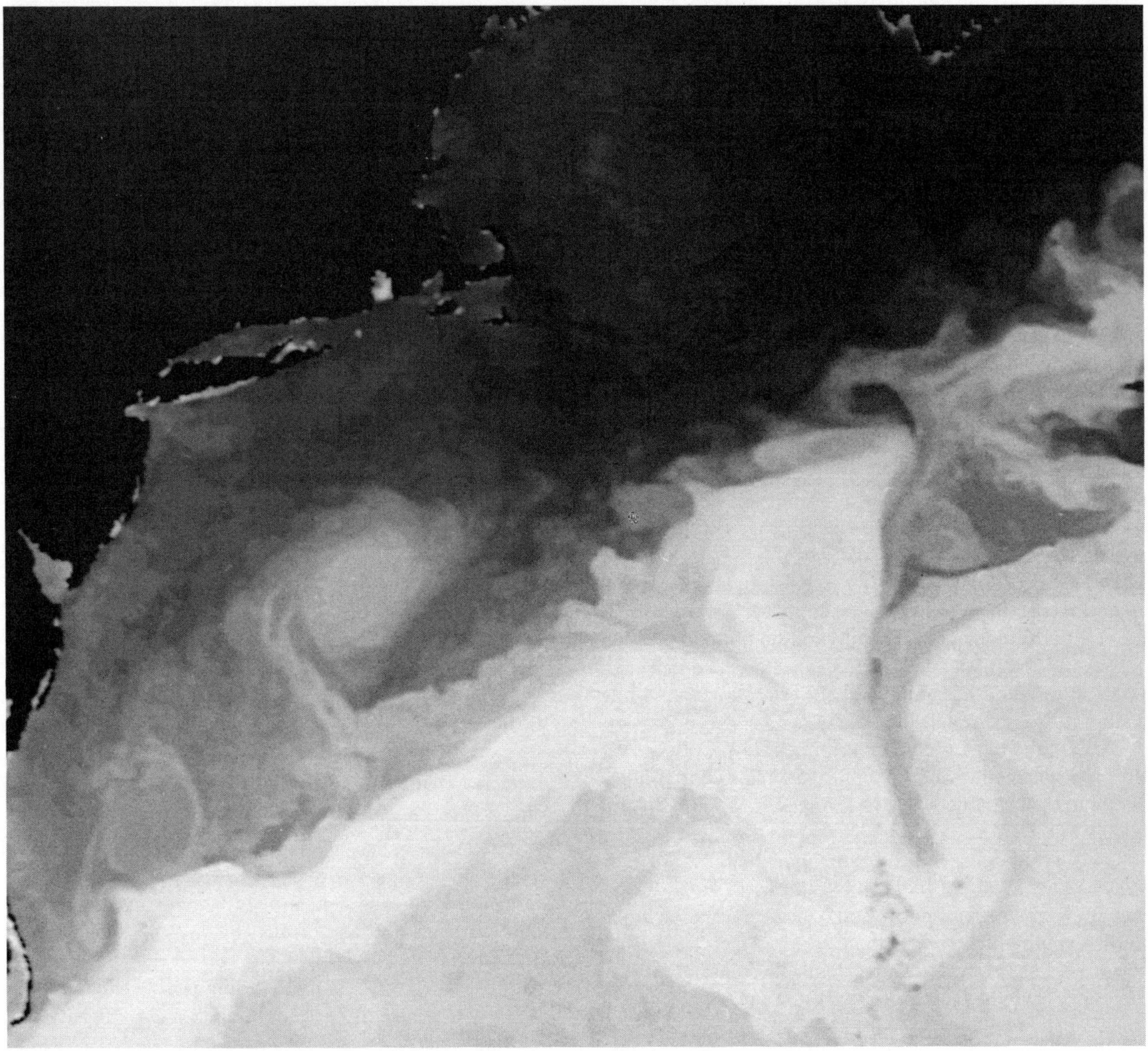

The image is of the surface temperatures of the ocean off the eastern coast of the United States. Sea surface temperatures are derived from the measurement of infrared radiation made by two satellite IR sensors. Based on the difference between the two readings, an estimate is made of how much radiation has been dispersed by the atmosphere and a final temperature is arrived at. This image shows a temperature range of 5-30 degrees Celsius. Cold water is depicted as gray, warm water as pale gray to white. The Gulf Stream is the wide band of warm (white) water starting in the lower left-hand corner. Warm and cold core rings can be seen. These rings can last for months to years before eventually being absorbed again by the Gulf Stream.

measures of sea-surface temperature, surface wind speed, surface roughness and color.

Satellite imaging provides a wide perspective on entire ocean basins. Areas to which ships or buoys have no access can be observed. The technique provides an opportunity to observe the dynamics of the oceans and the movements of the atmosphere. Although the results of satellite imaging have become quite useful during the last few years, there are still some flaws.

First, the sensing process itself is not fully understood because interpretation is not fully predictable. For example, scientists are striving to understand what effect the atmosphere has. They need to know what factors between the sensor in the sky and the ocean on Earth affect the measurements and thereby introduce a need for corrections.

Furthermore, there is a need to distinguish between the signal and the actual ocean process being sensed. For example, sensing the sea-surface temperature is comparable to, but not the same as, the emitted heat observed from the surface. The measurement is not a direct temperature reading, but an inference, an indirect interpretation of data.

Another example is wind speed. This measurement is made by translating the amount of surface roughness measured with a scatterometer or a special type of radar. Electromagnetic sensing does not make it possible to look into the interior of the ocean. Except for color sensors, which can "see" 65 feet down into the ocean, depending upon the water's clarity, sensors only glimpse a thin slice of the surface.

Interpretation of a satellite data map continues to require a degree of art on the part of scientists. Satellite data maps have not yet reached a level where every scientist looking at a map would interpret it in precisely the same way.

During the spring of 1987, RSMAS scientists working on a ship in the Indian Ocean took direct temperature measurements to make comparisons with satellite data. Over time, such comparisons will permit standardized interpretations of satellite observations. However, Dr. Brown believes another 10 years will pass before scientists can rely with full confidence on satellite data.

Despite its limitations, remote sensing has been used in many different applications. One is the tracking of fronts, places where the temperature changes abruptly. They are revealed by ocean color and sea-surface temperature.

An RSMAS graduate student, Guillermo Podesta, has used infrared satellite sensing to identify front patterns that might reveal the presence of hake, a commercial fish species found off the Argentine coast.

An RSMAS mammalogist, Daniel Odell, is using remote-sensing information to try to understand why whales strand themselves on beaches. Dr. Odell is interested in surface temperatures of the Gulf Stream and of loops of water called small eddies that measure about 6 miles across and are short-lived. Odell believes the small eddies are sufficiently large to carry smaller whales such as the pygmy sperm whale inshore with them. Virtually all the stranded pygmy sperm whales die of congestive heart failure, probably resulting from malnutrition. The eddies carry the whales away from their normal feeding ground.

Remote-sensing information is also used by oil companies to protect their exploration ships and rigs from the impact of temperature-created currents. With 5,000 feet of drill string dangling three-tenths of a mile beneath a ship, it is wise to avoid warm water eddies spinning at several knots, which can create tremendous drag.

Promised Improvements

Two satellites to be launched in 1990 should significantly improve the quality of sensor imaging of the ocean. The N-ROSS satellite (Navy Remote Ocean Sensing System) will carry a low-frequency microwave radiometer for measuring sea-surface temperature, a scatometer for deriving surface winds, and an altimeter for determining sea height. These will provide data for weather predictions and for ocean-circulation modeling.

NASA's Topography of Ocean Experiment (TOPEX) will be a part of a joint effort with the French Space Agency's POSEIDON. If launched on schedule in 1991, the mission will coincide with the World Climate Research Program, an international investigation of surface and subsurface phenomena conducted under the auspices of the United Nation's (U.N.) World Meteorological Organization and the International Council of Scientific Unions. The two big projects of the U.N. program will be the World Ocean Circulation Experiment mentioned earlier, and the Tropical Ocean and Global Atmosphere Experiment.

Along coastal areas, navigation depends on accurate knowledge of tides, currents, and surface winds, yet navigators still rely on incomplete tidal forecasts. For at least a century, data collection at sea has not changed. Ships move to fixed "hydrographic stations," where devices are lowered into the water on cables. The devices measure the water's properties from the surface to the bottom, and the collected data provides a basis for general circulation maps that show an average arrangement of water masses. A significant problem with the observations is that they have been collected over the course of decades, while ocean currents probably change from month to month.

The TOPEX/POSEIDON will crisscross 800 miles above the ocean for 3 years using radar to measure the precise distance from the ocean to the satellite within a few inches. The principal instrument aboard TOPEX/POSEIDON will be a radar altimeter that will send short pulses of energy toward the ocean surface. The length of time required for a round trip and the intensity and structure of consecutive returned signals will make it possible to determine the elevation of the sea surface, the height of the waves, and the speed of the wind as determined by its effect upon the surface. By knowing the height of the seas, oceanographers can extrapolate the size and direction of ocean currents. Ocean currents, in turn, are the power that drives climatic changes.

Even with TOPEX/POSEIDON in place, hydrographic maps would continue to be published, but the TOPEX/POSEIDON maps would provide up-to-date information as well as greater accuracy. It would also provide maps for regions where high-quality hydrographic stations are unavailable.

The TOPEX/POSEIDON data combined with the N-ROSS data would enable meteorologists to construct wind maps that would give a more accurate assessment of worldwide climate trends. Current knowledge of ocean winds is derived from information collected by ships confined to well-traveled routes.

TOPEX/POSEIDON could also help to chart the ocean's seafloor, because the ocean's surface is pulled into shape by the mountains and valleys of the sea floor. An undersea mountain heaps up water over it. The valleys on either side of a mountain become trenches.

Scientists further hope TOPEX/POSEIDON will enlighten them about recently discovered mesoscale eddies. Eddies are an oceanographic equivalent of meteorologic storms. Highs and lows build up and dissipate across the ocean surface, contributing to large currents. Along with the currents, they move the bulk of the earth's absorbed solar energy.

Improved tracking and mapping of the ocean would provide advance warnings of storms to shipping, predict the course of waterborne pollutants, and aid the fishing industry worldwide. Moreover, improved maps would aid the research of climatologists concerned about the potential impact of the greenhouse effect.

7

The Earth in the Past

COCKROACHES

Colonizers in Even the Nicest Homes

Many urban dwellers who turn off the kitchen light and retire to the living room for an evening of television can expect to be greeted by uninvited guests should they return for a snack. The shy German cockroach emerges from its hiding places when not repelled by bright lights or the presence of people. Given an opportunity, such as their human hosts going away on vacation, German cockroaches move out from their usual residences under kitchen sinks and bathroom fixtures and find their way into turned-off ovens and unopened drawers. Hungry roaches have been known to consume even the inner workings of televisions and refrigerators.

Cockroaches are also fond of the spaces beneath the cushions of vehicles. The size of the vehicle does not intimidate the cockroach. Along with passengers, the New York City Transit Authority transports thousands of cockroaches in its buses every day. Cockroaches have been riding the buses for at least 50 years.

In response to customer complaints about a recent minor population explosion of cockroach passengers, the Transit Authority tried insect bombs and fumigation, but the chemicals bothered the drivers more than the cockroaches. Other remedies also failed. Officials appealed to the Museum of Natural History for advice.

The request was turned over to Dr. Betty Faber, a research associate in the Entomology Department, who conducted research by riding the buses, visiting the terminals, and jotting down descriptions of the behavior of cockroach passengers. In developing her history of the problem, Faber learned that the Transit Authority had begun a new bus-cleaning program. It seemed that the more the buses were scrubbed, the more the cockroaches flourished.

Transit Authority officials had hoped that Faber would tell them how to eliminate the problem, but to their dismay, she concluded that the best the Transit Authority could do was to try to keep the cockroaches under control. Human bus riders, it seemed, would have to learn to live with their non-fare-paying fellow passengers. Like most roaches, the German cockroach is attracted to water. By providing a wet environment, the Transit Authority's scrubbing program had only worsened the problem. Faber's advice was to dry the buses after scrubbing and to cut down on the roaches' nourishment by keeping food off the buses as much as possible.

In all probability, the cockroaches did not board the buses on their own—a feat equivalent to mountain climbing. Each more than likely arrived clutching the clothing of a passenger. The German cockroach clings tenaciously when disturbed. Once carried safely on board tucked beneath a collar, or hidden in a cuff, the cockroach could loosen its grip and wander off to make a new home.

The cockroach is one of the most venerable creatures on Earth. A cockroach-like insect was among the first to colonize land, hundreds of millions of years ago. Fossilized roaches have been found within the same geological layer of rock as dinosaur bones, suggesting that roaches may have dined on dinosaur flesh.

The survival of the cockroach is due, at least in part, to its adaptability. Cockroaches have found urban settings to their liking and have resisted vigorous efforts to dislodge them. The German cockroach, an insect inclined to be mobile, emigrated to New York from Asia—not from Germany as its name would imply—at least 100 years ago. Since its arrival, the German cockroach has become the dominant cockroach species in the United States. The larger American cockroach—often referred to as a waterbug—though outnumbered is still very much in evidence.

A New, "Improved" Cockroach

A new cockroach immigrant, the Asian cockroach, has appeared in Tampa, Florida. The trip was probably made by plane or by ship—the most likely suspect being a freighter. The newest roach has quickly spread out to take up residence in lawns within a 500- to 600-mile area around that city.

The differences between the familiar German cockroach and the Asian cockroach are causing consternation. The reclusive German cockroach scuttles out of sight when a light is turned on; the Asian cockroach is attracted to light and light-colored surfaces. The German cockroach is active during the middle of the night; the Asian cockroach is active at sunset.

Yard lights, porch lights, and room lights draw the Asian cockroach toward people. Unlike German cockroaches, Asian cockroaches fly up to 120 feet, which makes it easy for some of those outside to find their way inside. Once in the house, the Asian cockroach will follow a homeowner from room to room as lights are turned on, rather than stay behind in the dark as do the German cockroaches. When the last light is turned off, the Asian cockroach likes to snuggle up in damp bathroom towels.

While the German cockroach reproduces rapidly, it hardly matches the ability of the Asian cockroach. If all the offspring of 100 female Asian cockroaches survived, within a year they would have produced an equivalent of 9 aircraft carriers' weight in cockroaches!

Asian cockroaches are about 5/8 of an inch long. As many as 150 to 300 of them may cover the pastel wall of a garage at a time, or cover the white surface of the side of a home. As many as 100,000 roaches per acre may take up residence in a lawn.

Asian roaches find Florida a near-perfect environment. There is plenty of moisture and plenty of food. Nevertheless some are moving on. Residents in Kansas, Virginia, and Alabama believe they have already seen Asian cockroaches. There is speculation that by hopping rides on trains or on interstate food trucks, the Asian cockroaches may easily spread throughout the South and Southwest.

Scientists are aware that in Asia the Asian cockroach has been found where snow falls periodically, in elevations as high as 4,000 feet. Thus the insects have the potential to also spread as far north as New Jersey on the East Coast and to the state of Washington on the West Coast.

Their size and their flying ability make the Asian cockroach's indoor presence unnerving. They also share with other cockroaches the ability to scamper quickly. When disturbed in a pile of lumber, or in a mound of leaf litter, their haste is apt to make them crawl up the legs of the unwitting human intruder.

Can the Cockroach Be Conquered?

Cockroaches are capable of transmitting more than 50 different disease-causing organisms. Roaches can also cause allergies. Entomologists report that roaches have been known to crawl on people, where they gnaw at calluses on hands and feet, and feed around the eyes and face.

Because cockroaches are more than a simple nuisance, the temptation is to attack the problem with pesticides. A pest-control manager, Alvin Burger, who appeared on ABC's news program "Nightline" on March 18, 1987, believes continuous control of a typical home in Tampa would require that pesticide be applied to the cockroach's shelters and breeding areas. The intent of Burger's treatment would be to wipe out existing infestations and to prevent recurring infestations. He suggests that chemicals selective to roaches, such as organophosphate, be used.

Richard Brenner, an entomologist with the U.S. Department of Agriculture, appearing on the same program, feels that a better approach would be to place toxic bait in shaded leaf litter, where the Asian cockroaches develop, in June and July, when the roaches are least mobile.

Environmental toxicologist Diane Baxter, a biologist with the National Coalition Against the Misuse of Pesticides (NCAMP), has serious qualms about the use of pesticides—in particular the use of organophosphate nerve poisons. Baxter points out that many pesticides, although registered with the Environmental Protection Agency

(EPA), have not been adequately tested, so that risk to humans from low-level exposure over long periods is still unknown.

Baxter recommends sealing cracks to prevent the cockroaches' access into the home. She also recommends that boric acid in a plastic catsup bottle be squeezed into crevices inside the house.

Pest-control manager Burger disagrees with Baxter's recommendations, arguing that moisture would render the boric acid ineffective and that the problem should be addressed at its source outside, where the cockroaches live and breed.

Science Enters the Fray

Not all the recent news about cockroaches has been dismal. Research on cockroaches by United States Department of Agriculture (USDA) scientists in Texas and California is part of an emerging field called insect neurochemistry. At the agency's Veterinary Toxicology and Entomology Research Laboratory in College Station, Texas, and at the Western Regional Research Center in Albany, California, most of the work has focused on the large Madeira cockroach, which is a problem in many American cities.

The focus of the USDA effort is the insect's brain, a complex organism that sends out chemical messages called neurotransmitters. The purpose of the research is to identify what processes—breeding, molting, egg laying—are regulated by the neurotransmitters, with a view toward developing a chemical to disrupt the processes.

The USDA scientists have chemically distinguished many neuropeptides, the amino-acid chain molecules, that are released from the roach's brain in extremely small amounts (probably less than 0.05 to 0.15 nanograms, depending on the specific chemical).

Scientists in Texas and California are particularly interested in neurochemicals that control the cockroach's digestion, blood flow, and water excretion. The neuropeptides themselves are not practical as a control agent, since to obtain an extract would require crushing from 78,000 to 2 million roach heads and since the neuropeptides are quickly broken down by the insect's digestive tract. Thus, USDA scientist Ronald Nachman in California is developing chemical mimics of neuropeptides that share the original chemical's structure but lack the unstable chemical bonds that make the originals vulnerable to enzyme breakdown.

The Asian cockroach.

As an alternative, researchers might also design antipeptides, which, once inside the roach's body, would attach to and neutralize the animal's natural peptides. The attractiveness of the mimics lies in their selective toxicity and the unlikelihood that the insects will develop a resistance to mimics of their own regulators.

But designing chemical interventions is only part of the scientists' problem. Carrying the chemicals to the insect is another hurdle. Conventional methods, which include crop dusting, irrigation, or traps, might be used. Scientist J. E. Wright of the USDA's Research Service for Entomology in Beltville, Maryland, foresees bacteria carrying chemicals into the field, where they would be picked up by the insects.

Environmentalist Diane Baxter of the NCAMP is not opposed to this research, but she is cautious. She fears that the peptides might be taken up by receptors in other animals, even humans. Jay Feldman, a colleague of Baxter's at the NCAMP, is less sanguine, pointing out that the EPA's monitoring of pesticide field tests has not been stringent.

Other researchers are studying the cockroach's immune system, which, along with its adaptability, may have been an important factor in the insect's longevity.

A University of Cincinnati scientist, Richard Karp, has reported that the cockroach's natural protection includes allograft immunity, the process responsible for rejecting transplants from donors of the same species. The rejection of grafts indicates that the insect has cell-mediated immunity, an ability observed in higher animals. Work done earlier at the Cincinnati lab found that cockroaches produce antibody-like substances against the venom of other insects. Research is continuing in this area.

While the USDA scientists and other researchers continue to seek an effective means of controlling the ubiquitous cockroach, it is clear that humans will have to share their living space with roaches for some time to come.

DINOSAURS

New Answers for Old Questions

A few young paleontologists are taking issue with some old theories about dinosaurs. Jack Horner, curator of paleontology at Montana State University Museum of the Rockies, and Robert Bakker, adjunct curator of paleontology at the University of Colorado Museum, are among those questioning currently held assumptions about these extinct former inhabitants of planet Earth.

Answers to the difficult questions that Horner, Bakker, and their colleagues are asking could shed new light on why dinosaurs flourished for 140 million years. The questions include: Were dinosaurs sluggish and cold-blooded like reptiles, as has long been believed? Might dinosaurs have been warm-blooded like birds and mammals? Did dinosaurs travel in herds, or did they live essentially alone and come together only in battle or for breeding? How were dinosaur offspring raised?

Dinosaurs prospered during their 140 million years on Earth, filling a variety of ecological niches. Some dinosaurs were the size of a chipmunk, while others weighed 10 times as much as an elephant. They included the *Tyrannosaurus rex*, a predator who ate meat, and *Brachiosaurus*, who cropped foliage from the tops of trees.

One factor contributing to the new theories is an unprecedented increase in information about dinosaurs over the past two decades. Forty percent of all known species of dinosaur have been discovered since the late 1960s.

Dinosaurs evolved during the Triassic period, from 248 million to 213 million years ago. Staurikosaurus, one of the first true dinosaurs, weighed about 70 pounds and measured about 6 feet, 6 inches. By about 190 million years ago, the dinosaurs had supplanted their immediate ancestor, the thecodont. Surpassing the existing reptiles and the emerging mammals, dinosaurs became the dominant land-dwelling animal until they died out 65 million years ago, at the end of the Cretaceous period.

The first discovery of dinosaur bones is often credited to Mary Ann Mantell in 1822. Mantell was the wife of an amateur fossil collector. However, a book published in 1677 by Robert Plot, *Natural History of Oxfordshire*, contains an illustration of a dinosaur femur.

Were the Dinosaurs Warm-Blooded?

Dinosaurs acquired their name from the British anatomist, Richard Owen, who called them *Dinosauria*, or "terrible lizard." He believed they were enormous reptiles. Owen's conception of dinosaurs as "lizards" persisted until the 1960s. Displays of dinosaur bones assembled by museum staffs inevitably depicted dinosaurs with reptilian characteristics. The elbows were bent, the tails dragged on

Plastic cast of a baby Maisaura peeblesorum, *the state fossil of Montana.*

the ground, and the noses were shaped to resemble those of lizards.

One night, in Yale's Peabody Museum, Robert Bakker began to doubt the prevalent view of dinosaurs. He became concerned with the front-end alignment of the Brontosaurus. The back end had been constructed to resemble an elephant while the front had been made to resemble a lizard. The front, to Bakker, did not seem to match the back.

In the summer of 1964, one of Bakker's Yale professors, paleontologist John Ostrom, found a preserved foot of a bipedal dinosaur. The foot, like that of many upright dinosaurs, resembled a bird's foot, except that an inner toe ended in a claw designed for ripping flesh. In Ostrom's view, the claw could not have belonged to an animal that behaved like a reptile. The animal had to have been instead an active, agile, fast-moving predator.

Reptiles are ectothermic, or cold-blooded. Their bodies are dependent on the sun to heat them, and on the shade to cool them. This dependence on the environment limits their activity.

Mammals, on the other hand, are endothermic, or warm-blooded. Their bodies are heated internally, freeing the mammals to be more active under a wide variety of environmental conditions. Ostrom's finding of a dinosaur claw that seemed compatible with a fast-moving predator suggested to him that dinosaurs might have been endothermic rather than ectothermic as had long been supposed. Ostrom admitted his theory might be hard to prove, but to Bakker, the idea made sense. He took up the cause.

Bakker calculated the cruising speed of dinosaurs. The Brontosaurus, he figured, could cruise at more than 3 miles per hour. In Bakker's view, this relatively fast pace was needed because, as the rainy seasons came and went, the dinosaurs migrated, following the greening of the trees they relied on for food. Reptiles, however, do not migrate, because they do not have the high metabolism needed for prolonged exercise.

Bakker looked at the climates of the southern tips of Africa and Argentina, where the winters were cooler at the beginning of the Dinosaur Age than they are now. No remains of other cold-blooded animals have been uncovered in those areas. However, there were many dinosaur bones.

Today, warm-blooded predators number about 1 to 6 percent of the total animal population in a given region. Bakker tallied the numbers of carnivorous (meat-eating) and herbivorous (plant-eating) dinosaurs in various museum collections and found that predators represented 1 to 3 percent of the total, within the range now found for warm-blooded animals.

However, colleagues, including Jack Horner, did not accept either Bakker's geographic distribution arguments or his arguments based on his count of museum fossil collections (though they do admit that Bakker's discounted ideas keep reappearing as plausible whenever new evidence is acquired). Horner disbelieved counts of fossil collections because he felt there were biases in the selection of animals to be preserved in collections. Also, there is an organizational problem connected with counting museum collections. Due to lack of staff and funds, many museums have substantial parts of their collections packed away unexamined. Therefore, Horner concluded, there is no way of accurately determining that predator dinosaurs actually represent 1 to 3 percent of dinosaur remains found to date.

Horner, though, did share Bakker's interest in the work of Armand de Ricqles, a French anatomist and paleontologist who was investigating ways to distinguish endotherms from ectotherms. Horner believed that a growth series—a collection of dinosaur fossils from all different stages of the life cycle—would help test de Ricqles's ideas. Thus he set out to find dinosaur babies.

Returning in 1977 to the site of his first childhood discovery of a dinosaur bone in the plains of northeastern Montana, Horner found something that looked like a smashed turtle. At the suggestion of a colleague, he compared his find with some black, bumpy bits of dinosaur eggshell in Princeton's Museum of Natural History. His squashed egg matched the dinosaur shells perfectly.

The following summer, Horner returned to the area. He collected dinosaur eggs in a rock shop, found a dinosaur nest with fifteen nestlings, and came upon an entire hill covered with dinosaur nests, eggs, and babies.

Every summer Horner returns to the area. Each year he has discovered more eggs, babies, and juveniles. (Twenty-eight eggs even had the embryos still inside.) In this way, Horner acquired a complete dinosaur growth series from embryo to adult.

The growth series suggested a way to settle the controversy over whether dinosaurs were endothermic or ectothermic. Ectothermic animals grow slowly. A crocodile, for example, grows only about a foot a year. Endothermic animals grow quickly. Horner's collection of embryonic, nestling, and juvenile dinosaurs exhibited a growth rate much faster than that of the ectothermic crocodile, suggesting that perhaps the dinosaurs were warm-blooded after all.

Horner and de Ricqles examined microthin sections of bone from nestling and juvenile dinosaurs, from modern birds, and from crocodiles. They found many vascular canals (passages for blood) in both bird and dinosaur bones, but few in crocodile bones, which suggested to Horner that dinosaurs were fast-growing, like the warm-blooded birds. (Vascular canals are plentiful in fast-growing bones in order to accommodate the rich blood supply needed for growth.)

Further supporting his theory, Horner has determined from his growth series that baby hadrosaurs, which were 13 inches when they hatched, reached 10 feet in size by their first birthday. This is a rate that can be matched by some baby birds, but not by cold-blooded animals. However, whether dinosaurs were warm-blooded or cold-blooded is still a question far from being settled.

Did the Dinosaurs Live in Tropical Swamps?

Undaunted by being out of step with accepted theory and with the views of colleagues, Bakker pursued his notion that museums created anatomically incorrect displays of dinosaurs. Moreover, Bakker was sure that the settings created for dinosaurs in museum exhibitions were also wrong. The dinosaur's world was routinely illustrated as tropical, filled with lakes and swamps.

Bakker concluded that the Brontosaurus's feet were unsuited for walking in moist earth. Instead of being a spreading foot to provide support on muck, the foot was firmly cushioned and was more suitable for walking in arid surroundings. Bakker looked for evidence to support his view in the area of the Dinosaur National Monument, which is in Utah and Colorado. He did an environmental survey of the Jurassic period, a time when the dinosaurs prospered. He also spent time with other researchers at the late-Jurassic dinosaur beds in Como Bluff, Wyoming.

In both places, there is an abundance of limestone nodules, called caliches, which are consistent with a monsoonal climate, that is, one where intense rain is followed by long drought. The Jurassic vegetation was an open-canopy forest. There was no evidence of a jungle or a rain forest. Bakker concluded that the dinosaur's habitat was not swampy.

How Did Dinosaurs Raise Their Young?

On the basis of the Brontosaurus's spacious birth canal, which is larger in relation to its body size than that of any

A helicopter lifts out dinosaur skeletons from a site in the Dinosaur Provincial Park in Alberta, Canada.

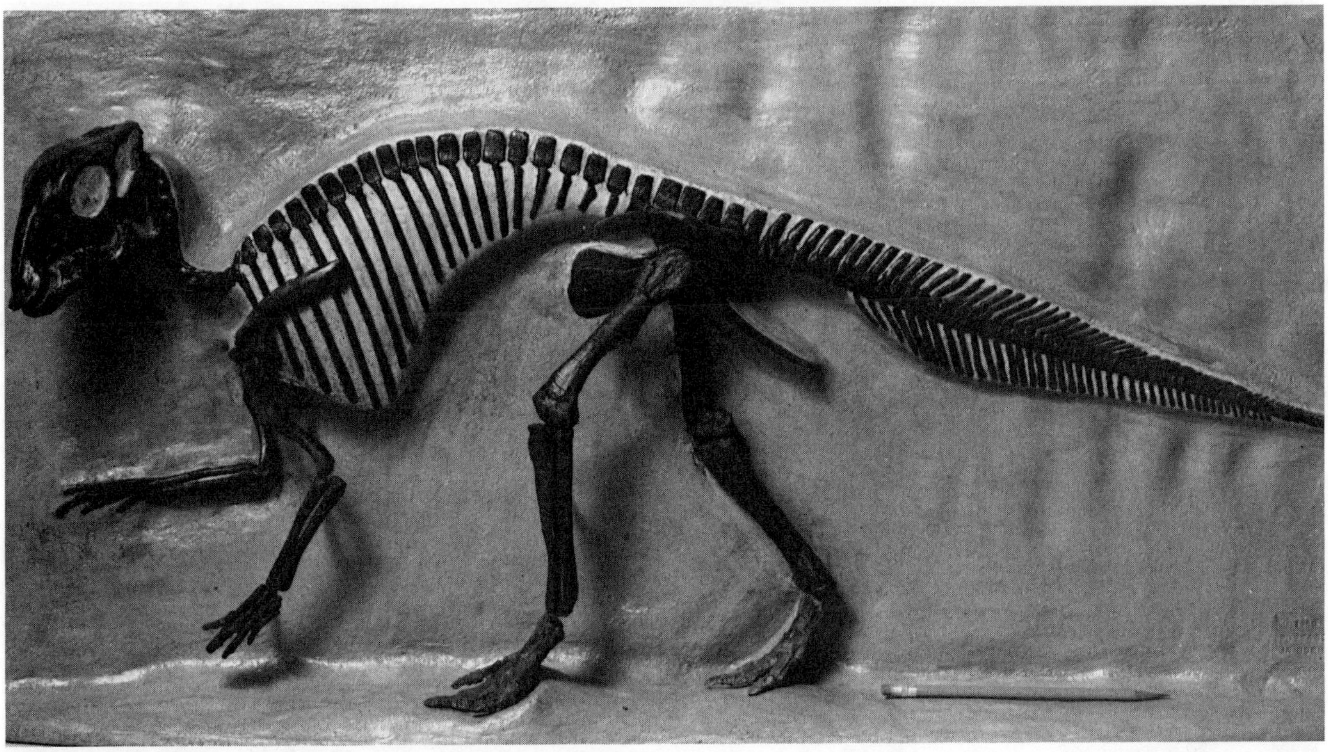

Reconstructed skeleton of the first baby dinosaur ever found in a nest. This skeleton was found with six other individuals and eggshell fragments. The species is Maiasaura peeblesorum.

other dinosaur, Bakker believes that the Brontosaurus gave birth to live young. In support of his conjecture, there have been no confirmed discoveries of Brontosaurus eggs.

Horner finds reasonable Bakker's theory of live Brontosaurus birth. He points out that for an animal destined to be enormous, it helps to be born bigger than would be possible from an egg. The bones of a young Brontosaurus are about one-fourth the size of an adult female, which is larger than would be expected if the young were hatched from eggs.

Bakker believes that sauropods (herbivores with a long neck, a small head, and five toes) were gregarious, herding together in the manner of African elephants, musk ox, and caribou. Phil Currie, assistant director of collections and research programs at the Tyrrell Museum of Paleontology in the Dinosaur Provincial Park in Alberta, Canada, thinks that ceratopsians (horned dinosaurs) and hadrosaurs (often called duckbills) spent part of the year herded together in small groups for mutual protection from predators. At some point during the year, Currie believes, the small groups joined together in a long march in search of food. From northern Canada, they may have migrated to the Arctic, where there would have been especially rich plant and animal life.

To test this theory, researchers are looking in the Arctic for herds similar to those found in the Dinosaur Provincial Park. An abundance of dinosaur bones was discovered on Alaska's northern slopes in 1986, suggesting that Currie's hypothesis may be valid. In February of 1987, Currie announced the discovery of a partial skull of a Troodon, a carnivorous dinosaur that lived 73 million years ago. Currie described the discovery as having delicate bone structures remarkably similar to those found in modern birds.

In June 1987, a twelfth-grade amateur paleontologist, Wendy Sloboda, reported to a University of Calgary scientist that she had found fossilized eggshell fragments. She led Currie and his team to the best site ever discovered of preserved duckbill dinosaur eggs—some with intact embryos. The setting, which the Tyrell Museum refers to as the Devil's Coulee Egg Site, is located near Raymond, Alberta, Canada.

The nesting sites Horner found in 1978 prompted him to propose a new theory of dinosaur parental behavior. He believes that the hadrosaurs, rather than depositing eggs in a sandy bank and leaving them as turtles do, dug nests and covered them with vegetation. As many shore birds do today, the hadrosaurs may have located their nests in a dry area, where there would have been fewer predators to disturb them. The nest's vegetation would have served as an incubator for the eggs, and once the eggs were hatched, the parents could have carried food to the young, perhaps regurgitating the food for their offspring, as many birds do.

An unusually well preserved skull of a Triceratops, found by Museum of the Rockies staff on the C. M. Russell Wildlife Refuge in Eastern Montana. "MORT" stands for Museum of the Rockies Triceratops.

Evidence that the dinosaur babies remained in their nests after hatching comes from the remains of broken eggshells found in the nests, because modern bird hatchlings who remain in the nest crush the shells in the same way as the dinosaur eggshells were broken. In fact, one of the reasons dinosaurs survived for so long, in Horner's view, is that they nurtured their young.

Why Did the Dinosaurs Become Extinct?

Dinosaurs dominated the planet for 140 million years. The dinosaurs' ability to survive over such a long period was probably due to their adaptability to environmental pressures. When seas moved in and destroyed animals and habitats, versatile species moved into the mountains, where they lived in small groups and perhaps even evolved into new species. When the seas withdrew, the dinosaurs moved back out onto coastal plains.

However, despite their nurture of their young and their adaptability, the dinosaurs did disappear from the Earth. There are several theories to explain what wiped out the dinosaurs, along with three-quarters of the species living on Earth 65 million years ago.

The most popular theory is one by Walter Alvarez, an astronomer at the University of California at Berkeley, who proposes that an asteroid crashed into the Earth at the end of the Cretaceous period, often referred to as the Cretaceous-Tertiary (K-T) boundary. The force of the impact, in Alvarez's view, threw into the atmosphere a blanket of dust, which circled the planet, blocking out the sunlight and causing famine and death.

The element iridium inspired Alvarez's impact theory. Although iridium is found only in small amounts on the Earth's surface, it is abundant in meteorites. Alvarez and other researchers found high iridium levels at the K-T boundary.

Another contending theory, held by Vincent Courtillot and Stanley Cosowski of the University of California at Santa Barbara and Charles Officer of Dartmouth College, suggests that a series of volcanic eruptions affected the Earth's environment and led to the dinosaurs' extinction.

Evidence to support the volcano theory comes from India's Deccan Traps, vast lava flows covering an area about the size of France. The researchers believe the Deccan Traps were the largest volcanic disturbance during the last 200 million years, consisting of about 100 flows over a 500,000-year period. Proponents suggest that the Deccan eruptions caused the K-T extinctions by spewing sulfur and other volcanic substances into the atmosphere, darkening the sky, cooling the earth, and creating acid rain.

However, Alvarez has expressed doubt that quiet, nonexplosive eruptions such as the Deccan Traps (similar to the Kilauea eruptions in Hawaii) could spew material high enough to contaminate the Earth's atmosphere. Other researchers argue whether the Deccan flood basalts could have released much sulfur and also been able to flow over such great distances.

However, Courtillot counters that his argument is strengthened by the existence of the North Atlantic Tertiary Igneous Province, an enormous plateau of basalts along the coasts of Greenland and Scotland. They are thought to have erupted at about the same time as the Deccan Traps.

Jack Horner, Phil Currie, and Robert Bakker have a different perspective. They believe the extinctions were not immediate, as has been assumed, but actually took place over millions of years. Currie points to a dwindling of species in the late Cretaceous period. There were 35 known species of dinosaurs 73 million years ago. By 68 million years, they had been reduced to 20 to 25 species, and by 64 million years ago, there were only 6 known species left. Fossil evidence from a study near Braggs, Alabama, found that only 36 percent of the site's 83 species disappeared at the K-T boundary. Similarly, only 3 of 19 turtle species in Montana disappeared at the K-T boundary. Such evidence lends credence to the idea of a gradual, or "stepwise" extinction.

Bakker believes that the dinosaurs did not suffer a mass extinction but were destroyed by illness. An absence of environmental pressures and a lack of diversification of species, in Bakker's opinion, rendered the dinosaurs vulnerable to disease. The immigrant Triceratops, which by the end of the Cretaceous period had spread to all the world's continents, may have brought parasites and disease into the dinosaurs' midst.

Whatever caused the extinction of the dinosaurs, arguably the most successful form of life ever to inhabit the Earth, one thing remains clear: Scientists will be disputing for a long time to come over how the dinosaurs died out—as well as how they lived.

VOLUNTEER SCIENCE
A Working Vacation

Thousands of volunteers pay up to $3,000 to spend their vacations working on a scientific expedition. The work site might be just up the road, or it might be on the other side of the world. The volunteers tend to be well educated and financially comfortable. Their ages range from 16 to 85, with occasional opportunities for some who are even younger. Joanne Edgar, founder and senior editor of *Ms.* magazine, spent her summer vacation mapping and measuring a peat bog in Ireland.

Much of science is dependent on the accumulation of discrete bits of information. The accumulation is likely to require either a few workers for a long time or many workers for a short time. But funding for research is often unavailable, so significant data goes uncollected.

Funding is not the sole impediment for some important scientific tasks that are left undone. On occasion, the nature of the project involves a task that must be done quickly due to seasonal constraints, or because the source of the data is threatened with extinction. These, along with the cost savings, are the conditions that make the services of volunteers useful to scientists.

The volunteer's reward for participation in an expedition is the opportunity to "try on" the workday of an unknown profession, to gain additional knowledge, and to spend time and money on a vacation that has a more meaningful result than an extra layer of tan.

How Volunteers and Scientists Find One Another

There are several routes by which volunteers can become linked with scientists. Earthwatch, the largest nonprofit organization to make the matchings, does substantial advertising. In 1987, they sent out 2,000 volunteers to join 422 research teams.

The next largest organization, University Research Expeditions Program (UREP), sends out only about one-tenth as many volunteers as Earthwatch. They recruit volunteers from around the country for projects conducted under the University of California system.

A wide variety of expedition opportunities are described in the annual *Archaeological Fieldwork Opportunities Bulletin*, published by the Archaeological Institute of America (AIA). The opportunities reported by the AIA are supplied by related organizations such as the American Schools of Oriental Research, Earthwatch, the UREP, the U.S. Army Corp of Engineers, the National Forest Service, local and state historical and/or archeological societies, municipal historic offices, and many universities.

The amount of time provided by the volunteer varies from one organization to another and according to the nature of the particular expedition. The volunteer's commitment of time for AIA excavations may be as little as 2 days or as much as a whole summer. The Foundation for Field Research offers several week-long excavations. Earthwatch volunteers generally sign on for 2 weeks. Although an Earthwatch expedition may last for many months, the work is performed by successive sets of 2-week volunteers.

Many projects accept both volunteers and students for field school as a prelude to, or as an ongoing part of, the project. A substantial number offer college tuition credits. Some fieldwork is entirely training.

The Over-arching Purpose

Many expeditions pursue "pure science" with no obvious immediate application. They are intended to gather knowledge. Other expeditions have results destined for almost immediate application on a broad scale.

In March of 1987, Earthwatch held a Principal Investigator's Conference to bring together scientists with staff, members, and press representatives. The theme of the conference was field research as a tool in solving global problems.

For some scientists, setting their work into a global context was an awkward task. Black-bear specialist Roger Powell said, "Only about 10 percent of research leads to direct, applicable results that have broad implications for the general public. The key is that nobody can predict that 10 percent ahead of time."

The AIA's unassuming purpose is to bring "student and amateur to actual excavation." The mission of Earthwatch is more complex. They aspire to achieve "a company of scholars and citizens working together."

Earthwatch solicits proposals from scholars whose fieldwork could appropriately use volunteer teams. Before approval, the proposals are reviewed by an affiliate, the Center for Field Research, an independent academic body that manages the peer review and screening and the final selection of an average of 350 proposals each year.

A Sample of 1987 Expeditions and Their Goals

One intriguing, though rather expensive, 1987 excavation reported by The AIA was sponsored by Harvard University Summer School. Fifteen summer field-school students, who had to be at least juniors in high school, were scheduled to "excavate part of the 17th and 18th century Harvard College complex buried in Harvard Yard." The focus of the study was the economic, social, and ideological aspects of student life at the earliest college in North America.

An example of a 1987 project in which the data gathered could have an almost immediate impact upon public health policy was a program to study infant diarrhea in Peru. The

Anthropologist Dr. Michael Crawford has made a career of searching out the small subdivision among people that affect genetic variation. In the summer of 1987 Crawford took volunteers to Hungary to measure the demographic and genetic effects of geographic isolation and religion on 17 villages on the Tisza River.

Volunteers floating over the Panamint Valley of southeastern California can see pictures, traced on stone, too large to see from ground level—giant birds, snakes, and complex geometrical patterns. These huge stone tracings are called geoglyphs.

program was led by a Peruvian physician and anthropologist, Hernan Zegarra.

Zegarra's interest focused on the estimated 5 million young children in developing nations, 1 every 6 seconds, who die from diarrhea each year.

Within a few days of the onset of diarrhea, a baby's body weight can drop by 15 percent. Given such a severe fluid loss, death follows quickly. Among Third World nations, the aggregate of potentially lethal episodes among children under 5 amounts to a billion cases each year.

A simple but underused remedy, oral rehydration therapy (ORT), is available to reverse the dehydration. A combination of sugar, salt, and water administered by mouth accelerates the body's rate of absorption of salt and water by 2,500 percent.

In 1987, in the third year of Zegarra's project, he proposed to target 100 families in two communities within 35 squatter settlements around Lima to determine the prevalence and favored treatment of common diarrheal infections. The findings from Zegarra's research promised public health officials an opportunity to shape their prevention and education policies effectively, not just in Peru, but in other developing nations as well.

An Earthwatch 1987 project with a less direct application was a study of Hungarian marriage in 17 villages that were isolated in 1945 by the demarcation of a new border between Hungary and the Soviet Union. Cut off by the new border from communities absorbed into the USSR, the villages were also separated from Hungary by a bend in the Tisza River.

The project's task was to look at the impact of isolation on the demography and genetics of the villages. Each volunteer was paired with a Hungarian scholar to interview families and to transcribe church and municipal records.

Fall 1987 found some of the more adventurous among Earthwatch volunteers gazing down from balloons over the Panamint Valley in southeastern California. The valley's prehistoric people who lived there 10,000 years ago adapted to a transformation from marshy lake to barren desert. The question under exploration by the expedition

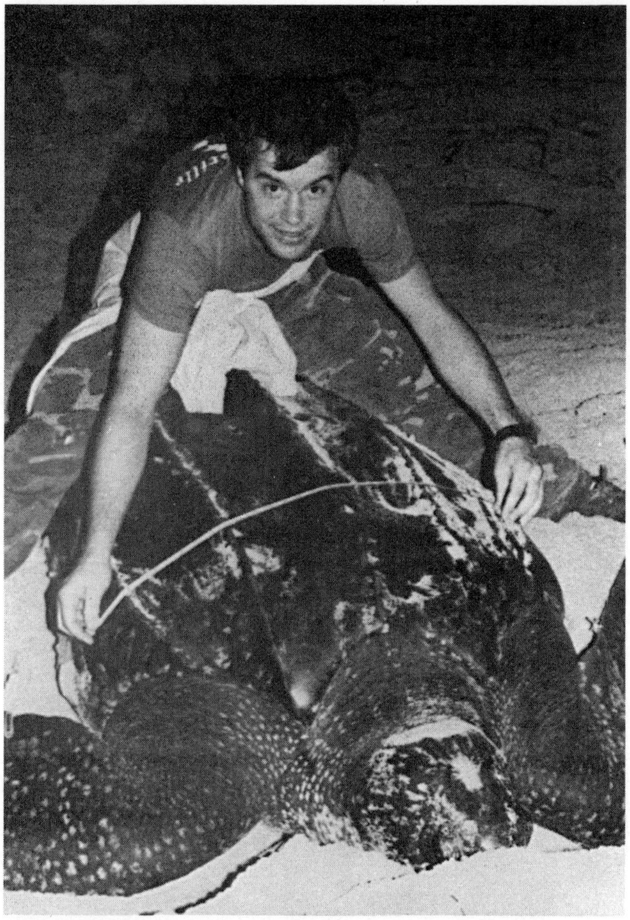

Earthwatch volunteer Jeff Trelegan measures a leatherback turtle coming to shore to lay her eggs. In September of 1987 Earthwatch was cited by the U.S. Dept. of the Interior for its efforts to preserve leatherback eggs and hatchlings.

was why the valley's foragers spent long hours building gigantic stone alignments (geoglyphs) recognizable from the air as birds, snakes, and geometric designs.

For Earthwatch volunteers who preferred their adventure beneath the water instead of up in the air, the summer of 1987 found them—provided they were open-water certified divers—in Bermuda, mapping harbor-seabed conditions and locating the remains of wrecks.

Financial Support for Volunteer Science

In private funding for field research, Earthwatch is among the top three sources, along with the National Geographic Society and the World Wildlife Fund. In 1986 the World Wildlife Fund's average grant was $25,000, Earthwatch's average grant was $20,000, and the National Geographic's average grant was $15,000.

About 51 percent of Earthwatch's volunteer contributions go directly to the field to pay for equipment, on-site transportation, and volunteers' food and lodging. Another 13 percent finances planning and evaluation. The rest covers the cost of recruiting volunteers, developing new expeditions, and running a central office and four field offices in the United States and Australia.

For some researchers, private funding means the difference between doing or not doing a project.

Many researchers consider volunteer funding a supplement to government grants and a source of nonspecialists who can be quickly trained to do specific tasks. Some researchers who do not really need additional funds participate because they believe the volunteers who join them are committed, interested, and hardworking.

Volunteer Living and Working Conditions

A perfect match between the project and the volunteer does not always happen. This is the area of strongest complaints from scientists. The volunteers tend to self-select the expeditions they want to join. Earthwatch staff brief them beforehand about all the negatives involved in their choice—snakes, or heat, or primitive living conditions—but many romanticize the discomforts until they arrive at the site. Some of the principal investigators stave off complaints by providing comfortable accommodations.

However, accommodations do vary widely. Volunteers in Pisgah Bear Sanctuary might sleep in group tents. In Italy, to study wolves and feral dogs, they might sleep in a rented house. In Alaska, to study musk ox, they might sleep in a newly built cabin. In Norway, to study moving glaciers, they might live in three-person tents and have an hour's walk for a hot shower and fresh food. In Israel, to study medicinal plants, they might sleep in a Bedouin household. In Wales, to study how archeological records are created, they might stay in a Welsh cottage. In France, to study the origins of urban Europe, they might camp in an orchard. In Africa, to study early humans, they might live in a bush camp equipped with trailers.

The tasks volunteers may do in the field are as varied as the locales and the living arrangements. At a Roman outpost in Yugoslavia, they might dig with trowels, plot and fine-clean artifiacts, bones, and frescoes, and map features. For a study of climate change in Hudson Bay, they might core trees, collect ancient pollen from peat samples, and look for evidence of forest fires in forest-encrusted dunes. For a study of Dusky dolphins in New Zealand, they might radio-tag some animals, take photographs for identification, and correlate dolphin distribution and behavior with food availability. For a study of China's wildlife, they might spend daytimes turning over logs and rocks looking for reptiles and amphibians, with nights spent collecting insects around a light, and they might scoop swamp water to measure salt and sulfur concentrations. For an effort to restore the *Edwin Fox*, an eighteenth-century merchant ship lying off Picton, western New Zealand, they might scramble over wet timbers to measure, photograph, and produce sketches to be fed into a computer.

Sometimes getting to the site presents more difficulty than any conditions after arrival. For a monkey study a few years ago, volunteers had to fly into a jungle village, travel 3 hours by canoe along a river, hike over a mountain, take a second canoe trip, and finish with another hike through the rain forest.

A New York tax attorney on his 1987 vacation traveled 40 hours in 5 buses and 4 planes to connect with his team in Zimbabwe. Five hours after his arrival, the team piled into Land Rovers for a 10-hour journey over gravel and dirt roads.

Participants Keep Coming Back

Whatever the living conditions, whatever the tasks they are asked to perform, and whatever the travel difficulties may be, most volunteers enjoy their experience. Repeaters make up about 30 percent of Earthwatch's annual volunteers and about 23 percent of the UREP's recruits. One veteran volunteer, by 1987, had been on 22 Earthwatch expeditions.

One of the attractions of the adventure appears to be the close relationships developed among the participants. A small group of individuals with varied backgrounds come together under sometimes rugged living and/or working conditions where they mutually solve problems. Social and emotional bonds are formed.

The *Wall Street Journal* called the group experience "potluck social chemistry." From a 5 year, ongoing effort to save endangered leatherback turtle eggs on St. Croix, the *Journal* described a typical incident on a beach in the middle of the night. While the turtle laid her eggs over a sandy hole, the eggs were caught before they touched ground by a Boston biophysicist, handed off to an airline attendant, and buried in a safer location by a Maplewood, New Jersey high school student.

Many Earthwatch veteran volunteers do more than just have their vacation adventure. During the rest of the year, they continue to benefit from two principal goals of Earthwatch: to introduce the public to the processes and findings of science, and to convince people that the pursuit of knowledge is self-fulfilling.

The volunteers involve the public by setting up programs at zoos, museums, libraries, and schools. And they mobilize foundation and corporate support to encourage minority teachers and students to train for careers in science. Lecture series are often arranged where principal investigators, sometimes joined by volunteer team members newly back from an expedition, present preliminary findings.

Volunteer science is not limited to the affluent. Some of the expeditions that appear in the AIA bulletin offer scholarships. Some even pay modest wages, particularly for those who have had prior experience or training. Several offer the opportunity of employment after initial participation as a volunteer or as a student. Many cost under $500 for room, board, and transportation from a central meeting point to the site.

Aside from the expense of transportation, compared with a typical vacation, the cost of participation in an Earthwatch expedition—which includes room and board—can be modest. The cost of hotels and restaurants in some exotic locations where the expeditions take place are apt to be expensive.

Volunteer science is not new. It has a venerable history. An example of an earlier project took place in Great Britain in 1928 when, with no external funding, ornithologist Max Nicholson organized the first nationwide survey of a bird population. Nicholson enlisted 500 volunteers to survey the nation's population of grey heron. Nicholson found the volunteer response quick, well done, and efficient. That effort eventually led to the British Trust for Ornithology.

No one involved in the volunteer science effort believes that scientists are created from a few weeks of experience. What they do believe is that an ever-increasing pool of citizens becomes scientifically literate.

8

Weather and Climate

WIND

A Boon, but Sometimes a Threat, to Life

At any given moment, the earth is wrapped in 5,600 million tons of air. When this air is in motion it is called wind. The Earth's gravity keeps the air from flaoting away, and no new air comes in from space. Thus, wind and weather take place in a closed system.

The physical conditions of land and water that create global winds also cause local variations in wind. As a part of Dennis Connor's strategy to win back the America's Cup in Australia, he chose to practice in Hawaii, where local winds and water conditions were close to those he would face in Perth during the Cup races. Although wind patterns may be similar in different parts of the world, they are rarely identical. Even the wind in a backyard with a tree, or at the bottom or top of a hill, can be quite different than the wind in a neighboring yard. These slight differences in wind can mean the difference between winning and losing a sailing competition. Although Connor was successful in his bid, there was an element of risk in his strategy that could have cost him the trophy. As it turned out, the steady 18- to 25-knot winds of Hawaii did not provide Connor with a true estimate of the speed of his boat, *Stars and Stripes*. During the initial races in Australia, where light winds blew at under 22 knots, *Stars and Stripes* was painfully slow.

Global air is set in motion by the Sun's uneven warming of the Earth. The envelope of air around the Earth, as well as the Earth's land and sea, absorb energy from the Sun, but the equator receives more heat than do the poles. The incoming rays at the equator are more nearly perpendicular to the Earth's surface and are able to penetrate the atmosphere more easily. This uneven distribution of the Sun's energy is the major cause of wind and weather.

Despite the equator's additional absorption of heat, the equator does not become increasingly hotter each year, nor do the poles become increasingly colder. This is because the movement of wind around the planet regulates the heat of the Earth and makes it inhabitable. Without the wind, moisture would be confined to the oceans, and all but the edges of the continents would be deserts. Without wind, life on Earth would be impossible.

Air that moves vertically is called a current. Air that flows horizontally, whether along the Earth's surface or high above it, is called a wind. A large body of air is often called an air mass. An air mass, contoured like a plump cookie, may be hundreds, or even thousands of miles across. Throughout the air mass, the temperature and moisture are about the same. During its formation, the air mass

America's Cup winner Stars and Stripes.

takes its temperature and moisture from the surface beneath it.

The Atmosphere's Layers

Air is at its most dense at the surface of the Earth. Moving upward from the Earth's surface, the pressure at each level of air must be just enough to support the weight of the column of air above it. Air at higher altitudes is under less compression from air stacked above it, and thus is more loosely packed. The thinner air at higher altitudes has fewer molecules. These molecules collide less often, and the air is cooler and lighter.

The temperature of air grows colder by about 1.8 degrees Farenheit for every 500 feet, up to the "ceiling." The ceiling over the poles lies at about 25,000 feet, where the temperature remains at about −76 degrees Farenheit. The ceiling over the equator lies at about 15 kilometers, where the temperature is usually lower because of its greater altitude.

Everything below the ceiling is known as the troposphere, from a Greek word meaning "to turn." Within the troposphere, 75 percent of the Earth's mass of air and virtually all the water vapor and weather are confined.

Above the ceiling begins a second zone, which continues up to an altitude of over 31 miles. This zone is called the stratosphere, from the Latin *stratos*, meaning "something flat in layers." The stratosphere is visibly layered. The stratosphere's density, the packing together of its molecules, is one-thousandth that of air at sea level. Scattered within the stratosphere are stable molecules of oxygen, which, under the influence of radiation from the Sun, have converted to unstable molecules called ozone.

The layer of ozone comes closest to the ground over the poles and rises to its maximum height over the equator. Without the ozone layer to filter out damaging ultraviolet radiation from the Sun, life on Earth may never have evolved.

Air and Weather

Air that has risen and become cool contracts. The molecules draw closer together, making the cool air heavier. Cool air sinks back toward Earth, filling in the areas where warm air has departed. Heavy, cool air pushes down on the Earth. Cool air generally means the air pressure is high. Warm, light air moving away from the Earth's surface generally means the air pressure is low. Another way to describe this phenomenon would be to say: Low-pressure areas are regions of less dense air on the rise, and high-pressure areas are regions of denser air that is falling. (Nevertheless, cold areas do not always have high pressure, nor do warm areas always have low pressure.) Air flows out from areas where pressure is high toward areas where pressure is low. High-pressure areas normally bring fair weather and light winds. Low-pressure areas generally bring bad weather and strong winds.

Of the waves of energy that leave the Sun, some eventually reach the Earth's surface and are absorbed. The Earth, in time, radiates this energy back into the atmosphere. It does so in long wavelengths, in contrast to the short wavelengths of the Sun with which the energy arrived.

These long wavelengths of energy being reradiated by the Earth are intercepted by molecules of water in the air. (On the incoming trip from the Sun, the shorter solar wavelengths bypass the widely spaced water molecules.) In effect, the water molecules act as a one-way valve by allowing radiation to flow freely downward from the Sun but allowing its escape back into space only gradually. This process, known as the "greenhouse effect," decreases the heat loss of the Earth to one-seventh of the loss that would occur in the absence of moisture.

When a body of water is in motion, some of its molecules escape into the air from the surface. Other molecules of vapor reenter the liquid. As temperatures rise, more molecules escape from the water than enter it. Whenever the Sun's energy is absorbed by water, evaporation takes place. When the temperature falls, the molecules come together rapidly, and their energy is released into the surrounding air. Water vapor thus stores energy, which is returned to the atmosphere when the water vapor condenses back to a liquid.

Warm air can hold more water in vapor form, because the rapidly moving molecules are less likely to clump together to a degree that would allow condensation to take place. The resistance of surrounding air molecules keeps minuscule droplets aloft in the form of clouds. The water vapor droplets that form a cloud are too small to fall as rain. They hold only about a millionth as much water as an ordinary raindrop. In turbulent air, bigger droplets collide with and collect smaller ones, and when a droplet grows to about 1/125 of an inch in diameter, it can fall out of the cloud.

Wind blowing down from the North Pole bends to the west as the earth rotates from west to east in the same way the pen line tilts to the right as the orange is rotated from the viewer's left to right.

Where ground temperatures are high, as in the tropics, the blanket of air above the ground warms quickly. Warm air expands, rises, cools, condenses, sloughs off moisture, and rises again, forming a thunderstorm that can drive energy high into the troposphere. Water vapor and warmth swarm upward until they collide with the troposphere ceiling.

From thousands of these heat towers, tremendous quantities of heat are released back into the atmosphere each day. The heat is distributed over the globe by the circulation of wind.

The Hadley Cell

For centuries, models have been put forth to explain the Earth's air movements. Present models are derived from a concept proposed in the 1730s by an Englishman named George Hadley. The concept is called the Hadley cell.

Hadley proposed a convective, circular model. He suggested that as the Sun heated the Earth's air, the air became lighter and rose. If the Earth did not rotate on its axis, Hadley suggested, each hemisphere would have only one large cell of air circulation. In other words, air in the vicinity of the equator would rise and move toward the North Pole in the Northern Hemisphere; and air in the

Southern Hemisphere would rise and move toward the South Pole. Cool air would descend and flow from both poles along the Earth's surface back toward the equator.

The Earth's winds do begin their journeys in accordance with Hadley's explanation. However, their route is diverted by the effect of the Earth's rotation and tilt.

A simple experiment to demonstrate the effect of the Earth's rotation and tilt upon wind can be done with an orange and a ballpoint pen. Holding the orange with its navel, representing the North Pole pointed upward, draw the pen straight down toward the equator while the orange is rotated from left to right. The drawn line veers away to the southwest. A similar line drawn from the orange's South Pole veers toward the northwest. This veering is called the Coriolis effect, named for the French physicist who first explained the phenomenon. The Coriolis effect deflects any moving body, whether it is a bullet being shot from a gun or a wind making its way around the world.

According to Hadley's model, warm ground temperatures in the tropics cause the blanket of air there to heat up quickly. When the rising air hits the troposphere ceiling, it turns and flows toward the poles. As a general rule, warm air traveling toward the poles flows over cooler surfaces and becomes bottom heavy and increasingly stable, unless rain is triggered when the air is forced up by higher land. As cold air moves away from the poles over warmer land or sea, it becomes turbulent and unstable, with squalls interspersed with fair periods.

The Three-Zone Model

Hadley's concept formed the basis of the "three-zone model." The first cell of the three-zone model is the wind in the tropics.

The upward flow of air from each side of the equator aimed in the direction of the poles loses its heat in the upper troposphere long before reaching the poles. The warm air is cooled so rapidly that it sinks back to the Earth at approximately 30 degrees north or south latitude, where the air flows along the surface back to the equator.

The cooled, sinking air is deflected by the Coriolis effect. In the Northern Hemisphere the wind flows from the northeast to the southwest. In the Southern Hemisphere, the air moves from the southeast to the northwest.

The winds at approximately 30 degrees North and 30 degrees South Latitude create large, relatively permanent circulations of air over the major oceans known as the trade winds (because merchant sailing ships used to take advantage of them) or the easterlies.

The second cell of the three-zone model is found between latitudes 30 degrees (high pressure) and 60 degrees (low pressure) in both the Northern and Southern Hemispheres. In these zones, surface winds travel toward the poles, then rise upward from the surface of the earth. Again the Coriolis effect deflects the winds toward the northeast in the Northern Hemisphere and toward the southeast in the Southern Hemisphere. These are the westerlies that push the mid-latitude weather systems in both hemispheres. Air temperature and pressure change more rapidly in the zone of the westerlies than in that of the easterlies.

Winds that blow from the same direction most of the time are referred to as prevailing winds. The United States is in the path of the prevailing westerlies. Thus weather in the United States, carried on the westerlies, usually travels from west to east. In the Southern Hemisphere, the prevailing westerlies, unhampered by land, blow over immense stretches of water, creating winds so fierce that sailors call them "the roaring forties."

A mobile band lies in the zone between the trade winds and the westerlies. This is where equatorial air sinks, becomes compressed as it sinks, and gains heat from the compression. These are regions of high pressure called subtropical highs. At sea, this fair-weather zone is known as the horse latitudes. The horse latitudes were named by sailors, perhaps because when becalmed in this relatively windless region, the mariners would be forced to throw their horses overboard to preserve the ships' supply of drinking water.

Above the ocean in this region, the air does not gain moisture from the cooler ocean surface. Most of the world's deserts lie along this belt of dry air. From the deserts, warm air masses sometimes flow toward the poles, colliding with advancing colder fronts and giving rise to an endless series of high- and low-pressure systems. These turbulences are carried around the planet by the westerly flow of the mid-latitudes.

Another factor in the movement of the Earth's air is "the equator of the winds." In contrast to the neat line drawn on maps and globes representing the equator, there is a moving band of air around the Earth's bulging middle that drifts north and south, and bends around continents and seas. This area, technically known as "an intertropical convergence zone," is known to sailors as the "doldrums," taken from the English word meaning dull. The doldrums are an area of low and uniform pressures where calms can leave sailing ships stranded.

The width and precise position of the doldrums are not constant. Seasoned ship's captains dependent on wind for their sails learned to predict when and where trade winds of each hemisphere might dip toward one another. Poised to catch each stray breeze, the captains would maneuver their ships across the equator. Less-experienced skippers might be left behind for as long as 4 weeks with limp sails.

Even at the equator, the land and the ocean areas absorb and radiate heat at different rates. Land and water heat and cool at different rates. The upper layers of the oceans are often vigorously stirred by waves, distributing heat gains and losses through various layers. On land, heat penetrates into the soil only to a shallow depth, and there is no mixing as there is with water.

As a consequence of the ocean-stirring process, marked temperature differences at the surface of the ocean—day to night, and summer to winter—are reduced. By contrast, the soil of the land warmed during the day cools quickly at night. The air above the soil is warmed and cooled equally rapidly. Thus the variation in temperature and wind is much greater over land than it is over ocean.

A typical interaction between land and water happens along coastal regions. The temperature of the land, under clear daytime skies, will rise. The temperature of the water will remain relatively constant. The land gains heat, warms the air above it, and the air rises. The cooler air above the ocean moves to take the place of the rising warm air over the land, producing a cool onshore breeze. At night the process is reversed.

Malevolent Local Winds

The winds and weather of some areas are much more predictable than are those of other areas. Local geography, vegetation, and climatic extremes can create marked differences. Even in areas not far from one another, one may have conditions that give rise to a characteristic local wind.

Many areas have benevolent winds as does Hawaii. There are benign winds such as the Feh, which cools Shanghai evenings. There is the Zephyr, a gentle west wind that blows on the West Coast of the United States and in Rome. In Greece, there is the Aura, the first breeze of early morning.

Many less fortunate areas, however, are plagued by malevolent winds. The existence of mountain barriers running east to west has a significant effect on the presence of malevolent winds. North America has no east-west range to

One of the more malevolent effects of the wind, a dust storm.

block the southerly flow of cold north winds. As a result, an occasional "norther" carries a wave of polar air as far south as the Gulf of Mexico, where the temperature can drop 27 degrees Farenheit in an hour.

Separate from the larger global currents of air, mountains may make their own indigenous winds. During the warmth of morning, the expanding air in deep valleys flows up the mountainsides. Cold air piles up over the valley, feeding the upward current of warm air. After the sun sets, the air cools rapidly, contracts, and with the help of gravity, tumbles back down onto the valley floor.

The upslope winds are called anabatic winds. The downslope, gravity-assisted winds are called katabatic winds. Not all the katabatic winds are kindly. An unstable wind can climb a mountain, leave moisture on the mountain's peaks or in hanging clouds, and, deprived of water content, rush down the opposite side as hot dry air in search of moisture.

Such an unwelcome wind is the *föhn* (from a Gothic word meaning fire) that pours into the valleys of Switzerland, Bavaria, and the Austrian Tyrol. The föhn sucks in air from the Mediterranean, pulls the air across France and up the southern slopes of the Alps, where it sheds its moisture on the Alpine peaks. The rise in heat is due to compression as the wind pours down into the valleys.

The föhn's dry wind in summer causes Alpine village leaves to crumble to dust. The winter föhn's dry wind siphons the snow right off the slopes. The temperature rises by 1.8 degrees centigrade for every 333 feet the wind descends. When it blows strongly, the föhn can cause terrible damage. The wind tears roofs off chalets, flattens crops, and uproots forests. Cattle stop eating, and people can become disgruntled and surly. Some hospitals in Switzerland and Bavaria postpone major surgery, if possible, during the föhn. Suicides, traffic accidents, and physical disturbances increase on the day before the föhn and continue until the wind has passed.

The desert heat of North Africa spawns the feared sirocco. Known as the "breath of the Sahara," *sirocco* in Arabic means "easterly." The wind appears most often in spring, with warm air drawn to the coast by low pressure over the Mediterranean. As a series of low-pressure systems, the wind moves eastward across the sea. The sirocco has many local names. Under any name, the wind carries a temperature more than 50 degrees Farenheit higher than the average for the season. And the wind is dry, with a relative humidity that is usually less than 30 percent, sometimes falling as low as zero.

In a study at Hebrew University in Israel, almost a third of the population tested experienced some kind of adverse physical reaction to the *sharav*, as the sirocco is known there. Almost 43 percent had an elevated concentration of serotonin in their urine. Serotonin is a powerful hormone that controls constriction of peripheral blood vessels, controls sleep, and affects mood. Another 44 percent had little or no adrenaline in their urine, and complained of fatigue, apathy, and depression. At least part of the ill effects of the sirocco winds must be due to the dust they carry. Eyes become swollen, lips are parched, inhalation of sand leads to chest pain. Collectively the siroccos are sometimes called *simoom*, which means "poison wind."

Wind carrying dust occurs as storms that come in three possible forms. The first is the wall. Preceded by an abnormal calm, the horizon is then blocked by a yellow mass that looms larger and larger as it approaches until it blots out the Sun. The category of wall dust storms includes the "black rollers" found in the western United States. One of the most unpleasant walls is the "karaburan," the black blizzard of the Gobi Desert.

The second form of dust storm, common in hot areas, is the "column," a whirling structure caused by conflict between two currents of air. In California, the columns are known as "sand augurs." In India, they are called "dust devils."

The third form of dust storm is the dust sheet, an all-enveloping haze of fine sand that covers everything. The dust sheet is a part of longer-lived weather conditions. In Iran, the "bad-i-sad-o-bist-roz," the wind of 120 days, blows from June to September.

One of the most famous malevolent local winds is the *mistral*, a strong, dry, cold wind that funnels through the valley of the Rhône between the Alps and Cevennes to wreak vengeance upon the French Riviera and the Gulf of Lyons. The howling wind, which has been clocked at 93 miles per hour, has been known to blow children into canals, overturn freight cars, and strip the clothes off those in its wake. The Provençal towns mount some defense against the mistral by laying out their streets at right angles to the wind and by building doors and windows only on the southeast side of buildings.

Microbursts

Not all malevolent winds cut the wide swath created by föhns and mistrals and their counterparts. Within all recognized climatic zones, there are more localized winds that can be just as dangerous. From a few one hundredths of an inch above the ground up to a height of 500 feet, air is prone to turbulence. Eddies produced by wind moving across rough surfaces sprawl and scatter. The faster the wind speed the more intense the turbulence. One of the most dangerous forms of localized turbulence is a microburst. They are the largest source of aircraft-related death in the United States. During a 12-year span, between 1975 and 1987, microbursts were responsible for three of the most catastrophic weather-related air accidents, resulting in 398 deaths. The sailing ship *Pride of Baltimore* is also thought to have been sunk by a microburst.

A microburst is a wind pattern that descends from rain clouds during the spring and summer months. The stream of falling air hits the ground, and the wind fans out horizontally into an outflow. The outflow resembles the pattern made by water from a kitchen faucet when it hits the bottom of the sink. The water bounces in the shape of a bowl. The outflow causes a condition described as "wind shear," a rapid change in wind speed or direction.

As an airplane enters a microburst, it runs into a head wind, that is, a wind whose direction is opposite to the plane's path of travel. The head wind increases the speed of air over the plane's wings, which gives the plane additional lift. After the plane has passed through the head wind, it travels through a down draft in the center of the microburst, where it encounters a tail wind. The tail wind, traveling in the same direction as the aircraft, robs the plane of lift. Should the microburst descend at a critical point in the take off or landing procedure, there may be no time to make the adjustments needed to keep the airplane aloft. To make matters worse, an unanticipated microburst can momentarily be mistaken for an ordinary head wind, causing the pilot to make a dangerous miscalculation.

Tetsuya Theodore Fujita of the University of Chicago is credited with being the first to discover the existence of microbursts. In doing an aerial survey of tornado damage in 1974, Fujita noticed a change in the pattern of fallen trees. Instead of the typical swirling tornado pattern, Fujita found that hundreds of trees were blown outward like spokes of a wheel. He investigated the 1975 crash of an Eastern Airlines Boeing 727 at New York's Kennedy International Airport and determined the cause to be a relatively small column of downward-rushing air. He gave it the name microburst.

In 1986, Fujita announced that microbursts were more common than had originally been assumed. And he reported that microbursts can be created even by small, harmless-looking clouds, which are so numerous that no pilot could choose to fly around all of them.

The mechanics of microbursts are not yet fully understood. The evaporation of raindrops cools an area of air. The air begins to fall as it grows heavier, thereby creating a down draft. Wet microbursts will produce a visible rain shaft, which can be hidden within a benign rain shaft. With dry microbursts from high-cloud bases, precipitation evaporates before the down draft reaches the ground, rendering the microburst invisible unless it picks up dust.

Microbursts are small, typically 0.6 to 1.9 miles across, and of short duration, generally 5 to 15 minutes. From the time the down burst hits the ground to the time the winds of the outburst have reached their highest speeds is an average of 5 to 6 minutes. In the case of wet microbursts, only 2 to 3 minutes may elapse.

In an effort to find a way to warn pilots of microbursts, scientists are using Doppler radar. Ordinary radar can see a storm but cannot track the winds within it. However, Doppler radar can reveal the direction of the winds as well as their speed by bouncing microwaves off objects that move with the wind, such as raindrops, ice particles, and even insects.

A single Doppler radar cannot measure vertical winds and thereby detect the descent of a down draft. But Doppler radar can give indirect evidence. Both above and below the cloud base, wind and rain will converge around the descending current of air. These do not prove that a microburst is forming, but they do serve as warning signals.

Scientists are developing computer programs to sift through incoming radar for signs of a microburst. John Anderson of the University of Wisconsin in Madison is working with the Massachusetts Institute of Technology's (MIT) Lincoln Laboratory in Lexington, Massachusetts, to develop computerized clouds to forecast a microburst before the down draft occurs. Forecasting the weather on a large scale has been practiced for many years. However, forecasting on the scale of a single cloud is a new idea.

Research at NASA Langley at Hampton, Virginia, is developing airborne sensor systems to enable aircraft to carry their own protection. Scientists are using a variety of approaches to learn how to predict microbursts. However, the installation of this type of equipment on airplanes is far off. Until then, microbursts will continue to wreak havoc, as do the föhns, mistrals, and other malevolent winds of the world. Although life on Earth would be impossible without wind, there are some types of wind that the world's inhabitants could well live without.

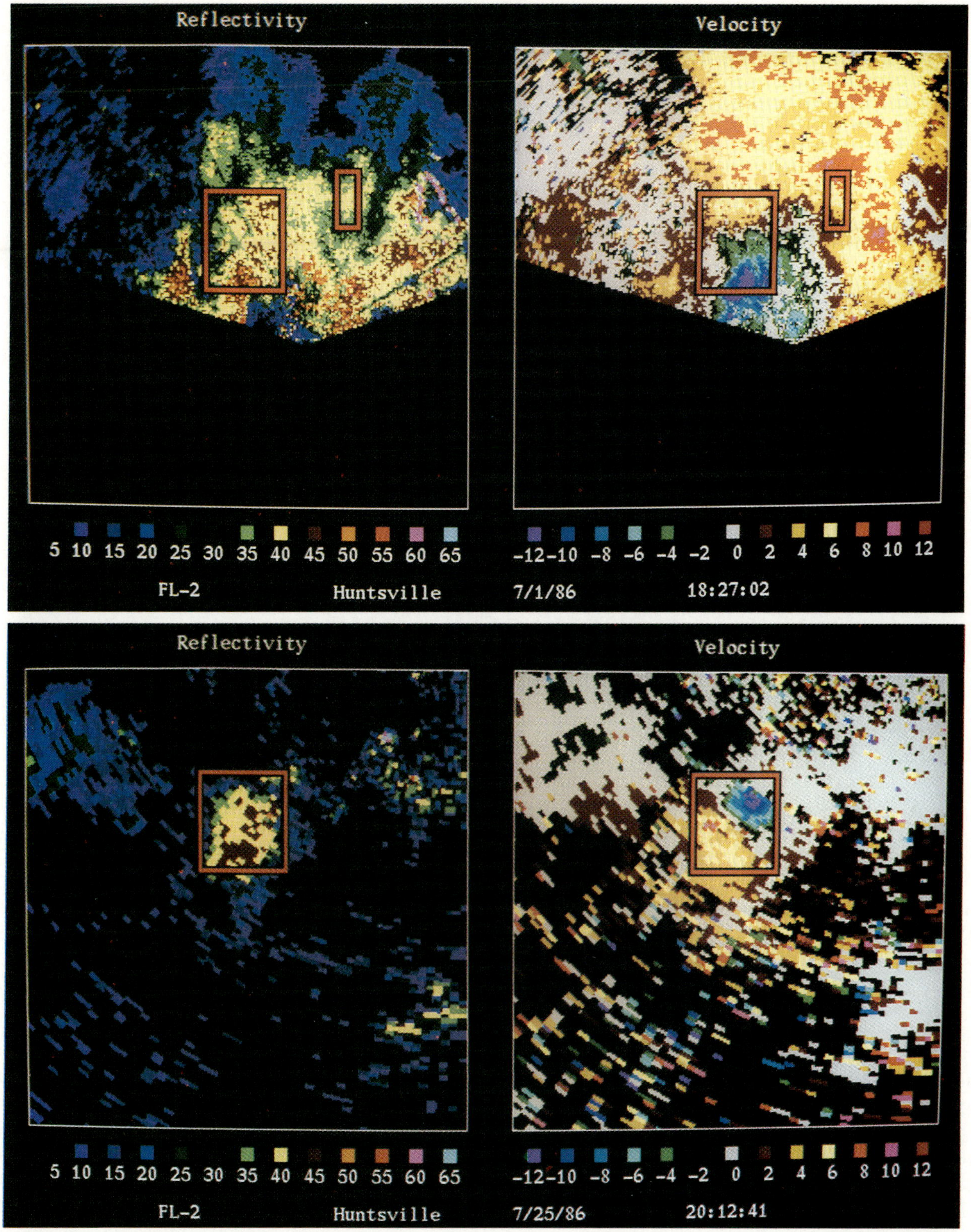

Radar images for typical microbursts. Images on the left are radar reflectivity, measured in units of dBz (30 dBz is light rain, 50 dBz is extremely heavy rain or hail). Images on the right are radial velocity, measured in units of meters per second where negative velocities indicate motion towards the radar. Each image depicts an area 26 kilometers square. The regions outlined in red are microburst algorithm alarms, where strong divergent shear has been detected. Both cases were observed with the FL2 radar, while it was located in Huntsville, Alabama.

9

The Stars and the Universe

SUPERNOVA 1987A

A Closer Look at a Collapsing Star

A Rare Opportunity

On the morning of February 24, 1987, astronomers reported sighting the nearest supernova known to scientists since Kepler's supernova in 1604. Visible to the naked eye in the Southern Hemisphere, the event could not be seen north of 20 degrees North Latitude.

The explosion was first observed at the Cerro Tololo Inter-American Observatory at La Serena, Chile. Shortly after 9 P.M. on February 23d, a University of Toronto research assistant, Ian Shelton, began making a 3-hour exposure of the Large Magellanic Cloud. (The Large Magellanic Cloud [LMC], about 170,000 light years away, and its companion, the Small Magellanic Cloud, are satellite galaxies to the Milky Way and our nearest galactic neighbors.) When Shelton developed the 3-hour exposure, he found a 5th-magnitude star within the Cloud where there had previously been none. After discarding other possible explanations, Shelton realized that the object must be a supernova.

Astronomers encounter between 20 and 25 supernovas each year, but most of them occur in distant galaxies. Although many supernovas take place in the Earth's own galaxy, the Milky Way, they are obscured by interstellar dust. Thus, the LMC supernova provides astronomers with a rare opportunity for close-up, unobstructed observation.

On the morning of February 24th, the astronomers in Chile sent a telegram to Brian Marsden at the Harvard-Smithsonian Center for Astrophysics in Cambridge, Massachusetts. Marsden is responsible for the International Astronomical Union's Central Bureau for Astronomical Telegrams, a service that keeps astronomers up to date on recent discoveries. As the first supernova seen in 1987, the phenomenon was officially named 1987A.

Robert McNaught of Siding Spring Observatory in Australia determined that the supernova was some 20 arc minutes southwest of 30 Doradus, also known as the Tarantula Nebula. (Arc degrees are units for measuring angles. A circle contains 360 arc degrees; a degree contains 60 arc minutes; a minute contains 60 arc seconds.)

Several observers placed the brightness of the supernova within a few tenths of Magnitude 4.5. (The brightest stars are of the 1st magnitude. Stars just visible to the unaided eye are of the 6th magnitude.) Many astronomers speculated about how bright the supernova would become. Most thought it would brighten to at least 1st magnitude. On May 20th it peaked at Magnitude 2.97. Subsequently it dimmed to Magnitude 3.4.

Supernova Shelton, 1987-A.

A Wealth of Data

Supernova 1987A's light curve (its brightness) did not behave as astronomers had expected. A normal pattern involves a quick rise to maximum brightness and a slow fading away into a prolonged "tail." Instead, 1987A brightened, faded, and brightened again. Neither did 1987A's brightness dominate the southern sky as a nearby supernova should have.

A supernova signals a final violent end in the life of some stars. When a star's core is no longer able to sustain the weight of the surrounding material, the core collapses, causing the star to explode. The explosion releases such energy that the supernova may outshine its entire galaxy.

At the outset, there was speculation that 1987A might be a Type I supernova. A Type I supernova is thought to originate in binary star systems (two-star systems) that contain a white dwarf (a star that has used up its store of nuclear fuel and has been compressed by gravity to about the size of the Earth). The core of the white dwarf is made up of carbon and oxygen surrounded by helium. Should the white dwarf grow by acquiring matter from its companion star, the internal pressure of the white dwarf is not great enough to bear the addition. The temperature in the core of the white dwarf rises. Carbon ignites. Nuclear fusion reactions rapidly spread outward. The star is destroyed. A supernova quickly brightens and slowly fades.

After several days of reports by astronomers in which the presence of hydrogen was observed in the star, a consensus developed that 1987A was a Type II supernova rather than a Type I. A Type II supernova occurs when a red giant star uses up its nuclear fuel. Many times the mass of our Sun, the massive star begins life—as do other stars—by converting hydrogen into helium in its core. The conversion proceeds at a rapid rate, so that within a few million years—in contrast to, say, the Sun's 10 billion years—the hydrogen is exhausted.

Devoid of hydrogen, the weight of the overlying gas raises the pressure and the temperature in the core high enough to burn helium. The rate of reaction increases as the temperature continues to rise. The process continues creating heavier elements and then using them in nuclear reactions. Carbon, then neon, oxygen, and silicon form. The helium burning may go on for half a million years, but silicon is converted into iron in only one day and the process stops. No energy can be generated by nuclear reactions in the iron core.

Without the internal energy to provide pressure to support the outer layers, the core collapses violently in less than a second. The collapse ends abruptly when the core is crushed into an ultradense mass of neutron particles. A small, dense neutron star or a black hole is all that is left—reduced to a size much smaller than a planet—more like the dimensions of a city. Shock waves rebound outward, blowing the rest of the star into space and creating a supernova.

Besides providing information about itself, the light from 1987A also provided a "flashbulb" illumination allowing scientists to examine material between the Earth and the LMC, because the light from 1987A passed through intervening clouds of gas. Depending on its composition, the intervening gas absorbed specific wavelengths of light. Thus each cloud left its own particular imprint in the spectrum of the supernova.

The brightness of the supernova when viewed with giant telescopes in the early months after the explosion concealed what was happening inside. Like nested balloons, shells of hot gas were expanding at a rate of thousands of miles per second, growing cooler and more rarefied as they traveled. At the outset, the expanding gases, most of them in the form of electrically charged ions, were not transparent, and they allowed neither light nor any other form of electromagnetic radiation to escape from inside the explosion. By June, observers had begun to detect absorption lines characteristic of barium and strontium, which they believed indicated that they were looking deeper into the explosion. The presence of barium and strontium confirmed predictions that those elements would be created in the process and that they would become evident in the underlying helium shell.

Other calculations involved the identity of the progenitor (the star that had existed before the explosion). The area of the sky was familiar and had been documented on photographic plates taken prior to the explosion. Intensive study narrowed the search to a single star, discovered in 1969 by Nicholas Sanduleak and named Sanduleak 69.202 (Sk69.202). The hot supergiant, 20 times the mass of the Sun, fitted the characteristics that would have led to supernova 1987A.

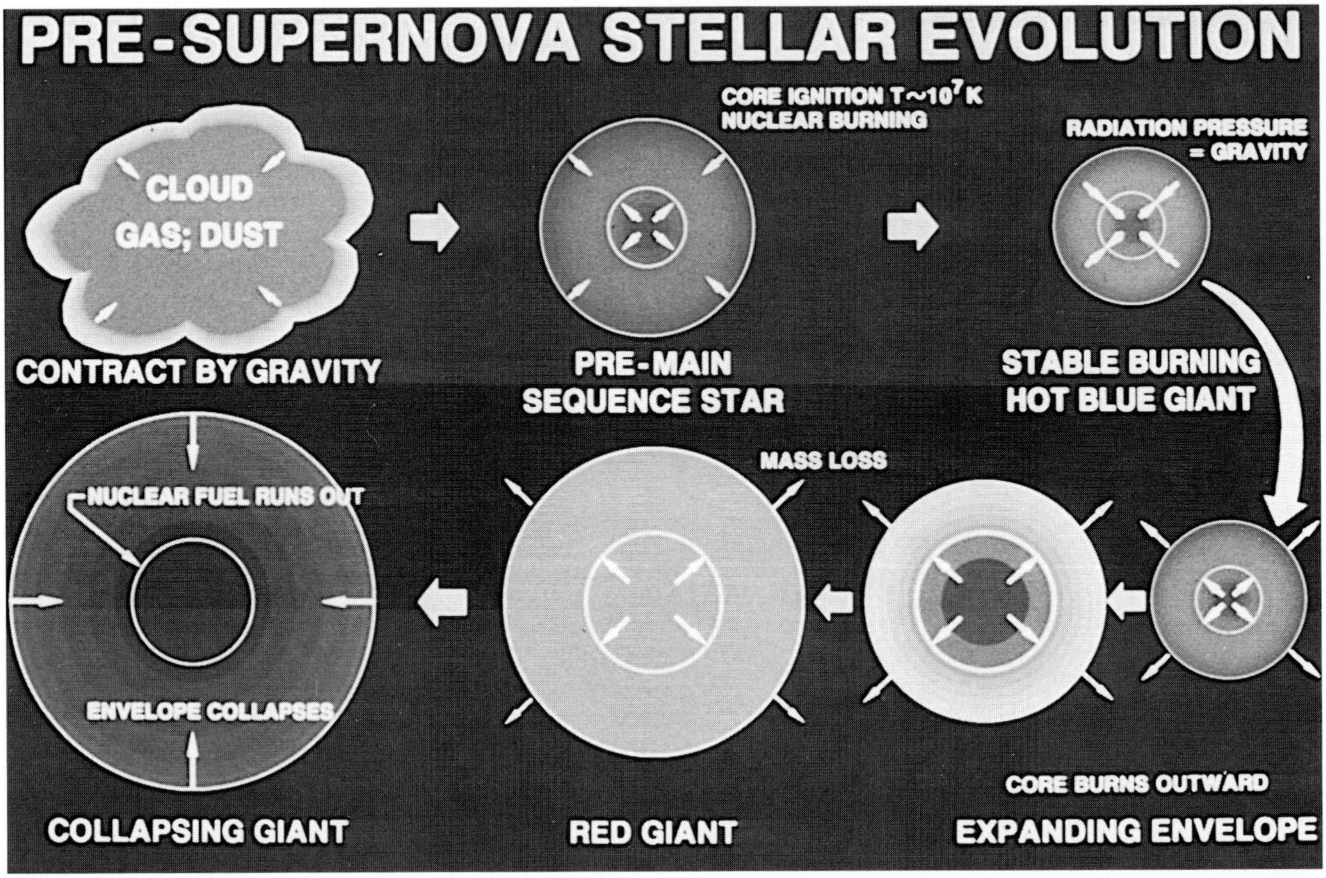

Evolutionary development of a star that would be expected to later turn into a red giant and undergo a supernova explosion.

The Elusive Neutrino

For scientists, the most rewarding aspect of 1987A was the detection of neutrinos, elusive particles critical in the study of supernovas and several other areas of physics and astrophysics.

Theorists had predicted that a supernova explosion would release an immense quantity of neutrinos, as huge numbers of the particles produced inside the collapsing core of the progenitor carried off most of the energy of the explosion. However, the theory had never been confirmed.

Neutrinos have little or no mass. They have no electrical charge. They travel at, or close to, the speed of light. They interact with matter so weakly that almost all the neutrinos emanating from a supernova are able to pass through the entire universe without being stopped by anything. Thus, despite their massive numbers, neutrinos are supremely difficult to detect. Detectors built to perform other tasks record only an occasional neutrino of the trillions that pass through them every second.

The discovery of neutrinos in connection with 1987A was almost accidental. For the past decade, experiments have been conducted around the world to detect the decay of the nuclear particle called the proton. The sensitive experiments had to be shielded from the effects of high-energy cosmic-ray particles striking the Earth, and to create the needed shielding, the experiments used deeply buried tanks containing thousands of tons of water, which are capable of capturing neutrinos.

On February 28th, the Mont Blanc Neutrino Observatory operated by the Instituto di Cosmogeofisica in Turin, Italy, and by the Institute of Nuclear Studies in Moscow, reported detecting a record of 5 neutrinos in a 7-second interval. Ten days later, the University of Tokyo, Niigati University, and the University of Pennsylvania announced the findings of their Kamiokande-II facility, which recorded 11 neutrino events over a 13-second interval. However, the Mont Blanc and the Kamiokande-II observation times were separated by 4 hours and 43 minutes.

An experiment of the University of California at Irvine, the University of Michigan, and the Brookhaven National Laboratory located in a Morton Thiokol salt mine near Cleveland, Ohio, corroborated the Kamiokande-II report.

The neutrino observations from 1987A jolted the theoretical models of the pre-supernova star. By measuring the time it took the shock wave to reach the surface of the star, astronomers could calculate the radius of the progenitor, and the radius calculated for 1987A better fitted a blue giant star than a red supergiant, the type of star predicted to be the progenitors of Type II supernovas.

The explosion of Sanduleak 69.202, which became supernova 1987A, and the neutrino pulses, which were detected on the night of February 23, 1987, are expected by some astronomers to lead to a new science of neutrino astronomy, which will address important questions such as whether neutrinos have a resting mass and whether neutrinos could be the "missing mass" holding galaxies together.

More Puzzles from 1987A

At a joint meeting of the American Astronomical Society and the Canadian Astronomical Society in June of 1987, discussions focused on some of the puzzling developments connected to 1987A. One such puzzle was the appearance of a companion object observed by means of "speckle interferometry" at Cerro Tololo on March 25th and April 2d.

Speckle interferometry is a method for circumventing twinkling caused by turbulence in the atmosphere of the Earth. The images of objects that lie close together are blurred by turbulence. Speckle interferometry takes a large number of short exposures and uses special camera apertures to sharpen the resolution.

An analysis of 50,000 frames of film revealed that the companion was 5 or 6 magnitudes brighter than the star that had been there before the supernova explosion. It was also about 3 magnitudes dimmer than the supernova itself and was about 2 light-weeks away from the supernova.

Theorists searched for an explanation: From its appearance, they were sure that the companion star was not a second supernova. They also knew it had not been ejected from the supernova because it was too far away. One explanation is that the spot represented some interstellar gas that had been in that location and had begun to reflect or to reprocess light or radiation from the supernova. Another explanation suggests that the spot was beamed radiation from a pulsar inside the supernova. Supernovas are expected to produce pulsars, and the observation of one here would provide direct evidence for that theory.

Richard McCray of the Joint Institute for Laboratory Astrophysics at the University of Colorado in Boulder pointed out that the companion could be a real object lit up by the supernova. If so, material flying out from the supernova will strike the object within 10 to 20 months, creating an exciting show for astrophysicists.

Observations of the supernova have been made in light, ultraviolet, and radio waves. Other forms of radiation are expected from the supernova. Among these is infrared.

Robert Gehrz of the University of Minnesota in Minneapolis is a specialist in infrared observations. He believes there is every reason to expect dust to form in a supernova. Because heated dust would radiate infrared, astronomers would be able to track a supernova in daylight, a feat not possible with visible light observation. However, dust would seriously hamper the observation of visible and ultraviolet radiation from the supernova.

Experts generally agree that gamma rays can be expected from the supernova. The nuclear fusion processes that synthesize some of the heaviest chemical elements produce gamma rays. The discovery of gamma rays from nuclear synthesis in 1987A would be welcomed by a wide range of theorists.

Searching for Other Supernovas

The nearness of 1987A in the Large Magellanic Cloud has provided astronomers with an unparalleled opportunity to study the supernova with many instruments they were never able to use before. Long-term observation of 1987A will continue to produce unique data. However, as more details accumulate, astronomers need a context into which to place the details. Since many aspects of 1987A have not been seen before, it is not clear whether the new information is unique to 1987A or common to many supernovas.

In order to distinguish between what is common and what is unique, astronomers need statistical information about other supernovas. The chances of another supernova exploding as close as 1987A any time soon are not good. But the odds are good in other galaxies. By August 22, 1987, 11 other supernovas had been detected elsewhere in the universe.

Automated observational patrols, planned long before 1987A, are now in operation. In the absence of automated patrols, most supernovas have been discovered by accident, and they are not usually noticed until the most significant early days are already past.

The University of California at Santa Cruz, during the summer of 1987, held a conference called Workshop on Instrumentation for Ground-Based Optical Astronomy. Carl Pennypacker of the University of California at Berkeley and Sterling Colgate of New Mexico Institute in Socorro and Los Alamos, described the supernova patrol programs that each of them direct.

Both programs use a 30-inch-diameter telescope, and both divide the sky into a large number of fields to be viewed in rotation. Each time a new image is taken of a particular field, the computer compares the new image with one already stored in its memory. Once fully operational, the New Mexico program expects to be able to perform an

At the top left is the Supernova Shelton, 1987-A. At the bottom right is the Tarantula Nebula.

average of 36,000 observations each month. The California program has comparable expectations.

Supernovas can be used as cosmological "standard candles." If supernovas of a particular type can be expected to have the same luminosity at maximum light, they can be used to measure cosmic distances, because the apparent brightness of such a standard candle equals its intrinsic brightness divided by the square of the distance. From such calculations are derived the Hubble constant, the expansion rate of the universe.

As automated patrols become routine and fully operated, they can be expected to help build a fund of information about the early days of supernovas. An accumulation of coordinated information can be expected to answer many questions that now remain unanswered, despite the explosion of 1987A onto the astronomical stage.

BIOSPHERE II

A Model Environment

The largest and most complex self-contained ecosystem ever attempted is in the advanced planning stages at an isolated patch of desert north of Tucson, between Oracle and Oracle Junction, Arizona. The project, called Biosphere II (the Earth itself is Biosphere I), will have its own miniature rivers, grasslands, forests, desert, ocean, and human population. The structure will cover approximately 2 acres, include 98,000 square feet in floor area, and encompass 5 million cubic feet in volume.

Ground breaking for construction took place in January of 1987. The project began in December of 1984 with an international conference of 50 scientists, followed by 2 years of design and engineering. In December of 1989, eight human volunteers will enter Biosphere II to be sealed inside by an air lock for a period of 2 years. Nothing material will pass into or out of Biosphere II, but information exchanges will be constant. Video cameras and computerized monitors will allow outside scientists to sample atmospheric and oceanic conditions, to examine diseased organisms, and to track changes within the Biosphere II system.

Conceived by the Institute of Ecotechnics of London and brought into being by Space Biospheres Ventures (SBV), the undertaking is a for-profit blend of high technology and earth sciences. Located on SBV's 2,500-acre SunSpace Ranch, the venture's primary financial support comes from Edward Bass, a Texas oil millionaire. The overall cost is projected to be $30 million.

A major purpose of Biosphere II is to examine the practicality of operating and living in a self-sustaining space station on Mars or perhaps beyond. But the founders of Biosphere II envision their project as more than a model for a habitat to be sent into space. They see it as a tiny, controlled world in which the unfolding of ecological and environmental events of the Earth can be tracked.

The atmosphere will be a single, continuous system throughout Biosphere II. Plans call for interconnected biomes: a human habitation biome; an intensive agriculture biome; a rain forest biome; a transition biome; and a desert biome.

The human habitation biome will be a domed, 4-story white building. Inside will be apartments for eight researchers, laboratories, workshops, offices, accommodations for computers and communications, and libraries.

A series of arched vaults to the south of the habitat will house the 20,000 square foot intensive agriculture biome. On broad terraces, crops for food, fiber, and other human uses will be grown. Behind the plant-crop area will be animal areas for chickens, goats, and aquaculture.

The rain forest biome, the tallest structure, will be approximately 80 feet high and will cover 20,000 square feet in floor area. This biome will include a small mountain, a rain forest, and a waterfall.

A transition section will receive a stream from the waterfall of the rain forest biome. Included in the transition section will be a tropical savanna biome (an open plain without trees and covered with grass or reeds), a freshwater marsh biome (very wet lowland overgrown with coarse grass), a saltwater marsh biome, and a marine biome.

The marine biome will contain a 35-foot-deep miniocean with a coral reef and a machine to make waves. A thorn scrub forest will mark the boundary between the savanna biome and the desert biome.

The desert biome, enclosed in glass and metal, will duplicate the conditions of a small coastal fog desert, with species adapted to low rainfall and high humidity.

The Biosphere II Test Module

In order to test Biosphere II, the Biosphere II Test Module was constructed. The model, 27 feet by 27 feet, although only a small fraction of the expected size of Biosphere II, upon completion became the world's largest sealed structure that admitted light.

An array of construction issues can be tested with the module. Some of the problems involve the proper materials for the structure, glazing techniques (methods of installing the building's glass), design for the louvers that will regulate sunlight, options for heating and cooling mechanisms, and the computer systems designed to keep track of the intricate activities.

On the module, and on Biosphere II, light entering through the glass canopy roof will be regulated by opening and closing louvers. Controlling light will also help to control temperature. The most likely cooling device will be air directed across water-filled coils. The water in the coils will have been chilled by a cooling tower attached to the agricultural biome.

The completed Biosphere II will use a "lung" that will allow the enormous form to expand and contract in reaction to changes in the atmosphere inside and outside the structure. Without such a system, the expansion and contraction of air in response to changes in temperature would cause the glass or seals to break.

Growing Food in Biosphere II

In addition to the module, a research facility was also built before construction of Biosphere II began. The research facility pursues greenhouse-agriculture techniques, aquaculture techniques, and tissue-culture techniques.

Among the greenhouse-agriculture techniques being used in the research facility are hydroponics, that is, growing plants in liquid nutrients, and aeroponics, the growing of plants in mists of nutrients rather than in soil. Small crops of a variety of vegetables, fruits, and herbs have been successfully grown using these methods.

An aquaculture technique uses complex interactions among plants, fish, algae, bacteria, and sunlight. In a farm of 45 tanks, fish eat algae and plants, and excrete ammonia into the water. The water is directed through a biofiliter where bacteria extract the ammonia and convert it into nitrates. The nitrates are then routed back as food for the algae and water plants, and the whole cycle begins again.

While producing crops of plants and fish that can be harvested, the system maintains itself. Among the fish grown is an ugly, but savory, fish called the Tilapia, which is predicted to become the chicken of the aquaculture industry.

The tissue-culture bank where plantlets are stored serves as a backup system. If misfortune or disease should destroy

Biosphere II's test module.

Fish farming in a Biosphere Ventures research facility.

any of Biosphere II's species, the tissue-culture bank would permit the ecosystem to be restarted. Biosphere II's library of frozen cells could regenerate replacement plants using a technique called micropropagation.

Once locked inside, the eight volunteers will be totally dependent on the ecology of the biosphere. Their food and their energy will come from renewable resources. They will raise selected animals and plants for food and will manage their own wastes.

Years of Planning

To replicate biological, geological, and chemical cycles of the Earth on a miniature scale requires reliance upon already existing knowledge from many fields. It also requires making educated guesses. For example, would the rain forest be better served by soil brought in from South America or by local sterilized soil inoculated with microbes from the Amazon? This is just one of thousands of decisions the research team will have to make.

Each biome had to be designed as it would look and feel in nature, including the proper light, humidity, and temperature. The two architects who designed Biosphere II, Margaret Augustine and Philip Hawes, continually worked with a variety of consultants retained by SBV.

During planning, the designers and consultants had strong disagreements. One argument centered on how to stock the ecosystems. The positions fell into two camps: "Species Packing" and "No Extinctions." The species-packers wanted to stuff each biome with different plant and animal species on the theory that if one plant or animal did not survive, four or five others would. The no-extinctioners argued for minimizing extinctions by installing well-understood species. In the end, the final choices were a compromise between the two positions, since both sides recognized that, given the limited data available, a high level of extinctions could probably not be avoided.

Each separate biome had its own distinctive planning problems. For example, in parts of some deserts, temperatures rise above 120 degrees in summer and drop below freezing in winter. To reproduce those extremes in Biosphere II would have been both expensive and difficult. Botanist Tony Burgess avoided the extremes by choosing a maritime desert with moderate temperature variance and high humidity. He found models in several parts of the world, including the west coast of Baja California, which he chose as his major source of inspiration.

To replicate Baja's Vizcaino desert, which has a rainy season in winter, and where most plants go dormant in summer, plans call for the Biosphere II desert louvers to be closed from 9 A.M. to 4 P.M. each day from late May to September. Burgess will take the bulk of the desert species from the Vizcaino, but will supplement them with species brought in from other regions. The importation of species requires permits from the Department of Agriculture, from the originating country, and in some cases from the Convention of International Trade-in-Endangered Species (CITES).

The design of the marine sub-biomes has a different set of problems. Each of the marine sub-biomes will include 300 or 400 species of plants and animals. In a typical marsh, several square meters may have more than 100 species, too many to collect one by one. Marine consultant Walter Adey approached his task with the intent of hauling in chunks of Florida mangrove swamp, and by transporting coral reef and sandy beach from the Caribbean.

Life in Biosphere II

All the biomes will require management. Rain forest trees cannot be allowed to grow through the biosphere's roof. A species of algae that might, in nature, temporarily take over an area for a many-mile-long coral reef cannot be allowed to dominate space on a reef only 50 feet in length.

Most vertebrates will wander from biome to biome. Birds and animals will affect plant distribution. Seeds might be buried and forgotten by an agouti, a rain forest rodent. Plants throughout the biomes will be pollinated by hummingbirds and omnivorous bats.

Because of space limitations, most of the species introduced into Biosphere II will be pygmy. A tentative species list includes monkeys, frogs, salamanders, snakes, birds, tortoises, and ungulates (hoofed animals), specifically small deer.

The handling of pests will be an especially critical issue in the small, contained world. An insecticide sprayed on the garden could be found in the drinking water within 2 weeks. Therefore, instead of chemical pest control, insects will be used to control undesirable insects: ladybugs for aphids; predatory beetles for spider mites; parasitic wasps for white flies; and lacewings for leaf miners.

To minimize the introduction of new pests into the state of Arizona and into Biosphere II, plants will be held in quarantine greenhouses, and then in propagation greenhouses. Unfortunately, there is no way to completely sterilize plants. The agriculturists hope pests will be prevented from migrating from the other biomes to the agricultural biome by a 60-foot tunnel equipped with several screen doors.

Designing Biosphere II

In the design of the overall building, ''form has followed function, and function has followed form.'' In other words, the shape of the structure has in part been determined by the conditions that needed to be created; and the conditions that could be created have been limited by the feasible shape of the structure. For example, the building steps down a hill, and a gradient is developed as the floor line is lowered about 40 feet. Hot air will be driven up the slope from the desert, pass over the savanna and marine biomes, and collect in the 80-foot-high tropical rain forest, where condensers will cool it and clouds will gather.

Ladybugs and other insects will be used for pest control rather than risk pesticides in the closed ecosystem.

The ecologists are intent on replicating conditions that will sustain life. Toward that purpose, Adey lobbied Biosphere II's designers to increase the surface covered by water in the sealed world from one-fifth to about one-half. On the Earth, the ocean stirs the atmosphere and keeps the temperature tolerable. Moreover, the Biosphere's savanna could serve as a carbon dioxide control: Too high a level of carbon dioxide should cause rainfall over the grasslands; the rain would promote swift plant growth; and the increased plant life would lower the level of carbon dioxide.

The glass-sheathed roof presents a formidable problem. Leaks are likely, yet from an engineering standpoint, an almost perfect seal of the glass panes in the roof is critical because without a tight seal, the model would not be usable for a space colony. From the horticulturists' perspective, however, the seal is not nearly as important as the amount of sunlight permitted by the roof.

Beneath the test module is expensive stainless steel intended to prevent water from seeping out. All of Biosphere II's water will pass through multiple physical and biological filters before it is recycled. From the cooling coils, drinking water will be piped to the living quarters. In order to make it drinkable, the pH balance will need to be adjusted.

Human waste will probably be passed through a composting toilet and undergo steam sterilization before being reentered into the system. Air pollutants will in all likelihood be removed by passing them through soil.

A Model for Earth As Well As Space

While yielding data for space colonization, Biosphere II could also direct public attention toward better management of the Earth's resources. The model could even be used to perform experiments of ecological hazards that the Earth may one day have to face. For example, a nuclear winter could be simulated by closing the louvers, mimicking the effect of clouds of soot and smoke blocking sunlight from the Earth. Or by raising Biosphere II's carbon dioxide level, the researchers could test the impact of the greenhouse effect, which is the warming trend predicted to partially melt the Earth's polar ice caps and raise the sea level early in the next century.

Tom Gould, firing site leader for the Center for Explosive Technology, and Phil Anthony, lab manager, prepare for a blast at CET's Eagle Lab.

Part Three

Physical Science and Mathematics

EVENTS AND TRENDS IN PHYSICAL SCIENCE AND MATHEMATICS

The ever-expanding involvement of computers in science and technology continued in 1987 to blur the boundaries between the physical sciences, mathematics, and the life sciences. Nowhere was that more evident than in the link between computer neural networks and brain science. The year was also one in which old materials and old techniques were rediscovered.

Physics

Socorro, New Mexico, has become a unique center for research in the physics and chemistry of explosions. In 1983, the New Mexico legislature established the Center for Explosives Technology Research, and in 1986 added the Research Center for Energetic Materials. A multinational team of explosives experts working at the New Mexico Institute of Mining and Technology create custom-tailored blasts from a wide selection of ingredients.

Up to 20,000 explosive substances are known, and the physicists and chemists who work at Socorro are constantly looking for new ones. One of their latest tools is a device called an explosive plane-wave lens. The lens is designed to slam fissionable components together with enough force to cause an instantaneous chain fission reaction.

To make an explosive lens, a thin cone of fast-detonating explosive is molded to surround a cone of slower detonating explosive. A detonation wave moving along the sides of the double cone has a longer distance to travel before it reaches the cone's base than does the detonation wave that moves straight down. By varying the ingredients and the geometry of the concentric cones, a detonation wave can be made to order, including a flat wave.

In an ordinary detonation of a high explosive, a spherical shock wave balloons outward more or less uniformly in all directions. A shock wave can be described as a swiftly moving boundary, in front of which matter is undisturbed, and behind which matter travels at almost the speed of the shock wave.

A spherical shock wave that strews, smashes, and distorts objects in its path is useless as a precision tool. Socorro's scientists are using plane waves, shock waves that move like the flat face of a rapidly moving hammer. Struck by hammerlike waves, materials experience physical and chemical changes not possible under normal circumstances.

The problem of piercing the laminated armor of Soviet tanks has spurred efforts to improve the hollow-charge warheads used in antitank missiles. In contrast to a lens, a hollow charge concentrates its shock energy in a thin penetrating jet. The forward face of the cylindrical cone is indented to form an internal cone. The cone is lined with metal and when the charge is detonated, the sides of the cone blow inward, crushing the metal between them and squirting it out as a high-speed jet of solid metal. Hollow charges can be shaped into grooves, instead of indented cones, to sever huge girders with foil-thin sheets of metal.

Chemistry

Supercritical fluid, discovered in 1822 by French scientist Charles Cagniard de la Tour, is central to the first "high-risk, high-return innovative research program" ever financed by the National Science Foundation. The research effort led by Erdogan Kiran, a professor of chemical engineering at the University of Maine in Orono, is looking for a practical and cheap method of dissolving and separating the main components of wood, cellulose, hemicellulose, and lignin. Besides revolutionizing the pulp and paper industry, the process would produce chemicals essential to making polymers used for plastic implements and textiles.

Most substances at low temperature are solids, at intermediate temperature are liquids, and at high temperatures are gases. But a combination of high pressure and high temperature can convert a substance into a state that does not ordinarily exist. The properties of the new state, called supercritical fluid, are intermediate between a liquid and a gas.

A supercritical fluid expands like a gas to fill its container and to suffuse everything in the container. But like a liquid, a supercritical fluid can dissolve solids. By manipulating the composition, pressure, and temperature of a supercritical fluid in which a solid is immersed, a skilled chemist can withdraw from a solid a single component, leaving the remainder intact.

Many substances, including water, can be used as supercritical solvents. But a chemist must choose a supercritical fluid that will not destroy the molecules it is intended to dissolve. The temperature of supercritical water is hot enough to set fire to wood or paper. Carbon dioxide, on the other hand, becomes supercritical at 88 degrees Fahrenheit and at a pressure of 73 times the atmosphere, and is capable of dissolving a variety of chemicals, including caffeine. Early in 1987, Sanka began having its coffee decaffeinated in West Germany using supercritical carbon dioxide.

For some applications of chromatographic chemical analysis, supercritical fluids have begun to replace conventional gases and liquids. The breakdown of unstable molecules that would be destroyed by conventional analysis is avoided with the use of supercritical fluid as a solvent.

The technique works particularly well with pesticides, narcotics, organic poisons, and some antibiotics.

Computer Science

A 65-year-old Nobel Prize-winning dipping technique has been rediscovered to create ultrathin film the thickness of one molecule on sterile glass plate. The thin film allows scientists to cram many additional transistors, diodes, and capacitors onto silicon wafers, a development that could make computers more powerful and faster.

The films being created by Scott Rickert, a chemical engineer at Case Western Reserve University in Cleveland, Ohio, and by other chemical engineers, are made from organic, carbon-based molecules containing metallic atoms. When the film dries, the metallic atoms of the crystallized molecules line up in a precise geometric pattern that conducts electricity while the carbon behaves as an insulator.

Because they create less resistance to the flow of electricity, and because they can be packed closer together, the thin film is able to process information thousands of times faster than conventional chips. The process is similar to the flow of electrical impulses in nerve tissue, or to the transport of electrons in photosynthesis.

Another development in computer chips not only promised more space but also greater safety. Very large-scale integrated (VLSI) circuits under development by TRW of Redondo Beach, California, will have the capacity to repair themselves, using diagnosis and repair software built into the computer chips. The VLSI chips activate spare features to replace malfunctioning ones. Upon command, they also can change functions while still installed, such as wiring in additional memory of circuits.

In applications such as fighter aircraft, the new chips will provide protection when failure of an integrated circuit would result in catastrophe.

Mathematics

The mathematical sciences board of the National Research Council brought together officials of the Strategic Defense Initiative (SDI), or "Star Wars," team with university mathematicians to discover what SDI is doing or can do for mathematics. The staff director of the mathematic sciences board reported that some basic math problems must be solved before SDI can become operative.

There is a need for finding short cuts that would enable computers to respond to continuously updated information about incoming missile tracks and to determine which warheads were real and which were decoys. In mathematical terms, the problem is one of "optimization." The SDI optimization problem is more difficult than any previously faced because of the volume of constantly changing data that must be processed simultaneously.

Mathematicians will need to look for solutions similar to the Karmarkar algorithm, which is used to route computers to the fastest solutions for minimizing costs and distributing resources. Branches of mathematics such as statistics would be faced with equally difficult tasks.

Mathematicians are divided in their opinion about the wisdom of calling the conference. Mathematicians who support the action are enthusiastic because they believe SDI funding could pay for computers on which to do research. They also believe breakthroughs made on behalf of the SDI could be applied to other areas such as artificial intelligence, telecommunications, and aerodynamics.

Mathematicians who oppose the action think neither they nor their colleagues should work on the SDI because the research is either impractical, too expensive, or immoral. Since the mathematical sciences board has no direct control over mathematicians, each individual's decision to accept or reject SDI funds will be based on his or her perspective about whether mathematics will be enhanced or diminished by the research.

10

Physics

SUPERCONDUCTIVITY

Research Heats Up

Superconductivity, the ability of everyday material to carry electricity without a loss of energy to resistance, was discovered in 1911 by Heike Kamerlingh Onnes of the University of Leiden, in the Netherlands. The phenomenon first appeared in solid mercury at a temperature of 4.2 kelvins, approximately 452 degrees below zero on the Fahrenheit scale. Whereas an ordinary conductor such as copper requires a battery or a generator to overcome losses to resistance, a superconductor can circulate electricity indefinitely without a power source, producing an intense magnetic field.

The drawback to widespread use of the discovery was the fact that a state of superconductivity could be achieved only at very low temperatures, close to absolute zero. Over the years following the 1911 discovery, scientists struggled to achieve superconductivity at warmer temperatures. Progress was painstakingly slow, and only industries that could justify the costly and difficult use of liquid helium as a coolant took advantage of superconductivity.

For years, German-born scientist Bernd Matthias was responsible, either directly or indirectly, for every improvement in the temperature at which materials became superconductors. By the 1980s only a few scientists continued to look for high-temperature superconductors. One of them was Ching-Wu Chu, known as Paul, who had been a student of Matthias.

The Breakthrough

But Chu was not the one to make the initial breakthrough in superconductivity research. The long-sought breakthrough came in Zurich on January 27, 1986. The barriers to superconductivity fell before an unexpected kind of material, a dark chunk of ceramic. Oxides like ceramics are normally poor conductors of electricity. However, two scientists at the IBM Zurich Laboratory in Switzerland, K. Alex Mueller and J. George Bednorz, believed oxides held interesting possibilities in superconductor research. For 3 years, the researchers mixed powders, baked them in hot ovens, then chilled them, hoping that each compound would lose its resistance to electricity. For their efforts the pair were awarded the 1987 Nobel Prize in physics.

Nothing happened until Dr. Bednorz read in a French journal about a new oxide that combined barium with lanthanum, copper, and oxygen. The French scientists who had created the substance were primarily chemists rather

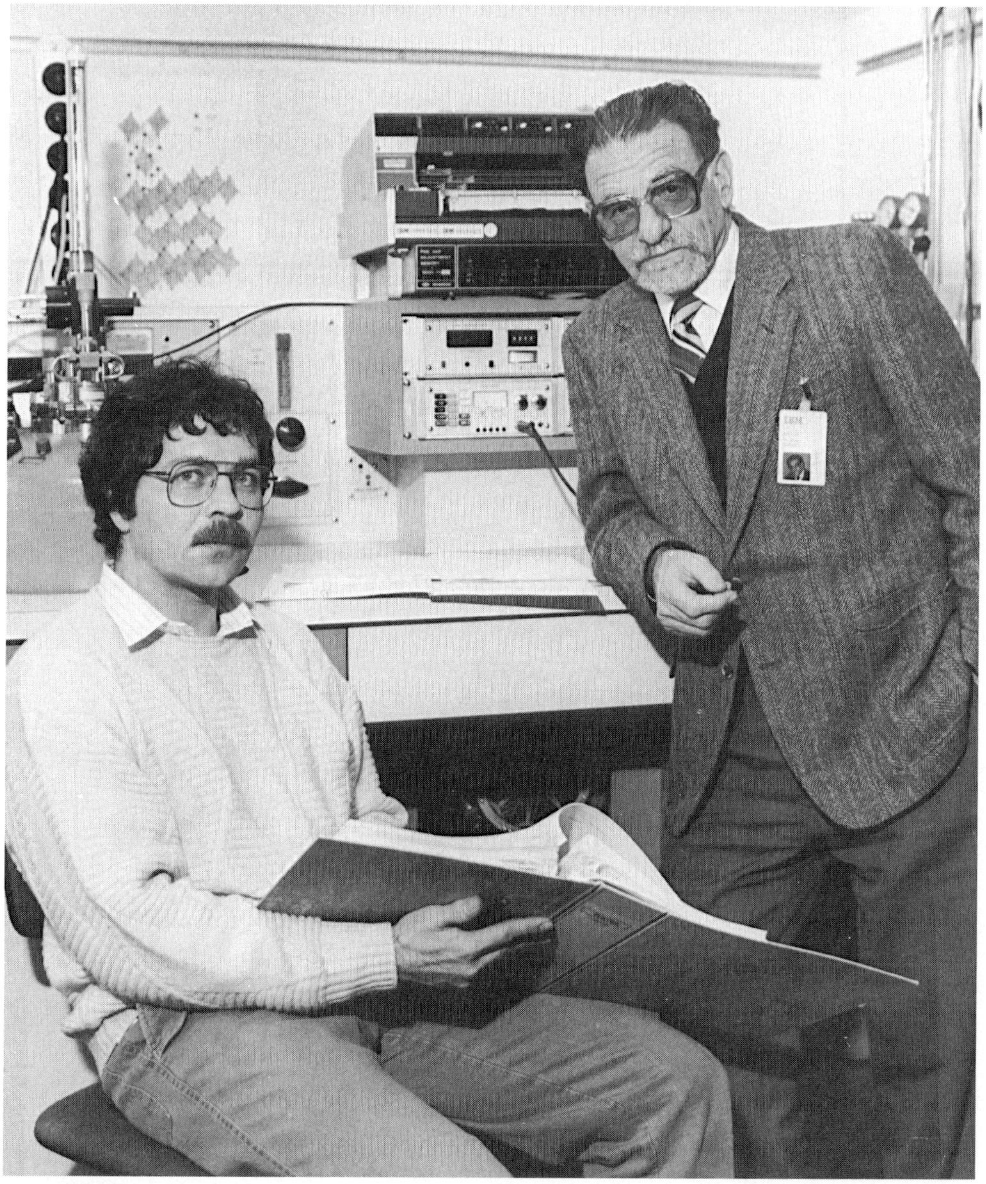

J. Georg Bednorz and K. Alex Mueller at IBM's Zurich Research Laboratory aroused worldwide interest with their discovery of high-temperature superconductivity in a class of oxide materials.

than physicists, so they did not test their discovery for superconductivity. Apparently no one who read the French journal considered the oxide as a potential superconductivity candidate—except Bednorz and Mueller.

On January 27th, using the new material, Mueller and Bednorz found that electrical resistance in the oxide plunged at about 30 kelvins, or approximately 406 degrees below zero Fahrenheit. Despite the breakthrough, the two scientists kept silent about their discovery until they were sure they could replicate the results. In April of 1986, Mueller and Bednorz submitted a tentative report to the German journal *Zeitschrift fur Physik*, which did not publish their findings for another 5 months. In the interim, unpressured by competition, the researchers continued their measurements.

In September, scientists who read Mueller and Bednorz's findings hurried off in two directions. Some tried to reproduce the Zurich scientists' results while searching for explanations of the unusual behavior. Others tinkered with the recipe, looking for a variety of substances that might produce superconductivity at even warmer temperatures.

Research Heats Up

By December of 1986, competition was becoming fierce. At the University of Houston, Paul Chu, who had previously worked on oxides and had studied the effects of high

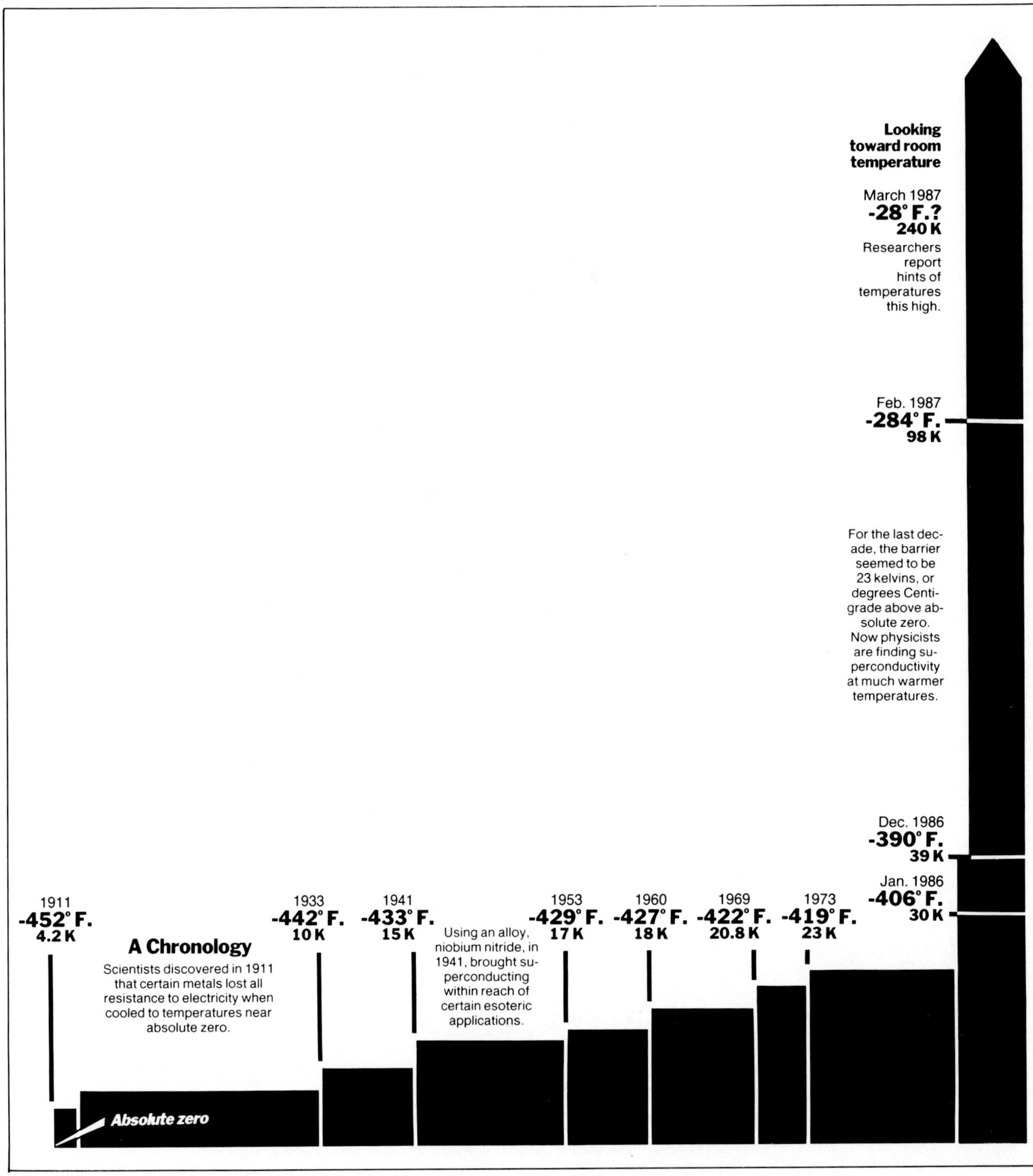

pressure in promoting superconductivity, squeezed the new substance with pressure amounting to thousands of times that of the atmosphere. With this technique he was able to achieve superconductivity at 40 kelvins, then at 50, and then at almost 60 kelvins, but there the limit was reached. No amount of additional pressure improved his results.

Next Chu and his team tried to mimic the effects of pressure by using chemical methods that involved the crystalline structure of the oxides. They tried replacing barium with strontium, a smaller atom. Again the transition temperature rose. But when they tried a still-smaller atom, calcium, the temperature fell.

Thereupon the team turned their attention to the purity of their samples. Most samples were not homogeneous but contained different phases, or chemical structures. Dr. Chu made his samples purer—but superconductivity disappeared.

Subsequently Dr. Chu replaced the lanthanum with yttrium. This material, containing many different phases in any particular sample, again produced high transition temperatures.

During the last week of December in 1986, Dr. Chu's group, and a group at Bell Laboratory in New Jersey, simultaneously made the first public announcements of the dramatic change that had begun in Zurich 11 months earlier. On January 8, 1987, Dr. Chu submitted a patent application for his work. In mid-February, Chu's group, and a group at the University of Alabama led by Chu's former student, Maw-Kuen Wu, announced a transition to superconductivity at more than 90 kelvins; or approximately 284 degrees below zero Fahrenheit. They refused to name the material that made superconductivity feasible before official publication of the findings in *Physical Review* on March 2, 1987. In the meantime, the race to duplicate Chu's findings grew heated. Many scientists pursued a provocative rumor that the key element was ytterbium.

The manuscript that Chu had submitted to *Physical Review* did specify ytterbium. Two weeks before publication, Chu corrected what he said was a typographical error. The final paper named a different element, yttrium. Some scientists claimed there had been a leak at the journal; others claimed that Chu had made a deliberate mistake to mislead competitors.

From a temperature in 1911 of 4.2 kelvins, or 452 degrees below zero Fahrenheit, to a temperature in 1987 of 90 kelvins, or 284 degrees below zero on the Fahrenheit scale, is a substantial warming. The warmer temperature represents a considerable savings in the cost of achieving superconductivity, since the liquid helium needed for cooling at 4.2 kelvins is rare, costly, difficult to work with, and is not a particularly effective coolant.

Within months after Paul Chu and Maw-Kuen Wu made public their findings, several laboratories were reporting that they had produced superconductivity at 321 degrees below Fahrenheit, a temperature at which they could use liquid nitrogen. Liquid nitrogen, essentially liquid air, is cheap, easy to obtain, and a much better coolant than helium.

Rises in temperature continued to be announced. In March, announcements were so frequent that they began to be dated by the hour at which they were made.

By April, physics students at Northeastern University, like fans at a play-off game, were standing outside laboratory doors waiting for superconductivity temperature scores to rise higher. A physicist at Northeastern described the discoveries of superconductivity as an event that comes not just once in a lifetime, but once in a century. Even the comic strip "Bloom Country" participated in the excitement when child prodigy Oliver Wendell had a success that warranted calling the Patent Office.

The new materials are fairly easy for a chemist to make. Any two or three physicists and/or chemists can launch their own efforts. Neil Ashcroft of Cornell University described the pursuit as "truly tabletop physics."

By June, Chu reported that his group was able to reproduce materials that could superconduct at 130 kelvins, or about 225 degrees below zero Fahrenheit. Chu reported that his earlier accounts of superconductivity at 90 kelvins, or about 298 degrees below zero Fahrenheit, had lost superconductivity quickly. His announcement of superconductivity at 225 kelvins, or 54 degrees below zero Fahrenheit, had not been reproducible.

In late summer of 1987, scientists at the University of Arkansas announced they had designed a new way of turning rare-earth elements into superconducting materials. In their technique, which made it possible to make the material in bulk, they melted their ingredients, thus avoiding the laborious technique used by hundreds of labs, which involved combining powders by grinding, compacting, and sintering (heating powders without melting them).

About the same time, scientists at the University of South Wales reported they had found a new way to raise the temperature at which compounds lost their resistance to electricity. They bathed the ingredients in an atmosphere of nitrogen gas while the materials were being made. Why the nitrogen helped was not clear, but a gain of as much as 70 degrees Fahrenheit was reported.

Among researchers there was widespread hope that superconductivity would be achievable at room temperature. A Japanese newspaper claimed that a group at Kagoshima University had in fact achieved this. The possibility of room-temperature superconductivity would make many existing electrical and electronic technologies obsolete. Many scientists view these discoveries as the most important in solid-state physics since the invention of the transistor.

The Uses of Superconductivity

Until the 1987 breakthrough, the chief commercial market for superconductivity was in magnetic resonance imaging (MRI), a medical technique for observing tissues within the human body. The superconducting coils produce an intense, steady field that shortens exposure time and produces sharper, higher contrast pictures than with conventional magnets.

By 1986, more than 300 MRI units were sold annually for $600 million. The MRI market was expected to rise to $1.4 billion by 1990. A quarter of the cost of MRI units has

A magnet floats above a superconducting disk; levitation is potentially one of the most practical traits of superconducting materials.

been the cost of superconducting magnets and their cooling systems. The new high-temperature superconductors are expected to promote a greatly expanded superconductivity industry with a wide range of new uses in the near future, such as smaller, faster computers; storage of electricity in huge magnetic coils; electric motors shrunk to one-tenth their current size; materials separation (removal of impurities); and high-speed trains levitated by magnets.

A peculiar characteristic of superconductors is that they float serenely in the air when placed above a magnet, which eliminates the friction of wheels on, say, railroad tracks. "Maglev" trains are already a reality. A monorail system near Bremen, West Germany, regularly carries 200 passengers at more than 200 miles per hour. At a maglev train test center 30 miles north of Miyazaki on Japan's southern island of Kyushu, researchers strive to create a train fast enough to compete with air travel. The train is moved by the interaction of superconducting magnets on the train with magnets along the sides of the track. Each train magnet is simultaneously pushed by a side magnet of the same polarity and pulled by a side magnet of the opposite polarity. The frequency of the continual reversal of the side-magnet polarity determines the speed of the train.

A particularly attractive superconductivity application is the large-scale transmission of electric power. Helium-cooled superconducting lines would be cost competitive if they could carry at least 3,000 megawatts of power. The largest transmission line presently in use, the Pacific Intertie, carries 2,000 megawatts.

Conventional electrical transmission lines sustain losses of about 1 percent per 100 miles of length. In the United States, it has been cheaper to build new power plants than to install long lines. Superconductivity could bring power into areas now considered too remote. Many scientists believe they have not even begun to imagine the applications of room-temperature superconductors.

Explaining Superconductivity

Although superconductivity was discovered in 1911, a successful theoretical explanation of the phenomenon had to wait until 1957, when the BCS theory (for its developers, John Bardeen, Leon Cooper, and J. Robert Schrieffer, who won the Nobel Prize for their work) was advanced. The BCS theory holds that superconductivity occurs when electrons travel in pairs through a material. Since electrons normally repel one another, an intermediary is necessary to induce them to pair. The intermediary is a phonon, a vibration or a ripple in the lattice of the crystal.

Scientists continue to believe that electrons are paired in the new superconductivity, but they speculate that the mechanism of pairing may be different. The first attempt at a theoretical explanation for the new phenomenon appeared in *Science* in early March, from Nobel Laureate Phillip Anderson of Princeton University. He sees as fundamental the fact that the new materials hover on the edge of being insulators. With the slightest change, they carry no electricity at all. He hypothesizes that a state is created without long-range order, with no regular structure, much like a fluid.

In mid-March of 1987, a most unusual session of the American Physical Society was held. The session lasted from 7:30 P.M. to 3:15 A.M., and addressed an audience of thousands about the progress being made in superconductivity. At the meeting, Dr. Anderson, an often controversial theorist, described a computer simulation of the crystal. Rather than a phonon as the intermediary, as in traditional superconduction, Anderson believes that in the new superconductivity there is a phenomenon called "resonating valence," in which valence electrons bind the atoms in a crystal. Anderson suggests that valence electrons jump from one atom to another, causing force distortions that bind the conduction electrons in pairs.

Other theorists who spoke at the meeting seemed to be in agreement that copper and oxygen and the chemical relationship between them are important for superconductivity. They did not agree whether the relationship involved planes of atoms or simply lines of atoms. They agreed that the rare-earth oxides seemed important, though paradoxical.

Rare-earth oxides are magnetic. Magnetism and superconductivity have usually been incompatible. For example, one rare-earth oxide used with success in superconductivity experiments, gadolinium, had previously been used in research to actually eliminate superconductivity.

Another factor that can eliminate superconductivity is too much current. A superconductor will convey current without resistance as long as the current density does not

Closeup of a ceramic substrate patterned with high-temperature superconducting wires made with a new IBM plasma spray technique. Such wire might be used to connect logic and memory chips in computers.

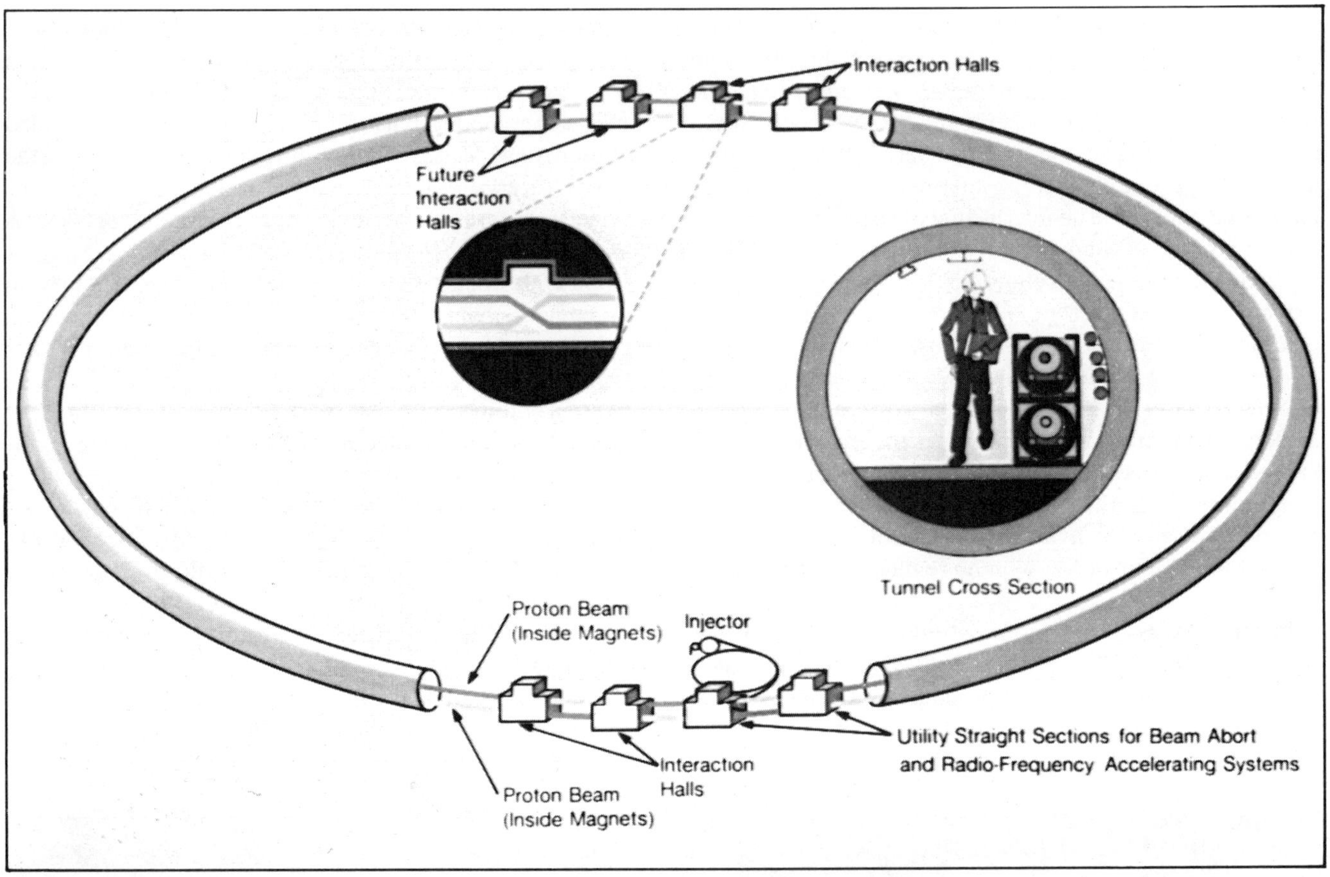

Schematic of the proposed SSC, 52 miles in circumference. The injection system is shown to scale, but the experimental halls and other components on the main ring are not.

pass a limit characteristic of the particular substance. But to be useful, a superconductor ought to be able to sustain substantial current. The IBM Watson Research Center in Yorktown Heights, New York, announced that their scientists had been able to pass 100,000 amperes per square centimeter through one of the new high-temperature superconductors.

The IBM studies found that the materials are anisotropic conductors; that is, they carry current more readily in one direction than in another. Household conductors such as copper are called either isotropic, bulk, or three-dimensional conductors; that is, they conduct electricity equally well in all directions. This anisotropic quality will be significant to theorists trying to explain superconductivity. It will also be important in the design of devices that make practical use of superconductivity.

With an industrial technique called plasma spraying, IBM scientists used superconducting materials to coat preshaped wires and lay down fine lines of film on the surface and through the holes of a ceramic chip. Many such chips joined together could form the basis of a small computer freed of heat caused by current flowing through connecting wires.

A Note of Caution

Despite the dramatic events of the year, by late summer of 1987, the initial euphoria of discovery had begun to dissipate. A note of caution began to creep into superconductivity news accounts. In the August issue of *Discover*, an article by Gina Maranto called "Superconductivity: Hype Vs. Reality," quoted a scientist who said it would be a long time before it became possible to run to the hardware store to buy a spool of superconducting wire. Each specific use of superconductivity could be expected to have both a generic and a unique set of scientific and engineering stumbling blocks. For example, scientists must develop unprecedented controls over ceramic processing. And for applications such as integrated circuits, engineers must find a way to make films only fractions of micrometers thick to carry a million amperes per square centimeter.

More than 1,000 business executives, laboratory directors, venture capitalists, and government program managers gathered in Washington, D.C., in late July of 1987 to discuss the future of superconductivity. Science officials laced their predictions of a bright future with warnings that industry should prepare for a long struggle and should also prepare for stiff international competition in superconductivity development.

Superconductivity and the Supercollider

The progress on superconductivity in 1987 proved to be a threat to the fate of the Superconducting Supercollider (SSC). On January 29, 1987, President Reagan gave formal approval of a project envisioned 20 years ago by physicist John Blewett.

Blewett suggested building a huge particle accelerator in a ring around Greater Berlin as a multinational project to ease international tensions. The planned particle accelerator, SSC, was never built in Berlin. Instead, it may be built in the United States.

The purpose of the 40-trillion-electron-volt proton-proton particle collider is to make it possible for physicists to better understand the properties of fundamental particles such as quarks and leptons as well as the forces that affect them.

Protons are made of quarks, which are held together by one of nature's strongest and least understood forces. With 20 times the energy currently available at the most powerful accelerator (the Tevatron at the Fermi National Accelerator Lab in Batavia, Illinois), the SSC would allow scientists to study quarks and their interrelations and other aspects of the ultramicroscopic structure of matter.

The accelerator site is planned to encompass 83 kilometers, or 52 miles. The magazine *High Technology* described the proposed facility as 20 times larger than the Indianapolis Speedway. The imaginary speedway's entire length would be lined with 10,000 superconducting magnets, each at the cost equivalent of a Mercedes.

Opponents of the project argue that construction of the SSC ought to wait for development of the warmer-temperature superconductors. They believe that the SSC's liquid-helium-cooled magnets would be obsolete before the facility was even completed.

Government officials and some particle physicists argue that delay of a project that has taken so many years of engineering would be a grave error. For those charged with shepherding the SSC project through the difficult route of congressional approval, opposition from within the physics community was a painful irony.

A simple description of an accelerator divides it into three parts: an accelerating section or sections in which radio waves convey energy to protons; a confinement system that compels the proton to travel in a circular path, moving through the same accelerating sections again and again; and an injector, a preactivator that delivers the protons to the main apparatus already partially energized.

The confinement system consists of magnets that bend the path of the protons so that they go in a circle. The SSC's superconducting magnets will carry stronger currents and generate more powerful fields than any previously constructed.

The magnets are simple in concept, consisting of flat niobium-titanium cable wound around a copper tube. They are secured with laminated collars of stainless steel or aluminum.

The cable must be prevented from moving in response to the huge magnetic force. Even a shift of as little as one-thousandth of an inch would generate energy resulting in a rise in the cable above its critical temperature. A rise in temperature would change the cable to a state of ordinary electrical resistance. This transformation, called a quench, would then heat the magnet to several hundred degrees, forcing a shutdown of the SSC.

Maury Tigner, head of the Design Group for the SSC, has said that even if the new superconductors were commercially available, he would keep temperatures as low as 405 degrees below Fahrenheit as a protection against quenching. That temperature would rule out the cheaper liquid nitrogen as a coolant at the SSC.

Critics of the planned SSC, among them theorist Phillip Anderson, point out that cooling is not the only limitation that calls for a delay until the new superconductors become available. Another important issue is that the new materials could make the magnets 10 times more powerful, which might allow the SSC to be only 5 miles in circumference rather than the more than 50 miles now planned. Proponents, however, counter that more powerful magnets create problems of their own, among them the need for protection of physical structures from the force of the magnetic fields.

Opposition to the SSC arose even before the new superconductor developments. The major complaint concerns the initial cost to build the facility, and the ongoing cost to operate it. In fiscal year 1988, the SSC's cost would be $35 million, all of which would come from the Department of Energy's (DOE) high-energy physics research budget.

In 1989, SSC spending would rise to $348 million and would continue to rise to a peak of $709 million in 1994. With inflation, total costs might reach $5.32 billion. With delays in construction, or higher inflation, costs might be as high as $6 billion.

Scientists who find themselves in the uncomfortable position of opposing a "pure science" research program are nevertheless concerned at the drain the SSC poses to funding of other valuable science programs, notably the Fermi National Accelerator Laboratory and the Stanford Linear Accelerator Center.

Despite all the uncertainties about the SSC, proponents felt the supercollider was the next logical step in particle physics. David Schramm, a physicist at the University of Chicago, described physics as being at a critical threshold. He characterized the Fermilab's 4-mile Tevatron accelerator, and the current generation of accelerators, as limited.

Proponents believed the SSC opened a new frontier onto elusive particles. They hoped to show whether the four basic forces of nature (strong, weak, electromagnetic, and gravitational) could be joined into a Grand Unified Theory.

Theorists, drawing on recent findings in physics, have created a multitude of new explanations for the order and harmony in the universe. Their theories carry an array of unusual names, Technicolor, Supersymmetry, and Compositeness. There is no way of knowing which—if any of these theories—might be correct. Physicists hope the SSC's discoveries may shed light on the various explanations.

In general, physicists hope the SSC will simplify the baffling complexity that has been found in the subatomic world. The growing particle "zoo" is viewed as a failure in simplicity, which in the past has proven to be such a powerful guide to the development of high-energy physics.

When Congress returned to Washington, D.C., from its August recess on September 9, 1987, it had to consider a special SSC appropriations bill. The bill was sponsored by 200 House members led by the chairman of the House Committee on Science, Space and Technology, Robert Roe, and by the ranking Republican member, Manuel Lujan, Jr. Such a bill is considered an unusual mark of congressional favor.

The unfolding fate of warmer-temperature superconductivity and of the massive SSC, whether or not their futures remain linked, can be expected to continue to be news items for many years to come.

11

Chemistry

ORDINARY CLAY MAY NOT BE SO ORDINARY

The Search for the Origin of Life

Shall We Throw Out the Primordial Soup?

The theory that life began when organic molecules came together in a ''primordial soup'' may have to move over for a theory that proposes that life may have had a more solid start in ordinary clay.

Proposed in the 1930s by Russian scientist A. I. Oparin, the primordial-soup theory asserts that the forerunners of life were organic molecules formed in the Earth's atmosphere and that events were set in motion when lightning or solar ultraviolet rays sparked chemical reactions among ammonia, nitrogen, methane, and water.

After their formation, the theory goes, the molecules poured into the oceans. Billions of random chemical reactions followed, and millions of years passed before a complex organic molecule evolved that was capable of reproducing itself.

The primordial-soup theory has been compromised by recent evidence from meteorites, and from ancient moon and Earth rocks, which indicates that the essential chemicals ammonia and methane were not abundant during the Earth's early years.

In any discussion of the origin of life, a pivotal problem is how simple combinations of atoms could have evolved into complex molecules that could process energy and reproduce themselves. Now clay has attracted attention as a possible link.

Was Clay Life's First Energy Source?

Clay is the end result of erosion. Rocks are squeezed, crushed, smashed, cracked, dissolved in water, then crystallized once again as particles to form clay. Clay's familiar clammy, pliant texture is due to the water that has filled the tiny spaces between the particles.

Clay has been found to have astonishing properties: A lump of clay smashed with a hammer will give off ultraviolet energy for a month. This ability to store and to give off energy intrigues scientists at NASA's Ames Research Center in Mountain View, California, led by Leila Coyne of San Jose University. Coyne believes that clay is able to store energy, such as that set free during natural radioactive decay, by capturing energetic electrons in irregularities in the clay's crystalline structure. When the clay was irradiated with gamma rays, fractured, ground up, dried, or wetted, the scientists found that it also gave off the light. It is thought that this brutal laboratory treatment of

Clay mineral crystals occur in diverse forms that could have offered different-shaped templates for the origin of life forms, suggests Dr. W. D. Keller, professor emeritus at the University of Missouri-Columbia. The scanning electron micrograph shown here is vermicular kaolinite weathered from feldspar in a sedimentary sand at a lacustrine deposit near Jacal, Villa Victoria, Michoacan, Mexico.

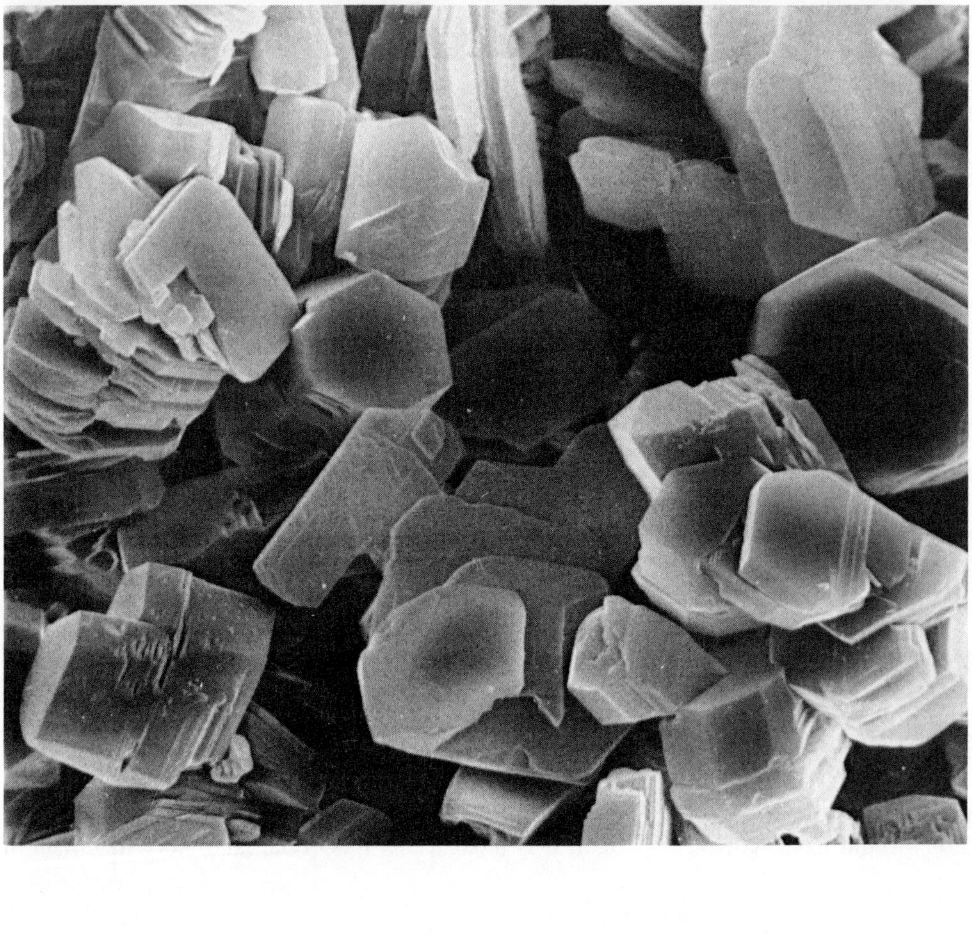

Clay is found worldwide, and Dr. Keller suggests that the variety in both form and location may be significant if clay played a role in the origin of life. Shown here is an unusually well crystallized example of kaolinite collected from within geodes at Keokuk, Iowa.

clay resembles the treatment nature might provide in the form of freeze-thaw cycles, earthquakes, tidal cycles, and erosion.

Dr. Coyne proposes that the most fundamental requirement of a living system is the collection, storage, and transfer of energy. A life-form must have the ability to extract energy from the environment and to use it to fuel its own chemistry. She suggests that the energy that clay can absorb, store, and transfer could have touched off the chemical reactions that formed Earth's first proto-organisms.

A theory proposed by Graham Cairns-Smith of the University of Glasgow in Scotland suggests that the evolution of life was not random. Clay has long been known as a catalyst (a substance that encourages a chemical reaction) and for its capacity to absorb certain chemicals. For example, observations suggest that clay could have served to absorb and concentrate the raw materials necessary for life, perhaps by extracting these chemicals from the ocean during high tide. Then clay could also have set in motion further reactions involving life's building blocks that, over time, may have produced elementary proteins and DNA.

The Source of Clay's Power

The crystals of clay form in layered sheets. This layered structure, resembling a deck of playing cards, gives clay a large surface area. A 1-pound lump of clay may have a surface area equal to 50 football fields. This abundance of surface area is what makes clay powerful, because molecular events take place on the surface of substances. Clay's large surface area makes it useful as a catalyst as well as a neutralizer of toxic wastes. For example, clay was the first catalyst used in oil refining, and the rate of chemical processes can be increased by a factor of 10,000 or more through the presence of small amounts of clay.

With the assistance of new microscopes and particle beams for examining small-scale structures, the complexity of clay is becoming apparent. Scientists expect breakthroughs when the new microscopes are used to examine clay, atom by atom.

Dr. Cairns-Smith points out that a perfect crystal is a blank. Disorder is necessary for the storage of information. The order-disorder quality of clay makes it unique. Clay holds a position somewhere between the monotonous

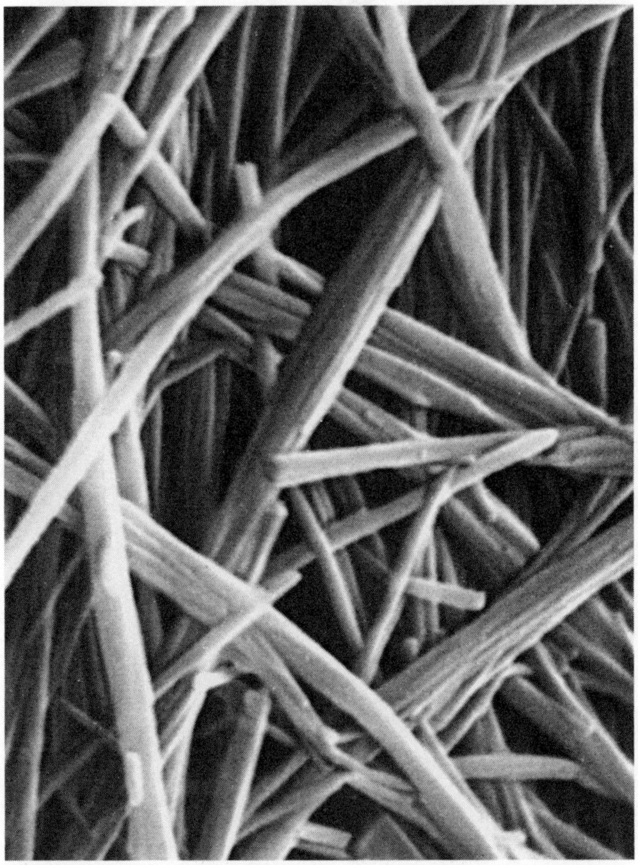

Dramatically filamentous halloysite, presumably hollow, weathered from a pegmatite in Piedade, Brazil.

These clusters of halloysite, standing on feldspar in a crack in the Sparta Granite, in Sparta, Georgia, have an uncommon morphology, a "wet grass" structure.

uniformity of crystals like salt, and the inconstant structures of living organisms. Clays have formless areas of disorder where atoms might be missing or where structures might be broken. These are the areas where chemicals bind and reactions occur.

Under the microscope, clay comes in an assortment of odd-shaped structures. At the molecular level, clay provides enormous surface areas and space that can be filled by water or other substances. The grid of atoms on each layer provides sites that attract molecules, setting off chemical events.

The mysteries of clay's behavior and the search to understand the arrangement of its surfaces are at the cutting edge of a branch of investigation known as materials science. Hyman Hartman of the Massachusetts Institute of Technology describes clay as the most complex area of all geochemistry.

Can Clay "Reproduce"?

Scientists describe clay's storage of information through patterns of ions as resembling checkers on a checkerboard. Some speculate that as crystals grow, they may repeat patterns in new layers. Researchers hope to discover whether particular patterns of ions in a piece of clay can replicate those patterns on other pieces of clay. Dr. Hartman synthesizes clays in the laboratory and then seeds them with other clays. The hypothesis behind the experiment is that patterns in one layer will repeat themselves as other layers pile up, and then a layer will separate in the manner that strands of DNA (deoxyribonucleic acid) separate.

Unanswered Questions

Cairns-Smith, a proponent of the idea that life began with clay, points out some of the difficulties posed by the theory. First, the sequence of properties needed to create life includes more than just the ability to make copies of information; the information must be able to transform the environment, to catalyze reactions, since the key catalysts in living organisms are enzymes.

Also, according to the theory, the evolutionary force of natural selection should play a role. If bigness or smallness,

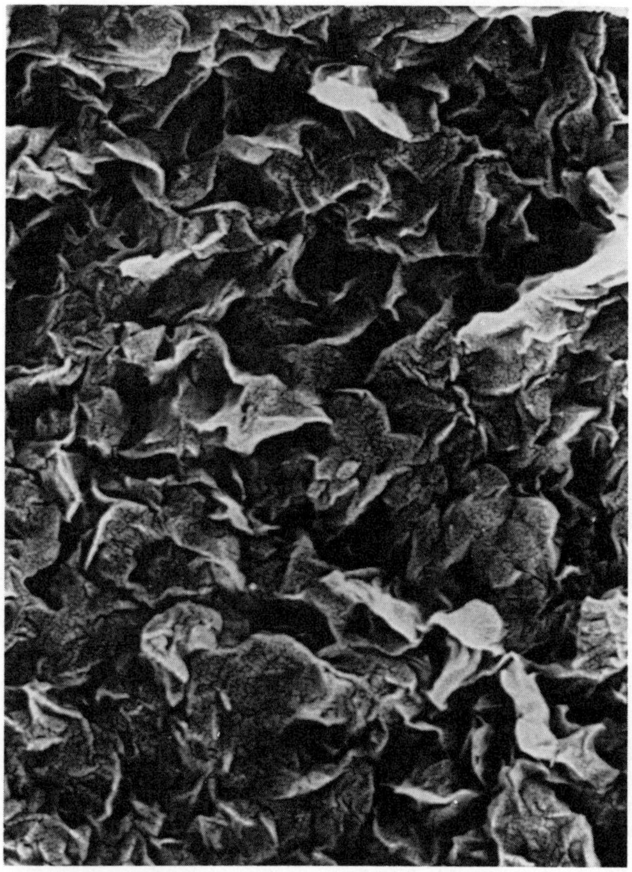

These "corn flakes" from Clay Spur, Wyoming, are Namontmorillonite.

Here are polygonal, hollow tubes of halloysite from Gardner Ridge, Indiana.

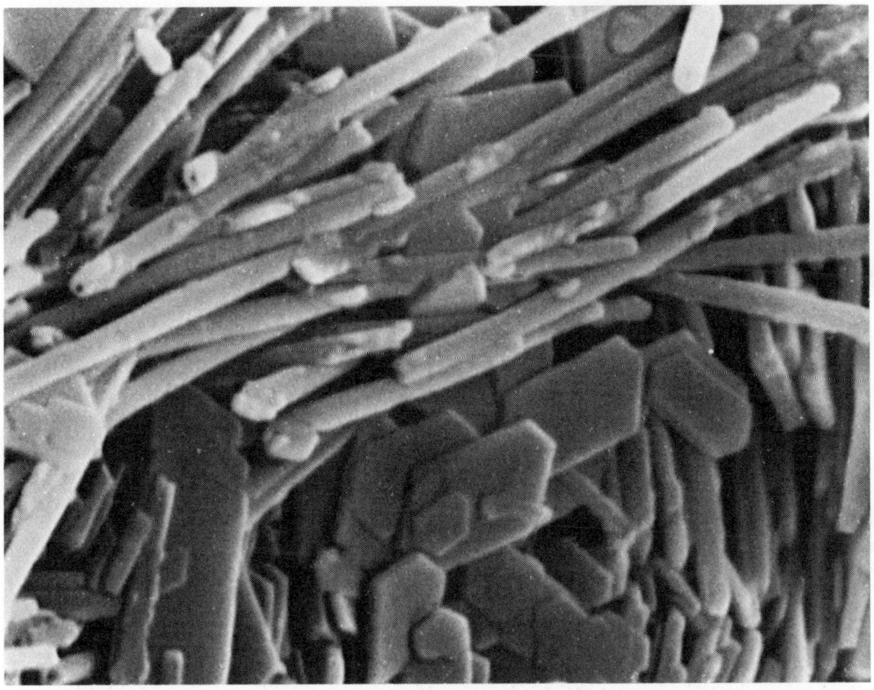

Weathered from a pegmatite near Kauling, China, this polymorph of kaolinite shows an intimate mixture of platy crystals of kaolinite with elongate crystals, presumably halloysite.

or a tendency to be absorbed in water, contributed to successful propagation, eventually a sort of proto-organism might form. Could the now universal complex genetic machinery have hitched onto such proto-organisms?

While there is now widespread skepticism about the primordial-soup theory of life's beginning, not all scientists are ready to credit clay as the likely source. Leslie Orgel of the Salk Institute for Biological Studies in San Diego, California, points out that there is no evidence yet that clay can duplicate itself and perform life-giving chemistry. Much work needs to be done before scientists will know whether clay is the cradle of life—or just clay.

12

Computer Science

NEURAL NETWORKS AND PARALLEL PROCESSING

Computer Systems that Learn from Their Own Mistakes

Conventional Computer Limitations

From their conception, conventional computers have been described as "electronic brains," when in fact their function is quite different than that of a brain. A conventional computer uses a single processor following precise instructions. Tasks are broken into components and processed rapidly in sequence. The brain, on the other hand, uses billions of neurons, each connected to thousands of other neurons, and they all operate in harmony.

In conventional computers, all incoming information is coded into symobls using the digits 0 or 1, which represent an "on" or "off" signal. For information that can be arranged into symbols, the conventional computer's performance is extraordinary. However, some forms of information defy precise definition. A three-year-old child can pick out a picture of a crudely drawn tree using a reservoir of experience with trees. The conventional computer asked to identify a tree on the other hand needs a precise description of a precise tree.

The sequential, step-by-step operation of conventional computers is rapid; however, if one of the steps is absent, even the fastest chip in useless. Conventional computers also suffer from a malfunction known as the Von Neumann bottleneck, named for John Von Neumann, who set down the basic principles of modern computers. The Von Neumann bottleneck has been likened to a traffic jam at a tunnel. Each car may be swift, and thousands of cars may rapidly move through the tunnel, but they can only do so one at a time.

The sequential design of conventional computers was adopted for pragmatic reasons. At the outset of digital computing, the computer's memory and central processing unit were made of different materials. Because memory was less expensive than processing, the efficiency of memory was sacrificed to maximize processing. In the intervening years since the adopting of the sequential computer design, however, materials have changed. Memory and central processors both are now made from etched silicon wafers. In a typical computer, more than 90 percent of the silicon is devoted to memory, the vast majority of which remains idle while the central processor stays constantly busy.

Other factors involving conventional computers that have changed during the intervening years are speed and size. Since 1947, there has been a thousandfold increase in the speed of the processor. That speed has been achieved by shrinking the electronic components and squeezing them into ever-smaller spaces. The single-processor design that has served so well for 40 years is fast approaching fundamental physical boundaries.

Electricity can travel no faster than the speed of light. In the Cray-2, a supercomputer, 4.5 billionths of a second must elapse between the beginning of one operation in the processor and the beginning of the next operation. During that time, light is able to move about a yard and a half. The avoidance of transmission delays requires that the processor's components be separated by no more than a yard and a half. The Cray-2's processor is almost that large, so even the most sophisticated technology is verging on its limits.

The Concept of Thinking Computers

The idea that the functioning of the conventional computer, in its use of numbers and symbols, and the functioning of the brain, in the process of thinking, were related to one another, had the effect of narrowing the focus of research. Attention was spent on looking into the nature of rules and symbols used by the mind. Scientists looked for rules such as how a word in the present tense is changed to the past tense, or how a chair is distinguished from a table.

The difficulty encountered in moving conventional computers from number- and symbol-crunching to tasks such as speech and vision led to the suspicion that perhaps thinking involved more than symbol manipulation. The biologically relevant task of image processing, that is, recognizing a familiar face, a feat easily done by humans, proved to be exceedingly difficult for a computer.

During the 1950s and 1960s, scientists tried to build computers that replicated the brain. Frank Rosenblatt, a scientist at Cornell University, designed the perceptron, a simple neural computer. But the various devices that were developed had serious limitations. In 1969, Marvin Minsky and Seymour Papert, leaders in the field of artificial intelligence, published a book containing an elegant mathematical critique of the perceptron that squelched further interest.

Despite the collective defection from replications of the brain, called neural networks, a few scientists maintained their interest. Using his own elegant mathematics, John Hopfield of the California Institute of Technology (Caltech) revived the field with a seminal paper published in the *Proceedings of the National Academy of Science* in 1982. Other scientists who figured in the resurgence of interest were David Rumelhart of Stanford and Stephen Grossberg of Boston University.

Until Hopfield, the idea of turning on hundreds of computing units connected to one another inspired the expectation of a wildly oscillating system. Hopfield established that a network of interconnected units would operate in a manner comparable to a heated bar of metal that hardens as it cools. A neural net whose switches are turning on and off at random will, like the metal, also go through a stabilizing process. Hopfield called his computing units, neurons, and the connections between them *synapses*.

A Confusion of Terms

Actual machines that function like a network of neurons are referred to as *parallel processors*, or *multiprocessors*. The term *neural network* tends to be used to describe computer-simulation programs that do parallel processing either on parallel-processing machines or on conventional computers. Discussions are apt to make parallel processing and multiprocessing sound as if they are interchangeable terms. They are not, however, exactly the same. In parallel processing, a single program is divided among multiple nodes. But in multiprocessing, the nodes run totally different applications or independent job streams of the same general application.

Parallel Processing

One approach to capture the use of idle computer memory, to go beyond the physical limits of traditional computers, and to have computers "think" brought about the major redesign called parallel processing. Parallel processing uses many small processors working simultaneously, each with a small memory of its own. One machine called the Connection Machine uses 65,536 simple processors, each much less powerful than a personal computer, but which in tandem can execute several billion instructions per second.

The Connection Machine was introduced commercially in 1986 by Thinking Machines Corporation in Cambridge, Massachusetts. Daniel Hillis, Massachusetts Institute of Technology (MIT) prodigy and co-founder of Thinking Machine, described his motive for building the Connection Machine as an attempt to understand how the human brain works. Although at least 100 other projects were under way at companies and universities around the world, the Connection Machine had succeeded in linking up tens of thousands more processors than anyone else.

Massively Parallel Processing

Just one sweep of a satellite sensor across a 100 mile swath of Earth produces a scene with a million pieces of potentially useful information. To deal with the volume of image-processing information, NASA scientists commissioned the development of a computer called the Massively

The Connection Machine and Data Vault built by MIT prodigy Danny Hillis and the Thinking Machines Corporation. Says Hillis, "I love to figure out how people think. It's going to be hard to do. We're not even positive that thinking happens in the brain."

Parallel Processor (MPP). The machine was designed and built by Goodyear Aerospace Corporation in Akron, Ohio.

To automatically analyze, within 20 seconds, a satellite picture of Earth, MPP studies the million or so pixels that make up a typical image and determine whether each spot represents water or land, forest or field, street or stream. To process the same image, a conventional computer takes hours.

The MPP is organized into a network of 16,384 simple processors that allow a computation to be divided up so that each processor performs the same operations on different pieces of data at the same time. The MPP is based on a nearest-neighbor network. Its 16,384 processors arranged in a 128-by-128 square array are each connected only to their four neighbors.

NASA invited researchers throughout the United States to suggest projects to exploit MPP's ability. In one of those projects, computer scientist John Barnden of Indiana University in Bloomington used the MPP to study how neural networks in the human brain process complex information.

In his model, Barnden used networks in two-dimensional arrays. Each processor handled one grid square and kept track of the square's "state" and "color," which represented properties of a small neural circuit. When new information was added and "reasoning" took place, the squares changed their properties as neighbors influenced neighbors according to a set of rules.

An earlier parallel-processor machine called the Distributed Array Processor (DAP) was developed by International Computers in England. DAP has 4,096 simple processors connected in a 64-by-64 array. As in the MPP, the processors respond at the same time to the same instruction while working on different pieces of data. Unlike the MPP, the DAP provides electronic highways for sending data across the entire array rather than just to neighbors.

Parallel processors fall into two broad categories: coarse-grained machines, which have numerous, weaker processors; and fine-grained machines, which have numerous, weaker processors. The Connection Machine with 65,536 processors each weaker than a microchip in a video game, falls into the fine-grained category. The machine is based on the concept of "cellular automata," tiny entities that communicate with their neighbors in some prescribed fashion.

In a coarse-grained machine, which is like a network of computers, the programmer has the difficult task of devising instructions that can be distributed among different processors operating simultaneously. In Hillis's fine-grained Thinking Machine, laborious programming is not needed. Data are distributed so that each data point is associated with one processor, and all processors follow the same instructions on their different data points. Working in concert, as does the human eye, the 65,536 processors can look at a whole image at once.

An area where the Connection Machine works particularly well is at modeling the flow of air over a proposed design for an airplane wing. Given the difficulty, even for a supercomputer, of solving airflow equations, most proposed designs are built to scale and tested in wind tunnels. The Connection Machine avoids the equations by simulating the airlfow itself. A particle of air is assigned to each processor. The particles are then made to bombard the wing, and the designer watches the results.

Parallel Processor Design

In the design of a parallel processor, four issues must be addressed. The first concerns the amount of parallelism needed—the large-grained versus the small-grained approach. The second issue is configuration of connections. High-performance connections in which each processor is connected to every other processor are expensive and complex. Nearest-neighbor-only connections are less costly but constrain the system.

The third issue is how to attach processors to memory. Will they share memory or each have a separate memory? The final, and most difficult, issue is the breakdown of the task into parallel parts. If the task is performed entirely by the computer and its language compiler, programming is simplified and performance is relatively inefficient. If the programmer makes the decision, performance is improved, but programming becomes extremely difficult.

The Connection Machine is set up so that it can be reconfigured to reflect the actual structure of a problem. Each tiny processor has a small piece of memory, and each processor can form connections through the physical (hardwired) network with any other.

During a search, the process by which connections are formed, one cell finds the address of another cell. If cell *Yellow* needs to call cell *Brown*, cell *Yellow* sends out a message wave to *Brown's* location. When the wave with *Yellow's* address reaches *Brown*, the *Brown* cell responds with its own address back to *Yellow*, which then cancels the still-spreading original message with a faster cancel wave.

Messages are passed from cell to cell and appropriately altered in each. A message with an address "up 4, across 7" would be handed on to the cell above with the message "up 3, across 7."

Neural Networks

Neurologists know that the human brain contains from 10 billion to 1 trillion neurons, each of which is connected with 1 to 10,000 other neurons. Each neuron discharges electrochemical impulses at varying rates. Through connections called synapses, each neuron is aware of the firing state of its neighbors. Whether or not a neuron fires is dependent on the aggregate of message received from its network of cells.

Neural networks are analogous to neurons, the nerve cells of the brain. Neural networks perform massively parallel computation, mostly on conventional computers using experimental chips or complex programming. Neurons consist of many processing units, or nodes, which receive and transmit electrochemical signals.

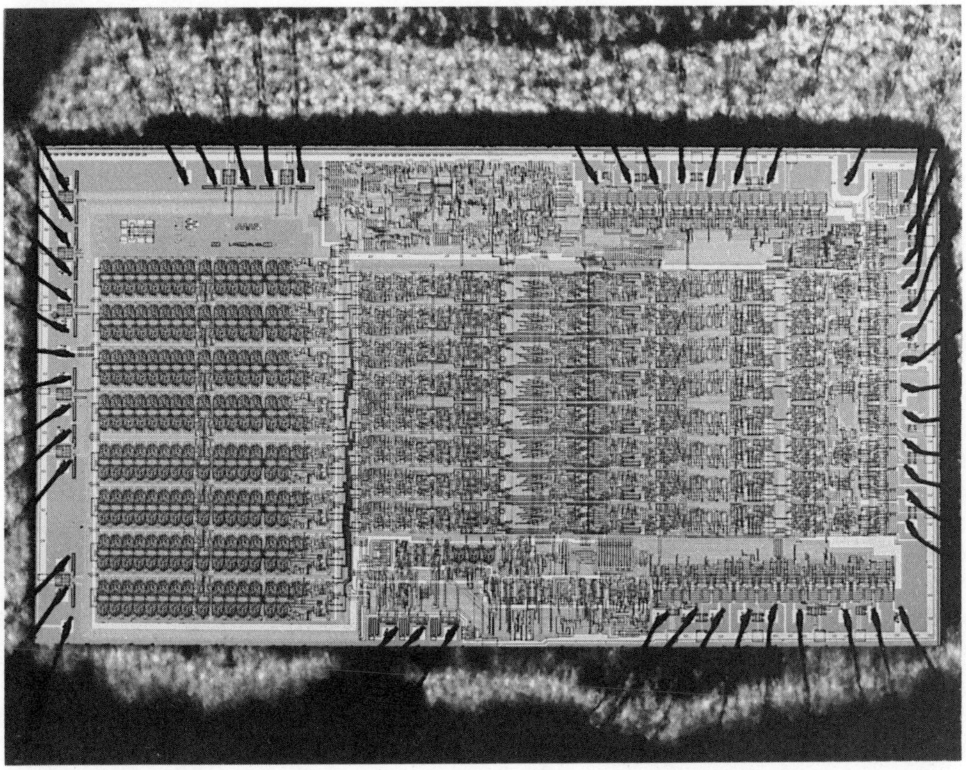

The array unit of the MPP consists of a square array of 128 x 128 processing elements (PE's). Pictured is a custom VLSI PE chip containing eight PE's. There are 2,000 such chips on the MPP.

Each node is connected to many other nodes. The strength of the connection varies. When the activation level of a node attains a minimum level, the node passes on a signal to other nodes with which it is connected. The product of the activation level and the strength of the connection determines the power of the signal passed on.

If a unit has an activation level of .7 and the strength of the connection is .2, the unit will send an input of .14 to a connecting unit. The receiving unit will receive similar inputs from other units. The sum of those inputs will be the receiving unit's activation level which, if they exceed an established threshold, will prompt the unit to send out a signal to other units.

Two layers of processing units might be set up to recognize letters of the alphabet. First-layer units might represent characteristics of letters such as a horizontal line on the bottom, or a vertical line on the left.

If a letter with a bottom horizontal line confronts the computer, a unit representing the characteristic of the horizontal line will be activated. That unit will in turn strongly activate units representing letters such as *L* and *E*, and mildly activate the units for letters such as *B* and *C*, which have a bottom line that somewhat resembles a straight line, and depress letters with no bottom line. At the same time the network will be sending out activations for other characteristics such as loops at the top. All the characteristics of the letter to be recognized are sent simultaneously through the units. The letter with the highest activation is selected.

Learning by Trial and Error

In identifications such as letters, activation weights are preset. But networks can be set to learn by trial and error. If a network makes the wrong choice of a letter, using a mathematical formula, the liability for the error is allocated to the different connections and the weights for those connections are changed. After hundreds or thousands of trials, the weights become adjusted so that most of the time they provide a proper response.

In a letter-recognition task, the computer's field of vision would be divided into a grid in which points on the grid would be light or dark. A unit might be strongly activated if all the dots in a grid row were dark, and less strongly activated if some but not all were activated. In this way, the network can recognize distorted letters or those whose position has shifted.

Since information does not reside in one place in the system, should a portion of a network break down, the system still retains its ability to reconstruct information. In this respect, the neural networks resemble brain activity, in which function continues even when some cells die.

Associative Memory

The collective behavior of neural nets provides it with another brainlike trait—associative memory—which is the ability to bring forth a collection of facts from a fragment or even from a partially incorrect input. An example used repeatedly to explain associative memory uses a doctor friend named Sally who has red hair and lives in Pittsburg.

If an assortment of related information—Sally, doctor, red hair, and lives in Pittsburgh—represents one stable arrangement of a neural net's on/off switches, given the input Sally and doctor, the units will settle into the configuration red hair and Pittsburg. The net will even make a reasonable guess on the basis of incorrect input. Offered a red-headed doctor who lives in Philadelphia, the system might still arrive at Sally.

Learning from Learning Rules

Neural nets can learn from a series of examples by using algorithms or "learning rules." The rules work on the principle that if two neural units cooperate to produce the right answer, the strength of the connection between them is increased. If two units produce a wrong answer, then the connection between them is decreased.

NETalk is a machine build by Terry Sejnowski of Johns Hopkins and Charles Rosenberg of Princeton to learn from learning rules. NETalk is a 200-unit neural net that learned to read aloud. Starting with an input of written text and the ability to drive a speaker, NETalk did not have any rules for matching letters with sound. Instead it had a learning algorithm.

The first training session began with a 500-word text of a first-grader's recorded conversation. A linguist had transcribed the correct sounds for the child's speech divided into units called phonemes. While NETalk read the text, its network selected phonemes to depict the letters. At the same time, the learning algorithm compared the selected phonemes with the linguist's transcription. When dissimilarities arose, the algorithm altered neural unit connections to try to create a better match.

At the outset, NETalk babbled. After a day of training, it could with about 90 percent accuracy read any text. Rather then put in rules as would have been done with a conventional computer, the scientists waited for the rules to emerge.

Researchers at Los Alamos National Laboratory, Alan Lapedes and Robert Farber, used a neural-net simulation with a learning algorithm to address a problem in genetics. The problem is how to determine whether a particular sequence of bases in a fragment of DNA (deoxyribonucleic acid) is coding for the production of a protein. The DNA bases A, C, T, and G (adenine, cytosine, thymine, and guanine) determine whether or not a protein will be made. Using a statistical approach, scientists can predict DNA-strand activity accurately provided the strand contains at least 200 base pairs.

For smaller segments, with 20 or 30 bases, the conventional method is no better than flipping a coin. Evaluation of fragments with as little as 30 base pairs is important because ribosomes, the "factories" where proteins are produced according to the DNA blueprint, are believed to operate on about 30 base pairs' worth of information at a time.

The scientists trained the net using 900 examples of active DNA fragments and 900 examples of inert strands. The net was able to predict with 80 percent accuracy whether or not the strand was active. Moreover, Lapedes reported that the net appeared to have learned some fundamental rules about genetics not yet clear to biologists. The next step for the researchers is to try to understand how the net did what it did and thus to extract the biological rules.

A factor that appears to capture the imagination of researchers working with neural nets is the "intelligence" that seems to arise from the collective action of neurons doing simple things. David Rumelhart, of the Institute for Cognitive Science at the University of California at San Diego, in experiments with a network, found that the network developed its own internal representation to distinguish plants as a group from animals as a group.

The Brain as an Architectural Model

The brain's pattern of connections, often called "wetware," is not just a handy analogy to make it easier for scientists to talk about neural nets. Researchers are drawing upon what is already known about neural systems such as the visual system, olfactory cortex (which controls our sense of smell), and cerebellum to build both hardware and software. The computer systems not only behave in certain ways like their biological counterparts, they enable scientists to screen theories about how the brain functions.

Brain researcher Ralph Linsker of the IBM Thomas J. Watson Research Center in Yorktown Heights, New York, modeled a self-developing, multilayered network that generated features qualitatively similar to those found in the first few stages of the mammalian visual system. Linsker modeled the visual system as a "layered self-adaptive network." Each layer was composed of hundreds or thousands of "cells," each able to receive hundreds of inputs from closely overlying cells.

Linsker built in a developmental rule: If the firing of a cell in one layer was usually preceded by the firing of a cell in the previous layer to which it was connected, the strength of the connection was increased and its "vote" about what the receiving cell would do would be stronger. In the absence of those conditions, the connection strength decreased and the vote had less influence.

In Linsker's model, several cell layers matured one at a time. Over time they emerged with biologically significant properties. As the cells of layer A fired randomly, their synapses with layer B reached maximum excitatory or inhibitory strength. If layer B developed into an all-excitatory layer, then the cells in layer C developed features like the specialized cells of the visual system called spatial opponent cells—cells identified long ago in the retina and in the brain.

One of the values to the brain scientist of models such as Linsker's is that they can lead to the generation and testing of ideas that might be much harder or impossible to test using experimental animals or models alone.

Less than Perfect Answers

Unlike a conventional computer, and very much like the human mind, neural nets provide good answers, but not always the very best answer. Perfect answers are often not

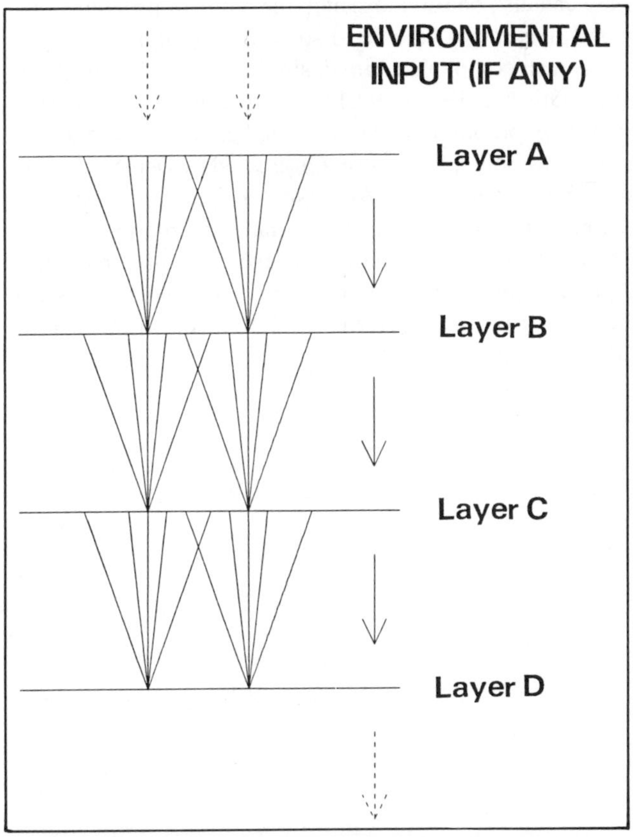

Schematic of Linsker's model. Each layer contains many cells, all of which receive inputs from an overlaying neighborhood of cells of the previous layer. Shown are input "arborizations" for two cells each in layers B, C, and D. The dotted arrow at the bottom indicates further layers.

worth the extra time and effort. A classic example is the often-used "traveling salesman problem," which is applicable to a wide range of everyday situations from the best routing for a sales representative to take for trips to 10 cities to the best approach in designing microchips.

It is mathematically possible to take 181,440 different routes to visit 10 cities. John Hopfield and David Tank at Bell Labs used a neural net to find answers to the traveling salesman problems. The neural net found answers a thousand times faster than did a conventional computer, but the answers were the very best only 50 percent of the time. However, the nets came up with 1 of the 2 best answers 90 percent of the time.

Robotics is an area in which neural nets offer promise. Conventional robots have difficulty coping with unpredictable environments. If the object a robot is programmed to pick up moves, or if the robot's arm is slightly off, the robot comes to a stop or thrashes around.

Wellesley College neuroscientist, Michael Kuperstein used a neural net to simulate a robot. The robot begins with random arm motions through every possible posture needed to pick up an object. At the same time the robot is in motion, the robot's two eyes rove. Whenever the robot "sees" its arm in a position where an object can be grasped, the robot stores the correlation of how the arm moves with where the object is located.

Varied Problem-solving Areas

Because the hardware is so difficult to design, most neural nets are simulated on conventional computers using complex programming. The neural-net simulations can be used to help solve the problems of their own hardware design. They can also be used to sketch the range of problems that neural nets might be able to solve in the future.

Several companies are designing special neural-net chips. Others believe optical computing might be a solution to wiring problems because light beams can cross one another without interference. Groups led by Demetri Psaltis at Caltech and Dana Anderson at the University of Colorado have built optical associative memories, which, when shown partial patterns, retrieved the entire memory. When not presented with a pattern, the Colorado system displays random patterns that the researchers call "daydreaming."

Future Prospects

This discipline, which until recently attracted only a handful of professionals, drew 1,700 researchers, designers, and engineers in June of 1987 to the First International Conference on Neural Networks in San Diego. Discussions included knowledge processing, cognitive science connections, vision and speech recognition, and robotics.

The range of proposed applications for neural nets and for parallel processing seems almost limitless. Proposals include: robots on Mars, underwater exploration, electronic circuit design, molecular modeling, oil reservoir modeling—almost anything consisting of many small elements in flux.

Most vendors who sell parallel processors share the belief that the machines will eventually prove more suitable than serial processors for most computing problems. They look at the world and see it as parallel rather than serial.

13

Mathematics

SRINIVASA RAMANUJAN

India's Mathematical Genius Finally Receives His Due

Srinivasa Ramanujan, born in 1887 in the small city of Kumbakonam in southern India, has become the source of whole new subdisciplines within modern mathematics. His contemporaries early in this century recognized Ramanujan's genius but found his elegant formulas obscure. Since then, computers with programs to manipulate algebraic quantities have enabled modern mathematicians to better follow Ramanujan's lines of thought.

In 1976, Dr. George Andrews of Pennsylvania State University found 130 unlabeled pages produced by Ramanujan in a box at the library of Trinity College in Cambridge, England. Andrew's discovery is referred to as the "Lost Notebook."

Those 130 pages represent an extraordinary output of work done while Ramanujan coped with the pain of a mysterious ailment that ultimately killed him at the age of 32. The 130 pages alone have been described as the equivalent of a lifetime's work for a great mathematician, but in addition to the 130 pages created during the last year of his life, between 1903 and 1914, Ramanujan filled three notebooks with mathematical formulas and relationships.

The notebooks are a source of wonder and frustration to modern mathematicians. Living in poverty, which made the cost of paper a burden, Ramanujan used a slate rather than paper to do his work. Only his final results were entered into his notebooks. Therefore, with none of Ramanujan's work sheets to guide them, modern mathematicians are spending years proving perhaps as many as 4,000 theorems that Ramanujan set down unembellished.

Ramanujan was born a high-caste but poor Hindu. His father and grandfather worked as clerks. Ramanujan received an adequate high school education. However, at college he repeatedly failed examinations in subjects other than mathematics.

In mathematics, Ramanujan had no teacher. His pursuit of what was to become his life's work began with old, second-rate textbooks, but with a cultural tradition that allowed him to aspire to the life of a scholar.

Working as a clerk, after several years of unemployment, Ramanujan wrote a series of letters to English mathematicians during 1912 and 1913. The letters offered carefully chosen samples of his theorems. Most of the offerings were in the form of identities; that is, they made a statement that a familiar quantity such as pi was the equivalent of some unfamiliar quantity, or that two unfamiliar quantities were equal.

In the letter he received from Ramanujan, English mathematician Godfrey Hardy recognized work that could have

Srinivasa Ramanujan

Illustration by Michael Ng

A Mysterious Formula for Pi

$$\frac{1}{\pi} = 2\sqrt{2}\sum_{n=0}^{\infty}\frac{(\frac{1}{4})_n(\frac{1}{2})_n(\frac{3}{4})_n}{(1)_n(1)_n n!}(1103 + 26390n)(\frac{1}{99})^{4n+2}$$

Mathematicians find many of Ramanujan's formulas to be both beautiful and obscure. To their surprise, the formula above provides an extremely rapid way to calculate the value of pi, an age-old preoccupation. Only last year, a computer scientist used a version of Ramanujan's formula to calculate pi to 17 million places. Only after this success were mathematicians able to prove why Ramanujan's insight was correct.

been done only by a mathematician of the highest caliber. Hardy arranged an invitation to Cambridge University for the Indian scholar.

In 1913, Ramanujan arrived at Cambridge, where he stayed for almost 6 years. During that time, Hardy and Ramanujan shared a preoccupation with numbers. They thought about numbers almost as if they were living beings or storybook characters. During his years in England, Ramanujan published a substantial number of papers and achieved a level of worldwide fame. Although Godfrey Hardy understood and appreciated Ramanujan more than his other contemporaries, even Hardy had difficulty looking beyond Ramanujan's inadequate education. Seven years after Ramanujan's death, Hardy expressed his disappointment with his former colleague by describing Ramanujan's work as strange and lacking in simplicity.

Hardy felt that Ramanujan would have been more at home in the great age of formulas a century earlier. By way of contrast, Richard Askey of the University of Wisconsin, who has collaborated with George Andrews in trying to understand some of Ramanujan's work, regrets that Ramanujan was not born 100 years later. Current unsolved mathematical problems involve multiple variables, and Askey believes they would have benefited from the intuition Ramanujan appeared to have.

Today mathematicians are engaged in a process of "forensic mathematics" as they struggle over Ramanujan's pages, trying to understand the formulas and to prove them. Bruce Berndt, a mathematician at the University of Illinois at Urbana-Champaign, has spent a substantial portion of the last decade working with Ramanujan's notebooks. His method involves looking for sources to support already known formulas and attempting to prove the work not already known. The bulk of Berndt's time is spent with the unknown work. George Andrews has been engaged in a similar task with the 130 pages of the "Lost Notebook." The notebook is not without errors, but the errors are few.

Andrews has described Ramanujan's work as intriguing and revolutionary, with real implications for current mathematics. After more than 65 years, much of what India's genius discovered has not been rediscovered or duplicated.

Many of Ramanujan's discoveries concerned a family of identities he called mock theta functions, simple assertions in arithmetic with profound implications. Such mathematics has helped to spawn one of the major new visions of theoretical physics, superstring theory.

Ramanujan loved infinite series. Mathematically, a series is simply the sum of a specified number of terms. One of Ramanujan's infinite series has become the basis for methods to compute pi. In 1985, Bill Gosper of Symbolics used the formula to calculate pi to 17.5 million digits.

Mathematicians are awed by Ramanujan's accomplishments. Even with today's deeper theoretical understanding and powerful computer software, mathematicians find it difficult to generate the kind of identities Ramanujan found.

Ramanujan was also fond of inventing and exploring structures called continued fractions. In this area, Berndt believes, the Indian scholar surpassed all other mathematicians. Continued fractions are fractions of fractions of fractions and so on, to infinity. In the expansion of the continued fraction, the terms as they succeed one another rest deeper within the fraction's denominator. An algebraic formula can be used to produce the terms.

An area in which Berndt believes Ramanujan developed his most provocative continued fractions is gamma functions, which concern the values of particular integrals in calculus. The topic is not entirely understood, nor do mathematicians understand how Ramanujan made his discoveries.

During the short span in which Ramanujan worked, his interest in formulas was out of fashion. The eighteenth and nineteenth centuries had been the period of discovery of such relationships. But uneducated in standard mathematics, and isolated in India, Ramanujan still possessed the optimism of earlier eras.

Undervalued during his lifetime, Ramanujan's work is now being absorbed into mathematics and science. Jonathan Borwein of Dalhousie University in Halifax, Nova Scotia, believes that Ramanujan's productions were not just curiosities but were evidence of a foundation, an underlying theory that Ramanujan never made explicit but that Borwein hopes mathematicians will in time reveal.

On the occasion of his centennial, mathematicians gathered during 1987 in conferences held in the United States and in India to honor Ramanujan and to discuss the implications of his work. At the meeting, physicist Freeman Dyson likened current work on superstrings to flowers that grew from seeds in Ramanujan's garden. It appears that mathematicians will be toiling in the great Indian theorist's garden for many years to come.

APPENDIX

1987 SCIENCE AWARD WINNERS

NOBEL PRIZE IN PHYSICS

J. Georg Bednorz, West Germany
K. Alex Mueller, Switzerland

In 1986, Bednorz and Mueller discovered superconductivity in a new class of ceramics at temperatures higher than had been possible previously.

NOBEL PRIZE IN CHEMISTRY

Charles J. Pedersen, USA
Donald J. Cram, USA
Jean-Marie Lehn, France

The discovery of how to make relatively simple molecules that mimic the function of much more complex molecules produced by living cells was first made by Pedersen in 1960, and later extended by Cram and Lehn.

NOBEL PRIZE IN PHYSIOLOGY OR MEDICINE

Susumu Tonegawa, Japan

Honored for creating new techniques to determine how the body's immune system is able to produce antibodies to millions of disease agents not previously encountered.

ALBERT LASKER MEDICAL RESEARCH AWARDS

These awards are to recognize and honor individuals who have made significant contributions in basic and clinical medical research.

Basic Medical Research Award—Susuma Tonegawa, Philip Leder, and Leroy Hood

Given a finite number of genes coding for antibody production, the three scientists, during the 1970s, independently determined how the immune system can produce antibodies to a lifetime of encounters with foreign substances (antigens).

Clinical Medical Research Award—Mogens Schou

For the conduct of clinical trials of Lithium therapy and prophylasis for manic-depressive illness, which initiated a revolution in the treatment of mental illness.

Public Service Award—none was given in 1987.

NATIONAL MEDALS OF SCIENCE

The highest science award given by the U.S. government. Conferred by the President's Committee on the National Medal of Science.

Winner	*Field*	*Affiliation*
Philip H. Ableson	Physics	*Science Magazine*
Anne Anastasi	Behavior	Fordham University
R. Byron Bird	Engineering	University of Wisconsin
Raoul Bott	Mathematics	Harvard University
Michael E. DeBakey	Biology	Baylor University
Theodor O. Diener	Biology	U.S. Department of Argiculture
Harry Eagle	Biology	Albert Einstein Medical College
Walter M. Elsasser	Physics	Johns Hopkins University
Michael H. Freedman	Mathematics	University of California, San Diego
William S. Johnson	Chemistry	Stanford University
Har Gobind Khorana	Biology	Massachusetts Institute of Technology
Paul C. Lauterbur	Physics	University of Illinois
Rita Levi-Montalcini	Biology	Lab of Cell Biology, Rome, Italy
George E. Pake	Physics	Xerox Corporation
H. Bolton Seed	Engineering	University of California, Berkeley
George J. Stigler	Behavior	University of Chicago
Walter H. Stockmayer	Chemistry	Dartmouth College
Max Tishler	Chemistry	Wesleyan University
James A. Van Allen	Physics	University of Iowa
Ernst Weber	Engineering	Polytechnic Institute of New York

GLOSSARY

absorption line a minute range of wavelength or frequency in the electromagnetic spectrum within which radiant energy is absorbed by the medium through which it is passing.

adrenal gland a triangular-shaped body atop each kidney that secretes compounds (catecholamines) that affect the sympathetic nervous system. It is particularly related to adjustments of the body in response to emotional states, mobilizing the physiological changes that occur in fight-or-flight emergencies.

akrasia implies that some individuals succumb to risky behavior even though safer alternatives are obviously available.

algorithm a set of well-defined rules in a finite number of steps for the solution of a problem

Alzheimer's disease involves progressive, irreversible loss of memory; deterioration of intellectual functions; apathy; speech and gait disturbances; and disorientation. The frontal and occipital lobes of the brain atrophy. The disease was named for Alois Alzheimer, a nineteenth-century German neurologist.

amphiphilic relates to any of many organic compounds such as surfactant, detergent, or phospholipids composed of hydrophilic (attractive to water) and hydrophobic (repellant to water) components.

anemia a condition in which there is a reduction in the normal volume of circulating red blood cells; the condition is not a disease, rather it is a symptom of various diseases.

antibody a protein substance developed in response to, and interacting specificially with, an antigen; antibodies may be present due to a previous infection, vaccination, transfer from mother to fetus in the uterus, or without any known antigenic stimulus.

antigen a substance that induces the formation of antibodies that specifically interact with it; this antigen-antibody reaction forms the basis for immunity.

anti-idiotypic antibodies (anti-ids) molecules formed in the body when challenged by a foreign cell or protein.

arborist a specialist in the care and maintenance of trees.

arbuscules fungal organs that allow the exchange of nutrients between fungus and plant.

art deco a decorative style of the 1920s and 1930s based generally on geometric forms.

associative memory the ability to bring forth a collection of facts from a fragment or even a partially correct input.

autoimmune disorder when the body's immune system becomes defective and produces antibodies against normal parts of the body to an extent that causes tissue damage.

autotransfusion a method of returning a patient's own blood that has escaped from blood vessels back into circulation.

axon the portion of a neuron that conducts impulses away from the cell body; they are usually long and straight, and most often end in synapses in the central nervous system, or in ganglia (a mass of nerve-cell bodies lying outside the brain or spinal cord), or in effector organs such as motor neurons.

B lymphocytes highly specialized cells that manufacture antibodies to help fight infections.

biome the replication of a habitat.

biomedical engineering the application of engineering technology to the solution of medical problems such as artificial valves for the heart, sensors for the blind, and automated artificial limbs.

braille a system of printing and writing for the blind, in which letters, numerals, and punctuation are made with raised dots distinguishable by the fingers. The system was named after Louis Braille, who invented it.

bubble clouds clusters of bubbles created by the turbulence of waves that slowly sink into deeper, colder water, diminish in size until they disappear; in the process, they lose their gases into the ocean.

bubonic plague an acute, infectious disease passed to human beings by the bite of rat fleas, characterized by enlargement of the lymph glands or pneumonia.

cachexia a wasting away of the body common in cancer and AIDS patients.

caliches limestone nodules consistent with a monsoonal climate of intense rain followed by a long drought.

calpain an enzyme activated by calcium, which is theorized to cut through the protein scaffolding of cell walls when platelets change shape and during the formation of a memory trace.

catecholamines biologically active amines, epinephrine and norepinephrine, that have a marked effect on the nervous and cardiovascular system, metabolic rate, temperature, and smooth muscle.

cellular immune network consists of patrolling cells called macrophages and killer T cells that directly attack and destroy foreign bacteria and viruses.

chain of infection six components a scientist would look at in an analysis of the outbreak of an infectious disease; they are: (1) the causative agent; (2) the habitat of the agent; (3) the exit of the agent from the host; (4) the mode of transmission; (5) the entry into the new host; and (6) the host's susceptibility.

chameleon a lizard having a prehensile tail, four feet suited for grasping branches, eyes covered by a single circular eyelid with an aperture in the center, and a capacity to change color.

cholera an acute infection involving the entire small bowel, characterized by profuse diarrhea and vomiting, severe loss of fluids, muscular cramps, diminished urine formation, dehydration, and extreme exhaustion.

clotting factors also called coagulation factors, are needed by hemophiliacs to prevent continued bleeding. There are a great number of terms to refer to the complex coagulation process as well as a set of Roman numerals: When blood is shed through an injured vessel, one factor, thromboplastin, is liberated from the injured tissue and from degenerating blood platelets to initiate the clotting mechanism; another factor, fibrin, forms a meshwork of fibers in which corpuscles of blood become entangled, thus forming a clot.

computer-aided speech systems that allow speech to be visualized graphically.

congestive cardiomyopathy a disease that kills thousands of cats annually brought about by the absence of an amino acid called taurine, the replacement of which corrects and prevents the condition.

Coriolis effect also known as the Coriolis deflection, the Earth's rotation and tilt deflect any moving body whether it is a bullet shot from a gun or a wind making its way around the world: An object moving horizontally is deflected to the right in the Northern Hemisphere and to the left in the Southern Hemisphere.

cortex of the brain the thin convoluted surface of gray matter of the brain hemispheres, consisting principally of cell bodies of neurons arranged in five layers.

Cretaceous-Tertiary (K-T) boundary a period 65 million years ago when three-quarters of the Earth's species were extinguished; there are several theories to explain what might have happened: The most popular is that an asteroid crashed into the Earth at the end of the Cretaceous period, blanketing the Earth in dust.

cryosurgery a technique of exposing tissue such as tumors to extreme cold, usually below −20 degrees centigrade, using a probe whose coldness is likely to be produced by liquid nitrogen.

cytoskeleton protein fibers composing the structural framework of a cell.

dendrite a branched structure of a neuron that conducts impulses to the cell body (there are usually several to a cell); they form synaptic connections with other neurons.

diabetes mellitus a disorder of carbohydrate metabolism, characterized by hyperglycemia (increase of blood sugar) and glycosuria (glucose present in the urine), resulting from inadequate production or utilization of insulin.

dialysis in cases of impaired kidneys, or in the absence of kidneys, the blood of a patient is diffused across a semipermeable membrane to remove toxic materials, and to maintain fluid, electrolyte, and acid-base balance.

dopamine a catecholamine synthesized by the adrenal glands and critical in the study of schizophrenia and Parkinson's disease.

dressage a method of training horses in obedience and precision of movement.

ectothermic an animal that obtains most of its heat and cooling from the environment; this dependence limits activity.

electrophoresis the movement of charged colloidal particles through the medium in which they are dispersed as a result of changes in electrical potential.

embryo transfer the removal of a fertilized egg from a mother who produced the egg to a mother who will carry the fertilized egg through labor and birth.

endotherm an animal that produces and retains enough heat from its own metabolism to keep its body temperature somewhat independent of the environment, freeing the animal to be more active.

entomologist a scientist who studies insects.

enzyme any of a group of catalytic proteins that are produced by living cells and that mediate and promote the chemical process of life without themselves being altered or destroyed.

epidemic the rapid spread of a disease or condition among people in a specified geographic area.

Epidemic Intelligence Service a division of the Centers for Disease Control, most of whose members serve 2 years as commissioned officers of the Public Health Service, learning and practicing epidemiology.

epidemiology the study of the occurrence of disease in human populations using a process that looks at three interactions; the causative agent, the host, and the environment; although the word is intended to refer to human diseases, it is sometimes used to describe the process of tracking down diseases in plants.

epilepsy a recurrent cerebral disorder characterized by sudden, brief attacks of altered consciousness, motor activity, or sensory phenomena. Symptoms vary according to the type of cerebral dysfunction and may range from a fleeting lapse of consciousness or twitching limb to a severe seizure lasting 2 to 5 minutes.

epitopes unique molecular projections of antigens that may serve as recognition and binding sites for one or more antibodies; the immune system in some way memorizes epitopes, thereby creating a lifelong defense against them.

Epstein-Barr Virus Syndrome an illness that leaves

its victims subject to debilitating fatigue, low-grade fever, muscle pains, depression, headaches, recurrent sore throats, swollen lymph glands, and allergies; medical opinion is divided about what role the Epstein-Barr virus plays, if any.

erythropoietin a hormone produced mainly in the kidneys in response to low oxygen levels that acts upon immature precursor cells in bone marrow to cause them to multiply, divide, and differentiate into adult red blood cells.

estrogen a hormone produced by the ovary that influences secondary sexual characteristics (such as body shape) and is responsible for cyclic changes in the tissues of the vagina and the uterus.

ethology the science of ethics, especially applied ethics.

exercise-induced pulmonary hemorrhage (EIPH) blood is sometimes found in the airways of horses after the completion of a short high-speed race: One theory holds that small terminal airways collapse during exhalation and do not reopen with the next inhalation, causing unequal expansion of the lungs, leading to the breakage of small capillaries.

explosive lens a thin cone of fast-detonating explosive is molded to surround a cone of slower-detonating explosive; by varying the ingredients and the geometry of the concentric cones, a detonation wave can be made to order.

Feline T-lymphotropic Lentivirus (FTLV) a recently discovered AIDS-like virus in cats.

forensic scientist a scientist who has specialized training and education in the recognition, identification, collection, and preservation of physical evidence to unravel a mystery or solve a crime.

gamma ray a high-energy photon, especially as emitted by a nucleus in transition between two energy states.

GIFT *g*amete *i*ntra*f*allopian *t*ransfer, a technique used on behalf of couples whose fertility is prevented by a blockage of one of the wife's two fallopian tubes; the egg and the sperm of the couple are placed into the unblocked tube for fertilization to take place in the natural setting.

glial cells the non-nervous or supporting tissue of the brain and spinal cord.

glycoprotein a compound consisting of a carbohydrate and protein; The carbohydrate is hexosamine, an amino sugar.

granulocyte leukocyte containing granules in the cytoplasm (protoplasm of a cell outside the nucleus); granular leukocytes have the power to ingest minute particles.

hematologic growth factors hormones that stimulate bone marrow, the soft tissue filling spaces in the spongy interior of bone shafts, into making red or white blood cells.

heme an iron-containing nonprotein portion of the hemoglobin molecule in red blood cells.

hemophiliacs individuals who, because of hereditary blood disease, have abnormal bleeding due to a failure of their blood to clot normally.

hepatitis inflammation of the liver from a virus or a toxin; jaundice (yellowness of eyes, skin, and urine) is usually evident, and sometimes the liver is enlarged.

herpesvirus a family of viruses including those which cause herpes simplex, herpes zoster, and varicella (chicken pox); the Epstein-Barr virus is a herpesvirus, and like all other herpesviruses persists in the body for life.

hertz a unit of frequency, also known as cycle per second.

hippocampus a ridge that extends over the floor of the descending horn of each lateral ventricle of the brain.

hormone a substance originating in an organ, gland, or part that is conveyed by the blood to another part of the body where, by chemical action, it stimulates increased activity or secretion.

hydrographic stations fixed points where ships lower devices to measure the ocean's properties from the surface to the bottom.

image processing the use of a computer to perform interpretation and recognition tasks usually performed by humans.

immunoglobulins any set of serum glycoproteins (a compound consisting of a carbohydrate and a protein) that has the ability to bind other molecules with a high degree of specificity; one of a family of closely related though not identical proteins that is capable of acting as antibodies.

immunology a branch of biological science concerned with native or acquired resistance to infection from microorganisms.

infectious mononucleosis an acute infectious disease characterized by enlarged, often tender, lymph nodes and an enlarged spleen, with a great increase of atypical mononuclear leukocytes in the blood; the disease is associated with the Epstein-Barr virus.

infertility the failure to achieve pregnancy despite frequent unprotected intercourse within an 18-month period. About one out of every nine couples has difficulty achieving a pregnancy or in carrying a pregnancy through to term.

infrared astronomy the study of electromagnetic radiation in the spectrum between 0.75 and 1,000 micrometers emanating from astronomical sources.

interferon a protein or proteins formed when cells are exposed to viruses; noninfected cells exposed to interferon are protected against viral infection.

intrauterine device (IUD) a device placed inside the uterus to prevent pregnancy that is thought to work by inflaming the lining of the uterus, impeding implantation of the egg.

in vitro fertilization a procedure to overcome infertility: after treatment with hormones to increase ovum (egg) production, through an incision in the woman's abdomen, mature eggs are withdrawn using a laparoscope, a lighted tube with a magnifying lens; the eggs are fertilized with sperm in a glass petri dish and after 42 to 78 hours, the fertilized eggs are placed in the woman's uterus where, if all goes well, they will become implanted and will develop.

iridium a metallic element found only in small amounts on the Earth's surface, but in abundance in meteorites; it is found in high concentrations at the Cretaceous-Tertiary boundary, lending credence to the theory that the mass extinction of three-quarters of the Earth's creatures may have been due to the crash of a meteor.

land-bridge islands geographic areas cut off from their surroundings in which full ecological diversity cannot be maintained, leading to the eventual death of animal species.

leach to dissolve and be washed into solution.

Legionnaires' disease a severe, often fatal, disease named for individuals stricken while attending an American Legion convention in 1976, characterized by pneumonia, dry cough, muscular pain, gastrointestinal problems and, with progress of the disease, dysfunction of other major organs.

lemur any of a family of small, nocturnal quadrumanous (all four feet adapted to function as hands) mammals, closely allied to monkeys, with large eyes, a pointed muzzle, and soft woolly fur.

lithics instruments made of stone.

magainins a substance in the skin of frogs that kills various, though not all, invading bacteria, while leaving the red cells intact.

Magellanic clouds two irregular clouds of stars in the Milky Way in the Southern Hemisphere.

magnitude the relative brightness of a celestial body; the smaller the number (algebraically) indicating magnitude, the brighter the body.

malaria an acute and sometimes chronic infectious disease due to the presence of protozoan parasites in red blood cells introduced by the bite of a mosquito.

microburst a wind pattern that descends from rain clouds during spring and summer to hit the ground and fan out horizontally into an outflow that resembles the bowl-shape of water hitting the bottom of a sink; the outflow causes a rapid change in wind speed and direction that is hazardous to aircraft.

microclimate the conditions of soil, water, temperature, winds, and geology of small areas.

modular cognitive separation the disregard of pieces of information because they are not compatible with previous experience or because they thwart unrecognized desires.

morbidity the number of sick persons or cases of disease in relationship to a specific population.

mortality the ratio of number of deaths to a given population.

mucous membrane membrane lining passages and cavities communicating with the air; consists of a surface layer of epithelium, a basement membrane, and an underlying layer of connective tissue, mucus-secreting cells or glands are usually present.

multiprocessing data-processing system capable of carrying out more than one program or more than one arithmetic operation at a time; in multiprocessing as distinguished from parallel processing, nodes run totally different applications or independent job streams of the same general application.

mustelids a large, diverse family of low-slung, long-bodied, carnivorous mammals, including minks, weasels, and badgers.

natural resource management the balancing of the interlocking needs of an environment by using the skills of a variety of specialties, such as wildlife, genetics, soil science, aquaculture, and arboriculture.

neonatal care care given to newborns, often because they are born immature and are not able to survive without additional attention.

nerve growth factors substances in the brain that help nerve cells survive, grow, and make new connections.

neural network computer systems that act on information all at once through interconnected units, in contrast to conventional computers that operate on data sequentially.

neurasthenia exhaustion commonly following depressed states, characterized by a sense of weakness or by symptoms of various types of organic disease without the existence of a degree of organic disease sufficient to justify the level of complaint.

neurobiology a branch of biology that is concerned with the anatomy and physiology of the nervous system.

neuron a nerve cell, the structural and functional unit of the nervous system, consisting of a cell body protruding structures, an axon, and one or more dendrites.

neuropeptides small proteinlike chemicals (including the body's own morphinelike chemical, endorphins) made by cells in the brain, which are viewed by some scientists as biochemical units of emotion.

neurotransmitters when neurons send an electrical impulse down a stalk called an axon, molecules at the end of an axon's branches called neurotransmitters carry the signal across a space to the next neuron.

neutrinos have been thought to have no mass (a concept that is now being questioned), to have no electrical charge, and to travel at or close to the speed of light.

oral rehydration therapy (ORT) a combination of sugar, salt, and water used to reverse the effects of dehydration brought on by diarrhea, a killer of 5 million young children each year in developing nations.

orthosis the straightening or correction of a deformity or disability.

ovum the female reproductive cell that is capable of developing into a new organism of the same species.

parallel processing in contrast to the use of a single, powerful processor, as in a conventional computer, a parallel processor has a network of processors that permit the same operations to be done simultaneously on different pieces of data (in parallel processing as distinguished from multiprocessing, a single program is divided among multiple nodes).

Parkinson's disease a chronic nervous disease characterized by a subtle, slowly spreading tremor, muscular weakness, rigidity, and a peculiar gait. The onset is generally gradual. The disease was named for an English physician, James Parkinson.

patch to modify a computer program or routine.

perceptron a pattern-recognition machine based on an analogy to the human nervous system, capable of learning from a feedback system which reinforces correct responses and discourages incorrect ones.

phonemes a class of closely related speech sounds (phones) regarded as a single sound and represented in phonetic transcription by the same symbol such as the *r* in bring, red, and round. Discernible differences are due to the influence of adjacent sounds.

photon a quantum of electromagnetic energy having both particle and wave behavior, it has no charge or mass but possesses momentum; the energy of light, X rays, and gamma rays is carried by photons.

plaque a gummy mass of microorganisms that grows on the crowns and spreads along the roots of teeth, unremoved it attacks gum and bone tissue, leading eventually to a loosening of the teeth.

platelet a round or oval disk, 2 to 4 micrometers in diameter, that plays an important role in blood coagulation, hemostasis (the checking of blood flow), and blood thrombus formation (clotting); when a small vessel is injured, platelets adhere to each other and to the edges of the injury to form a plug to cover the area.

polymer substance made of giant molecules formed by the union of simple molecules (monomers).

porphyrin any of a group of nitrogen-containing organic compounds that occur in protoplasm and form the basis of animal and plant respiratory pigments, obtained from hemoglobin and chlorophyll.

predisposition the potential to develop a certain disease or condition in the presence of specific environmental stimuli.

probe an instrument, usually flexible, for exploring the depth and direction of a wound or any cavity having a relatively narrow opening.

processing the manipulation of information to convert it from one format to another or to reduce it to manageable or intelligible data.

processor a device that performs one or many functions, usually a central processing unit.

progestin a hormone that prepares the endometrium (the lining of the uterus) to receive a fertilized ovum.

proton an elementary particle that is the positively charged constituent of ordinary matter and, together with the neutron, is a building block of all atomic nuclei.

psychoactive description used for drugs or chemicals that have a specific effect on the brain's functioning.

psychosomatic disorders that have a physiological component but are thought to originate in the emotional state of the patient.

pulsar a celestial radio source emitting intense bursts of radio emission.

quark one of the hypothetical basic charges whose magnitudes are one-third/two-thirds of the electron charge from which many of the elementary particles may be built up in theory.

raptor an order of birds of prey that live on other birds and animals, have strong, curved, sharp-edged, and sharp-pointed beaks, robust short legs, with three toes in front and one behind, and armed with long, strong, crooked talons: Eagles, vultures, and falcons are examples.

receptor a site or structure in a cell that combines with a substance to produce a specific alteration of cell function.

reconstructive surgery surgery performed to repair or restore defective or missing structures damaged at birth or through disease or accident, frequently involving the transfer of tissue from one part of the body to another.

redundancy the design of computer hardware and software to permit simultaneous output such as the simultaneous output of printed text on a screen and synthetic speech providing the same text.

rejection destruction of transplanted tissues and organs at the cellular level by the host's immune mechanism.

remote sensing the gathering and recording of information without actual contact with the object or area being investigated.

retrofit a modification of equipment to incorporate changes made in later production of similar equipment: The word is derived from the term *retroactive refit*.

riparian along the banks of rivers, lakes, or streams.

risk-taking behavior behavior that threatens the health or life of the risk taker, a few of the many possibilities: smoking, driving under the influence of drugs or alcohol, unprotected sex, intravenous drug use, skateboard acrobatics, suicide, accidents, and murder.

robot a completely self-controlled electronic, electric, or mechanical device.

schizophrenia mental disorder characterized by disturbances of thinking, mood, and behavior; an altered concept of reality and sometimes delusions and hallucinations are present; judgment, learning from experience, abstract reasoning, conformance with social norms, and sustained attention are all seriously impaired.

sensation-seeking scale a four-part scale that measures thrill and adventure seeking (physical risks), experience seeking (nonconformity), disinhibition (disregard for social controls), and boredom susceptibility.

sexually transmitted diseases disease acquired as a result of sexual contact with an infected individual; includes many diseases such as syphilis, gonorrhea, genital herpes, and genital warts.

speaker recognition systems computers that respond to spoken speech.

speckle interferometry the use of speckle patterns to study stellar objects distorted by the atmosphere's turbulence by taking a large number of short exposures and by using special camera apertures to sharpen the resolution.

sperm spermatozoa, mature male sex cells that measure about 51 micrometers in length, are self-propelled, and resemble tadpoles: The spermatozoan head pierces the envelope of the ovum and loses its tail when fusion of the two cells takes place in a process called fertilization.

spot map a map where dots or flags are used to indicate a number of households with a particular characteristic, especially useful in tracking epidemics.

squids superconducting interference devices that make it possible to detect the brain's magnetic field.

stochastic processing a family of random variables, dependent upon a parameter that usually denotes time, and an integral part of speech-recognition systems that are governed by probability.

stratosphere a zone above the troposphere that extends to about 50 kilometers: *Stratos* means layered and the stratosphere is visibly layered, the density of the air there is about one-thousandth that at sea level.

sudden-death syndrome unexpected death as a result of an abrupt onset of an uncontrollable increase in the heart's rhythm that deteriorates into a state where the heart trembles and jerks instead of pumping blood.

supercritical fluid a combination of high temperature and high pressure can convert a substance into a supercritical fluid, a state that does not ordinarily exist; a supercritical fluid expands like a gas to suffuse everything in a container, but like a liquid, it can dissolve solids.

synapse a site where the axon of one neuron comes into contact with and influences the dendrites of another neuron or a cell body.

syndrome a group of signs and symptoms that collectively indicate a particular disease or abnormal condition.

synthesized speech computer-produced spoken speech.

technology transfer the wider use of products invented for a special purpose.

tomography uses the technique of making radiographs of plane sections of a body or an object to show detail at a predetermined plane while blurring the structures in other planes.

toxicologist a scientist who studies poisons, including their nature, effects, detection, and methods of treatment.

transparency design of the parts of a computer that allow it to be used in a variety of ways by a variety of users without a need for adaptations.

troposphere the air between the Earth's surface and a ceiling at about 8 kilometers over the poles and at about 15 kilometers over the equator; within the troposphere, 75 percent of the Earth's mass of air and virtually all the water vapor and weather are confined.

ultrasound inaudible sound that has different velocities in tissues that differ in density and elasticity from others; this property permits the use of ultrasound to outline the shape of tissues and organs for diagnosis and treatment.

ultraviolet radiation electromagnetic radiation in the wavelength range of 400 nanometers, a range that begins at the short wavelength limit of visible light and overlaps the wavelengths of long X rays (some scientists place the lower range at 40 rather than 4); also known as ultraviolet light.

virology the study of viruses and viral diseases.

virus a minute organism not visible with ordinary light microscopy and a parasite dependent upon nutrients inside cells for its metabolic and reproductive needs; as seen under an electron microscope, it consists of a strand of DNA or RNA, but not both, separated by a covering of protein; viruses cause a variety of infectious diseases, among them most childhood illnesses, and the majority of upper respiratory infections.

water ranching the practice of buying land solely to use the water rights that accompany ownership; a method being used by cities faced with increased populations and projected future water shortages.

PHOTO CREDITS

p. 2 Rick Kruger/U.S. Fish and Wildlife Service; pp. 7-9 Teddi DiCanio; p. 11 School of Veterinary Medicine/University of Pennsylvania; p. 12 Teddi DiCanio; p. 13 School of Veterinary Medicine/University of California at Davis; p. 14 Teddi Di Canio; p. 15 School of Veterinary Medicine/University of California at Davis; p. 19 Nancy Anne Dawe; pp. 20-24 San Francisco Friends of the Urban Forest; p. 25 Walter Coker/University of Florida; pp. 26 & 27 Dr. Russell A. Mittermeier/World Wildlife Fund; p. 28 (top three) Dr. Russell A. Mittermeier/World Wildlife Fund; p. 28 (bottom) Walter Coker/University of Florida; p. 29 Walter Coker/University of Florida; p. 30 Preservation Consultants, Inc.; p. 31 Margaret Di Canio; p. 34 Sperm Bank of Northern Calif.; p. 35 Hank Morgan; p. 36 Wide World Photos; p. 38 Ortho Pharmaceutical Corporation; p. 40 (top left) Richard Feldman, Division of Computer Research and Technology/National Institutes of Health; p. 40 (top right plus bottom left and right) Dr. Tom Folks, National Institute of Allergy and Infectious Diseases; p. 42 National Institute of Allergy and Infectious Diseases; pp. 45-50 Centers for Disease Control; p. 52 Jeanne Fitzgerald/AMGen Corporation; p. 53 Bill Varie/AMGen Corporation; p. 55 Deborah Perugi/The Boston Globe; p. 57 National Institute of Allergy and Infectious Diseases; p. 59 Brigham and Women's Hospital; pp. 60-64 National Institute of Allergy and Infectious Diseases; p. 65 Dr. Anthony Fauci/National Institute of Allergy and Infectious Diseases; p. 66 National Institute of Allergy and Infectious Diseases; p. 68 Teddi DiCanio; p. 69 U.S. Department of Agriculture; p. 70 & 73 Centers for Disease Control; p. 74 U.S. Department of Transportation; p. 77 Adolph Brotman/Copyright © 1987 by The New York Times Company, reprinted by permission; p. 78 National Institute of Child Health and Human Development; pp. 79 & 81 Copyright © 1987 by The New York Times Company, reprinted by permission; p. 83 National Institute of Neurological and Communicative Disorders; p. 85 Barbara Lyter/University of California at Irvine; p. 87 Sergio Dorantes/New York Times Pictures; p. 88 Jim Wheelock/Wendy Maeda/The Boston Globe; p. 90 National Institute of Neurological and Communicative Disorders; p. 93 Eric Lesser/Gainesville Sun; p. 94 (top four plus bottom left) Teddi DeCanio; p. 94 (lower right) Department of Public Safety/Massachusetts State Police; p. 95 Teddi DiCanio; p. 97 Walter Coker/University of Florida; p. 99 Marshall Print/University of Florida; p. 101 U.S. Department of Transportation; p. 103 Dragon Systems, Inc.; pp. 104 & 105 Gallaudet University; p. 107 Teddi DiCanio; pp. 108-110 Wilson Rivera/Volunteers for Medical Engineering; pp. 113-118 Teddi DiCanio; p. 119 Bo Parker, NYC/Greenacre Foundation; pp. 120 & 121 Riverways Program/Massachusetts Department of Fisheries, Wildlife & Environmental Law Enforcement; p. 123 Courtesy of British Tourist Authority; p. 126 Teddi DiCanio/Courtesy of the Boston Public Library, Print Department; pp. 127 & 128 Teddi DiCanio; p. 129 Boston's City Archaeology Program; p. 131 Jean Courtin/University of Provence, Director of the Fontbrégoua excavation; pp. 132 & 133 Paola Villa/University of Colorado; p. 134 Pat Shipman/Johns Hopkins University; p. 138 & 143 Teddi DiCanio; p. 144 Harvard Gulfcasting Program, Division of Applied Science/Harvard University; p. 146 Graduate School of Oceanography/University of Rhode Island; p. 151 U.S. Department of Agriculture; p. 153 John Walper/Dinosaur Provincial Park, Alberta, Canada; p. 155 & 156 Museum of the Rockies/Montana State University; pp. 158 & 159 EARTHWATCH; p. 160 Scott Eckert/EARTHWATCH; p. 163 Wide World Photos; p. 164 Teddi DiCanio; p. 166 U.S. Department of Agriculture; p. 169 M.I.T. Lincoln Laboratory; p. 171 University of Toronto; p. 172 NASA; p. 174 University of Toronto; pp. 175-177 Peter Menzel; p. 178 New Mexico Tech; p. 183 IBM Corporation; p. 184 New York Times Pictures; pp. 186 & 187 IBM Corporation; p. 188 SSC Central Design Group; pp. 192-195 Dr. W.D. Keller, Professor Emeritus, University of Missouri-Columbia with a grant from National Science foundation; p. 198 Thinking Machines Corporation; p. 199 Loral Corporation; p. 201 Ralph Linsker/IBM Corporation; p. 204 Copyright © 1987 by The New York Times, reprinted by permission.

INDEX

INDEX